ESSAYS
on
JEWISH
BOOKLORE

ESSAYS
on
JEWISH
BOOKLORE

Articles Selected by **PHILIP GOODMAN**
Executive Secretary, Jewish Book Council of America

Preface by **JUDAH NADICH**
President, Jewish Book Council of America

Introduction by A. **ALAN STEINBACH**
Editor, Jewish Book Annual

KTAV PUBLISHING HOUSE, INC., NEW YORK

JEWISH BOOK COUNCIL OF AMERICA
Sponsored by
NATIONAL JEWISH WELFARE BOARD

Library of Congress Cataloging in Publication Data

Goodman, Philip, 1911-   comp.
Essays on Jewish booklore.

Articles selected from the Jewish book annual, 1942-
1971.
Includes bibliographical references.
1. Jewish literature--Addresses, essays, lectures.
2. Jews in literature--Addresses, essays, lectures.
I. Jewish book annual. II. Title.
PN842.G6 1972   809.8'8924   76-176055
ISBN 0-87068-142-7

SBN 87068-142-7

LIBRARY OF CONGRESS CATALOG CARD NUMBER: 76-176055
MANUFACTURED IN THE UNITED STATES OF AMERICA

IV

TABLE OF CONTENTS

All articles are reprinted from the Jewish Book Annual. *The volume and page numbers of each article follow the title and author.*

Books and the Holocaust

Love of Books

Makers of Books

From One Language to Another

Treasure Houses of Books

Bibliophilic Sidelights

CONTRIBUTORS

SHMUEL YOSEF AGNON, late Nobel laureate for Hebrew literature; novelist and short story writer.

DR. BERNARD J. BAMBERGER, rabbi emeritus, Temple Shaaray Tefila, New York; author of *The Story of Judaism* and other works.

DR. CHARLES BERLIN, Lee M. Friedman Bibliographer in Judaica and Head of Hebrew Division, Harvard College Library, Cambridge, Mass.; editor, *Studies in Jewish Bibliography, History and Literature in Honor of I. Edward Kiev.*

B. J. BIALOSTOTZKY, late poet, essayist, lecturer; writer for *Jewish Daily Forward* and literary journals; author of many volumes.

DR. JOSHUA BLOCH, late chief, Jewish Division of the New York Public Library; author of monographs on Jewish culture and bibliography.

ADAH BORAISHA-FOGEL, contributor to YIVO and other publications on literary research; translator and essayist; associate editor, *Anthology of Holocaust Literature.*

DR. MOSHE CARMILLY-WEINBERGER, professor of Jewish Studies, Yeshiva University, New York; author of books and articles on Hebrew literature and booklore and Jewish history.

DR. MORTIMER J. COHEN, author of *Pathways Through the Bible* and other works; rabbi emeritus, Congregation Beth Sholom, Philadelphia.

DR. SALAMON FABER, rabbi, Kew Gardens Anshe Sholom Jewish Center; library research intern, Library of Fordham University.

SOLOMON FEFFER, chairman, Department of Hebraic Studies, Rutgers University, Newark, N.J.

DR. LEE M. FRIEDMAN, late president, American Jewish Historical Society; honorary vice-president, Jewish Publication Society of America; member, Council of Massachusetts Historical Society; author of historical works.

DR. PHILIP FRIEDMAN, late lecturer on Jewish history, Columbia University, New York; research director, Documentary Projects of Yad Vashem and YIVO, New York; author of books and studies in Jewish history.

PHILIP GOODMAN, executive secretary, Jewish Book Council of America; author of *The Rosh Hashanah Anthology, Illustrated Essays on Jewish Bookplates,* and other books.

DR. SOLOMON GRAYZEL, editor emeritus, The Jewish Publication Society of America; author of *A History of the Jews*; professor of Jewish history, Dropsie University.

RICHARD GRUNBERGER, historian and writer; author of *Germany, 1918-1945*; and *The 12-Year Reich: A Social History of Nazi Germany, 1933-1945.*

DR. IRVING HALPERIN, professor of English, San Francisco State College; contributor to numerous publications; author of *Messengers from the Dead: Literature of the Holocaust.*

DR. BERNARD HELLER, rabbi and educator; author of *Odyssey of a Faith, Dawn or Dusk?* and other works; visiting professor, Jewish ethics and philosophy of religion, Hebrew Union College—Jewish Institute of Religion.

DR. MAURICE JACOBS, former executive vice-president, The Jewish Publication Society of America; vice-president, American Jewish Historical Society.

DR. JACOB KABAKOFF, chairman, Hebrew Department, Lehman College of the City University of New York; author of *Pioneers of American Hebrew Literature* (Hebrew).

DR. LOTHAR KAHN, professor of modern languages, Central Connecticut State College, New Britain; contributor to Jewish and general periodicals; author of *Mirrors of the Jewish Mind.*

JOSEPH LEFTWICH, author of *Yisroel, The Golden Peacock, Israel Zangwill, The Way We Think,* among others.

LUDWIG LEWISOHN, late novelist, critic, Zionist theoretician; editor of *New Palestine,* 1943-48; professor of comparative literature, Brandeis University.

DR. MORDECAI SOLTES, late executive director, Yeshiva University; director, Jewish extension education, National Jewish Welfare Board; author of *The Yiddish Press: An Americanizing Agency* and other works.

DR. A. ALAN STEINBACH, author of ten books; honorary president, Jewish Book Council; editor, *Jewish Book Annual* and *In Jewish Bookland*; rabbi emeritus, Temple Ahavath Sholom, Brooklyn, N. Y.

DR. SEFTON DAVID TEMKIN, staff editor, *Encyclopedia Judaica;* professor of Jewish history, State University of New York in Albany.

DR. ZEV VILNAY, author of *The Israel Guide, Legends of Palestine* and other books; educator and lecturer.

DR. TRUDE WEISS-ROSMARIN, author and lecturer; editor of *The Jewish Spectator*; contributor to English-Jewish and other magazines; author of *Judaism and Christianity: The Differences, Highlights of Jewish History,* and other volumes.

PREFACE

By JUDAH NADICH

On the occasion of the publication of *Essays on Jewish Book-lore,* consisting of selected articles reprinted from the *Jewish Book Annual* published by the Jewish Book Council of America sponsored by the National Jewish Welfare Board, it is fitting to recall the aims of the Council and to express appreciation to those who have made possible the issuance of the *Annual.*

Created in the dark days of the Holocaust when famous European Jewish scholars were annihilated and great Jewish libraries destroyed, the Jewish Book Council of America has steadfastly sought to aid in the creation of an American Jewish cultural renaissance. Sponsored by the National Jewish Welfare Board, the Council recognizes that without the Jewish book, the Jewish group cannot survive. Our goals have been formulated as follows:

To infuse in both young and old the traditional ardent zeal for Jewish knowledge through reading the Jewish classics as well as contemporary works.

To encourage the establishment of Jewish book shelves as an integral part of the home environment.

To help augment Jewish book collections in libraries of synagogues, schools, Centers, and other institutions, and to stimulate their utilization for enriching group programs, study circles, discussion groups, and the like.

To make available books of Jewish interest for promoting reciprocal inter-faith understanding and cooperation.

For three decades the Council has pursued the above aims through a wide variety of media. One of the most significant is the publication of the *Jewish Book Annual* of which twenty-nine volumes have been published since 1942. The most complete record of Jewish book productivity in America, the volumes of the *Jewish Book Annual* bear testimony to the growing literary creativity of American Jewry. It is my privilege to express deep appreciation to all those who, in one way or another, have made possible the publication of the *Annual*. The continuing support of the Lucius N. Littauer Foundation and its president, Harry Starr, has been a great boon. Past presidents of the Jewish Book Council, notably Dr. Mortimer J. Cohen, Dr. Gilbert Klaperman and Dr. A. Alan Steinbach, have been actively concerned with securing the necessary funding. We are also grateful to the numerous contributors of articles and the bibliographers who painstakingly compiled the booklists.

The first volume of the *Annual* came into being as a result of the initiative of the late Dr. Mordecai Soltes. Among those who served as "Section" editors when the book was divided into three lingual parts (English, Hebrew and Yiddish) were Dr. Bernard J. Bamberger, Dr. Abraham G. Duker, Dr. Hayyim Leaf, Harry Schneiderman and Moshe Starkman, and the late Dr. Pinkhos Churgin, Moses Feinstein, Jacob Levin, Dr. Jacob S. Minkin, Daniel Persky, Menachem Ribalow, Louis Rittenberg, and Dr. Jacob Shatzky.

Since 1952 the following have been associate editors: Hyman B. Bass, Dr. Menahem G. Glenn, Dr. Jacob Kabakoff, Dr. I. Edward Kiev, Dr. Yudel Mark, Dr. Lawrence Marwick, and the late Dr. Philip Friedman and Dr. Jacob Shatzky.

Rabbi Philip Goodman has been managing editor of the *Annual* for twenty-seven of the twenty-nine published volumes. The early editors who created the pattern for the book were Dr. Mortimer J. Cohen, Dr. Solomon Grayzel and Dr. Sol Liptzin. Since 1956, Dr. A. Alan Steinbach has been the editor and has not only maintained the high standards set by his predecessors, but has extended even farther the usefulness of the *Annual*. Throughout the world today it is regarded as a unique literary and reference work. His own rich literary talents have enhanced the high quality of each of the volumes published under his editorship.

Last but not least we wish to express our indebtedness to the National Jewish Welfare Board, its president, Morton L. Mandel, and its executive vice-president, Herbert Millman, for making it possible for the Council to function effectively and to publish the *Jewish Book Annual*. The Council itself depends for its daily far-flung activities upon its dedicated and able executive secretary, Rabbi Philip Goodman.

INTRODUCTION

By A. Alan Steinbach

I

The Jewish Book Council of America has published the tri-lingual *Jewish Book Annual* in a literary continuum encompas-sing almost three decades. It has striven to cultivate and to nurture its little cultural orchard in the world of books. The word "little" is used advisedly, for the Council is concerned only with Jewish books. We shall not revive the polemic as to what constitutes a Jewish book; but whatever definition one formu-lates, there is an incontrovertible distinction between *books* and *Jewish books*.

Books in general possess a personality and complexion, a pulsation and voice that reveal the author's portrait—his in-tellectual processes, his philosophy, the landscape of his mental topography. Jewish books limn more than the author's portrait. They are characterized by an interiority that transcends the author's mind, even of his philosophy; they partake of an im-ponderable, an indefinable mystique that is indigenous to the Jewish psyche. They are integral to the Jewish *modus vivendi*.

In psychology we find a parallel in Carl Jung's concept of a *collective unconscious*. Even when the Jew was ghettoized and forced into parochialism, his mind was circumferenced by broader cultural and spiritual lineaments that could not be obliterated by the passage of time. His mind orbited around a "remembered dream" voiced in ancient rabbinic prophecy: *Atidah Eretz Yisroel lehitpashet bekhal haarazot* "In some future day Eretz Israel will extend to all peoples."

This "remembered dream" was galvanized into an ineluctable vision that hovered over his cultural thematic blueprint. Through the primacy of study and learning for which Torah is the all-embracing generic term, through the ethical imperatives disseminated in a large corpus of Jewish writings as the basis for an authentic humanism, through the interpenetration of Jewish prophetic verities into the thinking of the Western world—all these original horizons cradled in Eretz Yisrael and channeled over the centuries through Jewish teachers, thinkers and writers, were assimilated onto the wider frontiers of mankind.

The Roman *patria* applied only to the city of Rome, not to the whole of Italy. The ancient Greeks concentrated their colonization on localities abutting great bodies of water. The ancient Hebrews always followed the changing centers of civilization. Ensconced at first around the shores of the Euphrates and the Tigris, they pulled up stakes and journeyed to the Nile when it became the hub of civilization. For a long period they settled in Egypt, but the magnetic, gravitational "pull" of onmarching civilization, operating like a centripetal force, again attracted them into its orbit, propelling them into centers that had been established along the eastern shores of the Mediterranean.

This pattern of migrating from one country to another, even from one continent to another, has been invoked by the Jews throughout their history. Although theocentrically inclined, they were not necessarily motivated by religious impulsions. Indeed, there is no equivalent in Hebrew for the term religion. The motivation stemmed from the Jewish intellect, which attained a planetary character at an early stage in Jewish history. It was the Jewish mind, the Jewish psyche, the Jewish ethos—all of which are fundamental ingredients of a culture rather than of a religion—that were from the very beginning universalistic, evolving a world that circumscribes the whole cosmos and a history that is sadly incomplete if it does not embrace the whole of humanity.

"In the beginning God created heaven and earth." Jewish history begins with cosmology, with our earth planet and with mankind. Christianity begins with biography; Judaism with the genealogy of the whole human race. This cosmic interpretation, which was fashioned into the Jewish metronome measuring the meter and rhythm of life, became the foundation of Jewish culture. The Jewish mind was a restless Columbus exploring for new intellectual continents.

Ancient Jewish culture proceeds from the Bible, and medieval Jewish civilization is found in the Talmud. (Digressing for a moment, it is little short of miraculous that two of our greatest cultural achievements, the Mishnah and the Gemara, were fructified by the Jewish mind on the eve and immediately after the destruction of ancient Judea by the Romans.) The Bible, the Mishnah, the Gemara, and subsequent writings from the Talmud to Maimonides, from Maimonides to the Gaon of Vilna, up to our contemporary period—these are all cultural barometers by which we read the Jewish mind. They bear enduring testimony to the breadth and depth, to the vigor and broad spectrum of the Jewish cultural efflorescence.

Ahad Ha-Am epitomized the survival potential of the Jew in his declaration: "Learning, learning, learning; that is the secret of Jewish survival." Reduced to a pragmatic postulate, we may paraphrase his statement: Books, books, books are the cultural bastion of the Jew. Rabbinic fancy went so far as to suggest that God Himself spends three hours of each day reading the Torah (Ab. Zara 3b).

II

The ubiquitous hunger of the Jewish mind for the cosmic and the universal engendered an optimistic world outlook that seems puzzling and paradoxical. It created the Talmud which the Gentiles sought to destroy in their autos-da-fé; and yet, it was this same Talmud that promulgated the humanistic dictum: "The righteous among the Gentiles have a share in the world to come." Certainly, the lamentable experiences of the Jew do not appear to justify even an iota of optimism; but the tribulations of the moment, which too frequently made living unbearable for the Jew, could not emasculate his belief in the inherent goodness of man. Original sin was repugnant to his rational mind. Through the prism of universality, the prophets looked to the *aharit hayamim,* not as an instrumentality of Divine destruction, but rather as a new beginning for man, when a just Messianic rule will hold sway and the whole of humanity will submit to it.

In the interim, while nations were deifying power and striving to construct great empires, the Jews were building *yeshivot,* expanding their culture.

In the context of the above observations, it is not difficult to understand the depth of Jewish reverence for books. This reverence runs like a gossamer thread throughout the vast Jewish literary thesaurus. (The Jewish Book Council and the editors of the *Jewish Book Annual* implement this attribute as a literary article of faith, endeavoring to vindicate their responsibility as a humble link in the cultural chain that has been transmitted from generation to generation.)

Not only reverence, but also a quality of sanctity permeates the Jewish attitude to books. The Talmud (Sukkah 26a) equated the acquisition, production and the dissemination of books with religious observance: "They who copy scrolls, and their wholesalers and retailers, are exempted from reading the Shema, the Amidah, and from wearing phylacteries." An old Hebrew writing admonished: "One should be meticulous to handle books with respect. Never put a book underneath when you line paper for writing." And another: "If you keep a box of books in your bedroom, place it at the head, not at the foot of your bed." Judah the Pious wrote: "They who loan books to students merit the same share in the world to come as do the students themselves." The 1736 Minutebook of the Latvian Community Council asserts that individuals who refused to loan their books were fined. This attitude brings to mind Yehuda Halevi's tender verse: "My pen is my harp and my lyre . . ./ Its library—my garden and my orchard."

III

The Jewish Book Council welcomes the collaboration of Ktav Publishing House in the production of this volume: *Essays on Jewish Booklore.* The proliferation of republications by Ktav of many scholarly works that are out of print, has assumed proportions of a mini-renaissance in the realm of Jewish culture. It has infused new vigor and vitality into our contemporary cultural kaleidoscope, thereby enhancing both the spiritual and educational frontiers of modern Jewish literature.

The forty-three essays in this volume were culled from the twenty-nine published volumes of the *Jewish Book Annual;* the first volume, published in 1942, was titled *Jewish Book Week Annual.* The trilingual pattern—English, Hebrew and Yiddish—was established at the very beginning, in order to embrace the whole linguistic gamut of Jewish cultural expression. A glance at the table of contents will reveal the wide spectrum of subject matter, divided into eight subheadings. Each essay was written by a specialist in the field to insure authenticity, and while each has its own individual organic character, it is also part of a whole which, we trust, will add illumination to the fascinating topic of Jewish booklore.

Great Jewish Books

THE BIBLE — ETERNAL BOOK*

By A. Alan Steinbach

I

THE English poet Shelley wrote in the Preface to his lyrical drama *Hellas*, "We are all Greeks; our laws, our literature, our religion, our arts have their roots in Greece." More than a century later Pope Pius XI, addressing a delegation of Belgian pilgrims in 1938, referred to Abraham as "our patriarch" and admonished the pilgrims that "spiritually we are Semites."

Both allusions were reminders not to forget the source, the matrix from which we spring. They point up Isaiah's exhortation, "Look to the rock whence ye were hewn and to the hole of the pit whence ye were digged. Look unto Abraham your father, and unto Sara that bore you."

It is universally conceded that for moral and spiritual truths, for sublimity of ethical precepts, for the ecstasy and profundity of its religious affirmations, for its majestic sweep of the heights and depths of human nature, and for its conspicuous role as great literature, the Hebrew Bible is the primer and textbook of humanity. Its moral maxims have marched like spiritual battalions across the map of history. In the whole compass of world literature there is no comparable book which looks with such profound compassion upon every phase of human life, which echoes such exquisite strains of poetry, which teaches man not only the best way to live, but also how to suffer nobly, and even how to die. The Book of Job is a notable example. It is such sublime literature that the English poet Swinburne is said to have memorized it completely. No wonder many regard it as an invaluable training manual for life's vicissitudes and vagaries!

The Bible Theme

There is a cogent reason for selecting the Bible as the theme for our forthcoming nineteenth annual nation-wide observance of Jewish Book Month next November 16 through December 16.

---

* Address delivered at Annual Meeting of the Jewish Book Council of America, May 15, 1962.

1

This year has witnessed a monumental achievement in Jewish
religious and cultural life. Under the aegis of the Jewish Publication Society of America, a committee of renowned Bible
scholars headed by Dr. Harry M. Orlinsky, Professor of Bible
at the Hebrew Union College-Jewish Institute of Religion, has
been working since 1955 on a new translation of our Holy
Scriptures. The first ripe fruits of their sowing are about to be
harvested—the Pentateuch is now being printed.

In token of this major accomplishment, the Jewish Book
Council salutes the Jewish Publication Society of America and
extends felicitations to the distinguished committee of translators
who have dedicated themselves to this prodigious undertaking.
Perhaps it should be pointed out parenthetically that Bible
translation was not always an uninhibited project. We read
this rather astonishing notation in Gerald Kennedy's *A Reader's
Notebook:* "For daring to translate the Bible into the language
of his country, William Tyndale was burned at the stake; and
Henry VIII did his best to keep the Book out of England. Public
notices gave the warning—'No women, nor artificers, nor ap-
prentices, journeymen, serving-men, yeomen, husbandmen, or
laborers shall read the Bible in England in English to himself
or to another, privately or openly, on pain of a month's imprisonment.' " Happily, such strictures do not confront Dr.
Orlinsky and his co-workers.

Beyond Semitic Frontiers

The Bible is, of course, a Jewish creation; the product of a
minuscule people desert-born and desert-bred. It grew out of
the struggles, the triumphs and defeats, the hopes and frustrations, the aspirations and wrestlings, the loyalties and apostasies
of this little people. The Hebrew canon of thirty-nine books,
compiled by Ezra the Scribe some 2400 years ago, is its permanent diary. Heine referred to it as "the portable fatherland
of the Jews." He might well have added that it is also the spiritual
fatherland of the whole human race. Not only is it the rock
from which Judaism, Christianity and Islam were hewn, but
also the quarry from which the ethics, the morality, the culture,
and the social blueprint of western civilization were sculptured.
Blossoming out of the deepest loam of the Jewish spirit, it
transcended the frontiers in which it was cradled and became
the pulsebeat of mankind, the systole and diastole of humanity's
throbbing heart.

The universal role of Scripture is emphasized in several fanciful
midrashim. Our ancient rabbis asserted (Exodus Rabbah) that
the truths reverberated on Mount Sinai were intended for the
whole human family. Why, they asked, was the revelation given

*Isaiah 57.17-59.8, from the Dead Sea Scrolls, now located at the
Hebrew University.*

in the wilderness of Horeb—No Man's Land? They answered: In order that no one could say, "It belongs to me." Another *midrash* declares that the Voice at Sinai split into seventy different languages so that it would address every nation in its own vernacular. Still another suggests that the Voice traveled throughout the universe—south and north, east and west.

This postulate of universality is a logical implementation of God's promise to Abraham, "In thee shall all the families of the earth be blessed." Such insistence that the Bible is Everyman's Book and belongs to every age, has set it apart as the spiritual compass directing man's tortuous, agonizing trek over the promontories of the gaping centuries. Goethe was correct when he wrote, "The Jewish Bible is not the book of one people, but the book of all peoples." Its substance and purport are the scaffolding for the higher divine law which controlled and guided the upward history of man.

The Book: Human and Divine

With very rare exceptions, the books men write have their day and grow obsolete. The Bible is the most memorable exception. Long and vociferously (sometimes acrimoniously) men have debated if it is *Torah min Ha-Shamayim*—the direct utterance of Deity. Such a debate is academic, indeed puerile. Whether or not the Bible is literally the Word of God in the old sense, it is indisputably divine teaching in its espousal of the lofty conceptions of truth, goodness, holiness and righteousness as ultimate sanctions of divineness in the human spirit. Even if one denies that the authority of the moral law lies in its supposed provenience from God, one cannot question the validity of the divineness of the good and the goodness of the divine. Thus interpreted, the Bible is the most human book; the Bible is also the most divine book.

This broader concept of divineness sustained man's quintessential faith in the Bible as the work representing a human-divine symbiosis, a sublime partnership between man and his Maker. Such a faith helps us to understand Chief Justice Jay's reply, when asked on his deathbed if he had a farewell address to leave to his children, "They have the Bible." He knew what countless millions had learned before him: one who kindles his spiritual taper at this altar draws nearer to the presence of God.

II

One can readily understand why this powerfully stirring book has excited more attention and commanded more study and

Joshua, from one of the earliest complete texts of the Hebrew Bible, Soncino, 1488.

contemplation than any other in man's history. It is the heart's unfailing chart; the inner eye enabling finite man to glimpse the infinite. It is a mine so inexhaustible that the more one pores over it the more abundant is the precious ore it yields. It exercises a mystical pull that prompts unceasing human effort to unlock its riches and to fathom its deepest meanings.

I should like to hold before you three types of ore I have found in this mine of incalculable wealth. I shall discuss briefly three aspects of the Bible that demonstrate its grandeur as the *principium et fons* of human aspiration. These will be subsumed under the headings: (1) The Humanism of the Bible; (2) Dialogue and Dialectic in the Bible; (3) Glory in Failure.

Humanism of the Bible

The cryptic rabbinic metaphor, "The Torah speaks in the idiom of man," is more significant than appears on the surface. It intimates that, although the overall configuration of the Bible is theocentric, its anthropocentric architecture is paramount. The human element is never relegated to a secondary status.

An interesting illustration of this emphasis appears in chapter 18 of the Book of Genesis. Let the Torah speak for itself. "And the Lord appeared unto him (Abraham) by the terebinths of Mamre, as he sat in the tent door in the heat of the day; and he lifted up his eyes and looked, and lo, three men stood over against him; and when he saw them he ran to meet them from the tent door, and bowed down to the ground."

So simple and unobtrusive is this seeming prosaic narrative that the human value it adumbrates may be overlooked. What was Abraham doing at his tent door? He was engaged in a conversation with God. Now what can be more important than holding communion with one's Creator? The answer is given here in Genesis. Undeniably, the quest for the divine is an inescapable mandate binding upon every individual. But the Bible hints at an even higher obligation, namely, the search for one's brother-man. Abraham, without so much as asking God's forbearance, breaks off his conversation and runs to meet the three strangers. God interposes no protest, utters no rebuke. The human equation becomes quite clear in the context of this episode. More important than folding one's hands in a colloquy with the Almighty is the opening of hands and heart to serve a fellowman. Abraham keeps God waiting while dispensing hospitality to three weary travelers. There is apparently no irreverence here. Human good deeds, no less than divine revelation, are plenipotentiaries of Deity.

Rashi presents a startling commentary on the first verse adverted to above: "He (Abraham) was sitting in the tent door." Says Rashi, *bikesh laamod* "Abraham wanted to stand up." "The Holy One blessed be He said, 'You sit and I shall stand.'" Abraham, a creature of human imperfection, receives special tender consideration from God, the Perfect One. So venerable, according to the Bible, is human worth in His eyes. What a glorious biblical concept!

Another comment by Rashi is noteworthy. On the phrase *pesach ho'ohel* "In the tent door" he remarks: "To see if there is a passerby whom he might take into his home." This exaltation of man seeking godliness through hospitality to others is a superb gem in the crown of the Torah. It reveals a priority of the humanizing component in Scripture teaching.

A rabbinic observation goes even further. The Midrash (Genesis Rabbah), commenting on "he lifted up his eyes and looked, and lo, three men stood over against him," presents this rather intriguing interpretation: "He saw the *Shechinah* (Divine Presence) and the angels." Here the proffer of assistance to a fellowman is equated with beholding the *Shechinah*.

Dialogue and Dialectic

There is a passage in the Jerusalem Talmud (Ber. IX), "If a man is in distress let him not call on Michael or Gabriel, but let him call direct on Me and I will hearken to him straightway." This expression of God's immanence paraphrases Psalm 145:18, "The Lord is nigh to all who call upon Him, to all who call upon Him in truth." There is a wide chasm between man's finite "I" and God's ineffable "Awnoche," but the gulf may be bridged through prayer, communion, worship, meditation and entreaty. However, the biblical concept of human-divine dialogue involves a spiritual dimension that transcends the conventional pattern of seeking God through prayer and communion. *It partakes of the nature of an actual visitation.* Buber's "I-Thou" philosophy furnishes a strong clue for the understanding of this concept.

Biblical examples of the human-divine dialogue are legion. Abraham pleading for Sodom and Gomorrah; Moses, after the golden calf incident, invoking the attribute of mercy God Himself had proclaimed in the theophany on Mount Sinai; David's apostrophe to the Lord after he had escaped from the hand of Saul; Isaiah's overture to God, "Come now and let us reason together"; Job's disputation with the Almighty; these were not casual remarks addressed to an unapproachable potentate enthroned in some ultramundane sphere. They were pure dialogue, a mutual exchange which actually *communicates*.

The character of this dialogue is Call and Answer. It is not merely a matter of speech; it is vibrant, direct, mutual communication. Psalm 118:6 furnishes an apt illustration: "Out of my straits I called upon the Lord, He answered me with great enlargement." I *called;* He *answered*. Here man seeks God. But the dialogue is completed when God seeks man. The formula for such a dialogue is outlined in Ex. 19:20—"And the Lord came down upon Mt. Sinai . . . and called Moses to the top of the mount, and Moses went up." If the human-divine dialogue is capable of inspiring such an absorbing spiritual experience, one may hope to understand the mystical reference in Deuteronomy that God knew Moses "face to face."

Biblical Dialectic

As has been pointed out above, dialogue involves communication between God and man and also between man and God. Dialectic in religion takes on a form of debate initiated by man. Thus Abraham challenges God (Gen. 18:23, 25), "Wilt Thou indeed sweep away the righteous with the wicked? Shall not the Judge of all the earth do justly?" Moses is even more insistent. He not only questions God's word but actually puts Him on the defensive. We read (Num. 11:21-23) after the Lord had promised to send enough meat to last a whole month:

> And Moses said: 'The people among whom I am are six hundred thousand men on foot; and yet Thou hast said: I will give them flesh that they may eat a whole month. If flocks and herds are slain for them, will they suffice them? or if all the fish of the sea be gathered together for them, will they suffice them?' And the Lord said unto Moses: 'Is the Lord's hand waxed short? Now shalt thou see whether My word shall come to pass unto thee or not.'

To envision God actually defending Himself taxes credulity, but such is the power of biblical dialectic.

Jeremiah makes no pretense at diplomacy when he delivers the challenge (Jer. 12:1), "Righteous art Thou, therefore I will argue with Thee and will speak in the name of justice with Thee. Why does the way of the wicked prosper?" In a similar vein the pious Job, overwhelmed by a series of misfortunes, laments in his agony (Job 21:7), "Wherefore do the wicked live, become old, yea, wax mighty in power? How long wilt Thou look away from me?"

Genesis, from the Complutensian Bible. Alcala de Henares, Arnaldo Guillen de Brocar, 1514-17 (under the auspices of Cardinal Ximenes). It includes Septuagint, Targum, Vulgata and Latin translations of Septuagint and Targum.

These poignant plaints bear witness to two exalted biblical doctrines: (1) Man may engage in a dialogue with God; (2) man may engage in a dialectic with God; he need not hold his peace when he feels that the Author and Architect of the principles of justice and righteousness seems to be contravening one of those principles.

Glory in Failure

Judged by its impact on mankind through the ages, the Bible is the most successful book in history. It is, however, far from being a "success story" in the light of modern criteria. It is replete with records of failure and defeat, human and divine. Genesis 6:5-7 presents an extraordinary confession of divine failure.

> And the Lord saw that the wickedness of man was great in the earth, and that every imagination of the thoughts of his heart was only evil continually. And the Lord regretted that He had made man on the earth, and it grieved Him at His heart. And the Lord said: 'I will blot out man whom I have created from the face of the earth . . . *for I regret that I have made them.*'

Man, creature of flesh and blood, cannot escape the frailties and imperfections of his fallible creaturehood. However, when one contemplates the highly gifted biblical personalities who tower like spiritual mountain peaks in the Bible, one might expect a special preferred relationship of success in their lives. Their lives and labors contributed immeasurably to the unfolding social, moral and ethical sense undergirding civilization. They were the conduit for the eternal verities which were infused into human consciousness. As the elect of God, they might have been expected to be crowned with triumphs befitting their status.

Such, however, was not the case. On the contrary, many of them drank deeply from the bitter flagon of failure. Indeed, one sometimes wonders if failure was deliberately injected as a paradigm for biblical leadership. Perhaps this is what Rabbi Alexandri meant (Lev. Rabbah), "If a person uses broken vessels it is a disgrace to him; but God uses broken vessels, as it is said (Ps. 34:19), 'The Lord is nigh unto them that are of a broken heart.' "

Let us commence with our first patriarch Abraham. It would be hard to conceive of agonies, disappointments and frustrations more devastating than those he experienced. He came within a hair's breadth of sacrificing his son Isaac, the apple of his eye.

לֹא הָיָה: אֵזְרַע יַעַבְדֶנּוּ יְסֻפַּר לַאדֹנָי לַדּוֹר: יב יָבֹאוּ וְיַגִּידוּ
צִדְקָתוֹ לְעַם נוֹלָד כִּי עָשָׂה: כג א מִזְמוֹר לְדָוִד יְהוָה רֹעִי לֹא
אֶחְסָר: ב בִּנְאוֹת דֶּשֶׁא יַרְבִּיצֵנִי עַל־מֵי מְנֻחוֹת יְנַהֲלֵנִי:
ג נַפְשִׁי יְשׁוֹבֵב יַנְחֵנִי בְמַעְגְּלֵי־צֶדֶק לְמַעַן שְׁמוֹ: דַּגַם כִּי־

רש"י

מצודת ציון

מצודת דוד

פירוש ע"ם

משלי חכמים

Psalms, from Hebrew Bible with Rashi and commentaries, a translation in Ivri Taitch and Meshalim in Ivri Taitch taken from various sources. Lublin, 1912.

He failed to maintain *sholom bayis* in his household; at Sara's insistence he had to drive out his son Ishmael, together with the boy's mother Hagar, into the wilderness of Beer-sheba and exposed them to possible death. One can only surmise what utter desolation must have scarred his sensitive nature. Yet, despite these lacerating defeats, despite his mental anguish, he found the pathway to God's presence.

Moses! How many defeats he sustained in dealing with his people! Moses, the lawgiver who brought discipline out of chaos and anarchy, co-worker with God in creating a free people and a new civilization—surely he deserved the fruits of triumph. But they eluded him. His two monumental achievements—the Exodus and later his role at Sinai—loom higher than Mt. Everest athwart man's spiritual topography. His personal life, however, was saddened by a plethora of galling disappointments. Scorned by the people he sought to serve, he drank the dregs of failure after failure. His most crushing disenchantment and disappointment came in his old age—he was denied entrance into the Promised Land and died with his work uncompleted.

David! Slayer of gargantuan Goliath, composer of transfiguring psalms, ruler over Israel for forty years, intrepid conqueror, empire builder—what a phenomenal success! But was he a success? Twice a fugitive in headlong flight for his life: first from King Saul, later from his rebellious son Absalom seeking to usurp the throne. What dirge can match in torment the broken-hearted father's lament over his dead son: "O my son Absalom, my son, my son, my son Absalom, would I had died for thee, O Absalom, my son, my son!"

This was not the end of his wretchedness. Another son, Adonijah, attempted to seize David's throne, and again the saddened father wallowed in an ocean of despondency. And finally, the overwhelming failure—God did not permit him to build the Temple: "Thou shalt not build a house unto My name because thou hast shed much blood . . ."

This pattern of failure appears too frequently to be fortuitous. All the prophets experienced it. Jeremiah hounded from pillar to post, Ezekiel carried into captivity, Hosea betrayed by an adulterous wife—the entire coterie of prophets fought but failed. Leprous, helpless, hopeless Job groveling in the dungheap, bereft of children, stripped of affluence, taunted by his friends, is the paragon of human suffering.

It was in the labyrinth of their failures that the biblical giants garnered whatever success they could wrest from life. Who will attempt to envision the abject loneliness of their lives, the pain of deeps and heights warring within them, the solitude of their doubts and disappointments, the intensity of their spiritual

בראשית
א

בְּרָא אֱלֹהִים אֵת הַשָּׁמַיִם וְאֵת הָאָרֶץ: וְהָאָרֶץ הָיְתָה תֹהוּ וָבֹהוּ
וְחֹשֶׁךְ עַל־פְּנֵי תְהוֹם וְרוּחַ אֱלֹהִים מְרַחֶפֶת עַל־פְּנֵי הַמָּיִם: וַיֹּאמֶר
אֱלֹהִים יְהִי אוֹר וַיְהִי־אוֹר: וַיַּרְא אֱלֹהִים אֶת־הָאוֹר כִּי־טוֹב וַיַּבְדֵּל
אֱלֹהִים בֵּין הָאוֹר וּבֵין הַחֹשֶׁךְ: וַיִּקְרָא אֱלֹהִים ׀ לָאוֹר יוֹם וְלַחֹשֶׁךְ
קָרָא לָיְלָה וַיְהִי־עֶרֶב וַיְהִי־בֹקֶר יוֹם אֶחָד: פ   וַיֹּאמֶר אֱלֹהִים
יְהִי רָקִיעַ בְּתוֹךְ הַמָּיִם וִיהִי מַבְדִּיל בֵּין מַיִם לָמָיִם: וַיַּעַשׂ אֱלֹהִים
אֶת־הָרָקִיעַ וַיַּבְדֵּל בֵּין הַמַּיִם אֲשֶׁר מִתַּחַת לָרָקִיעַ וּבֵין הַמַּיִם אֲשֶׁר
מֵעַל לָרָקִיעַ וַיְהִי־כֵן: וַיִּקְרָא אֱלֹהִים לָרָקִיעַ שָׁמָיִם וַיְהִי־עֶרֶב וַיְהִי־
בֹקֶר יוֹם שֵׁנִי: פ   וַיֹּאמֶר אֱלֹהִים יִקָּווּ הַמַּיִם מִתַּחַת הַשָּׁמַיִם אֶל־
מָקוֹם אֶחָד וְתֵרָאֶה הַיַּבָּשָׁה וַיְהִי־כֵן: וַיִּקְרָא אֱלֹהִים ׀ לַיַּבָּשָׁה אֶרֶץ
וּלְמִקְוֵה הַמַּיִם קָרָא יַמִּים וַיַּרְא אֱלֹהִים כִּי־טוֹב: וַיֹּאמֶר אֱלֹהִים
תַּדְשֵׁא הָאָרֶץ דֶּשֶׁא עֵשֶׂב מַזְרִיעַ זֶרַע עֵץ פְּרִי עֹשֶׂה פְּרִי לְמִינוֹ אֲשֶׁר
זַרְעוֹ־בוֹ עַל־הָאָרֶץ וַיְהִי־כֵן: וַתּוֹצֵא הָאָרֶץ דֶּשֶׁא עֵשֶׂב מַזְרִיעַ זֶרַע
לְמִינֵהוּ וְעֵץ עֹשֶׂה־פְּרִי אֲשֶׁר זַרְעוֹ־בוֹ לְמִינֵהוּ וַיַּרְא אֱלֹהִים כִּי־
טוֹב: וַיְהִי־עֶרֶב וַיְהִי־בֹקֶר יוֹם שְׁלִישִׁי: פ   וַיֹּאמֶר אֱלֹהִים יְהִי

*Genesis, from Hebrew Pentateuch, Soncino Verlag, Berlin, printed by
the Officina Serpentis, 1930-33.*

struggles? Their lives were a gloomy, gray mosaic of despair and melancholy. They knew they could not conquer, but an inner compulsion deterred them from abrogating their responsibility. They found the prescription to mitigate their failures. The clarion tolled by the prophet Amos possessed them too: "The lion hath roared, who will not fear? The Lord hath spoken, who will not prophesy?" This became an ineluctable urge in all of them. Each of them felt he was a site upon which God had reared His tabernacle.

The possibility of harvesting glory from failure is an enheartening concept in the Bible, proclaiming that the pathway to God is not necessarily along the road of success. Often it emerges out of the abyss of failure. Only when Job had lost all was he able to exclaim, "Now I know that my Redeemer liveth." Whether one moves in light or in shadows, whether one's efforts succeed or miscarry, whether one reaps fulfillment or frustration, the true interpretation of success consists in establishing a dialogical relationship with God.

The infinite love and infinite wisdom, the challenging messages and invincible truths clarioned in the Bible diffuse light into every age. Its ideals are not ephemcra; they are a spiritual curriculum that teaches us who live in time how to apprehend, albeit vaguely, the timelessness of biblical pedagogy. They proclaim that in the lexicon of the spirit the word "failure" does not exist. To labor and fight for the right, not necessarily to triumph, is a divine beckoning to every individual. This is the eternal teaching of the Eternal Book.

שִׁיר הַשִּׁירִים אֲשֶׁר לִשְׁלֹמֹה: יִשָּׁקֵנִי מִנְּשִׁיקוֹת פִּיהוּ כִּי
טוֹבִים דֹּדֶיךָ מִיָּיִן: לְרֵיחַ שְׁמָנֶיךָ טוֹבִים שֶׁמֶן תּוּרַק שְׁמֶךָ
עַל כֵּן עֲלָמוֹת אֲהֵבוּךָ: מָשְׁכֵנִי אַחֲרֶיךָ נָּרוּצָה הֱבִיאַנִי
הַמֶּלֶךְ חֲדָרָיו נָגִילָה וְנִשְׂמְחָה בָּךְ נַזְכִּירָה דֹדֶיךָ מִיַּיִן
מֵישָׁרִים אֲהֵבוּךָ: שְׁחוֹרָה אֲנִי וְנָאוָה בְּנוֹת יְרוּשָׁלָ͏ִם
כְּאָהֳלֵי קֵדָר כִּירִיעוֹת שְׁלֹמֹה: אַל תִּרְאֻנִי שֶׁאֲנִי שְׁחַרְחֹרֶת
שֶׁשֱּׁזָפַתְנִי הַשָּׁמֶשׁ בְּנֵי אִמִּי נִחֲרוּ בִי שָׂמֻנִי נֹטֵרָה אֶת
הַכְּרָמִים כַּרְמִי שֶׁלִּי לֹא נָטָרְתִּי: הַגִּידָה לִּי שֶׁאָהֲבָה
נַפְשִׁי אֵיכָה תִרְעֶה אֵיכָה תַּרְבִּיץ בַּצָּהֳרָיִם שַׁלָּמָה אֶהְיֶה
כְּעֹטְיָה עַל עֶדְרֵי חֲבֵרֶיךָ: אִם לֹא תֵדְעִי לָךְ הַיָּפָה בַּנָּשִׁים
צְאִי לָךְ בְּעִקְבֵי הַצֹּאן וּרְעִי אֶת גְּדִיֹּתַיִךְ עַל מִשְׁכְּנוֹת
הָרֹעִים: לְסֻסָתִי בְּרִכְבֵי פַרְעֹה דִּמִּיתִיךְ רַעְיָתִי: נָאווּ
לְחָיַיִךְ בַּתֹּרִים צַוָּארֵךְ בַּחֲרוּזִים: תּוֹרֵי זָהָב נַעֲשֶׂה לָּךְ
עִם נְקֻדּוֹת הַכָּסֶף: עַד שֶׁהַמֶּלֶךְ בִּמְסִבּוֹ נִרְדִּי נָתַן רֵיחוֹ
צְרוֹר הַמֹּר דּוֹדִי לִי בֵּין שָׁדַי יָלִין: אֶשְׁכֹּל הַכֹּפֶר דּוֹדִי
לִי בְּכַרְמֵי עֵין גֶּדִי: הִנָּךְ יָפָה רַעְיָתִי הִנָּךְ יָפָה עֵינַיִךְ יוֹנִים
הִנְּךָ יָפֶה דוֹדִי אַף נָעִים אַף עַרְשֵׂנוּ רַעֲנָנָה: קֹרוֹת בָּתֵּינוּ
אֲרָזִים רַהִיטֵנוּ בְּרוֹתִים:

ב

אֲנִי חֲבַצֶּלֶת הַשָּׁרוֹן שׁוֹשַׁנַּת הָעֲמָקִים: כְּשׁוֹשַׁנָּה בֵּין

מ. א' ש'ו'ה'ם ד'ל'ה משכני אחריך י'ו' וחסר לגס"א ב'קרי

א · דאָס געזאַנג פֿון געזאַנגען, װאָס פֿון שלמהן.
· קושן זאָל ער מיך מיט די קושן פֿון זײַן מויל;
װאָרום בעסער פֿון װײַן איז דײַן ליבשאַפֿט.
· װױל צום ערוך מיט װײַן דײַנע אײלן,
געקלערטע בוימל איז דײַן נאָמען,
דרום האָבן יונגפֿרױען דיך ליב.

· צי מיך נאָך דיר, לאָמיר לױפֿן! —
זאָל דער מלך מיך ברענגען אין זײַנע קאַמערן,
מיר װעלן זיך לוסטיק און פֿרײלעך מיט דיר,
מיר װעלן לױבן דײַן ליבשאַפֿט
מערער פֿון װײַן.
אמת ליב האָט מען דיך.

· שװאַרץ בין איך, אָבער שײן,
טעכטער פֿון ירושלים,
װי די געצעלטן פֿון קדר,
װי די פֿאָרהאַנגען שלמהס.
· ניט קוקט מיך אָן װאָס איך בין שװאַרצלעך,
װאָרום די זון האָט מיך אָפּגעברענט.
די זין פֿון מײַן מוטער האָבן זיך געצערנט אױף מיר,
זײ האָבן מיך געמאַכט אַ היטערין פֿון די װײַנגערטנער;
מײַן אײגענעם װײַנגאָרטן האָב איך ניט אָפּגעהיט.

· זאָג מיר דו װעמען מײַן זעל האָט ליב,
װוּ פֿיטערסטו,
װוּ מאַכסטו הײַרן װי מיטן טאָג
װאָרום נאָך װאָס זאָל איך זײַן װי הי ...
בײַ די סטאַדעס פֿון דײַנע חבֿרים?

· אַ הענגל ציפּערבלומען אין עין-גדיס װײַנגערטנער
איז מײַן געליבטער מיר.

· ביסט שײן, געליבטע מײַן, ביסט שײן,
דײַנע אױגן זײַנען טױבן.

· ביסט שײן געליבטער מײַן, און ליבלעך,
גרין אױך איז אונדזער געלעגער;
· אונדזערע הױבבאַלקנס צעדערן,
אונדזערע האַנצבערגעטער ציפּרעסן.

ב · איך בין אַ רױז פֿון שרון,
אַ ליליע פֿון די טאָלן.

· װי אַ ליליע צװישן די דערנער,
אַזױ איז מײַן געליבטע צװישן די טעכטער.

· אױב דו װײסט עס דיר ניט,
דו שענסטע פֿון פֿרױען,
בײַ דיר אַרױס אין די טריט פֿון די שאָף,
און פֿיטער דײַנע ציקעלעך בײַ די פּאַסטוכס
געצעלטן.
· צו אַ פֿערדין אין פֿרעהס רײַטװאָגן
האָב איך דיך גלײַכיכן, געליבטע מײַן.
· שײן זײַנען דײַנע באַקן אין די קײטלעך,
דײַן האַלדז אין די שנורן.
· מילדערנע קײטלעך דיר װעלן מיר מאַכן,
מיט פּינטעלעך פֿון זילבער.

· בעת דער מלך איז געװען אױף זײַן הסב-בעט,
האָט מײַן נאַרד געגעבן זײַן ריח.
· אַ בינטל מירא האָט מיר רוט צװישן מײַנע בריסט,
איז מײַן געליבטער מיר.
· הקרוסטעוויל: שֵם שֵם.

*Song of Songs, from the Bible with Yiddish translation by Yehoash.
New York, Yehoash Farlag Gesellschaft, 1941.*

GREAT JEWISH BOOKS AND CIVILIZATION*

By Mortimer J. Cohen

IF THIS title were phrased more accurately, it would be "Books Are Enemies of Civilization," "*Great* Books Are Enemies of Civilization." Books are not merely pieces of paper with print upon them encased in attractive bindings. Books are centers of power and great books are centers of concentrated power. Because great books are centers of concentrated power, books may be dangerous to the status quo.

The history of mankind's reaction to great books proves their potential dangerousness. Books have been burned; books have been put on indexes; books have been locked behind doors; books have been kept in sacred languages; books sometimes have been chained to stands so that people could not take them away and read them.

Yes, books have always been centers of dangerous power and human beings, instinctively fearing danger, are suspicious of books and sometimes hate them. Books have often been enemies of the prevailing civilization in which they were born.

We use the word civilization broadly to mean the rigid forms into which the human spirit hardens as institutions. Though for a time they provide the channels through which human beings fulfill their lives, they grow old and become prisons that crush the spirit. They must be broken to let the spirit flow on to new forms on which it can reach to heights beyond. Not every book proves dangerous to its contemporary civilization. The few that are germinal, that burst out of the hot fires of genius, these burn their blazing pathways through the hampering forms and so make ready for the new advance. Books, like penicillin, are dangerous; penicillin to germs, books to the spiritual diseases of mankind. Great books are agents of change. Insofar as these changes spell progress, books are creators of new orders of being, new worlds for men to dwell in.

Let me discuss briefly a few such books. I shall mention altogether just three books, but in these three we can find witnesses of the dangerousness of great books.

* Address delivered at the Annual Meeting of the Jewish Book Council of America, Wednesday, May 21, 1952, New York, N. Y.

I.

The first book which I think is the most dangerous book ever written in the history of human civilization is the Bible. The Bible is the most dangerous book that has ever appeared upon this earth. If I were a dictator, I would gather every copy of the Bible in the world in every language in which it has been published and I would destroy that Book because that Book stands as an eternal challenge against the civilizations of mankind.

It is a lucky thing that people do not read the Bible. It is very fortunate that those who do read the Bible do not always understand it. It is most fortunate that for a long period of time the Bible was written in languages that the common man could not understand. Indeed, at one time in the history of western Europe, there were revolutions when men proposed to translate the Bible into the common language of the people of the country.

The Bible has been a dangerous book because it was born in the midst of a civilization which it determined to undermine and destroy. The civilization in which the Bible was born was a civilization which could be summed up in one word — idolatry. The idolatry-system was the civilization that the Bible writers determined to root out and utterly destroy. Read through the pages of the Bible and on almost every page you will read exhortations against idols, idol worshippers, idolatry as a system of life.

Now, when we speak of idolatry and the worship of idols, remember the people who lived in that civilization were not different from ourselves. They had a great deal of intelligence and they had a large understanding of the world. But the idolatry-system implied much more than people merely bowing before stone and wooden images.

The idolatry-system involved a whole complex of institutions, the outer garb of which was religion. There were, of course, the great god Moloch and all the other gods of the ancient pagan world. But the idolatry-system within its religious garb was also an economic system; it was also a political system; it was also a human system.

The idolatry-system implied the private ownership of land by powerful individuals led by and protected by the king. The king gave large portions of land to his nobles. The nobles let the people within their power toil upon the land. The system was owned by the king. The king was the ruler of it all; and not only was the king the ruler of it all, but the king was at times the god manifest of the system.

Pharaoh was not simply the king of Egypt. He was its god. He was the god against whom the God of Israel fought. Moses led a theological war of God against god, of system against system. So, too, the king of Babylon, and the king of Assyria, and the kings of the ancient world were gods upon the earth. In their hands they held the power of the state. They held in their hands the control of the land, and the people upon the land were merely serfs and slaves. These had no human rights. Their only right was to die in the wars that the god-kings engaged in when they wanted more land and more power.

It was a cruel system. It was a system that created great pyramids and temples, but those pyramids and temples were founded upon human suffering and human lives and the bitterness of men and women who had no rights whatsoever upon this earth.

It was against the idolatry-system that the Bible fought a relentless war. To the Bible the land did not belong to the king; the land belongs to God. And the people had their equal rights in the land, tribe by tribe and family by family. So that the economic system within the Bible waged war against the economic system on which the idolatry of the ancient Bible world was based.

The king of Israel ruled with the consent of his people. He had to study the Torah which was the Constitution and he had to govern his people by it, for he was only a constitutional king. He was not the representative of God upon earth. He was elected by the people and he could be rejected by the people.

The people upon the soil had rights, not rights that the king gave them or the parliament of the times. They had rights inherent in themselves, rights written in the pages of the Bible. Within the Bible existed a totally different system, a system that made for human well-being, for freedom, for human dignity, for the right of the individual to his own life and his own way of life; so that a citizen could defy his king to take away his ancestral land. Only a cunning princess and queen from the pagan world dared to deprive him of his rights in the land, of his dignity as a human being. Meanwhile her Jewish husband-king lay on his bed in the palace and sulked because he could not get the land so that he could enlarge his hunting grounds and his gardens of pleasure.

If you lived in the ancient world when the Bible was written and were a king, you would not have liked the writers of the Bible. You would not have liked their teachings. You would have hated them. If you were part of the pagan world and you saw this Book challenging the very existence of the things in which you believed and the idolatry-system from which you profited, you too would look upon that Book and the people who wrote it as dangerous to the peace of the world.

II.

Let us turn to another era in human history; we will understand again why books are dangerous. We come to the Middle Ages, somewhere around the thirteenth century. In western Europe, in which we are for the most part interested, the people were dominated by what we might call the faith-system. The Church ruled the whole of Europe and the Church asked the peoples of Europe but one thing: Believe in me. It did not encourage the common people of Europe to read, to think, to discuss, to criticize. It was a system based purely upon faith: Believe in me and you shall be saved.

Somewhere about the twelfth century out from the East came messengers, messengers from the Arab world. They had met and had been mastered by Greek philosophy, Greek science and Greek wisdom. The Jews who came in contact with that eastern world translated scientific and philosophical books from the Arabic into Hebrew, and from the Hebrew those books began to appear here and there in the prevailing Latin.

These books symbolized a new, upsetting force in the western world. It was the force of reason, the force of intelligence, inquiring intelligence and questioning curiosity.

There appeared a great Jew, the greatest perhaps since the close of the days of the Bible, Moses Maimonides. Maimonides wrote his "Guide For the Perplexed" in Arabic. His task was to make Aristotelian philosophy, which was the philosophy of the curious mind, the philosophy of the supremacy of reason, accommodate itself to the Bible of his ancestors.

In the *Moreh Nebukhim* Maimonides wrote another of those books, which if I had been Pope at that time, I would have destroyed utterly and ruthlessly every copy of it in every language it was translated into. I would have utterly destroyed it, for it was a source of danger, a destroyer of the faith-system of western Europe.

Hardly had the *Moreh Nebukhim* appeared, when it was translated into Latin. Among the great minds of the time one man in particular read it and made it his own. It was Thomas Aquinas. Thomas Aquinas was one of the most brilliant minds of the Church. He had studied and absorbed the whole Maimonidean philosophy. That influence, together with his researches in Aristotle, forced the first breaks in the walls of the faith-system, the breaks that culminated in the Reformation and the coming of reason into the realm of religion.

The faith-system was not only a Church. It was also the feudal system, for the faith-system owned lands and power. It could make kings. It could unmake kings. It held the keys not only of this world; it held the keys to heaven and the keys to hell, so that whether a man lived here upon this earth or whether he hoped to ascend into heaven or whether he feared the burning flames of hell, he had to reckon with the faith-system.

It was against this faith-system that Maimonides' *Moreh Nebukhim* proved itself to be one of the most dangerous forces that ever appeared in the history of human civilization. It fought against this faith-system by its emphasis upon reason, the right of the individual to think, the determination to harmonize reason and faith. Ahad Ha-am, in one of his essays, "The Supremacy of Reason," says:

"Only a few (in his time and ours) understood that Maimonides' teaching was revolutionary not because of his attitude on this or that particular question, but because he dethroned religion altogether from the supreme judgment-seat, and put reason in its place: because he made it his basic principle that whenever a Scripture is contradicted by proof we do not accept the Scripture, but *explain* it in accordance with reason."

"This emancipation of reason," continues Ahad Ha-am, "from its subordination to an external authority is the great and eternal achievement which has so endeared Maimonides to all those of our people who have striven after knowledge and the light."

Through Thomas Aquinas' great work, *Summa Theologica*, where Maimonides' teachings about God, the soul, the reason and man, found lodgement, the faith-system of the Middle Ages received its mortal blow. The walls crumbled and the modern age may be said to have begun. When Thomas Aquinas absorbed the Maimonidean and the Aristotelian philosophy of reason, reason for the first time was raised to challenge faith and the teaching became this: One can acquire truth not only through faith, but through the reason that God implanted in man's mind.

Then began the self-criticism of western Europe by men. They asked why should they be chained to the earth which they plowed and out of which they painfully drew their sustenance. They questioned the divine right of kings. They challenged all authority. Finally the faith-system broke. Out of that struggle, rooted in a dangerous book, came the Renaissance, the Reformation, the French Revolution (it even worshipped the Goddess of Reason) and the democratic world that we have today, itself now being challenged and put to the test.

III.

Finally, we come to our own time. What kind of a civilization do we live in and what is the great danger that we face, not only we here in the United States, but the whole of the western world;

the western world for the most part dominates world civilization, although its dominance is being questioned by the peoples of the East.

We might well ask ourselves: What is the supreme enemy that we must face in our time? It is not Communism and it is not Capitalism. It is the machine. The machine is our common enemy today. We live today in the machine-system and the machine-system demands automatic action. The machine is the antithesis of all that is human. It would dehumanize men; it would rob them of their individualities, of their personalities, of their spirit. The machine today is the common enemy of mankind. As idolatry was not merely an act of worship but was a whole system of life, and as the Church was not merely a place of worship but was a whole system of living, so the machine is not merely the specific machine in the factory or the particular machine that communicates for us or that takes us from place to place — the machine involves the techniques of our whole common way of life today from the form in which we take our leisure amusements to the very structure of Government. The machine is a state of mind.

Some years ago there was a play on Broadway called *R. U. R.* written by a well-known European dramatist, Karel Capek. This play struck deep into the consciousness of that time for it stood as a prophecy and a warning. *R. U. R.*, standing for Russom's Universal Robots, pictured a thoroughly mechanized world where men, in the name of cold efficiency, became soulless, spiritless mechanisms — robots. These human robots had no hearts, no feelings, no minds. They were merely the tenders of machines. This represented the ideal fulfillment of the machine-system.

Another memorable play was produced by Eugene O'Neill and was called *Dynamo*. It was short-lived because perhaps the American people could not take the play. The dynamo was set up as on an altar. It was worshipped. It was the symbol of power. It was the symbol of our world where the people were reduced to nonentities.

The novel called *1984* by George Orwell, contained a new word, the "unperson." The unperson is the person who fits into the machine of the state; he fits into the machine of industry; he fits into the mechanisms of a mechanical world. George Orwell holds up his book as a warning and says: "Remember, the eye of the big brother is on you, and you must think his thoughts; you must do his deeds; you must fulfill his will."

Today the mechanization of our world with its dehumanization of our Society is the greatest enemy we face. For the machine spirit threatens our basic ideals of personal freedom and the dignity of the human spirit. It is not the gadgets that we love to trifle with that confound us. Nor dare we reject the countless tools and instrumentalities that modern science has invented to make life easier and more comfortable for us. It is rather the creation of social machines which regiment our thoughts, our education. Men are reduced to saying "Yes!" or "No!" as the superior wills who operate the social machinery would have them answer. Thought-control, censorship, cultural boycotts, inquisitorial committees — all are manifestations of one common determination, namely, the determination to reduce men mentally and spiritually to cogs in a machine.

We have entered such an advanced stage of the mechanization of life where indeed in one great country of the world, Russia, man may not think his thoughts nor write his thoughts. In our own United States committees are set up to see that men's thoughts follow the proper line. And woe unto the man or the woman who does not think according to the line that is set up by the state.

The enemy of our world is the threatened mechanization of man, his total dehumanization. It is making him "unpersoned." He is being reduced to a robot.

The dangerous books of our times are the books that are fighting against this. One cannot mention all of these books, but I want to mention one — the most dangerous book that has recently appeared. It may not be recognized as such. Most of us have not even read it.

We have had the pleasure of having in our midst during these past few months a great spiritual teacher, Martin Buber. In his book called *I and Thou* (and in his later volume, *Between Man and Man*), Buber has not taught an escape from this world, but a confrontation of the machine world that is crowding in around us by the human spirit. In this book Dr. Buber writes, and I tried to reduce it to two or three sentences (I know that this is inadequate to express his rich contribution to our thinking) that there are two possible relations between the person and the world about him. He summarizes these two relations in simple terms: The I-It and the I-Thou relationships.

The I-It or the thing relation requires in no way that the I should interpenetrate into the thing. A chair is a chair and it is accepted as such, I and It. For me to know the great universe as a scientist, I need only the I-It relationship, but when I meet a human being, a kindred spirit, the I-It relationship which is purely surface and superficial no longer has validity.

I-Thou, I-you, you and I together influence each other and in the interplay between person and person, an insight, an idea, a reality is discovered that is unique.

And Dr. Buber expands this to the relationship of the individual to the world about him, the vast universe of which he is a part, for then I and Thou, Thou the spirit of the universe, you and I, O God, we meet, and there is a confrontation of the individual with the universe.

That cannot be mechanized. Dr. Buber represents a philosophy of life that is a protest against and a danger to the mechanization of the world in which we live.

Our machine-system, as it expresses itself in totalitarian governments with all the evils of regimenting the individual and suppressing freedom of thought and denying the ultimate postulates of freedom itself, cannot stand before the sovereignty of the individual, which is the corrolary of Buber's mystical philosophy. Buber's fundamental emphasis is on the individual, even in religion. "Meeting God in inwardness in person," is the basic religious experience. The individual person is the object of God's love and affection.

In a charming little volume called *The Way of Man*, Buber devotes a chapter to the precious uniqueness of the individual in Judaism and especially in Hasidic teachings. He writes:

"Every person born into this world represents something new, something that never existed before, something original and unique . . . ! Every single man is a new thing in the world, and is called upon to fulfill his particularity in this world. For verily: that this is not done, is the reason why the coming of the messiah is delayed."

And elsewhere in the same volume, Buber tells this Hasidic story about Rabbi Zusya. It happened a short time before his death when he said: "In the world to come I shall not be asked: 'Why were you not like Moses?' I shall be asked: 'Why were you not Zusya?'"

In an interview Buber granted just before he left the United States, he spoke of this growing mechanization of man's spirit and strongly denounced it. The interviewer's words are these:

"He is disturbed by the thought that, in our complex society, the path of least resistance leads to the support of those organizations and philosophies which dehumanize and depersonalize our basic relations with God and our fellow-men. In this respect he expresses constant concern with the fate of the individual who has been caught up in the organized machinery of Church, State, Party, Union or Business. The result is that the individual gets to behave like a machine and treats every other being, animate or inanimate, as a mere object . . . rather than as a subject or person."

Martin Buber's great contribution through his writings — and they stem from the Bible, embody the supremacy of reason of Maimonides, lead through Hasidism, and reckon with modern thought — is his rebellion against the machine-system, asserting the sacredness of the individual soul in whom is reflected God's glory.

Dr. Buber would not be permitted nor his books be permitted in Soviet Russia, where they are more alerted to the danger of books than we are. We in America still permit such books to be published. For the most part they are kept in German so that the masses may not get the books and the people cannot read them, but there will be persons who will delve into Dr. Buber's book and the time may come when this lonely thinker, who already has influenced Christian theology and whose name appears in index after index of theological books as the authority and the source for a new insight, an insight that man is hungry for, in the midst of this increasingly impersonal, mechanized and dehumanized world, will be more recognized.

To sum it all up: Books are centers of dangerous power. Great books are the eternal enemies of prevailing civilizations. We of the Jewish Book Council of America, who are dedicated to books, if we do our work well, must know that we are given to dangerous living and to dangerous lives. The book, the Jewish book, is still the most vital influence that we can give to human civilization. Whether it was the Bible in the ancient world, or whether it was The Guide for the Perplexed by Maimonides in the Middle Ages, or whether it be the mystical books that are written by Buber and his followers today, the Jewish book is no friend of any civilization that would deny the human spirit.

Great books are the carriers of the human spirit. The old and worn Midrash, that when Israel stood at the foot of Mt. Sinai, a hand appeared to descend from the darkened clouds of the heavens and in that great hand rested a book and a sword, is eternally true. The book and the sword were bound together, and God's voice was heard speaking, and the voice said: "Choose! choose!"

Every generation and every civilization must choose between the book and the sword. The book is still the most dangerous weapon that man has created with which to defeat the sword in human affairs.

GREAT JEWISH BOOKS: OLD AND NEW*

By LEON ROTH

AS I pondered the theme set to me for this evening's discourse, there came to my mind two sayings from two English authors of recent times. The first was that of Mr. E. M. Forster, who remarks somewhere: "Books have to be read (worse luck, for it takes a long time); it is the only way of discovering what they contain." That seems to me to cover most of what needs to be said under the heading of *one* word in our theme, the word Books. The second was that of G. K. Chesterton, who is reported to have said: "The *Iliad* is great because all life is a battle, the *Odyssey* because all life is a journey, the *Book of Job* because all life is a riddle." That seems to dispose of the word Great: a 'great' book is a book which stirs us by its treatment of a prominent and persistent aspect of experience. It rather looks as though all there is left for me to do is to settle the word Jewish.

I wish I could but, alas, I can't. I used to think I knew what Jewish meant but now I am not sure. You all know much more about it, and much better about it, than I; and if I were honest I should ask for our positions to be reversed — I should go down there and all of you would come up here. It did occur to me to suggest that to the Chairman, but I saw that the procedure, however enjoyable for both parties, might lead to some confusion. And so I had to set to work myself. The problem was, how?

I had to start somewhere, so I took the first publishers' list I could lay my hands on of the Great Books of world literature and asked myself which of them were written by Jews. The list happened to be that of the 990 volumes of the well-known and justly admired Everyman's Library. On search I found the following: *Ancient Hebrew Literature* (the Old Testament and Apocrypha); the *New Testament;* and then, in alphabetical order of authors, Disraeli's *Coningsby,* Heine's *Prose and Poetry,* Josephus' *Wars of the Jews,* Marx's *Capital,* and Spinoza's *Ethics.* That's a fairly mixed bag but it's hardly comprehensive; and it's not all what is commonly known as Jewish.

So I started again. I saw that I had used the wrong criterion:

* This lecture, delivered at a 1955 Jewish Book Week celebration in London, was published by the Jewish Book Council of England and is reprinted with permission.

a book is not necessarily Jewish because it happens to be written by a Jew. And, of course, the contrary also holds. There might be books fairly to be called Jewish which were written by non-Jews. So I widened my compass and turned to the list a second time — a standard list, remember, of Great Books actually published and put into common circulation — and I looked for Jewish books in a broad sense. The first example I came across (it was in the Bs) may appear to many of you trivial, but I give it to you all the same. It's a favorite book of my own and, however little you may think it to our present purpose, I might perhaps induce some of you to turn to it and enjoy it.

One of the most wayward of the many wayward eccentrics who make up the richness of English literature is George Borrow. Borrow was a wanderer with a taste for boxing and philology; and he cherished all wandering peoples, particularly Gypsies, Armenians, and Jews. True, he did not like the Jewish bruiser (as indeed, I may remark in parenthesis, I don't either), and he spent a whole chapter of *Lavengro* in dispraise of the great Daniel Mendoza. But this is as nothing compared with his descriptions of the mysterious Jews of all kinds who are made to pass before our eyes on his crowded pages. Let me read you a short section from his *Bible in Spain*, an alleged record of his travels in Spain and Portugal in the service of the British and Foreign Bible Society in the eighteen-forties. He has just described a figure he came across when riding at night near Talavera. He then goes on:

There was something peculiarly strange about the figure; but what struck me the most was the tranquillity with which it moved along, taking no heed of me, though of course, aware of my proximity, but looking straight forward along the road, save when it occasionally raised a huge face and large eyes towards the moon, which was now shining forth in the eastern quarter.

'A cold night,' said I at last. 'Is this the way to Talavera?'

'It is the way to Talavera, and the night is cold.'

'I am going to Talavera,' said I, 'as I suppose you are yourself.'

'I am going thither; so are you, *Bueno*.'

The tones of the voice which delivered these words were in their way quite as strange and singular as the figure to which the voice belonged. They were not exactly the tones of a Spanish voice, and yet there was something in them that could hardly be foreign; the pronunciation also was correct, and the language, although singular, faultless. But I was most struck with the manner in which the last word, *bueno*, was spoken.

I had heard something like it before, but where or when I could by no means remember. A pause now ensued, the figure stalking on as before with the most perfect indifference, and seemingly with no disposition either to seek or avoid conversation.

'Are you not afraid,' said I at last, 'to travel these roads in the dark? It is said that there are robbers abroad.'

'Are you not rather afraid,' replied the figure, 'to travel these roads in the dark — you who are ignorant of the country, who are a foreigner, an Englishman?'

'How is it that you know me to be an Englishman?' demanded I, much surprised.

'That is no difficult matter,' replied the figure; 'the sound of your voice was enough to tell me that.'

'You speak of voices,' said I. 'Suppose the tone of your own voice were to tell me who you are?'

'That it will not do,' replied my companion. 'You know nothing about me. You can know nothing about me.'

'Be not so sure of that, my friend. I am acquainted with many things of which you have little idea.'

'*Por exemplo*,' said the figure.

'For example,' said I, 'you speak two languages.'

The figure moved on, seemed to consider a moment, and then said slowly, '*Bueno.*'

'You have two names,' I continued, 'one for the house and the other for the street. Both are good, but the one by which you are called at home is the one which you like best.'

The man walked on about ten paces in the same manner as he had previously done. All of a sudden he turned, and taking the bridle of the burro gently in his hand, stopped her. I had now a full view of his face and figure, and those huge features and herculean form still occasionally revisit me in my dreams. I see him standing in the moonshine, staring me in the face with his deep calm eyes. At last he said —

'Are you also of us?'

Remember this was written over a hundred years ago, a full eighty years before Schwartz came again on the tracks of the still-existing Marrano communities during the First World War. But I'm not thinking of that. My point is that here we have a great book of permanent, although peripheral, Jewish interest because of the human character of its many Jewish episodes, a book which may therefore be included, with charity perhaps rather than with pedantic accuracy, in our tentative list of Great Jewish Books.

Borrow is unique, but the triumph of uniqueness is that it admits the existence of other varieties of uniqueness; and now that we see the sort of thing we may look out for in our Everyman list, we can find plenty more. I shall not delay you with the names of well-known compositions of Byron, Dickens, Marlowe, Scott, or Shakespeare. But I think we can fairly call the Jewish reader's attention to, say, Matthew Arnold (the chapters on Hebraism and Hellenism in *Culture and Anarchy*; Spinoza and the Bible and other essays in his *Essays in Criticism*); and while we're mentioning critics, there is Quiller Couch's *Cambridge Lectures* with the admirable essay on reading the Bible. Then there's Browning — Rabbi Ben Ezra, Cleon, even Bishop Blougram's vindication of the United Synagogue (though you won't find it by that title in the table of contents); George Eliot's *Daniel Deronda* and Macaulay's *Speeches;* and after Macaulay (I am still on the Index of Everyman) I see Milman's *History of the Jews*, a book not to be sneezed at even now. Talking of history reminds me that all history has a background, and the background of Jewish history is illumined by such books as Ford's *Gatherings from Spain*, De Joinville's *Memoirs of the Crusades*, Irving's *Conquest of Granáda* and the *Life of Mahomet*, and of course Gibbon's *Decline and Fall*, and Mommsen's *Rome*. But I see we're going too far afield and I must pull up. But I shall first, greatly venturing, point a moral.

It is this. I doubt whether there is at all a book of *purely* Jewish reference, much less of purely Jewish *greatness*. A great book, as we saw, is a book which deals worthily with a prominent and pervasive human interest. It may deal with it in its Jewish aspect or in its Jewish connections, or purely in its Jewish manifestations; but it is great only if, in the particular Jewishness, it manifests the universally human. That is why the Bible is great. As the rabbis say of the Book of Genesis, it is the "Book of the Generations," not of Priest or of Levite or of Israelite but "of man."

I say this in view of a theory which is widely held and to which in practice I have given some support myself. Those who hold it will tell you that in my search for Great Jewish Books I have started from the wrong end altogether. A Great Jewish Book, they will say, is only in Hebrew; and if by inadvertence it allows itself to be written in any other language, it becomes its real self, as it were, only when translated (they say: translated *back*) into Hebrew. The standard example is offered by Maimonides' *Guide for the Perplexed*. The Arabic in which it was written (they say) moulders in libraries. It is the Hebrew version which is great and which lives.

I think I can fairly dodge the issues raised by that interesting, but not necessarily sound, theory, for two reasons. The first is that tomorrow you will have the opportunity of listening to a special lecture on Hebrew literature. The second is that, for all our interest in Hebrew, we are most of us (regrettably) not Hebrew scholars. It is therefore just the translation from the Hebrew into English rather than the repatriation (as it were) of the English, or whatever language it may be, into Hebrew, which is important for us. I shall then, if I may, beat a retreat, using as a smoke-screen the old Rabbinic dictum on the Shema, the "Hear O Israel" . . . "Hear in whatever language you *can* hear;" and turn to the possibilities offered by translation.

Translations are of two kinds. We may start with a glance at the easier and more obvious.

And first let us express our gratitude to the men who have labored so successfully that we have now, in addition to Ḥumash, a Bible, Prayer Book and Maḥzor, Mishnah, Midrash, Talmud, Zohar, and a whole series (in extract) of Jewish philosophers, in English dress for English readers. This work has been done for Anglo-Jewry in our own day and is just cause for pride. Nor should we forget the Schiff Library published in the United States by the Jewish Publication Society of America. These pocket volumes, modelled on the Loeb series of Greek and Latin Classics, offer in admirable form editions of some typical Rabbinic texts and of some poets and moralists of the later period, in both the Hebrew original and English translation. I need only instance the delightful Zangwill *Gabirol*, the Nina Salaman *Jehudah Halevi*, the Israel Abrahams *Hebrew Ethical Wills*, in witness of the vigor and attractiveness of the English side; whilst the names of Brody, Malter, and Davidson on the Hebrew side are sufficient to quieten (I do not say silence) the suspicions of the experts. This series, so admirably planned, so carefully executed and so charmingly produced, has one fault only: it stopped almost as soon as it started and comprises no more than about twenty volumes.

I said it has one fault only. I was wrong. It has two; and I feel so strongly about the value of this series, and of the more ambitious Rabinowitz series inaugurated by Yale, and of the versions of the classical literature made in this country which I mentioned to start with, that I'm going to risk a ride on an old and favorite hobby-horse and be, for a moment, apparently — but not really — ungrateful.

You will remember my opening text from Mr. E. M. Forster: "Books have to be read (worse luck . . .); it is the only way of discovering what they contain." May I add the rider that, if books are to be read, they must be easily procurable, that is, be cheap. The books I've mentioned, with their wonderful paper and print and binding — I am not being ironical: they *are* wonderfully produced — are magnificent but too dear.

Now I know what I'm going to be told, and I'm not going to argue about it because I can't. In these days no books, and certainly not fine books, can be produced cheaply, especially when the market is so restricted. But a way out exists, and it must be noted. It is an intermediate way, and like most intermediate ways it is far from being the best. But it is a refuge from the worst. The best is, of course, that everybody should have his own books. The worst is that nobody (except the rich) should have any books at all. The middle way is that libraries should be provided everywhere possible, and thoroughly and generously stocked.

I happen myself to be living in a city where there is a synagogue on the walls of which there are bookshelves; and on the bookshelves are books, rows upon rows of them. On my first visit I inspected them and found they were — quite rightly — sets of prayer books and Pentateuchs; admirable books and in their place. I am not grumbling or contemning or criticizing; very much to the contrary. But suppose that *in addition to* the rows upon rows of prayer books and Pentateuchs (I am reminded of the old jest which I shall not translate: ותמלא הארץ חמס. חומש, מחזור, סדור.) — suppose that *in addition to* the prayer books and Pentateuchs there were sets of the Schiff Classics, of the various Soncino Press publications, of the East and West Library, even of the books from the Everyman list I have mentioned — let them be in a separate room but let that room be properly equipped; and the center chosen need not be only a religious one although the synagogue is a, if not the, natural place to start in: — boys' clubs, committee rooms, dance halls, night clubs, Woburn House — any place where Jews go: I myself should like to see such collections in the public libraries; suppose ...

How to do it? One obvious and easy way is to devote to it the next *Kol Nidrei* collection. But alternatively you can look out for a Jewish Carnegie, or run Book Clubs, or start a Publication Society, or consult Mr. Gollancz; anything you like: but so long as your Schiff Classics cost what they cost and your Soncino Midrash costs what it costs — and I say yet again that with conditions as they are these books are not overpriced — the only way to get Jewish books into Jewish hands is by a collective effort whereby the individual, if he can't have all of a book all of the time, can have all of a book, or a part of a book, at least part of the time. Jewish libraries everywhere and the books in many copies — what better investment for the Jewish communities of any country! We cannot, of course, force the horses to drink, and it may be difficult even to bring them to the river; so we must bring the river to them.

I said there were two sorts of translation, and one of them, the more obvious one, has been mentioned. The second is the translation of a classic not only into the language, but in terms of the thought, of the present time. In order to avoid confusion, I shall call this kind of translation, interpretation, with the remark that, without this second sort of translation, interpretation, the first sort, which is often not much more than transliteration, is (regrettably) useless. Putting a translation of the Talmud (for example) into the hands of untrained everyman is like giving him a ticket for a visit to a coal-mine when he asks for fuel for his sitting-room fire.

Of interpreters Anglo-Jewry has had very few. Schechter was one, Israel Abrahams was another. These scholars realized that although erudition is the foundation, it is not the end, of scholarship. An interpreter brings books home to men's "business and bosoms." He re-lives, and helps others to re-live, them. In Greek studies this is what Gilbert Murray has been doing (in addition to some other things) for over half a century. We need similar work, that is, similar workers, in Jewish studies. Our scholars must be taught that this work, what the French call "vulgarization," is not, as many of them seem to think, something to be ashamed of; but it is not, as they also suppose, easy. It demands the most finished scholarship, the keenest sympathy, and the most profound understanding. It is the finest and possibly the most rewarding, as it is certainly the most requested, fruit of the tree of learning.

But we cannot hope for many Schechters or Israel Abrahams, and I should like to mention a few examples of books written by scholars-on-holiday, or intelligent laymen, which seem to me to be of the type required today. I take them at random from the bookshelf. Here is the unforgettable (but, alas, forgotten) volume of essays, *Jewish Ideals*, by the Australian-English-American Jewish scholar Joseph Jacobs, whose centenary has just been celebrated by the Jewish Historical Society; here the translations by Elkan Adler of the largely autobiographical *Jewish Travellers of the Middle Ages;* here that splendid account of Biblical and post-Biblical Jewish moral ideas *The Old Testament and After* of Claude Montefiore; here the fascinating collection of historical sketches called *Dreamers of the Ghetto*, by Israel Zangwill. No one of these books is a work of pure scholarship though much scholarship went to their making; yet every layman will remember them with gratitude. They come from great Jewish hearts and are full to bursting with great Jewish themes. They are, each in its own way, interpretations, of one kind or another, of great episodes in the Jewish tradition; and they are all stimulating in the real sense that they make the reader want to know, and even to think, more. What we need today is the stimulating book in this sense, the book that helps us to make our first plunge.

A subject in which this need is especially urgent is our own greatest original book, the Bible itself. My own interest was first aroused by my form-master in the City of London School before the First World War who, when we were all tired at the end of term (and sometimes in the middle) of Cicero and Demosthenes, used to read out in class chapters from the Bible (and, alternatively, George Meredith). He afterwards published a small book, *The Literary Genius of the Old Testament*, which I heartily commend to you. The author is P. C. Sands; the publisher, the Oxford University Press. Another most stimulating little book, published by the Cambridge University Press, is E. G. King's *Early Religious Poetry of the Hebrews*. It was this book which first brought home to many of us the fact that a great deal of the Hebrew Bible is in recognizable verse form. Your expert will point out that these books are by amateurs, that they are no more than a hundred small pages each, and that anyhow they are out of date; and he will endeavor to persuade you, as I have been persuaded recently, to spend a vast sum on the 909 octavo pages of a Harvard professor. My advice to you is, don't. Avoid professors. They know too much. And they're so anxious to put you right on every detail that they smother any live interest you might have ever had. We ordinary folk can afford to be wrong. We cannot afford to have our interest smothered.

And how exciting the Bible has become with all the new discoveries. Take the latest book of M. Dupont-Sommer carefully translated for us from the French by Mr. R. D. Barnett of the British Museum and produced at a human price by Vallentine, Mitchell — for 10s. 6d. you get a story which for anyone with a mite of imagination opens up undreamed of vistas. We've all heard dimly of the Essenes; but here we are told of the contents of a huge Essene library (or so the author thinks), and together with it, in other caves which have now been found and investigated, data and information affecting most subjects connected with Judaism and Jewish history for a whole hitherto almost unknown epoch covering, possibly, some hundreds of years. Fancy reading in a casual footnote that a portion of a pre-*First*-Destruction book of Leviticus has been found! And whether we accept M. Dupont-Sommer's views or the even more exciting theory of the Reader in Rabbinics at Cambridge who thinks that the library is Jewish-Christian and that at least one now famous document contains references to the central figures of the New Testament, we have ample opportunity to follow out ideas — Jewish ideas — which have touched and influenced the world, and, incidentally, to sharpen our wits in a field where even scholars disagree.

This leads me to note that the new finds, and the controversies over their history and significance, only serve to emphasize, what is sufficiently obvious from other considerations too, that we Jews ought to interest ourselves in, and know more about, the documents and doctrine of Christianity. I shall not labor the point that its authors were Jews and that its subject-matter — how man should live — (although not necessarily its conclusions) is Jewish. I only ask you to remember how closely the new finds, the Apocrypha and the so-called Pseudepigrapha, the New Testament, the writings of Philo (available in the old Bohn version and in the Loeb library), the works of Josephus, the earliest Church Fathers, the Midrashim, both Halachic and Aggadic, and the Mishnah and Tosaphta, all hang together and illumine one another in the panorama of Jewish and world history. And this epoch was crucial not only in the social and political, but also, and far more importantly, in the *religious* history of Jewry; for the understanding of which by English readers we have the incomparable *Judaism in the First Centuries of the Christian Era*, by the great student of Rabbinics and the history of religion, the late George Foot Moore, of Harvard, a book which I hope will be found in many copies on the shelves of all our community libraries.

I have had several occasions to mention Josephus. Anyone interested in Jewish psychological types should read and re-read Josephus' *The Wars of the Jews*. To one who has been at all mixed up in modern Jewish public affairs it reads, in its majestic way, like a contemporary satire. But Josephus is more than *The Wars of the Jews*; and I earnestly draw your attention to the second part of his short work *Against Apion*. (It is not available, unfortunately, in Everyman, but it forms part of the first volume of the Loeb edition by the late St. J. Thackeray). It is strangely ignored by Jewish writers but it contains one of the best accounts ever written of the genius of Judaism. It is extraordinary how firmly the essentials are grasped and how clearly and boldly they are expressed. I say, turn to the *second* part. Scholars of course will send you to the first with its citations from long-forgotten authors, and so weary you before you get to the real point. The second part, where Josephus, instead of quoting other people, speaks in his own name and on things for which he cares deeply and intimately, is not only readable; it is genuinely alive and fine; and that, I suppose, is a principal reason for our scholars to ignore it.

Another reason may be that it is an attempt to set out the meaning of the great themes of Judaism in plain terms. Josephus is not a theologian, but he has observed the basic fact that Judaism is primarily a theology in the strict sense of the word, that is, a doctrine of God. This doctrine of God leads to a doctrine of man; and Josephus describes in some detail the main features of the way of life which the Jewish doctrine of God involves. In particular he explains, and follows out in its practical consequences, the root idea of regulation and law.

I mention this because it seems to me that one of the main (and many) deficiencies in modern Jewish life is an appreciation of the necessity of giving positive, though not necessarily dogmatic, information on these and similar themes. We seem to be concerned to spread knowledge about everything except the nature and doctrine of Judaism.

And that leads me to some wider points which I feel it essential to touch upon. The first is the general question why we should worry about books at all; and on that I shall have some reasonably conventional remarks to make although I may have to give them an irritating application. Another, which I propose to take first, is a little more elementary and obvious, although necessary. You may take it as the effete moralizing of a former pedagogue, or the death-bed growlings of a dying Tory, or the last fling of an Enemy of the People. But addressing myself in particular to the younger and more important elements in this audience, may I say that in matters of books, or if you like, literature and particularly great literature, or, in general, things of the mind, nothing can be achieved without personal effort. And by personal effort I mean something more than the turning of a knob. Unless you're prepared to give your time and your brain and your will, all talk about books is empty. I'm afraid of using the word Study. But I looked up my old Latin dictionary the other day and found that the word *Studium* from which Study is derived means application, assiduity, zeal, eagerness, fondness, inclination, desire, exertion. Well, I can only tell you that without application, assiduity, zeal, eagerness, fondness, inclination, desire, exertion, you won't get anywhere with books. Reading a book isn't just flipping over pages. And reading once only isn't reading. There's a great deal to be said

for the old-fashioned Jewish practice of שנים מקרא ואחד תרגום,
reading, translating into your own idiom, and then reading a
second time; or even (again the recommendation is Rabbinic)
setting aside so much of your spare time every day to a regular
grind — say, an hour a day, and two hours Friday evening, and
three hours Sabbath afternoon: that makes ten hours regular
reading a week; and try learning a Psalm, or a chapter from Isaiah,
by heart every day. It'll stand you in good stead, both in good
times and in bad.

For I am afraid that we shall have bad times as well as good,
and that will serve as introduction to the final, and cardinal, point
I want to raise with you this evening: Why read at all, and if we
do, why Great Books?

I have first to return a general answer; and having stated why
we, as human beings, need books, I shall ask why we need them
as Jews. And I shall now have to take the word Great in my theme
a little more seriously: not only, Why books, but Why Great
Books? If one must read at all (and the necessity is not demonstrated), why should we not be satisfied with the daily, and (of
course) the weekly, press?

I should say in brief reply that books are necessary, first, as
nourishing the conservative element in life; they keep before us
the best that has been felt and thought in the past: and, second,
as offering a platform to the progressive elements in life; they give
expression to new vision. Books — all books — both preserve old
standards and are the occasion of the creation of fresh ones.

The *Great* Book, I should say, is the book which fulfils either,
or both, of these functions in a conspicuously successful manner.
It keeps our eyes fixed on the horizon; but it may also have to
point out where the horizon is or may be hoped to be. And it
reflects basic themes in a way which invites re-interpretation in
every age. If I may crib the words of my title — and I congratulate
its framers on their power of definition — a Great Book is a book
which is at once both old and new.

And now that we know what a great book is, it is obvious what
is our interest as Jews in great Jewish books. Our deepest need,
now more than ever before, is to keep hold of ourselves; to know
what we are and what we can be because we have been it; to hold
tight to our best when there is danger that we are falling to our
worst; to retain in fact our better selves. In the turmoil of the
transitory (however real) crises in which we find ourselves continuously embroiled, we need, more than any other people and

more than at any other time, the strength that comes from self-recognition.

Such self-recognition and such strength will come, as they have always come, only from the books. From them we shall learn that the crises are not so critical and the forces making capital of them not so unusual. We have outlived many hopes and survived many disappointments. We have learned by experience the sad wisdom of the Latin saying that there were kings before Agamemnon.

I have urged you to read Josephus. You may remember that he tells us that in the last siege the defenders built a second wall behind the first so that the Romans, having effected a breach in the first, were amazed to find a second wall waiting in its place. I suggest that the present generation of Jews relies too much on one wall; and that if we were wise we should busy ourselves while there is yet time with the erection of a second wall to act as a substitute in case the first does not hold. The last word on this too is to be found in Josephus, and in the mouths of the Zealots themselves: for he tells us that, recognizing that their real strength was not in the Temple wall or indeed in any wall or any physical or geographical consideration, they cried out to Titus: "The world is a better Temple for God than this one." We are sometimes told today that our generation is so busy building the future that it need not worry to read about the past. To which it is a fair retort that greater attention to the past might suggest better methods of construction.

I come to my last point.

The most tentative list of Great Jewish Books brings a reader in contact with a dozen literatures and languages and civilizations. He is caught up in the life of Alexandria and Rome, of Cairo and Baghdad, of Troyes and Narbonne and Montpellier; of Toledo and Cordova, Naples and Palermo, Padua, Venice, Amsterdam. He treads the streets of Prague and Wilna and Odessa as well as of London and Paris and New York. The finds at Elephantine and Ras Shamra, Lachish and the Roman Catacombs; Demotic Greek, Norman-French, Hoch Deutsch, Old Castilian; Roman Law; Gnostic heresies; Scholastic philosophy; medieval geographers — he meets all these and much more as he is drawn to follow out leading threads in Jewish literature. There is much truth in the Rabbinic saying that the Torah was given in the desert — that is, everywhere and anywhere — and in every language. If to be an educated man is to have the chords of one's mind attuned to the greatest number of human sounds, Jewish literature is one of the great instruments of education.

So may I conclude with a word of practical advice? Start anywhere and read anything. Start — why not? — with the *Bible in Spain*, and you are plunged at once into the story of the Marranos which will lead you to the story of Spain, of the Inquisition, of the discovery of the New World, of a hundred episodes and incidents of the Old. Start with *The Wars of the Jews* of Josephus and you are introduced to a whole ancient civilization in its variety and its stresses and tensions, as well as to the universal phenomenon of militant messianism so tellingly analyzed for our own day by M. Albert Camus in his *L'Homme Révolté*. Start even with a page of the ordinary Ḥumash (and by a page I mean the whole of a page, all the contents of a page), and see where it will bring you. Take the marginal Masorah, and it leads you to the history of the text on which so much has been written and so much remains to be written. Take the *Toldot Aharon*, and you are led to consider the use made of the text in Talmudic literature which is in fact Talmudic literature. Take the Aramaic versions and ask what they are, and where and why they were made, and what is their relation to others in other languages. Take the commentators: the French school, Rashi, Rashbam; the Spanish school, Ibn Ezra, Ramban, and ask yourself in what they are alike and how they differ, and how their views stand today, and what is the aim and character of exegesis in general. Note even the different sorts of type used; and you are brought to the general history of typography and, eventually, to the general history of the alphabet on which an eminent Jewish scholar in this country has just produced a standard book. Begin on any one of these lines (and they are all bursting to view on every page of the most ordinary Rabbinic Pentateuch) and you are embarked on a hobby for life which, unlike some other hobbies, will make you at home in all periods and all times and places.

And read the books and don't trouble about the greatness. Greatness is a quality, I sometimes think, imputed to things by us. A book for us is great, I have urged, when we perceive its human significance and are stirred by it; but what we perceive depends on our powers of sight. I always think of the story of Whistler who, when he heard a critic say of one of his pictures "But I've never seen the Thames like that," retorted: "Don't you wish you had?"

The retort is of universal application. Our powers of appreciation, like our muscles, need developing, and, like our muscles, they are developed by exercise. We grow through activity. Books cannot be great to us unless we make them so, and we cannot make them so except by reading and re-reading them. He who reads a book for the hundredth time, goes the old Rabbinic proverb, is not to be compared with the man who reads it for the hundred and oneth. G.K.C. was certainly right when he said that the Iliad is great because life is a fight, the Odyssey because life is a journey, the Book of Job because life is a riddle. But the prosaic statement of Mr. E. M. Forster is to the point even more: "Books have to be read (worse luck, for it takes a long time); it is the only way of discovering what they contain."

Judaica Americana

AMERICAN JEWISH LITERATURE

A Tercentenary Review

By Joshua Bloch

LITTLE is known of the intellectual life of the handful of early Jewish settlers on Manhattan Island and nothing of their literary taste or interest. The fact that they came to a new land in search of opportunity to live a Jewish life without interference from persecution leads to the conclusion that such books as they had for their exclusive use represented texts essential for their liturgical needs and for the advancement of the religious education of their children — the kind of books that sprang from the Jewish heritage of the past — bibles, prayer books and works offering guidance in religious belief and practice. These they brought with them or imported from abroad.

Prior to the coming of the new arrivals to these shores, books had found their way to colonial America or were published in the New World which had an obvious appeal to Jews. Such a publication was the now exceedingly rare *Bay Psalm Book*, which appeared almost a decade and a half before the arrival of Jews on Manhattan Island. This book was the harbinger of many others which brought Hebrew spiritual ideas to colonial America. Printed in Cambridge, Massachusetts, in 1640, it represented an English version of the Psalter made directly from the Hebrew. It also included the first dissertation on the Hebrew language and on Hebrew poetry to be published in America. Almost a century later there appeared in Boston (1716) *Psalterium Americanum, The Book of Psalms*, in a translation exactly conforming to the original.

The publication of the *Bay Psalm Book* and the early attempts at the introduction of a Scriptural calendar in the colonies were motivated by a desire to plant on the American continent ideas and institutions the character of which was distinctly Hebraic. The appearance of Hebrew letters and Hebrew words in the pages of early colonial imprints sufficed to impress upon the minds of early Jewish settlers on American soil the fact that their non-Jewish neighbors shared with them a common love for the Hebrew Scriptures. Though not written or published by Jews, these publications nevertheless served as the foundation upon which was reared the structure of American research in the Hebrew Bible and the literature it engendered.

Hebrew was the Sacred Tongue, the language in which the earliest and major portions of the Sacred Scriptures were written. There was a keen interest in the study of its rudiments. It was taught in virtually all institutions of higher learning in colonial days. In many a publication in which Scriptural texts were used to support or to refute one view or another, their authors drew upon the Hebrew originals of such texts. Thus, George Keith in his tracts *New England's Spirit of Persecution* (Philadelphia or New York, 1693) and *Truth |Advanced in the Correction of many Gross and Hurtful Errors* (New York, 1694) drew upon Hebrew learning and employed Hebrew types in defence of himself and of his associates against persecution.

But no adequate mastery of the Hebrew language is possible without systematic instruction in its rudiments. Text books for this purpose were generally imported from abroad. In 1726, however, Samuel Keimer published a booklet *A Compleat Ephemeris* and attributed it to Jacob Taylor. It contained a brief introduction to Hebrew and included the first Hebrew alphabet published in Philadelphia. Helpful as the publication was for an elementary acquaintance with Hebrew, it could not serve adequately the needs of the more serious student. Such needs were admirably met by the appearance in 1735 of Judah Monis' *Dickdook Leshon Gnebreet, a grammar of the Hebrew Tongue ... published more especially for the use of the Students of Harvard College at Cambridge*. This publication was the forerunner of several text books on Hebrew grammar by Stephen Sewall (Boston, 1763).

Not only the Hebrew language and the books of the Hebrew Bible fell within the orbit of the cultural life of the early settlers in colonial America but other subjects of kindred interest were pursued by the settlers with the same avidity as applied to sacred lore. The antiquities of the Jews and early Jewish history fascinated them. They turned to such writings as those of Josephus Flavius, the earliest of Jewish historians. Next to the Bible, his works became the most popularly read Jewish books in this country. The importation from England of copies of Josephus was evidently insufficient to supply the ever rising American demand and before long publishers in this country vied with one another in printing his works. The first American edition of *The War of the Jews*, epitomized from the works of Josephus Flavius and translated into English by Sir R. L'Estrange, appeared in Boston in 1719 and again in 1721. Editions of the *History* and *Antiquities* were also published in Philadelphia (1773) and in New York (1773–75).

In the several discourses in defense of his conversion to Christianity which Judah Monis published in 1722, he drew upon rabbinic and cabbalistic learning. These discourses appeared in Boston, a community which had a considerable number of his former co-religionists, mostly transient Jewish merchants and traders. Their Puritan neighbors, themselves victims of religious persecution, often showed a ruthless intolerance of the religious beliefs and practices of others. The vigorous attempts of the Puritans at proselytism were often directed at the Jews. The tracts of Monis, in which rabbinic and cabbalistic lore was drawn upon in support of Christian teachings, were aimed at gaining Jewish converts for the new faith their author had embraced. The Jews of Boston, though less learned than Monis, remained steadfast in their attachments to the faith of their fathers. Nevertheless, accounts of the rare conversion of a Jew to Christianity were frequently published in those days and Christian preachers now and then discoursed on aspects of the Jews and of Jewish destiny. Thus, in one of his early publications *Discourses on Saving Knowledge* (Newport, R. I., 1770), Ezra Stiles draws upon rabbinic and cabbalistic texts pertinent to his discourse on the Trinity. Incidentally, before Ezra Stiles became president of Yale University, he lived in Newport, R. I., and there he met Rabbi Hayim Isaac Karigal of Hebron, who was visiting the North American colonies. *A Sermon Preached at the Synagogue in Newport . . . on the Day of Pentecost 1773* by Karigal in Spanish was translated into English by Abraham Lopez and appeared in Newport. It was the first Jewish sermon printed in America.

The friendship between Rabbi Karigal and Ezra Stiles presents the earliest contact in this country between two divines of different faiths — a Jew and a Christian — who, with mutual respect for one another, indulged in conversations on religion and made use of rabbinic and other post-biblical Hebrew texts. Similar conversations of Jews with other Christian divines followed. Rabbinic texts were often referred to when they tended to support or to refute one argument or another. As the Jewish community rose in numbers, their non-Jewish neighbors sought an understanding of Jewish religious practices and teaching. There arose the need for literature with the aid of which such knowledge could be disseminated. Learned Jews — itinerant preachers and rabbis — who found their way to this country discussed aspects of Jewish law and lore and contributed to the gradual rise in the demand for Jewish literature. With the growth of the Jewish population there came a corresponding growth in its interest in Jewish cultural values. This was particularly noticeable from the last quarter of the eighteenth to the middle of the nineteenth centuries when large numbers of Jewish immigrants from Central Europe found their way to the New Land. They carried with them their native culture, including a wide interest in Jewish literature and in modern Jewish learning which had its rise and early development in their native lands.

The interest in Jewish literature of the Spanish-Portuguese Jews who preceded them was confined largely to works bearing upon religious practices and synagogue worship. Works which they contributed to the making of American Jewish literature were therefore mostly popular treatments of religious subjects and were designed to meet Jewish religious and communal needs. Manuals for the teaching of beliefs and practices and text books for instruction in Hebrew comprised the major output of the literature. Most of the liturgical texts were imported from abroad. The German immigrants were, however, not willing to depend upon importations. They began to publish in this country religious text books in German and in English. Some of their congregations did not hesitate to adapt their respective order of worship to their special requirements and had liturgical texts published in this country. More than that, they launched a vigorous campaign for the strengthening of the position of the Jews and Judaism in America by infusing their religious and cultural life with the results of modern Jewish learning. They were not satisfied merely with publishing religious texts and works defending Jewish religious teachings and practices against frequent attacks upon them from Christian missionary quarters. They concentrated upon efforts to give Jewish religious and cultural values an opportunity to strike root in the New Land. They planted Jewish learning on American soil.

Many works in American Jewish literature were not written originally in English but were translated from other tongues. Each wave of Jewish immigrants brought to these shores gifted men of talent and learning, who of necessity often employed their native tongue in addition to the English language of their adopted land. This made the cumulative output of Jewish books a polyglot literature, a characterization which, indeed, applies to Jewish literature as a whole.

Towards the end of the nineteenth century, when this country was still hospitable to the influx of Jewish immigrants from East European countries, Jewish scholars, who had already gained fame in their native lands, found their way to these shores. Not a few of them were men whose names shine in the annals of modern Jewish learning. Due to their efforts, the turn of the century witnessed an intensified American interest in all branches of Jewish literary creativity and especially in the advancement of Jewish learning in this country.

The works discussed below represent but a small number of titles of a large output of meritorious publications. Though selected at random, these are representative examples of durable value; a few, though obsolete, are nevertheless of historic value, for they served as mileposts in the development of Jewish lore and learning in this country. Though replaced by more recent books, they nevertheless contributed immensely to the arousing of interest in Jewish knowledge. Moreover, they stimulated further growth in American Jewish literature and learning.

American Jewry can point with pride to the fact that at the beginning of the present century it gave to the world what is no doubt the greatest achievement of modern Jewish learning — *The Jewish Encyclopedia* (New York 1901–1905), a work in twelve sumptuous volumes, profusely illustrated and compactly printed. It incorporates a tremendous amount of information on every phase of Jewish life, literature, lore and learning, brought together by competent hands and presented authoritatively. Leading scholars, Jews and non-Jews, all over the world shared in its making. Each of its editors and contributors represented a writer or a scholar whose specialty in a given field was widely recognized. Virtually all the major articles represented veritable monographs by specialists. Even though half a century has gone by since its publication, it is still an indispensable work of reference to which one may turn with confidence. Although some articles now need revision and enlargement and others are obsolete, the work as a whole has not been superseded by any work of a similar nature in any other language. Virtually all subsequent attempts at similar undertakings in other lands and languages were dependent upon its contents. It is a monumental contribution to the systematic presentation of Jewish knowledge, which American Jewish generosity and scholarship made possible.

The Jewish Encyclopedia set the pattern for similar Jewish reference works issued in this country and abroad. Within a decade, there appeared a Russian Jewish encyclopedia, *Yevreiskaia Encyclopedia* (St. Petersburg, 1908–1912) which incorporated translations of several hundred leading articles from *The Jewish Encyclopedia*. In a like manner, Judah David Eisenstein, aided by other scholars, was able to present in Hebrew *Ozar Yisrael*, a useful reference work in ten volumes (New York, 1907–1913), which has gone through several editions in this country and abroad. Simultaneously, another American Hebrew scholar, Abraham Hayyim Rosenberg, singlehandedly produced a remarkable Hebrew encyclopedia of the Bible in five volumes entitled *Ozar Hashemot* (New York, 1923). It dealt with every phase of experience reflected in the Hebrew Bible. Unlike other encyclopedias of the Bible, Rosenberg incorporated a wealth of material drawn exclusively from rabbinical and other Jewish sources. *The Universal Jewish Encyclopedia*, in ten volumes, (New York, 1939–1943) owed to *The Jewish Encyclopedia* much more than is generally recognized. Monumental, too, was Israel Davidson's *Thesaurus of Medieval Hebrew Poetry* (New York, 1924–1933), a work in four sumptuous volumes and supplements. It represented a daring but successful venture in the compilation of an extraordinary index to the vastly dispersed Hebrew poetic compositions, sacred and secular, written during a millennium and a half, from the fifth century to the present. However, it recorded no secular poems written after 1740. Virtually all the entries were richly annotated with critical and bibliographical data in which authorship, sources, form, content and character were dealt with. Dr. Davidson carried out a stupendous task with acumen, diligence and a wonderful sense of proportion.

These great reference works which American Jewish scholarship produced within the first half of the present century represent comprehensive treatments of branches of Jewish knowledge. They comprise a rich contribution to the totality of Jewish literary endeavor.

Jews have never neglected the study of the Bible. Wherever Jews settled they brought with them their Scriptures and sooner or later had them translated into the vernacular of their new settlements. At an early date, Isaac Leeser, a diligent worker in advancing Jewish knowledge, undertook the task of making the first American Jewish version in English and published it in Philadelphia in 1853. Drawing heavily upon the King James version, it nevertheless reflected the traditional Jewish interpretation and retained the Jewish spirit though often at the expense of good style. It became the accepted version in all synagogues and Jewish religious schools in virtually every English speaking country. It was not successfully challenged until 1917 when the Jewish Publication Society of America produced its version *The Holy Scriptures according to the Masoretic text, a new translation*. Largely the work of Max L. Margolis, this Jewish version made full and advantageous use of the results of modern literary and archaeological research in Scriptures without in any way removing from the text the genuine Jewish spirit and the authoritative traditional Jewish interpretation.

The publication of the first American printed text of the Hebrew Scriptures (Philadelphia, 1814) and of the first American Jewish version of those Scriptures in the English language (Philadelphia, 1853) marked definite steps in the rise of American Jewish interest in biblical studies. The flow to these shores of Jewish commentaries on biblical texts from European countries stimulated that interest and encouraged American Jewish scholars to vie with their colleagues abroad in advancing Jewish studies in the Bible. Their contributions are notable and of durable value. The commentary on the Book of Job by Rabbi Benjamin Szold (Baltimore, 1888) was the first written in good Hebrew and printed in this country. It conveys much of the traditional Jewish views, yet not without some originality in the explanation of many passages, often adding a homiletical flavor. It was followed by American Jewish studies in Scriptural texts in Hebrew, English and German. Most notable are the exegetical notes of Arnold B. Ehrlich published in Hebrew *Mikra Kipeshuto* (3 vols., Berlin, 1899–1901) and in German *Randglossen zur hebräischen Bibel* (6 vols., Berlin, 1909–1913). They comprise a rich collection of brilliantly conceived notes on selected passages from the Scriptures. Their publication made a profound impression in the world of scholarship because of their display of the author's brilliance and originality. In his *Sprachgefühl* for Hebrew, Ehrlich was surpassed by none of his contemporary Bible exegetes. No wonder his German commentary on the Psalms (Berlin, 1905) as well as his *Randglossen* had such a profound influence upon the modern elucidation of the biblical text.

Ehrlich was also the author of *Rahshe Perakim*, a manual for the study of the Talmud (New York, 1900). It was designed to overcome difficulties students meet in efforts to master the elements of Talmudic study. A similar work by Moses Mielziner *Introduction to the Talmud* (Cincinnati, 1894) has gone through several editions. The last edition, revised and enlarged by Joshua Bloch and Louis Finkelstein, appeared in 1925. These books have done much for the advancement in America of the study of the Talmud and its commentaries. While American editions of the original text and of translations of the Talmud did not make their appearance before the twentieth century, they were preceded by important reference books by eminent American scholars, without which the study of rabbinical texts is difficult. Alexander Kohut's *Aruch Completum* (Vienna, 1878–1892), an exhaustive lexicographical work in nine volumes, was originally

begun abroad but completed in this country. It still maintains
its position as a work of reference without which the study of
the language of the Talmud would be more difficult than it is
now. This, to a lesser degree, is also true of Marcus Jastrow's
*Dictionary of the Targumim, The Talmud Babli and Jerushalmi
and the Midrashic literature* (London, 1886–1903). Both works
have gone through several editions and have made possible a
better understanding of the language employed in rabbinical
texts.

Michael L. Rodkinson's venture to translate into English the
Babylonian Talmud (New York, 1896–1902) was disappointing.
Neither the editor nor his collaborators were competent for the
task. It remained for British Jewry to perform the task with
good taste, skill, sound scholarship and fine style (London,
Soncino, 1935–1952). American scholars shared in the translation,
which found a large market in this country. American scholarship
also took a leading role in establishing scientific principles for fixing
the accuracy of early rabbinic texts. *Tractate Taanit of the Babylonian Talmud*, critically edited by Henry Malter, was published
by the American Academy for Jewish Research (New York, 1930),
while his popular edition of the same text, provided with an
English translation and notes (Philadelphia, 1928), was included
in the Schiff library of Jewish classics. Louis Ginzberg's edition
of *Yerushalmi Fragments from the Genizah* (New York, 1909)
presented a model worthy of emulation. His sumptuously published *Commentary on the Palestinian Talmud*, of which only the
first three volumes have thus far appeared (New York, 1941) is,
no doubt, the greatest work of its kind.

An outgrowth of Dr. Ginzberg's studies in rabbinical lore is
the remarkable collection of *The Legends of the Jews* (Philadelphia,
1909–1928), a monumental work in seven volumes in which extraordinary talent is displayed in the presentation of the classical
folklore of the Jews in a popular manner calculated to serve the
need of the general reader. It is supplemented with learned
notes of interest to the scholar. The enormous legendary lore
of the Jews revolving around biblical events and personalities
culled from a variety of sources, Jewish and non-Jewish, is brought
together in systematic order and presented readably and interest-
ingly. Like *The Jewish Encyclopedia*, this work, too, yielded
a vast amount of material upon which many a literary work
has been based.

The Geonim continued the tradition of Jewish learning which
the sages of the Talmudic era developed. Their writings and
the conditions under which the Geonim flourished are not suffi-

ciently known. In *Geonica*, a two volume work (New York, 1909), Louis Ginzberg paved the way for subsequent studies in the period and in the literature it produced. In addition to editing and elucidating a number of Genizah fragments of heretofore unpublished writings of the Geonim, the work includes a critical survey of their writings shedding light on problems which the subject presents. Ginzberg deals with a cloudy period in Jewish history. Virtually all knowledge of this period was heretofore derived from scanty sources. Ginzberg not only removed the historical contradictions presented in the primary sources — the Letter of Sherira and the report of Nathan the Babylonian — he also defined the character of the writings of the Geonim and determined their respective authorship. In addition, he discussed a variety of obscure subjects. In all of these, he displayed extraordinary mastery of the pertinent literature and succeeded in solving brilliantly problems with which scholars had wrestled for a long time. Some of the notes and the introductory remarks to the texts are in themselves models of literary composition, veritable monographs on the history and literature of the Geonim. No wonder Ginzberg's *Geonica* engendered a rich literary output by scholars in this country and abroad, all of which concern themselves with the reconstruction of the Geonic period and with highlighting some of the events.

Beyond any doubt, the greatest of the Geonim was Saadia. His life and works form the subject of a biography by Dr. Henry Malter (Philadelphia, 1921), the like of which is hardly equalled in Jewish literature. It is a complete and well-documented account of the life and achievements of the many-sided and colorful personality of Saadia. It includes a well-balanced evaluation of his works as well as an adequate bibliographical appraisal of the extensive pertinent literature. The factual material was drawn from many sources, especially from the scattered Genizah fragments, and the author displayed a command of the entire literature. With great skill, he combined the scattered data into an harmonious and glorious picture of the Great Gaon, who more than any of his peers contributed to the molding and shaping of the beliefs of Judaism.

American scholars have had a proportionately larger share than that of their peers in other lands in the investigation of problems bearing on the development of Jewish philosophical speculation. David Neumark daringly ventured to show the historical development of various philosophical problems in Jewish thought and literature. He was more than the historian of Jewish philosophy; he was also an original religious thinker. He did not live long enough to complete his projected ten volume work which he had hoped to publish in English, German and Hebrew. Of the German *Geschichte der juedischen Philosophie* (Berlin, 1907–1928) only three volumes and a supplement appeared, while of the Hebrew *Toldot ha-Pilusufiah be-Yisrael,* no more than two volumes were published in New York (1921–1929). Of the English some portions were issued in monographs and in scattered contributions to learned periodicals. Neumark's writings had a profound influence upon several younger scholars such as Nina H. Adlerblum, Z. Diesendruck, Israel Efros, Meyer Waxman, Philip D. Bookstaber and others whose contributions to Jewish philosophical writings have all been published in this country. Isaac Husik's *History of Mediaeval Jewish Philosophy* (New York, 1916) presents a general but dependable survey of the subject within the compass of a handy one volume work. Unsurpassed are the writings of Harry A. Wolfson. Brilliant in thought, elegant in literary expression and supported by testimony drawn from primary sources which he masters fully, Wolfson has unfolded the background and described the impact upon religious ideas of the philosophical teachings of *Philo* (2 vols., Cambridge, 1947), *Crescas' Critique of Aristotle* (Cambridge, 1929) and *The Philosophy of Spinoza* (2 vols., Cambridge, 1934).

Jewish philosophy is in a very large measure theological in character. No system of Jewish theology can be properly evolved without recourse to the writings of the Jewish philosophers. There is an affinity which binds the two together.

If Jewish theology in modern times has assumed a more or less definite form it is in no small degree due to the publication of outstanding works by Jewish theologians in this country. Solomon Schechter's *Some Aspects of Rabbinic Theology* (New York, 1909) conveys in fine language a goodly measure of Jewish theological speculation revealed in classical rabbinic lore. On the other hand, Kaufmann Kohler, no doubt the leading Jewish theologian American Jewry possessed, presented in German and English *Jewish Theology* (New York, 1918). It gives comprehensively and in systematic form the essential beliefs and doctrines of Judaism. It has had a profound influence upon modern Jewish religious thought. Mordecai M. Kaplan, in his attempt to define Judaism anew and to interpret its teachings in broad sociological terms, conceives it as a civilization. His *Judaism as a Civilization* (New York, 1934), *Judaism in Transition,* (New York, 1937) and *The Future of the American Jew* (New York, 1948) have gained for him many followers in all camps of American Jewry and the Jewish Reconstructionist movement guides itself largely by his ideas. The theological writings of Schechter, Kohler and Kaplan have enriched the religious thinking of modern Jewry not only in this country but in other lands as well.

The development of Jewish philosophical speculation and of religious ideas and institutions in Judaism cannot be well understood unless their growth can be traced within the realms of history. In these circumstances Jewish history cannot be neglected. It plays an important part in the literature by and about Jews. Except for the writings of Flavius Josephus, the early American publications dealing with Jewish history were all by non-Jewish authors and were not intended for the exclusive use of Jews. The first substantial Jewish presentation of Jewish history by an American author was the *History of the Israelitish Nation*, from Abraham to the present time, by Isaac M. Wise (Albany, N. Y., 1854). Evidently it represented the first volume of a projected larger work which was not completed, since it does not go beyond the Babylonian Exile. The author resumed the task in later years and published another volume, *History of the Hebrews' Second Commonwealth* (Cincinnati, 1880), intended as a continuation of the earlier work and bringing it up to the destruction of the Second Temple in the year 70 C. E. A little over a decade later The Jewish Publication Society of America began the publication in this country of the *History of the Jews* by H. Graetz (6 vols., Philadelphia, 1891–1898). Actually, it represents a condensation of the author's monumental *Geschichte der Juden* which ends with the turbulent year of 1848; the American edition, unlike the original, is brought down to 1870. In later years the work was brought up-to-date by the publication of a supplementary volume, *A Century of Jewish Life*, by Ismar Elbogen (Philadelphia, 1944). It brings the record almost up to the reestablishment of the State of Israel. A classic in modern Jewish historiography, Graetz's *History* remains the leading work on the subject. Written with warmth and enthusiasm it is comprehensive in scope and remains unsurpassed by any other work of its kind. It represents a major American contribution to the popularization of Jewish history. Another significant contribution to the historiography of the Jews is the *History of the Jewish People* by Max L. Margolis and Alexander Marx (Philadelphia, 1927). Though intended for the general reader, it manages to present within the confines of one closely printed volume the entire history of the Jews, covering every phase and recording every important event in the long span of three thousand years of Jewish experience. Whatever shortcomings are inherent in a one volume condensation of the diversified story of Jewish life in all ages and in all lands, this work cannot be charged with inaccuracy of presentation of matters factual. The volume is imbued with that spirit of Jewish loyalty, characteristic of the respective roles its authors played while they were among the living.

Regional history has been considerably neglected in American Jewish historiography. It is only in recent years that efforts are being made to emulate that example of accuracy, thoroughness and fine writing achieved in the story of *The Jews in South Carolina* by Barnett A. Elzas (Philadelphia, 1905) which remains unsurpassed by any other history of an American Jewish community thus far published.

In dealing with an appraisal of the basic work in American English-Jewish literature, it is difficult in this restricted space to cover the entire field. An attempt has, however, been made to survey only a few books, selected at random, which represent major achievements of American Jewish scholarship. It is clear: American Jewry, despite the short span of merely three hundred years of communal life, can point with pride to a record of literary achievements which can hardly be matched by older Jewries in other parts of the world.

AFTER THREE HUNDRED YEARS

The Literary Legend of the Jew — and the Reality

By Sol Liptzin

THE three hundredth anniversary of the first Jewish settlement in the United States is being celebrated in 1954. This celebration offers a suitable occasion for a review of the Jewish past on the American scene, a survey of the Jewish present, and a prognosis of possible developments in the years to come.

There is no doubt that, despite discomforts, prejudices, difficulties and resentments, we Jews in America are now experiencing a healthier relationship with our neighbors, a happier coexistence, than at any time anywhere in the Christian world during the past thousand years. Utopia is not with us — not even around the corner. Ups and downs may still await us. Greater knowledge should, however, help us in our quest for a continuing satisfactory relationship in the years ahead. The Jewish Book Council of America, in its activities, which reach their climax annually in Jewish Book Month, seeks to add to our knowledge of historic Jewish values, to further our insight into contemporary Jewish problems, to make us aware of the many complexities involved in our survival as a minority cultural group in the midst of a non-Jewish majority.

For a thousand years, from the early Middle Ages up to the founding of the United States, Jews and their neighbors lived distinct lives, separated from each other by religious and historic differences. There could be no question of complete integration of Jews into Christian Europe, because neither side desired it. Jews did not eat with their neighbors and certainly did not intermarry with them, and Christians at best accepted the Jews in their midst as a necessary evil. When Jews fulfilled certain economic functions, they were tolerated; otherwise, they were massacred, forcibly baptized, or expelled.

In 1492 the Jews were expelled from Spain. In that year America was discovered. But it was not until more than a century and a half later, that the first group of Jews landed in the territory that is now the United States. They were Sephardic refugees fleeing from the Inquisition. They came from the colony of Recife, Brazil, where the Portuguese had succeeded the Dutch and re-

53

ligious fanaticism had replaced religious tolerance. They arrived in 1654 in New Amsterdam, a settlement in which the somewhat familiar Dutch language and Dutch customs held sway. It is true that the governor, Peter Stuyvesant, was not too happy with the newcomers and sought to hem them in with petty restrictions. But there was always the possibility of an appeal to his masters, the Dutch West Indies Company, in which Jewish capital was invested, and the governor's decisions were at times overruled.

In 1664 the English replaced the Dutch and New Amsterdam became New York. The Jewish settlers were allowed to continue their trades and professions. They were felt to be an asset, fulfilling certain needs of the growing colony. They prospered and increased in numbers. Their ships sailed the seas with precious cargoes and their trappers roamed the wild hinterland in search of desirable furs. Their children and children's children became integrated into the life of the community. Soon the wall of religious separatism began to be breached by more and more individuals, as the spirit of Enlightenment spread from European centers to the New World.

The story of the Jewish settlers of New Amsterdam repeated itself in colony after colony until the War for Independence broke out. During this War, a number of Jews remained loyal to the British Crown. The majority, however, espoused the cause of independence.

Between the Revolutionary and the Civil Wars, Jews increased in numbers and rose in the social scale. The Sephardic Jews, who were the dominant strain during the Colonial period, continued to prosper. Their wealth opened all doors to them. In an atmosphere of freedom they became more and more assimilated into the American cultural pattern. The Spanish and Portuguese tongues of the immigrant ancestors yielded to typically American English and the tragic Marrano-experiences survived only as vague memories of a remote past. Intermarriage became more frequent. Conversion to Christianity by the sons and daughters of the most prominent families threatened the gradual decline and possible extinction of the Jewish group as an important cultural entity in America.

From the very beginning, the New World offered a hearty welcome and limitless opportunities to Jews who shed their Jewishness. Racial anti-Semitism was undreamed of. The earliest settlers of New England, the Puritans, were lovers of the Old Testament. They idealized the Jewish past. Upon the old English legends of the Jew as Christ-killer and Shylock, they superimposed their own legend of the angelic, patriarchal Hebrew. Though they did everything possible to keep the living, unconverted Jews away from their towns and villages, they retained an unbounded admiration for the ancient chosen people and testified to their affection for the old Hebrews by choosing Hebraic names for themselves and their children. Believing that the Messianic Era would dawn when the last Hebrews would cease to be Jews and would accept Christianity, the Puritan settlers were ready to receive as their equal and brother any Jew who became converted to their faith. They publicized each conversion as one more step toward the goal of universal salvation. When Judah Monis was baptized in 1722, they hailed him as a Jewish witness of the truth of Christianity, appointed him to a professorship at Harvard, and for four decades listened to his lectures on Hebrew. The influential Puritan ministers John Eliot, Samuel Sewall and Jonathan Edwards identified the Indians with the Lost Ten Tribes of Israel and saw in the conversion of these natives an omen of the nighing day of world-deliverance.

The poets of New England continued far into the nineteenth century the traditional Puritan attitude of admiration for Jews. In almost all cases, however, these were either biblical Jews or else dead Jews. Typical of this approach is Longfellow's poem, *The Jewish Cemetery at Newport*, composed in 1852. The poet ponders on the persecution and suffering of the Jews. He recalls the Christian hate that drove them over the sea to Rhode Island, the first Puritan colony to offer them asylum. He adds, however, that there is no longer any future for the Jews. Just as the Sephardic Jews who came to Newport were assimilated to the American way of life and disappeared as Jews, so it will be with all other Jews in the free world. The portals of the once flourishing synagogue at Newport are closed. Gone are the living. Only the dead remain, silent beside the never-silent waves, at rest, at last. After reviewing the glorious past of the Jews, Longfellow concludes:

> "But ah! what once has been shall be no more!
> The groaning earth in travail and in pain
> Brings forth its races, but does not restore,
> And the dead nations never rise again."

The attitude of the best American writers, a century ago, towards the Jews was to accept them as individuals while waiting for them to become assimilated to the way of life of the majority group and gradually to give up their Jewish traits, even as all other minority groups were giving up their distinguishing minority characteristics. The impression was wellnigh universal that Israel was a skeleton of withered bones, beyond hope of resurrection, and that the Jews of the New World, who as late as 1840 still numbered less than one in a thousand, could not and would not want to continue a separate cultural existence indefinitely. They were picturesque wayfarers who would succumb to the melting-pot of America. Longfellow described a Sephardic Jew in *Tales of a Wayside Inn.* This exotic survivor of an ancient people had the grand and grave appearance of an old patriarch or High-Priest, with lustrous eyes, olive skin, and flowing beard. He was garbed in aromatic garments which breathed a spicy scent of cinnamon.

"Well versed was he in Hebrew books,
Talmud and Targum, and the lore
Of Kabala; and evermore
There was a mystery in his looks."

The process of Jewish adjustment to the point of complete identification with the majority population, a process regarded as inevitable by Longfellow and other sensitive New England writers, was, however, arrested in the pre-Civil War decades by the influx of a large group of Jewish immigrants from Central Europe. German-speaking Jews, who had tasted of freedom and prosperity during the Napoleonic period, could not easily adjust themselves to the burdensome economic restrictions and the affronts to human dignity again imposed upon them after the defeat of Napoleon and the restoration of the ancient regime under the Holy Alliance. They looked wistfully to America, whenever their freedom was threatened. In the New World there was a promising haven for human beings of all races and creeds. Heinrich Heine, the literary spokesman of German Jewry, voiced their attitude a century ago, when he wrote: "Even if all Europe should become a single prison, there is still another loophole of escape, namely America, and, thank God! the loophole is after all larger than the prison itself." Heine noted that America was sound, America was resplendent, America was not attached to mouldy symbols and outworn traditions. America was the last hope of a dying Occident.

German Jews quickly outnumbered the Sephardic Jews in the United States and, even before the Revolution of 1848, which hastened the pace of their immigration, they were exercising a dominant role in Jewish communal life. They, too, grew in wealth and prestige from decade to decade. Some, who had begun as penniless peddlers with packs on their backs, became department store owners. Others, who had started as workers, became affluent industrialists. The success-stories told of Adam Gimbel, Lazarus Straus, Meyer Guggenheim, Samuel Rosenwald, and their descendants were paralleled on a somewhat smaller scale by many other German-Jewish immigrants. America was indeed the land of opportunity. Americanization, assimilation remained popular slogans. The process of complete integration to the point of baptism and intermarriage, which had decimated Sephardic Jewry, also made inroads upon German Jewry in America. But the process was slower because the numbers involved were larger. Besides, some resistance on the part of non-Jews to Jewish infiltration began to make itself felt. For example, in 1877, the Jewish banker Seligman was refused lodging in Saratoga Springs because he was a Jew. This incident was aired in the world's press. The virus of modern anti-Semitism had apparently crossed the Atlantic. Jews began to worry: how were they to eradicate the first symptoms of the infection before the moral disease had a chance to spread? Or, to take another example, Lafcadio Hearn spent the summer of 1884 vacationing at Grande Isle near New Orleans. Because his hotel did not discriminate against Jews, this philo-Semitic writer, who adored the people of the Talmud in the abstract, wrote for the New Orleans *Times-Democrat* a series of such vicious anti-Semitic articles about Jews in the flesh that the editor had to refuse to print them.

These isolated incidents of anti-Jewishness, however, had no lasting effect upon the tendency towards assimilation. They may even have hastened the obliteration of minority characteristics on the part of those Jews who were not too strongly attached to their ancestral heritage. Only among a few Jewish intellectuals did a questioning arise: was it really wise to give up traditional values of many centuries in order to be like unto their neighbors?

The first writer to face the problem boldly was Emma Lazarus, the poetess of New York, who was born in 1849 of Sephardic ancestry and who in her early works showed no desire to associate herself with Jewish strivings. She treated Greek themes, German themes, international themes, but carefully avoided Jewish themes. Goethe was closer to her than Moses. Admetus, King of Thessaly, meant more to her than David, the conqueror of Jerusalem. Even Heine, whom she greatly admired and translated, was in her eyes a German poet and not a Jewish poet. She aroused the interest of William Cullen Bryant and Ralph Waldo Emerson with her verses. She corresponded with the poet Edmund C. Stedman. To her surprise, this non-Jewish poet reproached her for her indifference to her own people. John Burroughs, another non-Jewish writer, asked her to follow the example of Walt Whitman, who was the greatest American poet because he had a biblical sweep. Let her, the Jewess, also find her way back to her biblical roots.

The pogroms of 1881 did, indeed, lead Emma Lazarus to find her way back to Jewishness. Visits to Ward's Island, predecessor of Castle Garden and Ellis Island, brought her into contact with hundreds of Jewish victims who were knocking at the gate of

America. She began to feel a kinship with these displaced and uprooted human beings. When these Eastern European Jewish immigrants were attacked in an anti-Semitic article in the *Century Magazine*, she rushed to their defense in a series of essays. She organized protest meetings. She wrote, in 1883, in behalf of the immigrants the sonnet, which is engraved on the pedestal of the Statue of Liberty, and which ends with the verses:

> "Give me your tired, your poor,
> Your huddled masses yearning to be free,
> The wretched refuse of your teeming shore,
> Send these, the homeless, tempest-tost to me.
> I lift my lamp beside the golden door."

Emma Lazarus went further. She took up the idea that George Eliot had launched in 1876, twenty years before Theodor Herzl, the idea of Zionism. She championed the restoration of Palestine as a Jewish homeland. In her poem *The New Ezekiel*, she cried out:

> "The Spirit is not dead, proclaim the word,
> Where lay dead bone, a host of armed men stand!
> I ope your graves, my people, saith the Lord,
> And I shall place you in your promised land."

While Emma Lazarus, however, was dreaming of Israel as the promised land, where Jews could experience historic regeneration, the masses fleeing from pogroms were directing their gaze westward to America as their Promised Land. These immigrants arrived in the New World with a legend of America constructed out of romantic tales and wishful dreams, a legend so glowing, so colorful, so entrancing, that reality could never approach it. We can reconstruct the contours of this legend from the works of Sholem Aleichem, the most popular interpreter of this Yiddish-speaking generation. His Jews envisage America as a land of marvels somewhere far, far away, a land of breath-taking progress. There people do not walk. They run. They write fast, they talk fast, they speed from place to place under the ground. It is the only land of true freedom and equality. It is built on foundations of truth, justice, dignity, honesty, tolerance, humanity, faith, and mercy. A mere mortal ought to wash his hands — as one does before saying one's prayers — before uttering the sacred name of America, God's finest handiwork. America was created by God as a place of refuge and solace for human beings who are hunted, persecuted, and expelled from all corners of the earth, and especially for Jews who can find there the only safe asylum when unexpected calamities, pogroms, or wars overtake them. "It is almost inconceivable that nowadays there should still be on this earth a sober spot where human beings are not blood-intoxicated and do not kill each other by the thousands, as we kill chickens before Atonement Day, and do not cut off each other's heads as we cut off the heads of herring and do not chop away at each other as we chop away at cabbage."

America is an unsophisticated land. A person says what he means and he means what he says. There no one ever breaks his word. There thieves are non-existent. There the poor are not poor for any length of time because all engage in physical labor and can work their way to the top. There a person can learn any trade he pleases and a tailor ranks with the elite. "All American millionaires and billionaires began by working hard in their youth either in a shop or on the street. Just ask Rockefeller, Carnegie, Morgan, or Vanderbilt about their early years. Didn't they, too, sweep the streets? Weren't they, too, newsboys or bootblacks? Or, take as an example Mr. Ford, the present king of the auto-industry — wasn't he once a mere chauffeur?"

The contrast between Eastern Europe, from which Jews were fleeing, and the legendary America, for which they longed, was best voiced by Sholem Aleichem in the speech of an immigrant at the moment of first stepping on the soil of the New World. Turning his face towards the ocean and clenching his right hand, this immigrant shouted back: "Listen, you jackasses, scoundrels, drunkards, hooligans, and murderers! We must thank you for finding ourselves now in such a free and happy land! If not for you and your wicked laws, persecutions, and pogroms, we would not have known about Columbus nor would he have known about us. You can wait a long, long time before we ever come back to you. Just as you don't see your own ears, so you won't see us as long as you live. Some day you may realize that you once had a Jewish people in your midst and didn't know how to take care of it. You will meet the same vile end as Spain once did. You will long for us. A Jew will be a precious rarity among you. You will call us back, but we will never, never return."

The immigrants of Eastern Europe went through a spiritual cycle that was in many respects similar to that of the two preceding groups, the Sephardic and the German-speaking Jews. Their slogan, too, was Americanization, complete integration. A best seller of 1912, two years before the First World War, was Mary Antin's autobiography, entitled *The Promised Land*.

The first sentence of this book reads: "I was born, I have lived, and I have been made over." What Mary Antin means is: I was born a Jewess, I lived the life of a Jewess in Russia, I came to America, and I have been made over as an American. She continues: "I bear the scars. But I want to forget . . . I want now to be of today. It is painful to be consciously of two worlds. The Wandering Jew in me seeks forgetfulness. I am not afraid to live on and on, if only I do not have to remember too much. A long past vividly remembered is like a heavy garment that clings to your limbs when you would run. And I have thought of a charm that should release me from the folds of my clinging past. I take the hint from the Ancient Mariner, who told his tale in order to be rid of it. I, too, will tell my tale, for once, and never hark back any more. I will write a bold *Finis* at the end, and shut the book with a bang!" And so she does. She writes her book about America, the Promised Land, where the Wandering Jew can at last find the death he yearned for and become a pure American. Thereupon she marries a non-Jewish professor of Columbia University and lives far removed from Jewishness ever after.

The dream of complete assimilation entranced many young Jews and Jewesses, both those of the immigrant generation between 1881 and 1914 and even more those of the second generation between the two World Wars. However, because of the great numbers involved and the low economic status of the newly arrived group, the process of integration was more difficult than it had been in earlier periods. For example, Anzia Yezierska, who came to America at about the same time as Mary Antin and who had the same dreams of the golden land beyond the Atlantic, found the process of adjustment fraught with much suffering. In her book *Hungry Hearts*, which followed Mary Antin's book by eight years, she, too, told of her childhood dreams of the Promised Land: "When a little baby in my mother's arms, before I was old enough to speak, I saw all around me weary faces light up with thrilling tales of the far-off 'golden country' ... Visions of America rose over me, like songs of freedom of an oppressed people." The hunger for America was the hunger to live and laugh and breathe like a free human being. "In America you can say what you feel — you can voice your thoughts in the open streets without fear of a Cossack. In America is a home for everybody. The land is your land. Not like in Russia where you feel yourself a stranger in the village where you were born and raised — the village in which your father and grandfather lie buried ... Everybody is with everybody alike, in America. Christians and Jews are brothers together ... An end to the worry for bread. An end to the fear of the bosses over you. Everybody can do what he wants with his life in America ... There are no high or low in America. Even the President holds hands with Gedalyeh Mindel. Plenty for all. Learning flows free like milk and honey."

Anzia Yezierska describes her ecstasy in catching sight of America: "Land! Land! came the joyous shout. America! We're in

America! cried my mother, almost smothering us in her rapture. All crowded and pushed on deck. They strained and stretched to get the first glimpse of the 'golden country,' lifting their children on their shoulders that they might see beyond them. Men fell on their knees to pray. Women hugged their babies and wept. Children danced. Strangers embraced and kissed like old friends. Old men and women had in their eyes a look of young people in love. Age-old visions sang themselves in me — songs of freedom of an oppressed people. America — America!"

But, after Anzia Yezierska lands in New York and, as a child, has to go to a sweatshop in order to earn her bit of bread, sadness comes over her: "Where are the green fields and open spaces of America?" she asks. "Where is the golden country of my dreams?"

A generation later, Anzia Yezierska, as a woman of seventy, asks the same question in her autobiography, entitled *Red Ribbon on a White Horse*, a profoundly moving document of the travails of the immigrant generation.

The first stage of idealization of America by the immigrants was generally followed by a second stage, disillusionment. The golden dreams of America as a veritable heaven on earth are dissipated when the immigrant finds himself face to face with the practical problems of earning his bread. The necessity of working from dawn to sunset and even far into the night in a sweatshop or as a peddler left the newly arrived person little leisure to enjoy the vaunted freedom of America. In the writings of Abraham Cahan, Morris Hillquit, Lillian Wald, Jacob Riis, and Hutchins Hapgood are found harrowing descriptions of the life of the Jewish masses on the East Side of New York. The Yiddish lyrics of Eliakum Zunser, Morris Winchevsky, David Edelstadt, Isaac Reingold, and Morris Rosenfeld mirror the disillusioned mood of these masses. Zunser laments that in the Golden Land there are men and women who collapse of hunger and families who are thrown out into the gutter when their rent is unpaid. "Look down upon New York's Downtown, where the air is pestilential, where human beings are pressed together like herring in a barrel . . . Who can calmly watch children jump from streetcars with batches of newspapers in their hands, risking their lives for a penny? The bitter need in their homes takes them from school prematurely and condemns them to coarseness and ignorance. Yet this is called the Golden Land." Morris Rosenfeld bewails the degradation of the newcomers to machines. In his poignant lyric, *The Sweatshop*, he writes: "I work and work and work endlessly. I toil and toil and toil ceaselessly. Why? For whom? I know not. I ask not. I am an unthinking machine."

The third stage in the adjustment of the newcomers was their

successful integration into American life. It followed the first
stage of idealization and the second stage of disillusionment. It
denoted recovery. The peddlers became storekeepers, the sweatshop workers became manufacturers.

The first half of the twentieth century witnessed a general as-
cent of the Jewish masses in the social and economic scale. The
former proletarians became members of the middle class and the
middle class took on the traits of the nouveau riche. Integration
was generally accompanied by a shedding of the characteristics
that the Greenhorn had brought with him from the Old Country,
the good along with the bad. The ideal of the children of the
immigrants was to be like unto their neighbors, indistinguishable
in every respect. Often, in the two decades before Pearl Harbor,
it reached among intellectuals the pathological state of Jewish
self-hatred, as is evident from an examination of such popular
novels of the period as Michael Gold's *Jews Without Money* (1930),
Ben Hecht's *A Jew in Love* (1931), and Budd Schulberg's *What
Makes Sammy Run* (1941). But, perhaps, the grimmest panorama
of the morass into which American Jewry then seemed to be heading was unfolded by the Yiddish novelist David Pinski in his
novel, *The House of Noah Eden* (1929), a genealogical novel comparable to Thomas Mann's *Buddenbrooks* or John Galsworthy's
Forsyte Saga. It portrayed three generations of a Jewish family
which emigrated to America in the 1880's from a little town in
Lithuania.

In the old country, Noah Eden lived as a member of a Jewish
enclave in non-Jewish territory. When he arrived in America, he
tried — as far as possible — to continue his traditional cultural
life. He was a Jew whose Jewishness was enriched by his American environment and experiences. His children, on the other
hand, were raised in the New World. They were Americans of
Jewish background. They fell under the spell of the brighter,
freer, gayer life which opened up before them, full of golden opportunities but also full of perilous allurements. They prospered and
rose in the social scale. One became a wealthy businessman, another a corporation lawyer, a third a prominent physician. With
each year they became more estranged from the Yiddish idiom
which they spoke when they first set foot on American soil. They
learned to live without God. They did not normally attend synagogue or temple on the Sabbath. Nor did they differentiate in
their homes between a Friday evening and any other evening.
But they did send their children to the finest schools and colleges,
where these third-generation Americans could be trained to be
perfectly-mannered ladies and gentlemen.

When the aging Noah Eden in his sixties came together with

his *Landsleit*, his old cronies of the immigrant generation, all of them had but one complaint: their children and grandchildren had left them and the ancestral ways. A world had arisen that knew not God. The road on which they and their forefathers had trodden for untold generations was coming to an end. They alone were left, a remnant of old men surviving as a traditional Jewish enclave in the great American metropolis, Noah's ark amidst the deluge. The youngest generation was smiling indulgently at the spectacle of the old men gathering daily in the basement of a synagogue to study Gemora and the strange ways of a strange people in a remote age. But, poring over the yellowed pages of a Talmud tract, these greybeards were rejuvenated. They seemed to live beyond time and space. They felt triumphant, despite the jeering laughter or the sophisticated jests directed at them, because they had the courage to be true to themselves and to live in accordance with their inner needs. In the depths of their heart, they hoped for a turning of the tide, for a return of their estranged children, for a reversion to God and to the ways of Israel. Or, if their children were too far gone, too completely immersed in the spirit of their non-Jewish environment, the grandchildren might be won back. One Friday evening, when the grandchildren of Noah Eden came to spend the Sabbath eve with their grandparents, one of them confessed:

"There is an emptiness in me; often despair overtakes me. I don't know why I'm living in this world. I don't know what to do with myself. My work amidst the skyscrapers is merely a way of killing time. This emptiness, this uselessness, must lead me astray, must lead me to weakness, folly, and immorality. I believe, religion could help me; it could fill my life with content; it could calm me."

Because these grandchildren were raised without religion, however, this insight came too late. Their splendid homes in the finest sections of the city had many books, usually arranged on mahagony shelves according to an artistic color-scheme, but the Bible was not among these books. If it happened to stray there as a Bar-Mitzvah gift, it was unread and its message unheard and unheeded. These Americans of Jewish origin were no longer embedded in Jewish tradition. Each of them was a detached fragment in the body of America, living a lonely life and facing a lonely death.

Pinski's novel of American-Jewish life, completed in 1929, when prosperity was at its height and when Jewishness seemed to be in precipitous decline, ended in despair, in suicide, double suicide, triple suicide. Its conclusion was as pessimistic as the conclusion of Peretz's story *Four Generations — Four Testaments*. upon which it was based. Its author held up a mirror to the generation of 1929. He presented a horrible object-lesson. He called for a stemming of the tide of assimilation. He begged: don't let a generation grow up that is emptied of Jewish content. He pleaded with American Jews that their survival not merely as human beings, not merely as Americans, but also as Jews, as a distinct ethnic and cultural entity on the world scene, was desirable, was necessary, was worth fighting for.

Throughout the quarter-of-a-century since the appearance of Pinski's novel, the problems he raised have been at the forefront of discussion. In 1954, the tercentenary year, we still face the question: can we enrich coming generations with sufficiently strong Jewish experiences so as to insure Jewish cultural survival in America? Can we make alive for them religious rituals, historic memories, and family habits which are our traditional treasures, our distinct heritage? Can we prevent their succumbing to the dominant trend towards cultural monism on this continent, a trend to which almost all non-Anglo-Saxon groups have already succumbed or are rapidly succumbing? Can we influence them to prefer the heroic life of biculturalism — the living in Jewish time and American space — to the more comfortable life of the mono-cultural majority about them? Can we substitute the slogan of cultural crossfertilization for the slogan of the melting pot?

The Jewish Book Council of America believes that it can make a contribution towards possible answers, or, at least, that it can bring greater clarity to the basic issues now under discussion. It can do so by bringing to bear upon current debates the wisdom of the past which is encased in the Jewish classics and the insight of contemporary sages now published in English, in Hebrew and in Yiddish.

The Jewish Book Council seeks to serve the entire Jewish community. It recognizes that we are no longer an immigrant group with common minority characteristics that are easily definable. It sees us in our present complex configuration as five million individuals of Jewish origin on American soil, individuals whose identification with Jewishness ranges from zero at one extreme to 100% at the other extreme. It recognizes that at one end of the scale there are men and women who are dreaming of inter-marriage, religious dissociation, release from bondage to ancestral values which to them are no longer meaningful. It recognizes that at the other end of the scale there are individuals who are dreaming of exchanging the most glamorous land of the Diaspora for the humblest fireside which Mother Zion offers to her children. But, it also recognizes that between the two extremes, between minimal and total identification with Jewishness, there exists a wide range of possibilities and that every person of Jewish origin on American soil will have to decide for himself, after painful soul-searching, where, on this scale of possibilities, he belongs.

The Jewish Book Council wisely refrains from offering advice but it tries to be helpful in opening up the sources of information to all who seek guidance in wrestling with Jewish values and problems.

The Jewish Book Council does not engage in polemics. It is tolerant of all currents in American Jewish life. It does not withhold its services even from the ultra-assimilationists who consciously disown all kinship with the Jewish people as a people, for even these, despite their flight from Jewishness, are unconsciously bringing to America Jewish traits which are part of the structure of their personality. They are doing so by their very existence, though they themselves may be unaware of their function as carriers of Jewish sensitiveness, as bearers of Jewish approaches to experience.

The Jewish Book Council certainly does not withhold its services from those Americans who are Israel-oriented and who are preparing to give up lightheartedness and ease for stern duty as they see it and peace of mind as they would have it. These dreamers and builders of Zion are not unfaithful to the American values among which they were born and reared. Though their objective is reintegration in the land of our historic origin, they are enriching it with American know-how. They are pouring their Americanism into the blood-stream of Israel, making Israel more virile, more practical, more efficient, more Western, more democratic, more freedom-loving.

The chief concern of the Jewish Book Council, however, as of the National Jewish Welfare Board under whose auspices it functions, must be the overwhelming majority of the five million who wish to live a rich bi-cultural life as Americans and as Jews, who wish to make their contribution to eternal human values right here on the basis of their Americanism and Jewishness. By means of Jewish Book Month, Jewish publications, and program aids to Jewish community centers, synagogues, and other organizations, the Jewish Book Council will continue to stimulate Jewish creativeness in thought and word, so that we may remain a wise and articulate group in America.

On the three hundredth anniversary of the first settlement of Jews in the United States, we stand at the apex of an uninterrupted growth in numbers, in prestige, in affluence, and in influence. We are presently experiencing the Golden Age of American Jewry. This is one of those rare historic moments when the guardian of our destiny puts our fate in our own hands and gives us the opportunity freely to choose our future. The choice we make, involving the character of our cultural survival as Jews in America, will reecho down the generations and will affect the lives of our descendents until the end of time. Let us not be indolent in our thinking. Let us acquire all the knowledge available to us. Let us accept gratefully the help extended to us by the Jewish Book Council. Let us read the great books of our past, from our original guiding light, the Torah. Let us ponder on great works of the present, which incorporate the conclusions of our rabbis and philosophers, our priests and prophets, our orators and imaginative interpreters. And then let each of us alone, or in association with others, make our decision in the light of our needs and the needs of humanity.

May it be a decision of knowledge and not of ignorance, of wisdom and not of folly, of dignity and not of convenience, of moral greatness and not of apathy! And may it lead to peace in our souls and happiness for all mankind!

A PANORAMA OF A HALF-CENTURY OF AMERICAN JEWISH LITERATURE

By Ludwig Lewisohn

JEWISH literary productivity in non-Jewish languages remains one of the enigmatic aspects of Jewish destiny. What is a Jewish book written in English? A book written by a Jew? Does that criterion suffice? In what sense is Mr. Walter Lippmann's *Preface to Politics* a Jewish book? Or Miss Edna Ferber's *Show-Boat?* Or a play by Mr. S. N. Behrman or Mr. George S. Kaufman or a poem by Mr. Kenneth Fearing? To call these productions Jewish is to imply a definition that has dangerous enough inferences — dangerous by virtue of possibly malicious assumptions, though it is sound enough to feel, at least, that the Jewish psyche has a more or less characteristic structure, as has that of a Frenchman or a Chinese. I am unwilling to embark upon these deep and perilous waters; I am equally unwilling to discuss the tragic and equivocal subject of the position of a Jewish writer in a non-Jewish society, never wholly accepted, unless it be on the shallowest plane of mere entertainment, by that society, and deprived of his natural audience, the Jewish community, by servile fears and environmental pressures. I shall pursue neither problem. But no one can write honestly of Jewish writing in a given land and period without stating these problems and being tacitly guided by their existence.

One other preliminary remark must be made. I am asked, as it were, to write literary history, in however modest a fashion, without any of the usual tools and researches. There are no extensive bibliographies; there are only tentative *Vorarbeiten*, except the admirable recent Surveys of Dr. Joshua Bloch.* I can do nothing that has scholarly soundness and completeness. I can do nothing that is adequately organized. Perhaps this preliminary survey — for it can be no more — will encourage some young Jewish literary scholar to engage in the research and interpretation of Jewish writing in the United States in the twentieth century.

If it may be said that tendencies are discernible at all, then a keynote was struck early by two books of very different value:

Jewish Book Annual, Volumes II–VIII.

the facile, superficial *The Promised Land* by Mary Antin (1912) and the grave, thoughtful, solidly wrought *The Rise of David Levinsky* by the venerable Abraham Cahan (1917). As was, alas, to be expected of a community, so to speak, "on the make," it was *The Promised Land* which pointed a way. To this day we are embarrassed and grieved by the novels of second-generation American Jews who carry the Mary Antin motif to morbid lengths of self-degradation, raging against their residual Jewishness (Norman Katkov's *Eagle at My Eyes*) with flamboyant illiteracy, exalting not the noble and elevated aspects of American culture, but its very dregs and sewage at the expense of all that was glorious and sacred in their ancestral tradition (Sam Ross's *The Sidewalks Are Free*).

Following this tendency backward for a moment from its latest and feeblest manifestation, we come upon Samuel Ornitz's *Haunch, Paunch and Jowl,* Michael Gold's *Jews Without Money,* Jerome Weidman's *I Can Get It For You Wholesale,* certain earlier performances of Ben Hecht (*A Jew in Love*). Allied thematic material, placed, as it were, upside down, inspired such things as Laura Z. Hobson's *Gentlemen's Agreement* and Jo Sinclair's *Wasteland.* All these books, fortunately and inevitably quite without literary merit, represent a frantic escape from Jewishness and Judaism under various aspects: *all* Jews are morally shabby or there *are* no Jews. In the first instance they and the Jewishness within the writer are to be repudiated; in the second instance not even repudiation is needed. The reason why this unsavory subject had to be treated is because, precisely now, at the middle of the century, we are flooded by documents of this character and innocent Christian publishers send one complimentary copies with the hilarious notion that, having published a "Jewish" novel, they have performed a graceful act.

Let us turn now to a generation which, whatever the specific aspects of its work, produced men of letters of honorable character: Louis Untermeyer, Jean Starr Untermeyer, Waldo Frank, the late James Oppenheim, Franklin P. Adams, Walter Lippmann, George Jean Nathan, Horace Meyer Kallen, the late Morris Raphael Cohen.* I am tempted to add the eminent scholars in the ranks of that generation, with some assurance that the works, for instance, of Harry A. Wolfson will, even as

---

* Since I cannot obviously discuss myself, I may be permitted to list my specifically Jewish books: *Up Stream* (1922), *Israel* (1925), *The Island Within* (1928), *Mid-Channel* (1929), *The Last Days of Shylock* (1931), *This People* (1933), *Rebirth: A Book of Modern Jewish Thought* (1934), *Trumpet of Jubilee* (1937), *The Answer* (1939), *Renegade* (1942), *Breathe Upon These* (1944) and the forthcoming *The American Jew — Character and Destiny* (1950).

literature, outlast the books of most of the practitioners of *belles lettres*. But I have not the space nor the knowledge required. Of the others it is to be said that Walter Lippmann, George Jean Nathan, Franklin P. Adams have consistently ignored their Jewishness. They have done so conspicuously and I, at least, consider it beneath Jewish dignity to wish them other than they desired to be or to devaluate on that account the moderate eloquence of Mr. Lippmann's earlier books, the wit and vivacity of Mr. Nathan or the graceful versifying of Mr. Adams.

Another story is to be told of the other members of that group — of Mr. Louis Untermeyer's highly accomplished literary skill, of his frequent re-alliance (*Roast Leviathan*) with the Jewish spirit, of the solid services he has rendered to the study and criticism of poetry; of Jean Starr Untermeyer's few but piercing Jewish lyrical cries; above all, of the nostalgic and aspiring spirit of Waldo Frank. His is a puzzling figure. He has desired to be a true man of letters and a truly Jewish man of letters. He has been thwarted by literary eccentricities adopted early and by an inveterate aversion to acquiring such Jewish knowledge as is fundamental to Jewish writing. The two philosophers, Horace Kallen and Morris Cohen, belong in this brief record: Mr. Kallen by reason of his titanic struggle with all Jewish problems in his many books, the late Morris Cohen, whose Jewish attitudes were tragically negative, by virtue of his accomplished style and wide influence.

I come to what might be called the popular entertainers of that general group or generation, of whom the earliest and in certain ways not the least effective was Montague Glass. The Potash and Perlmutter stories and stage adaptations were superficial enough. But they were warm and kindly. They did offer Jews to *condescending* Gentile appreciation, but so did the tales of Zangwill often enough. They omitted all the sterner aspects of Jewish destiny and character, but the historic period was one when that, though foolish and feeble, was not yet necessarily contemptible. The succeeding Jewish entertainers of a vast American public are very varied in quality and temper. We need not be detained by Octavus Roy Cohen. It is to be noted in mere justice that among Miss Edna Ferber's early stories there are some sound delineations of minor Jewish characters. The same is true in a lesser measure of Miss Fanny Hurst. Later both of these writers, especially Miss Ferber, tightened the assimilatory masks upon their faces and deliberately courted popularity on the lowest plane. I have been accused of being harsh in my dealing with these ladies. It is neither their wide sales nor the non-Jewish character of their later works that I deprecate. Jacob Wassermann's *Mauritius Case* shared both marks. It was a world success and not a Jewish novel. But it was a tense and lofty exercise of the creative imagination. *If* we had an American Jacob Wassermann, no critic would mention the *virtuosi* of mere entertainment.

The generation immediately following exhibited undoubtedly a very genuine improvement in literary *quality*. We are in a quite different world of style and manner and bearing when we come to, let us say, Robert Nathan, Elmer Rice, Babette Deutsch, Irving Fineman, Max Lerner, Irwin Edman, S. N. Behrman, Marie Syrkin, the English writings of Hayim Greenberg, of Will Herberg, above all, when we come to the work, the *oeuvre*, of Maurice Samuel. It is as though this generation, whether of native or of foreign birth, had suddenly in the deeper and higher sense learned English and moved with ease and grace within the moods and methods, to whatever subject applied, of the fundamental traditions of the literature of the English tongue. One may sorrow over the silly radicalism of Elmer Rice. One remains persuaded that at least in *The Adding Machine* he added a memorable work to the American drama. So sagacious a critic as Joseph Wood Krutch has constantly supported the claim of S. N. Behrman to be a comic dramatist in one of the classic English traditions. The slight but elegant fictions of Mr. Robert Nathan, the firmly wrought verses of Miss Babette Deutsch, the vigorous and trenchant political essays of Max Lerner — all these are on the higher levels of contemporary American literature. Slightly above even these levels, though all such immediate judgments must be tentative, stands the work of Irwin Edman and Irving Fineman. Mr. Edman, after a dash into Jewish autobiography in the *Menorah Journal* some years ago, withdrew entirely into neutral realms. His philosophical attitudes are not mine. But his witty verse and luminous prose in which he has, without unworthy concessions, made philosophy seem a friendly thing in a "middle-brow" world, are to be mentioned with respect and kindness.

With the work of Mr. Fineman we enter the tragic realm of the Jewish creative artist. The wide American public does not want to read about Jews, which is understandable; literate Jews prefer the psychical security of reading what everybody else is reading. In these simple statements is summed up the fragmentization of the career of this extraordinarily gifted novelist. Had he not chosen the honorable and spiritually fruitful part of writing out of the depth of his Jewish heart, he would rank with the most conspicuous American novelists today, none of which are above him in endowment or skill.

I come to Maurice Samuel, the one quite outstanding man of letters whom American Jewry has produced in the twentieth century. What are the marks of eminence in a man of letters? Intellectual power and mastery of language. I wish to assert that, except in the purely creative realm in which, of course, at least Hemingway and perhaps one other outshine him, he is *qualitatively* the ablest American writer of our time. By the tests of intellectual power and mastery of English his books, from *You Gentiles* (1924), through *King Mob* (1930), *The Great Hatred* (1940) to those recent, exquisitely poetic and creative resuscitations of a perished culture in *The World of Sholem Aleichem* and *Prince of the Ghetto*, are the American books most worthy of endurance. Nor is this all. Even in his earlier fictions, even in *Beyond Woman* (1934), there were, despite the warping of the total intention, pages that few other Americans would have been capable of writing. His massive historical novel *The Web of Lucifer* (1947), though again, perhaps, the embodiment of the subject choice was not sufficiently destined, is the finest example of continuously great and grave English prose in this period of American writing. It remains to be added quite objectively that the name of Maurice Samuel appears in no account of American literature, in no anthology, in no critical appraisal.

A still younger generation, at least equally gifted, serves to illustrate the same situation. The early, brilliant, acridly partisan plays of Clifford Odets, the firm and bitter tragi-comedies of Lillian Hellman, all written from behind a non-Jewish mask, have had perhaps more than their due upon the American scene. The struggling, aspiring effort to devote himself to the subjects closest to his heart and befitting his character have left in darkness and neglect the delicacy and sensitiveness of Meyer Levin. What one can still do with impunity, as in the days of Montague Glass, is to be amusing on Jewish subjects. Thus Leonard Q. Ross yesterday and Arthur Kober today have worked this vein not without talent. In the realm of humor this may be the place to record, at least, the name of S. J. Perelman.

As I approach the immediate present, my unhappily improvised task becomes more and more difficult. Omissions, too, throng upon the mind: the wry, Heinesque verses of the late Samuel Hoffenstein, the ambitious imaginative structures of Manuel Komroff, the tiny classic *A Cycle of Manhattan* by Thyra Sampter Winslow, the single novel of Leonard Ehrlich, *God's Angry Man*, the steady efforts of Mr. Myron T. Brinig. And perhaps I ought not to omit the not at all despicable productions of the two unequivocally Jewish writers who call themselves Ellery Queen.

Conspicuous on the immediate scene of American letters are

Mr. Howard Fast, Mr. Arthur Miller, Mr. Irwin Shaw, Mr. Norman Mailer. Of these Mr. Miller seems to me the most gifted as well as the most scrupulous. His delicacy of perception in *Focus* would have served him better with just a little more Jewish knowledge added; *Death of a Salesman*, too, is delicately felt rather than profoundly thought through. But his talent is evident and his possibilities of development are great. Mr. Shaw is often betrayed by a "slickness" of execution which in the milieu of the *New Yorker* passes for elegance, but of his talent and of legitimate hopes for his development there can be no question either. Mr. Norman Mailer, author of *The Naked and the Dead*, is a man of ruder, heavier execution and more sombre temper. What is true of all three is a very honorable attempt at least to include their people and that people's fortunes in their works. Everywhere among the younger writers the assimilatory mask is being lifted. What makes this honorable attitude futile is the pretty complete lack of Jewish knowledge, which none of them seems willing or able to supply. It is perhaps at this point that I should mention the brief, subtle, oddly shadowy dealings with Jewish life of Mr. Delmore Schwartz (*The World is a Wedding*), the modernist sketches of Mr. Paul Goodman, the promising beginnings of Mr. Saul Bellow.

There are moments when it seems to me as though we have in the immediate present done best in poetry. I have already mentioned Kenneth Fearing. To his name should be added at least those of Muriel Rukeyser, Delmore Schwartz, Karl Shapiro and Hyam Plutzig. These poets all belong, of course, to the contemporary movement of "difficult" poetry, poetry *as such* (*an sich*), which has abandoned direct communication in the older sense. Within this framework, however, all of these poets are authentically gifted and all, except Mr. Schwartz, are escaping from the framework of a total despair in the possibility of meaning. Miss Rukeyser has always been capable of startling clarities of lyric expression; Mr. Shapiro, despite his defense of the school and *cénacle*, writes with increasing communicative force, as he did in that salute to Israel which he wrote for the birth of the State.

> When I think of the battle for Zion I hear
> The drop of chains, the starting forth of feet . . .
> I look the stranger clear to the blue depths
> Of his unclouded eye. I say my name
> Aloud for the first time unconsciously . . .
> Speak the name of the land,
> Speak the name only of the living land.

A profounder and more authentic poet than any of these is

Abraham M. Klein of Montreal. He has not been reckoned publicly among the poets of various groups, partly because he is a citizen of the Dominion of Canada, where he has not been unhonored or unappreciated, and partly because the substance of his poetry is wholly and instinctively and learnedly Jewish.

Critical prose, in which Jews have often excelled in various literatures, has not been neglected among us. In the middle generation there is the accomplished, learned, witty Marvin Lowenthal; among the younger and youngest men mention should be made at least of Mr. Lionel Trilling, Mr. David Daiches, Mr. Harry Levin, all in conspicuous academic posts at Columbia, Cornell, Harvard, and of such free lance critics as Mr. Alfred Kazin and Mr. Louis Kronenberger. Mr. Trilling finds it hard and uncomfortable to be a Jew, which is bound to impinge on his total intellectual integrity. This leads in his and other cases — *not* in that of Mr. Daiches — to escape into a rootless liberalism, a nonqualitative universalism, which muddles all thinking and blunts all point. There seems, however, to be arising a still younger generation of critics and literary scholars which, by spontaneously accepting its Judaism and its Jewishness, is likely to produce deeper, richer, more fruitful work.

Is any summing up of this account either in place or possible? Desultory and unorganized as it has been because, it is worth repeating, no bibliographies, no preliminary studies, no exploration of the field of American Jewish literature exist, it yet seems to me that one very simple conclusion may be drawn. Given the character and history of American writing within which American Jews have had to work, we have not done ill either qualitatively or quantitatively. This is not the place to institute the comparison with what other Jewries in other lands have accomplished in literature in the twentieth century. When that comparison comes to be made it will be found that only the Jews in Germany, whose productivity was tragically interrupted in 1933, have surpassed American Jewry. We tower above the Jewries of both England and France. We have not been sterile or inactive. We have made a more than honorable showing.

A final remark is in place. Between the two World Wars there arose in the lands of German speech a group of men who created within that speech an illustrious *Jewish* literature. The names of Franz Rosenzweig, of Martin Buber, of the poets Karl Wolfskehl and Ludwig Strauss, of Bin-Gorion and Hugo Bergmann, of the living and the dead within that group, are already electric names in all Israel. Am I wholly wrong in hoping that such a development is possible in American Jewry and that, indeed, we are on the threshold of it? At all events, while these lines were being written there appeared among us two books that *could*, that *might* fore-shadow a development so ardently, so deeply to be desired as both symbol and means of Jewish redemption in America. Those two books are: *The Earth is the Lord's* by Abraham Joshua Heschel and the book of poems *Jerusalem Has Many Faces* by Judah Stampfer. Dr. Heschel's book is a great and poignant prose elegy on our martyrs — a commemoration, a monument, a prose *piyyut*. But it is more also. It is a humble yet unshaken reassertion of the nobility of our estate, despite our sufferings and our anguish. "We are God's stake in human history." Such is Dr. Heschel's piercingly true, immortally significant conclusion. And the poems of Judah Stampfer, almost a lad, yet rabbi and teacher and warrior in Israel, as well as accomplished scholar in English literature, sound the same consecrated note: they strike fire from the flint of our tradition and send abroad the kindling sparks:

> Over a web of light,
> And freezing steel,
> Sometimes I had to climb
> And sometimes kneel,
>
> Till I could rest my thoughts,
> Like ascetic mutes,
> Upon the starry needles
> Of God's attributes.

AMERICAN JEWISH LITERARY "FIRSTS"

By Lee M. Friedman

IN THIS tercentenary year when we are commemorating the arrival in 1654 of twenty-three Jews in New Amsterdam, establishing the first Jewish community in what is today the United States, many astonished Americans are discovering that American Jewish history dates back to the days of Columbus.

Today, United States history is being rewritten. Historians have come to realize that our history is the study of the weaving of the different strands of race and creed into a united nation, the blending of many heterogeneous peoples into something new and progressive in human experience, which we call Americanism. In a land of action, of conflicting social, political, economic and moral experiences, the coalescence of many peoples abolished insularity and created not only new ideologies but new human relationships. Differing stocks and races are seen bringing to our shores their traditions, cultures, philosophies and inherited characteristics into a free competition of ideas and ways of life to create an Americanism which is the contribution of no one group in the national makeup. American history may, therefore, be defined as the study and understanding of this progressive development and the contributions of each of these constituent peoples integrated into American national life.

American Jewish history is thus the presentation and analysis of Jewish contributions to American life and at the same time the showing of the changes, development and reaction of the Jews in America as they became acclimated, free citizens, integrated into the life of their communities. Therefore, this presentation of the facts and incidences of Jewish participation in the founding and developing life of the land, and Jewish contributions to American thinking, ideals and living standards, should be the aim of American Jewish historians.

In this American Jewish history, the topic of Jewish "firsts" is not of vital importance. While it may be interesting to know of the first Jewish settler in any community, it is of no great significance to record that Samuel Isaacs was the first Jew to settle in Texas, or that Simon Valentine lived in Charleston, S. C., in 1697, or that Alexander Levi was the pioneer Jew in

75

Iowa, or that Joseph Jonas settled in Cincinnati when it was still but a pioneer Western outpost. It is even unimportant that some five years before the twenty-three Jews landed in New Amsterdam the Great & General Court of the Province of Massachusetts Bay paid Solomon Franco to leave Boston when he proposed to settle there, or even that Jacob Barsimson had shortly preceded them. The emphasis on Jewish "firsts" is perhaps due to a new crop of authors responding to the call that, to celebrate the Tercentenary of our national Jewish history, all that is needed is pen, ink and paper, and in any particular part of the country you can show that Jews were pioneers, important and indispensible to the founding and upbuilding of the community — a prideful, filiopietistic, sectarian propaganda by exaggeration and false illusions seeking to bolster up a defensive neurosis for frustrated American Jews.

There are, however, certain Jewish "firsts" which have real significance in American history. When Oscar S. Straus became the first Jew to be a member of a President's Cabinet, or when Brandeis became the first Jew to sit on the United States Supreme Court, it indicated a certain status that American Jews had attained in their relationship with their fellow citizens. It also showed that in its development the American people had grown to that stage of assured confidence in itself that it could accept the fact that our conglomerate intermixing of many differing races had become a cross-fertilized social, political, and economic united nation. In this self-confidence, the people, outfacing an ancient prejudice, accepted as a natural national point of view that fellow Jewish citizens should share equally in the safeguarding and developing of American national ideals and ambitions.

Perhaps nowhere do American Jewish "firsts" shed a ray of light better upon how Jews and Jewish ideals played a part on the American scene than by examining the literary products which appeared in earlier days. Hebrew learning starts with the Pilgrim settlement in Plymouth. In his manuscript "History of the Plimouth Plantation," Governor William Bradford used eight of its blank flyleaves to write out most carefully over a thousand Hebrew words with their English translations "to see how the words and phrases lye in the holy texte; and to discerne somewhat of the same for my owne contente," and that Hebrew learning should be safeguarded for coming generations. From this very beginning, knowledge of Hebrew and acquaintance with the Old Testament and Jewish history was a requirement of learning and sound theology in Massachusetts. So when the first printing press, set up in Cambridge in 1639, printed the first book to be published in English in America, the "Bay Psalm Book," to convince the public of its authoritative authenticity, Hebrew words were printed in Hebrew type and the entire Hebrew alphabet was reproduced. The printing was crude and there are those who believe that the Hebrew type was locally handcut. It is known that there was not a set of Hebrew type in America until 1735 when Harvard imported such type from England to print Judah Monis' *Hebrew Grammar*, the first such grammar to be printed in the United States, that Harvard might educate future clergymen to be able to read the Holy Bible in the language they believed the Almighty spoke.

From 1669, when Increase Mather published *The Mystery of Israel's Salvation Explained and Applied*, "An Epistle" addressed to the Christian reader being "the substance of several sermons preached," it was but the first of a flood of printed sermons and pamphlets from the Puritan clergy dealing with the Jews of the Old Testament. Indeed, so intense was the admiration of the founding fathers of the Massachusetts Colony for Jewish ideals that as early as 1641 they sought to establish their theocratic government on "the modell of the Judicall lawes of Moses." At the same time, seeking and proclaiming religious liberty for themselves, they had no will to allow Quakers, Papists, Jews or Heathens to settle in their midst.

One of the beautiful survivals of Jewish literary works in America is *Parafrasis Comentado sobre el Pentateucho por Illustrissimo Sr Ishac del K. K. deAmsterdam* of 1681, a commentary on the Pentateuch written by Isaac da Fonseca Aboab, who died in 1693. When, in 1642, the Jews of Brazil became sufficiently prosperous to have a rabbi, they sent to Amsterdam and had Rabbi Aboab come out to them. After war broke out in Brazil between the Dutch and the Portuguese, Aboab returned to Holland, and, as the first Jewish author who had lived in America, not only wrote this book, but, described by Kayserling as "an excellent Hebrew poet," he left us other works worthy of his talents and learning.[1]

The first Colonial Jewish publication was an English translation of a Hebrew prayer of Rabbi Joseph Yesurun Pinto "performed at the Jews Synagogue in the City of New York," October 23, 1760, as a "Thanksgiving to Almighty God, for the reducing of Canada to His Majesty's Dominion," printed in New York at the new printing office of W. Weyman. In the following year,

---

[1] M. Kayserling, "Isaac Aboab, The First Jewish Author in America," *Publications of the American Jewish Historical Society*, No. 5 (1897), pp. 125–136.

W. Weyman printed an anonymous translation of the *Evening Service of Roshashanah, and Kippur, or The Beginning of the Year, and The Day of Atonement,* which has been described as being "the earliest Jewish prayer book printed in America." But the outstanding Jewish publication of early days is that volume of prayers which John Holt of New York published for Shearith Israel in 1766 (5526). Translated by Isaac Pinto, it was entitled *Prayers for Shabbath, Rosh-Hashanah, and Kippur; or The Sabbath, the Beginning of the Year, and The Day of Atonements; with the Amidah and Musaph of the Moadim, or Solemn Seasons. According to the order of the Spanish and Portuguese Jews.* In the preface to this prayer book, Pinto stated, among other things, his reason for making this translation:

> ... it has been necessary to translate our Prayers, in the language of the Country wherein it hath pleased the divine Providence to appoin our Lot. In Europe, the Spanish and Portuguese Jews have a Translation in Spanish, which as they generally understand, may be sufficient; but that not being the Case in the British Dominions in America, has induced me to Attempt a Translation in English, not without Hope that it will tend to the Improvement of many of my Brethren in their Devotion; and if it answer that Good Intention, it will afford me the Satisfaction of having contributed towards it.

A second issue was produced almost immediately.[2] Thus, in a little over a hundred years after their first coming, these Spanish and Portuguese Jews were already so American that they wanted their prayer books in English.

The first sermon preached by a rabbi in the Western world to be published was that of Rabbi Samuel Mendes deSolla, preached at Curaçao in 1750 and published in Amsterdam. But the first sermon to be both preached and published in the United States dates from 1773. Rabbi Haim Isaac Carigal, who excited much attention as he travelled around in that year, preached at the Newport Synagogue a Pentacost sermon which so impressed his hearers that the great merchant, Aaron Lopez, had it translated from Spanish into English and caused it to be published as the first of Jewish sermons published in America which was preached here.

There is a whole literature dealing with the Ten Lost Tribes, in many of which the authors discovered and proved to their entire satisfaction that the Indians were the dispersed Israelites.

[2] See *PAJHS*, No. 30, Item Nos. 41 (1761), 45 and 46 (1766).

The Reverend John Eliot was sent out to convert Indians in the belief that by Christianizing these Jews he was both delivering them from Hell and at the same time hastening the millennium.

In 1812 John Eliot, Jr., of Boston published *The History of The Jews from the Destruction of Jerusalem to the Nineteenth Century*, in two volumes, written by Hannah Adams. Hannah Adams was the earliest of Boston Blue Stockings, a learned lady and much interested in religion and in the conversion of Jews. This was the first history of the Jews written by an American and published here. It was not a very good piece of work. Largely borrowed from Basnage's *The History of the Jews from Jesus Christ to the Present Time* (1708) which had appeared in an English translation, it devoted but a single chapter to American Jewish history. A great missed opportunity. The book, however, had a good circulation. Republished in London and translated into German, it has its place as a "first" in American literary history.

In 1824 appeared the first Jewish "defence" publication in America; Solomon H. Jackson edited in New York the first number of his magazine, *The Jew; Being A Defence of Judaism Against All Adversaries*. This was offered as an answer to the publication *Israel's Advocate* and the activities of the American Society for Meliorating the Condition of the Jews, which was engaged in an active proselyting campaign and setting up of a community for converted Jews in upper New York.

Although Emma Lazarus is outstanding amongst American Jewish poets, the first Jewish poetess in American history is Penina Moise, born in Charleston, South Carolina, in 1797. An ardent Jewess, she wrote hymns, taught in the religious school of Beth Elohim, and was a voluminous contributor to the press of her day — not only with poems, but with a wide variety of articles. This American Jewish literary "first" lived on until almost our own day, until September 18, 1880.

It was in the year 1853–54, that the first English translation of the Hebrew Bible, by an American Jew, made its appearance in Philadelphia. It was the crowning literary effort of the Reverend Isaac Leeser. His translation was not superseded in this country until the appearance of the new version of the Jewish Publication Society of America in 1917. Leeser, in the opening lines of his Preface, outlined what motivated him in making this translation:

> In presenting this work to the public, the translator would merely remark, that it is not a new notion by which he was seized of late years which impelled him to the task, but a desire entertained for more than a quarter of a century, since the

day he quitted school in his native land to come to this country, to present to his fellow-Israelites an English version, made by one of themselves, of the Holy Word of God. From early infancy he was made conscious how much persons differing from us in religious ideas make use of Scripture to assail Israel's hope and faith, by what he deems, in accordance with the well-settled opinions of sound critics, both Israelites and others, a perverted and hence erroneous rendering of the words of the original Bible. Therefore he always entertained the hope to be one day permitted to do for his fellow-Hebrews who use the English as their vernacular, what had been done for the Germans by some of the most eminent minds whom the Almighty has endowed with the power of reanimating in us the almost expiring desire for critical inquiry into the sacred text.

The first Jewish book publisher was Benjamin Gomez of New York (1769–1828), who began publishing in 1792 and produced a large variety of books. Not the least important of these was a reprint of Dr. Priestley's letters to the Jews urging them to be converted, and the answering letters of David Levi which appeared in 1794.

No enumeration of Jewish American "firsts" could properly be brought to a close without mentioning Major Mordecai M. Noah. He was the champion holder of "firsts." The first articulate American Zionist (1843); the first American Jewish dramatist (1808); first Jew to be an American Consul abroad. If not first, certainly amongst the first of our Jewish journalists, sheriffs, politicians, and finally the first Jew whose portrait was reproduced in a book (1819).

After all, it is not difficult to select "firsts" for this article out of the far-flung and diversified assortment which history presents. No collection of them can be but a backdrop of a cyclorama of American life, showing how from the days of the founding fathers, as the years rolled on, Jews, changing and developing with their experiences on the American scene, preserving individuality and inherited characteristics yet integrated in the surrounding life, united with their neighbors in building, upholding and cherishing a new nation.

HEBREW LITERATURE IN AMERICA AT THE TERCENTENARY

By Eisig Silberschlag

I

THE three-hundred-year-old literary record of American Jews does not match their high achievements in the field of economic and philanthropic endeavor. Modest beginnings have reached a phase of modest accomplishments. That is all that can be said with justice on the eve of the tercentenary.

The fragmentation of intellectual effort and energy in three main languages — English, Yiddish and Hebrew — and in a few subsidiary ones may account for the slow growth of our literature in this country. But there are additional causes: paucity of Jews in the first two centuries — there were probably not more than 16,000 Jews as late as 1825 — economic pressures and social compulsions which drove Americans of all creeds and persuasions to concentrate on the material development of their country rather than on cultural refinements.

II

Hebrew literature in this country must be viewed within the context of world literature including Anglo-American literature and Hebrew literature in its predominant centers. Neglect of these factors can only result in parochial appraisal and distorted evaluation.

Colonial America had a religious interest in the Hebrew language. The Old Testament, so dear to the Puritans, was more to them than a divinely inspired document: it was the alpha and omega of knowledge and wisdom, the guide in personal habits and social relations, the inspirational force in just government. Respect for the "divine authority of the Sabbath," reference to Boston as the "Jerusalem of this land," reference to New England as the "New English Canaan," names of towns like Salem, names of persons like Israel and Samuel, Abner and Melchizedek, attest to love for the Bible — love which was fostered by temporal and spiritual rulers, by schools and colleges.[1]

---

[1] Six centers of learning were established before 1760 — Harvard, William and Mary, Yale, the College of New Jersey (later Princeton), King's (later Columbia)

81

Governor William Bradford of Plymouth[2] studied Hebrew because he would see with his own eyes "something of that most
ancient language and holy tongue in which . . . God and angels
spoke to the holy patriarchs of old time . . ." And the old lady,
who is said to have learned Hebrew in the ninth decade of her life
in order to converse in the inevitable meeting with her Maker in
his native tongue, is merely a humorous illustration of a predominant interest.

Colonial America even toyed with the adoption of Hebrew as a
national language. H. L. Mencken quotes William Gifford as
authority for the story that "at the close of the Revolution certain
members of Congress proposed that the use of English be formally
prohibited in the United States, and Hebrew substituted for it."[3]
But this enormous interest in the Hebrew language had a meagre
influence on the productivity in Hebrew both on the part of Jews
and on the part of other segments of the population.

Serious attempts at a native Hebrew literature date from the
latter part of the nineteenth century. It was then that the first
Hebrew periodicals like *Ha-Zofeh ba-Erez ha-Hadashah, ha-Pisgah,
ha-Zeman* and *ha-Ivri* were founded and kept alive for a number
of years against tremendous odds. Then and now editors and
writers, with few exceptions, had to pursue their literary labors in
spare time. Since Hebrew writing was not lucrative they had to
derive their livelihood from other sources. These economic reali-
ties were responsible, to a certain extent, for an overproduction
of three literary genres: lyric poetry in a romantic vein, the short
story in a sentimental mood and the essay in a protean variety of
forms.[4] Works of fiction and philosophy are still few and far
between.

III

As soon as Hebrew literature reached a degree of maturity in this
country with the publication of Benjamin Silkiner's narrative poem
Mul Ohel Timmurah ("Before the Tent of Timmurah") in 1909,

and the Charity School of Philadelphia (later the Academy and College of Philadelphia, and eventually the University of Pennsylvania).

[2] The majesty title does not correspond to the modest number of the population:
of the 102 people who had arrived on the Mayflower at the end of 1620, 56 were left
in the spring of 1621.

[3] *The American Language*, Fourth Edition (New York, 1936), p. 79; also *Supplement* I (New York, 1945), pp. 136–138.

[4] The excellent anthology of Hebrew poetry in America, compiled and edited by
the late Menachem Ribalow, should be complemented by an anthology of Hebrew
short stories and an anthology of Hebrew essays in America.

the influence of Anglo-American literature became a pervasive factor in Hebrew prose and poetry. The structure and the imagery of that poem were permeated with reminiscences of English romantic poetry. And the lines from Byron, preceding the poem, indicate a direct source of inspiration and a love for the interplay of nature and ethics which is a distinguishing mark of English poetry:

> ... The sun makes
> Sweet skies just when he rises, or is set ...

The subject-matter of the poem was also a bold innovation in Hebrew literature. For the first time a Hebrew poet built his poem out of native material — out of intertribal quarrels in early America, out of fights of Indians and Spaniards. Against a background of iron and blood he revived the defunct civilization of the Red Man: the cruel custom of human sacrifices to the Great Spirit, the tender cult of the God of Peace and Purity, the Soul-God, the wisdom and wiles of chiefs and priests, and the ancient splendors of the American landscape.

The contemporaries of Silkiner and younger Hebrew writers eagerly seized upon the new and native ores of poetry. The preoccupation with the Indian and the Negro in the poetry of Lisitzky, Efros, Ginzburg, and Bavli opened up a new folk-world of imagery and ideas to Hebrew literature. And the potent resources of English and American classics invigorated Hebrew writers. In the nineteenth century they had been nurtured by German and Slav literatures. In the twentieth century, they not only translated Shakespeare and Milton, Poe and Whitman; they wrote essays on American and English literatures and reflected their extensive studies of English and American authors in their writings. In the future the literary historian will be able to cultivate an interesting field of research in cultural fertilization. For a sensitive investigation of the works of Silkiner and Schwartz, Lisitzky and Bavli, Halkin and Regelson, Ginzburg and Feinstein, Friedland, Preil and Grossman-Avinoam will disclose an indebtedness to Anglo-American literature far beyond present premonitions or assumptions.

IV

Hebrew literature, in mid-century, radiates from the major center in Israel and the minor center in the United States. In other countries it is so insignificant as to be almost non-existent. This dual center, recognized by the historian and given only grudging assent by current opinion in Israel, is a recent development. Until the Russian Revolution in 1917 Hebrew literature was concentrated for more than one hundred years in the vast land-mass of Eastern Europe. Palestine was then only a minor center of literary activities. At the end of the First World War the inimical attitude of the communist government to Hebrew as a reactionary, counter-revolutionary instrument almost stilled the voice of Hebrew literature in Russia. Palestine, with its pioneering settlers and pioneering writers, quickly emerged as the new home of Hebrew literature. At the same time a young Hebrew literature of considerable import developed in the United States. Both in Palestine and in the United States, Hebrew literature was chiefly a literature of immigrants — people whose roots were not in the lands of their sojourn. Laboring in tension which was perhaps a contributory factor to creative efforts, the writers reflected a multiloyal attitude to the world: they either reconciled the import of their youthful experiences under different skies with the impact of their new milieu or drew on the successive layers of their lives and the lives of their forebears as if they had been separate and unrelated lives. It was A. D. Berkowitz, the master-translator of his father-in-law, Sholom Aleichem, into Hebrew, who became the voice of the uprooted in America while history-conscious Sackler recreated Canaanite and medieval ancestry, the world of Hasidism and the world of early American Jewry in drama and fiction. Recently a native literature has asserted itself in Israel, but there are only sporadic evidences of native Hebrew writers in America. New names appear with rare intervals in the Hebrew periodicals of this country — in *Hadoar* and in *Bitzaron*.

V

In Israel Hebrew literature draws its sustenance from the soil and the sky, from the language and the life of the land. In America it is an exotic growth, satisfying primarily the needs of the writer and a comparatively small Hebrew-speaking group: hence a marked degree of introspection and a preponderance of poetic output in America — not necessarily a disadvantage. In Israel there is an overwhelming concern for the immediate; in America there is a leisurely yearning for the eternal. A "realistic," soil-bound literature is predominant in Israel; in America, Hebrew literature is more "romantic," more soul-bound.

There is also a marked difference in the Hebrew language as it is being spoken and written in Israel and in the United States. There, the Hebrew language already boasts a healthy, picturesque slang and some not very healthy barbarisms and colloquialisms which have been imported in unabashed literal translations from Yiddish, German, Arabic and other languages. Here, the Hebrew language tends to be more bookish and more classical. It could and should serve as a corrective for the untamed flights of the language in Israel.

A comparison of Hebrew literatures in Israel and America will disclose the melancholy fact that neither there nor here does a marked personality dominate the literary scene. After the death of Bialik in Palestine, no man of similar stature usurped the vacant seat of his recognized eminence. Uri Zvi Gruenberg, lone poetic prophet of doom in Israel and nearest pretender to the throne, is too isolated, too self-centered to win the unchallenged admiration and affection of the Hebrew public. Yet it is a significant fact that poets predominate — as they always have — in Hebrew literature both in Israel and in America. Even the foremost prose writers in Israel — Hazaz and Agnon — lapse into a poetic lilt. And this can also be said of such Hebrew prose-writers of America as Twersky who spent his formative years in this country and developed a staccato style for romanticized biographies à la Maurois and Ludwig; Blank who in his novels preferred the idyllic life of the Bessarabian Jews to the hectic drive of American Jews; and Sackler whose re-creation of the past imparts poetic overtones to his style. Even the critical essays of Brainin, Ribalow, Epstein and Isaiah Rabinowitz, the educational essays of Touroff and Scharfstein, the discerning essays of Maximon and Ovsay, the light-hearted essays of Persky and Goldberg, the well-documented essays of Rivkind and Malachi, and the scholarly essays of Tschernowitz, Mirsky, Feigin, Federbusch, Waxman, Churgin and Bernstein, are charged with poetic overtones.

VI

Strangely, Jewish life in America has been meagerly exploited by Hebrew writers. Only Wallenrod, a realistic portrait-painter of immigrants in America, depicted with eager alacrity the baffled and bewildered Jews in the New World. Other writers either neglected them or approached them with timid caution. Though this service remains to be rendered to Hebrew letters, a word of caution is not out of place: no pursuit of regionalism or *couleur locale* can compensate for the timeless elements in literature. Before American Judaism crystallizes an indigenous tradition, it will not develop a genuine American-Hebrew literature. In the interval it is worth remembering that the flashing flight of a bird across the sky at dawn or the sight of a tree at sundown, deeply felt and deeply realized in a poem, is worth more than pages of arid descriptions and even fascinating approximations to real situations.

AMERICAN YIDDISH LITERATURE

By B. I. Bialostotzky*

AMERICAN Yiddish literature is truly American and not merely a transplantation from across the sea. Though intimately connected with Yiddish literature abroad, drawing sustenance from ancient Jewish traditions and the creative spirit of the Old World, it contributed motifs and ideas, types and portraits, which could not have been created in Warsaw, Odessa or Vilna, the main European centers of Yiddish creativity — a fact which deserves to be emphasized on the tercentenary of American Jewry.

The dominant theme of early American Yiddish literature was the immigrant's struggle for an economic foothold and his painful adjustment to the new environment. This theme, which has still not been exhausted, depicted the suffering sweat-shop workers, the more prosperous worker, and the boss who had graduated from the picket line. Realistic fiction of the closing nineteenth century portrayed comic and tragic situations, the slums of Attorney Street on New York's East Side and the glamorous homes on wealthy Riverside Drive, the idealistic laborer who fought for justice and the lonely or ne'er-do-well boarder around whom were woven all sorts of entanglements, humorous and pathetic.

The East Side of the Yiddish-speaking immigrants comes to life in the short stories of Z. Libin, who blended tears and laughter; in the tales and dramas of Leon Kobrin, who probed deeper conflicts of love and life; in the lyrics of Morris Rosenfeld which depicted the harshness, suffering and grotesqueness of the sweatshop, masterful lyrics of such poignant quality that they were immediately translated into English and aroused unusual attention on the American literary scene. Sholom Asch was then acclaimed for his portraits of "landsmen" in *Uncle Moses*, although later on he was to write *East River*, a novel of the mingling of Jew and non-Jew, synagogue and church, idealism and materialism, a novel of intermarriage.

Sholom Asch is one of a number of writers who pioneered in dealing with new phases of the economic conflict. Farm and prairie are treated by David Ignatoff and A. Raboy. The lonely

---

* Translated by Philip Rubin.

86

life of Jews in the South among Negroes, on an island outside of New York, or in strange communities throughout various states are treated by J. J. Schwartz, B. Glassman, Noah Goldberg, B. Demblin, Haim Pat, Z. Sher, L. Treister, A. A. Ayalti and F. Bimko.

But it was not only the economic struggle which found expression in Yiddish literature. Hardly less important was the spiritual adjustment to America. Poetry especially emphasized the struggle against the abandonment of Jewishness. We find this motif in the Broadway poems of the tradition-rooted A. Liesin, in the verse of the poet-dramatist H. Leivick, in the poems *Among Strangers* by M. L. Halperin, *Father's Shadow* by Jacob Glatstein, and *From the Old Source* by Ephraim Auerbach, in the verse of Menachem Boraisha, A. Leyeles, M. Schweid, A. M. Dilon, Kadya Molodawsky, and in Melech Ravitch's latest poem *The Coronation*. But we also find this motive in David Pinski's novels *Noah Eden* and *Arnold Levenberg*, in his one-act plays *The Woolen Idol* and *Money*, in Peretz Hirschbein's *Babylon*, and in the stories of J. Opatoshu.

East Side! The average American has only a faint idea of what these two words signify. He associates East Side with poverty and dirt, pushcart peddlers, salami and pickled herring. But one who reads Yiddish prose, drama or verse, gets an entirely different view. He sees vigorous folk life, deep ideological wrestling with Americanism, nationalism, internationalism, problems of ethics, aesthetics and human relations generally and, above all, a groping toward universalism.

American Yiddish literature includes not only rebelliousness and realism but also an emphasis on the dignity of the common man, an insistence that human value should not be measured by material success but rather by a person's spiritual resources. In part, this idea came from the socialistic tendencies then current but in greater part it derived from the ancient Jewish idea expressed in the Psalms: "He raises the poor from the dust."

This idea found expression in belles-lettres and in Yiddish journalism between 1880 and 1920. Such journalists as Philip Krantz, Morris Hillquit, S. Yanofsky, Abraham Cahan, Benjamin Feigenbaum, Zivion, Yitzhak I. Hurwitz, H. Rogoff, M. Olgin, R. Abramowitz and B. Charney-Vladeck identified themselves with the themes and ideas of the Yiddish prose and poetry that was created here in America.

American Yiddish literature had its start during the Eighties with the first wave of East European Jewish immigration when a Jewish working class came into existence. That chapter of early American Yiddish literature is usually referred to as the realistic one. But when one takes into consideration the poetry of those days, its most valuable part, it was not entirely realistic. It also was animated by romantic visions of world liberation, liberation not only from the sweat-shop but also from other evils that beset mankind.

There are literary historians and sociologists (such as Bezalel Sherman in his book, *Jews and Other Ethnic Groups in the United States*) who hold that these proletarian-revolutionary moods and strivings were transplanted motives, mainly derived from Tsarist Russia, from the Russian revolutionary *Narodniki*. This opinion is only partly true and does not take into consideration that, during the last quarter of the Nineteenth Century labor struggles, rioting and bloodshed took place in this country. It was the era of industrialization as well as of labor organization, of struggle on the part of the laboring masses whom the money-magnates, such as Gould and Vanderbilt, regarded as dust. In those days there were hunger riots and strike riots in San Francisco and Chicago. There were parades of homeless in New York in 1873. All this took place before the earliest Jewish labor and revolutionary poets, such as Morris Winchevsky, David Edelstadt, Morris Rosenfeld and J. Bovshover, appeared upon the American scene. Those were the years of the first great steel strikes in Homestead, Pennsylvania, and of the Chicago strikes in the McCormick factories. Eugene V. Debs organized the American railroad workers. The struggles of the mine workers with their employers even went back to the Forties and Fifties when the group of miners led by Molly Maguire engaged in terrorism. To claim that our first American Yiddish proletarian-revolutionary poets brought over here only the revolutionary mood from across the seas is, therefore, certainly not the whole truth. When these Yiddish poets came here they already found a rebellious mood. Hence, their notes of rebelliousness were not alien ones but were immediately linked with the American environment of those days.

NOSTALGIA FOR THE OLD COUNTRY

As we leave that early era we find that the rebellious mood quieted down and new moods came to the fore: nostalgia for the Old Country, for the quieter life of the *shtetl*, surrounded by fields and forests that had been left behind, idealization of the poor, pious Jew and his semi-medieval, semi-rural life. This nostalgia has not vanished to this very day and has even increased after the Nazi destruction of East European Jewry. It appears in dramas, tragi-comedies, novels and poetry. We feel it in the poetic cycle *Around the Mill* by Joseph Rolnick, as well as in the latter's memoirs, which often rise to symbolism; Rolnick's poetry resembles America's nature poet, Robert Frost. We find that nostalgia too in the poem *Tarnov* by Reuben Eisland; in the tenderly lyrical hometown portraits of Mani Leib (*Snow Area, Ukrainian Steppe*); in Daniel Charney's memoirs of Dukar; in *By the Rivers of Polessia* by N. Brusilov; in *A City Full of Jews* by S. Bikel; in the novel *On Grandfather's Fields* by I. Metzker; in the memoirs, interwoven with much folklore and historical facts, by M. Osherowitz; in the half-realistic, half-fantastic stories of M. J. Shelubsky; in the volumes of memoirs called *Poland* by I. I. Trunk; in *My Father's Inn* by I. Horowitz; in poems about the town of Michaelishok by Meinke Katz. Some writers produced works in the form of fiction and poetry while others wrote in the form of interesting memoirs.

Permeating these writings was a longing for the traditional Jewish holiday celebrations, for the wholesomeness of Jewish folklife of the past, for the high ethical traditions of that East European Jewry which, alas, is no more. As by-products of home-sickness most of these literary creations needed the long perspective of time and place and could not have been produced in former Jewish centers, such as Warsaw, Vilna, Odessa and Cracow, when Jewish life was in full bloom there.

We find a longing for the old Sabbath, for the singing of *Zemirot* and for the Prophet Elijah in the ballads of Mani Leib; in the Hassidic motifs of J. J. Sigal; in the poem *Youthful Years* by J. J. Schwartz; in such poems as *Queen of Sabbath, The Strikover Rebbetzin,* and *The Holy Baal-Shem Tov* by Zisha Landau; in the vigorous prose of *A World That Is No More* by I. J. Singer; in the Baal Shem poems of M. Bassin; in the two volumes, *Yidden,* by Naftali Gross; in the poem *Raisha* by Berish Weinstein; in *Longing for Mother* by Malka Lee; in the work of A. Berger and in the poetry written since the Nineties by A. M. Sharkansky and Joseph Yaffe. Even in those days, in the turmoil of radical, revolutionary agitation, there sprouted, like grass beside a fence, these tender songs of nationalistic and folk longing.

Beside the lyrical and Sabbath motifs there also appeared poems of a grotesque nature, written by poets who in that manner, it would seem, wished to overcome in some degree the home-sickness which smacked of too much sentimentality. These include the satiric poems on the Galician town of Zlotschew by M. L. Halperin; comic reminiscences by Moishe Nadir; and *Kumarna Types,* by Kalman Heisler.

This represents wide literary creation which depicts for us human lives, folklore, folkways, and the landscapes of Ukraine,

Lithuania, Poland, Bessarabia, Rumania and Galicia. Such nostalgic works were created here in America where the contrast with the former quiet, idyllic life of the *shtetl* was so great for the overwhelming majority of East European immigrants who settled in the large cities. They were created amid the turmoil of New York, in that melting pot of immigrant nationalities where the individual often succumbed to loneliness. They were written as an inner poetical protest against the standardization of life in the American metropolis. There are also works wherein can be found a more sharply expressed protest against the rush and turmoil of the city, such as the book *New Yorkish* by the terse storyteller L. Shapiro and the writings of Sh. Miller.

Thus the mood of nostalgia, the deep longing, as well as the mood of resignation, is a product of American circumstances and characterizes not only Jewish immigrants but other immigrant nationalities as well. In Yiddish it found stronger expression, since American Yiddish literature is richer and more colorful than the literature of the American Irish, Poles, Finns, Germans, Russians and Chinese.

YIDDISH LITERATURE AS PART OF AMERICAN CULTURE

Though Yiddish literature is part of general American literature and American culture, unfortunately, not all American literary critics and literary historians realize this fact.

In American Yiddish literature there are descriptions of noted American Jewish personalities, entirely Americanized, who had little or nothing to do with Yiddish. Some time ago there was published a play, *Major Noah*, by H. Sackler, and only recently there appeared a long novel, *Mordecai M. Noah*, by S. Erdberg. There are Yiddish sketches of Haym Salomon. There is a novel by S. Apter on the first group of Jews who landed in New Amsterdam in 1654. Yiddish literature, too, contains poems on Abraham Lincoln, such as *Lincoln in Richmond* by R. Eisland and *Gettysburg* by Berish Weinstein. There are also descriptions, in prose and verse, of other great American personalities.

American Yiddish literature also contains portraits of immigrants who are non-Jews, such as the poem *Pan Jablowski* by M. L. Halperin, or vivid portraits of American Gentile people in some of the works of B. Glassman, or *The Russian Shliapnikov* in the three-volume novel *Upon Distant Roads* by David Ignatoff, or Tom in Noah Goldberg's book, *A Light Comes Up*.

Negroes and Indians are often the subject of Yiddish poetry and prose. Typical are the Indian poems of A. Ludwig, who died young, the Negro poems of H. Leivick and the theme of Negro lynching dealt with by J. Opatoshu, M. L. Halperin and Aaron Kurtz.

It should be remembered, too, that in American Yiddish poetry and prose there are wonderful descriptions of the American landscape, such as *An Arm of The Sea* by A. Raboy, the verses of H. Roisenblat, the descriptions of the seashore and the Hudson by J. Bovshover and Mani Leib, descriptions of American cities by Eliezer Greenberg, Alef Katz and Anna Margolin, of Pittsburgh smokestacks, of Chicago stockyards, of sunny Florida, of forests, rivers, American skies and American seas. The Grand Canyon is described by Sholom Asch, Peretz Hirschbein, B. Charney Vladeck and, in a long poem, by Z. Weinper.

There are certainly big city motifs in general American poetry ever since the days of Longfellow and Walt Whitman. But there are in Yiddish literature no less important poems about the growth of New York and of American cities generally. The New York motif is perhaps depicted more strongly in Yiddish than in American poetry written in English.

In American Yiddish poetry are to be found new rhythms which did not find expression in Vilna or Warsaw, where the rhythmical romanticism of the well-known swinging amphibrach ruled poetry. The new rhythms, in part irregular ones, have been influenced by general American poetry. It would be an important contribution if a large anthology of American motifs in Yiddish poetry were issued in this country in English.

INFLUENCES ON AMERICAN YIDDISH LITERATURE

The first Yiddish poets to be influenced by Anglo-Saxon literature were Morris Winchevsky in his London silhouettes, who was influenced by Thomas Hood and William Morris, and J. Bovshover, who was influenced by Shelley, Walt Whitman and Edwin Markham.

Influences from Russian poetry were brought into Yiddish by A. Liesin, though he was a deeply nationalistic Jewish poet, and by some of the poets of the modernist group known as *Yunge*, such as Mani Leib, Zisha Landau, B. Lapin and J. Rolnick. Later on one finds Russian influences in L. Feinberg and Nochum Yood, and in N. B. Minkoff, who, though quite Americanized and intimately connected with American culture and literature, yet shows strong traces of Russian mysticism.

The group of poets and prose writers who came immediately

after the so-called *Yunge* was more under purely Jewish influence and followed the pattern and moods of literature created in Yiddish since the time of Mendele Mocher Sforim. They were pupils of I. L. Peretz, H. N. Bialik, Morris Rosenfeld, S. Frug and Abraham Reisen. Poets who preferred Yiddish to alien influence included Ephraim Auerbach, Z. Weinper, J. J. Sigal, A. Nisenson, Naphtali Gross, A. Lutzky, Levi Goldberg and B. I. Bialostotzky.

Another distinct group of writers centered around the literary journal *Arrows*. They included the poets Abba Stolzenberg and M. Shtiker, who were influenced by modern German poetry, and A. Tabachnik, who is also a good critic. A group known as *Prolet-Pen*, consisting of leftist American Yiddish writers, was influenced by modern Soviet writers.

The group known as *Introspectivists* or *In-Zich*, which started about 1918, was influenced by modern American and British poetry, primarily the American Imagists of the days of Amy Lowell. They emphasized the urban and intellectual approach to poetry; they called not only for sentiment and song but also for ideas, for a poetic message. Their main representatives are N. B. Minkoff, A. Leyeles, Jacob Glatstein and B. Alquit.

In defining the specific Americanism of American Yiddish literature, one should bear in mind that writers who developed their talents on American soil have more Americanism in their writings than others whose talents matured in Europe, such as the gifted writers I. J. Singer and I. Bashevis, who wrote important works about Jewish life in Eastern Europe, and Jonah Rosenfeld.

Sholom Asch, it is true, displayed a good deal of Americanism as regards theme and motif, although he had attained literary maturity in Europe before he came to these shores. Abraham Reisen, on the other hand, did not add much to his collection of charming short stories during his years in America. But Reisen the poet did create in New York a considerable body of excellent verse, perhaps deeper poetry than he had written during his youth in the Old World. And some of the verse Reisen wrote in America is filled with American experiences and yearnings and breathe universalism rather than the provincial air of the East European *shtetl*.

To sum up, American Yiddish literature includes many works, in poetry as well as prose, which express not only American landscape and American spirit but also express a strong universalism, an all-embracing humanitarianism. Nevertheless, American Yiddish literature is in the main animated by Jewish motifs, by the Jewish folk and national spirit. It not infrequently happens that in one's own national motifs, even in one's very folklore, there is more universalism than in particular universalistic themes which often suffer from too much intellectualism. This writer is strongly inclined to milieu, to environmentalism, in literary creation.

As to the broadly national motifs and works that appeared in this country in Yiddish I would like to say the same as with regard to the nostalgic works. Here too the depiction of many Jewish historical personalities and eras in American Yiddish literature was to a large extent a product of American Jewish life, a result of the moods that animated the American Yiddish writer who was worried over Jewish survival. Not having found in the American Melting Pot a firm enough basis for Jewish national life, Yiddish writers called upon the past for inspiration and the Jewish heroic figures in whom they could find comfort and hope for Jewish survival. In their uneasiness over the Jewish future they were like King Saul who in a moment of fear called the Prophet Samuel from his grave.

I know that the newly-aroused Jewish national yearnings and visions stem in large measure from Zionism and from the progressive Jewish nationalism preached by the historian Simeon Dubnow and the philosophers-publicists Chaim Zhitlovsky and Nachman Syrkin. But in Yiddish works created in America there is also a search for a Jewish base in this land of many nationalities. This can be felt in the historical works of J. Opatoshu, the personalities depicted in Menachem Boraisha's *Wanderer*, the poems of martyrdom by A. Liesin, Sholom Asch's *Witch of Castille*, David Ignatoff's *The Hidden Light* (based on the stories of Rabbi Nachman Braslaver), David Pinski's *The Eternal Jew*, David Einhorn's religious poems, Leivick's *Maharam of Rothenburg*, the Cabbalistic tones of Aaron Zeitlin's verse, many poems of A. Almi, the long novel, *The Gaon of Vilna*, by Pesach Marcus, and the Hassidic drama by Zvi Cahan.

One should also underscore that in the United States and Canada, as might be expected, many Yiddish translations were made of ancient and medieval Jewish literature. There was the monumental translation of the Bible by the great poet Yehoash, followed by renderings of the *Five Megillot* and the *Psalms* by Naphtali Gross, the *Mishnah* by S. Petrushka, portions of the *Midrash* by Sh. Z. Setzer, the medieval Hebrew poetry of Spain of the so-called Golden Era by J. J. Schwartz and Mordecai Jaffa; Talmudic *Aggada*, by Tashrak; ancient Jewish legends, particularly from the *Midrash*, by Chaim Shauss; *From The Babylonian Exile to Rome* by B. I. Bialostotzky; *Moses, Our Teacher* by J. J. Schwartz; a book of legends about Elijah the Prophet by A. Menes, and many others. This inclination to go to ancient and medieval

Jewish sources for literary creativity is partly a result of the feeling of the American Yiddish writer that he must hold on to the thread of Jewish continuity, that he must not lose Jewish historical perspective.

Revolving around Jewish historical figures many Yiddish dramas were created here, both for the melodramatic and the modern-artistic Yiddish theatre. Dramas of the Jewish milieu were also written. Here one should mention the works of Jacob Gordin, David Pinsky, Peretz Hirschbein, H. Leivick and others noted above. New York grotesques, very fine theatrical pieces, were written by Ossip Dymov in *Bronx Express* and Chone Gottesfeld in *A Livelihood*.

SCIENTIFIC AND PUBLICISTIC WRITINGS

Thus the thread of Yiddish literary creativity in America was being woven which embraced realism, romanticism, universalism and nationalism, historicism and folklore, symbolism and Messianism, and purely human individual longings.

In close connection with new moods and new ideas that stirred the Jew in the western world new and important Yiddish historians and publicists came upon the scene. Among them were Sh. Rosenfeld, Chaim Greenberg, Jacob Leschinsky, Dr. S. Margoshes and Baruch Zukerman, whose writings revolved mainly around Zionist problems, and Dr. Zhitlovsky, S. Niger, A. Coralnik, Dr. A. Mukdoni, Dr. S. Simon, Dr. I. N. Steinberg, Leibush Lehrer, Dr. I. Knox, Eliyahu Shulman, Moshe Starkman and Abba Gordin, who were more concerned with the survival of Jewish traditions and folk life. Such publicists as Ephraim Kaplan, Gedalia Bublick and David Eidelsberg wrote about problems of Jewish religion. Talented columnists and publicists like B. Z. Goldberg, Moshe Katz, Chaim Lieberman, David Shub, Dr. Herman Frank, B. Sherman and I. Levin-Shatzkes devoted their main attention to sociological problems. Historians included Dr. Jacob Shatzky of whose monumental history of the Jews of Warsaw, three volumes have already been published; Raphael Mahler; Chaim Shauss, historian of the Biblical epoch; A. Menes, historian and publicist; and Philip Friedman, historian of the recent Hitlerite era of destruction.

Eminent literary critics who contributed much to American Yiddish literature over many years are Samuel Niger, who recently issued important volumes of literary criticism; A. Coralnik, a beautiful stylist; B. Rivkin, visionary; Dr. A. Mukdoni, acute observer; Nachman Meisel, critic and researcher; N. B. Minkoff, a literary critic with an historical sense; Kalman Marmor, who searched into the beginnings of American Yiddish literature; Pesie Kahane, S. Bickel and S. D. Synger.

Besides works of historical research on past Jewish eras there have appeared in Yiddish works on American history by Abraham Cahan, H. Rogoff and B. Z. Goldberg and histories of the Russian Revolution and of the Jewish and general labor movement in America. There have also been published several volumes of a Yiddish encyclopedia.

Among those who occupy themselves with Yiddish linguistic problems are Yudel Mark, A. A. Roback, Nahum Stutchkov, Max Weinreich, and Judah Yaffe.

Yiddish literary humor included magazines, such as *The Big Rascal*, edited by Jacob Marinoff, which existed for about 20 years. Among its contributors were H. Gutman (Der Lebediger), Moshe Nadir, B. Kovner and many others.

Some fine Yiddish books were written for children of the Yiddish afternoon schools. Today there are in existence two Yiddish children's magazines, both of which are well edited and make a fine appearance.

To many Yiddish poems music was written by such composers as Zavel Silberts, Michael Gelbart, Solomon Golub, Jacob Schaeffer, Lazar Weiner and Vladimir Heifetz. This music contributed much to the enrichment of Yiddish culture in America.

Ever since the 1880's there have appeared in Yiddish a good many translations of world literature and science. Walt Whitman, Jack London, Edgar Allan Poe and Longfellow are available. Recently there appeared a new Yiddish translation of Shakespeare's sonnets by the poet B. Lapin (years before a similar translation had been made by Dr. A. A. Eisen) and a Yiddish translation of the Finnish epos, *Kalevala*, by Hersh Rosenfeld.

The above-mentioned poets, like most Yiddish writers, were intimately connected with the American Yiddish press which today still has 300,000 readers. One must bear in mind that each newspaper that is bought is read by more than one person. Today there appear in New York two large Yiddish daily newspapers, *Forward* and *Day-Morning Journal* and the smaller *Freiheit*. Another daily, *Canader Adler*, is published in Montreal. There appear also eight Yiddish weeklies, three bi-weeklies and six monthlies.

During the post-war years a number of well known Yiddish writers came over to this country with the refugees, after years of wandering through various countries. Among them are Itsik Manger, Chaim Graade, Nachum Bomze, Joseph Rubinstein, B.

Sheffner and Ch. S. Kazdan. They chronicled their experiences of the Nazi destruction of European Jewry, thus giving greater prominence to the *Hurban* (destruction) motif, the martyrdom and heroism of the Jewish victims.

American Yiddish literature has recently added the theme of the rise of the State of Israel, particularly in the poetry of Ephraim Auerbach and in the prose of Benjamin Ressler and Sh. Izban. But because the Yiddish language has, for many years, been frowned upon in Israel and regarded as a foreign tongue, many Yiddish writers have not become psychologically involved to a greater extent with the Israel motif.

American Yiddish literature kept renewing itself in the course of the years and avoided stagnation as it maintained contact with international Yiddish literature and American life.

American Yiddish literature was developed by men of great intellectual and creative force. From the Eighties of the past century until the present day around three hundred talented and creative writers participated in the creation of an American Yiddish literature. Among the new American Yiddish writers there are also a few who were born in the United States and Canada.

In the treasure-house of world Yiddish literature American Yiddish occupies a very large place, perhaps the largest. In America there also resided for a while one of the three great classic Yiddish writers, Sholom Aleichem. He lived in New York during 1914–15 and died there. It was in this country that Sholom Aleichem wrote his fine comedy *The Great Winning*, part of his important autobiographical work *From the Fair* and the second part of *Mottel, the Cantor's Son*.

On the occasion of the tercentenary of Jewish settlement in the United States, American Yiddish literature appears with its banner uplifted. It appears on the American Jewish scene breathing Jewish life, calling for social justice and filled with love for the "land of the free and the home of the brave."

THE LITERARY CONTRIBUTIONS OF JEWISH
COMMUNITY CENTERS

By Mordecai Soltes

THE Jewish Community Center, currently celebrating the centennial of its movement inaugurated in 1854 with the founding of the Young Men's Hebrew Association in Baltimore, Maryland, has always manifested interest in literary and cultural activities. Its original name reflects this objective. According to Benjamin Rabinowitz, in *The Young Men's Hebrew Associations (1854–1913)* (New York, 1948), Jewish youth movements assumed the form of literary societies in the early 1840's. These were forerunners of the Y.M.H.A.'s and the modern Jewish Community Centers. The first to adopt the name Young Men's Hebrew Literary Association (Y.M.H.L.A.) was a Philadelphia organization established in 1850. Later, mergers of these youth groups were effected to broaden the scope of the organizations into community-wide "Y's."

The programs of the early Y.M.H.A.'s encompassed lectures, debates, dramatics and social activities. The larger Y.M.H.A.'s had libraries, reading rooms and assembly halls to enrich the intellectual background of the clientele. *The Israelite* of November 23, 1855, tells of the founding of the Hebrew Young Men's Literary Association in New Orleans, which paid primary attention to lecture courses on "Ancient and Modern History," from Abraham to the present, and which had a library of more than 600 volumes. The *Occident and American Jewish Advocate*, a monthly edited by Isaac Leeser and devoted to Jewish literature and religion, reports in its December, 1858, issue that the newly formed Buffalo Hebrew Young Men's Association aimed to advance the members' knowledge of Hebrew and general literature, to engage in debates on diversified subjects and to afford the members opportunities for "mental recreation" and "literary training."

The Cincinnati *Jewish Times* of December 10, 1869, quotes from the constitution of the local Y.M.H.A., founded in 1867: "The association was organized for the purpose of cultivating and fostering a better knowledge of the history, literature and doctrines of Judaism; to develop and elevate our mental and moral character; to entertain and edify ourselves with such intellectual agencies as we may deem fit." The program of the short-lived "Y" in New

York, organized in 1870, included cooperation with the newly organized American Jewish Publication Society. The *Jewish Messenger* of October 16, 1874, reports that the first entertainment of the Y.M.H.A. of New York City over which Oscar S. Straus presided included a lecture on "Books and Reading," by A. L. Sanger. The newspaper urged as the primary objective of the organization "the cultivation of true literary and oratorial taste by our young men."

Eagerness for the literary enrichment of youth groups led the American Hebrew Association, the first national body of Y.M.H.A.'s and kindred societies, founded in 1880, to welcome literary associations as members. The *Association Bulletin* featured program material on literature, such as, "Hints to Library Committees" and "Books to Buy" by H. P. Rosenbach and "Chips from a Talmudic Workshop" by Marcus Jastrow. The 1881 convention of the American Hebrew Association considered a proposal calling for the exclusion of organizations "not having a permanent reading room and library."

The first professional employee in the Young Men's Hebrew Associations was the librarian. The constitutions, adopted in 1874 and 1875, respectively, of the oldest still existing Y.M.H.A.'s in New York and Philadelphia, provided for the employment of librarians. These provisions were duly executed. When, in 1876, the paid librarian of the Philadelphia "Y" required assistance, young Cyrus Adler volunteered his services and catalogued Isaac Leeser's collection of books which had been deposited in the "Y." Among the aims of the St. Louis Y.M.H.A. embodied in its constitution of 1880 was "the establishment of a reading-room and a library." When, in 1886, the Aguilar Free Public Library, which later merged with the New York Public Library, was formed, its nucleus was the library of the New York "Y," which had over 7,000 volumes. A report issued in 1915 by the Council of Young Men's Hebrew and Kindred Associations, the third national organization, stated that libraries and reading rooms were maintained by 116 associations.

Encouragement to Jewish scholars and authors has been an integral part of the program of Y.M.H.A.'s. Both the constitutions of the New York and Philadelphia "Y's" included provision for "lectures on Jewish History and Literature." During the early years of these associations the following distinguished authors were among the lecturers: Cyrus Adler, Emil G. Hirsch, A. S. Isaacs, Marcus Jastrow, Alexander Kohut, Mayer Sulzberger, Henrietta Szold and Simon Wolf. In 1884, Oscar S. Straus spoke at the New York Y.M.H.A. on "The Origin of the Republican Form of Government." This lecture attracted wide attention and was published in book form the following year.

The first two national organizations made serious efforts to establish lecture bureaus. In 1882, the American Hebrew Association organized a national literary bureau to help affiliated groups arrange courses and to furnish speakers at low cost. When the United Young Men's Hebrew Association of America was established in 1890, its constitution included, as one of six objectives: "To form a lecture bureau from which to supply the various local associations with lecturers." In 1921, when the National Jewish Welfare Board merged with the Council of Young Men's Hebrew and Kindred Associations which had come into being in 1912, it established a lecture bureau in its capacity as parent organization of the Y.M.H.A.'s, Y.W.H.A.'s and Jewish Community Centers. Today this Jewish Center Lecture Bureau sponsors forums, symposia, debates, institutes, courses, recitals and concerts. Above all, it furnishes platforms for authors who constitute the majority of the lecturers, and focuses the attention of audiences upon the books which they have written.

When the Department of Jewish Extension Education was established by the National Jewish Welfare Board in 1924, Jewish Community Centers applied for lists of books of Jewish interest for their libraries. The compilations prepared ranged in cost from $50 to $3,000. It was the Jewish People's Institute, now the Jewish Community Centers, of Chicago which utilized the $3,000 list to acquire a wide range of Jewish books for its library. Continuing stress on the importance of adequate collections of Jewish books for Center libraries has brought significant results. In recent years, many Centers have received library citations presented by the Jewish Book Council of America for meeting established criteria for a Jewish library.

To stimulate literary creativity, essay contests were conducted regularly by "Y's" and Centers. In the early days, Emma Lazarus and Solomon Solis-Cohen were among the prize-winners. In conformity with a resolution adopted at the first Biennial Convention of the National Jewish Welfare Board, recommending the conduct of competitions of a Jewish literary character, a play contest was launched in 1924. Seventy-one plays in one and two acts on Jewish themes and suitable for production by senior casts were submitted. The judges of the contest were David Pinski, Dr. Elias Lieberman and Gustav Blum. The first three prize-winning plays were presented successfully at the 49th Street Theatre and the Board made printed copies available to its constituent societies. The Board also published the first play by Herman Wouk, author of *The Caine*

Mutiny. Mr. Wouk believes that he was encouraged by the cooperation of the Board.

There has been an intensification of the Center literary program in the past quarter of a century, touching, influencing and growing out of all phases of activities. Adult courses and group discussions on Jewish writings and exhibits of Jewish books have been among the ways in which the program of the Center has been furthering an interest in Jewish literature. As an aid to Center workers in planning group and mass celebrations for the observance of the civic and Jewish holidays, plays and program bulletins have been made available by JWB. Special program material was also issued in connection with significant anniversaries of outstanding Jewish authors, such as Rashi, Moses Maimonides, Moses Mendelssohn, Baruch Spinoza, Achad Ha'Am and Isaac L. Peretz.

The interest of Jewish Community Centers in Jewish books led to widespread and wholehearted cooperation in observing Jewish Book Week, inaugurated by Miss Fanny Goldstein of Boston, and later expanded to Jewish Book Month, when the National Jewish Welfare Board became the sponsor-coordinator of the Jewish Book Council of America. This observance served as a springboard for enriching all-year round experiences. As all-embracing community-serving agencies the Jewish Community Centers, by providing professional skill and leadership, have helped to convert the Jewish Book Month programs into community-wide undertakings.

The present writer, when he served as president of the Jewish Book Council of America, succeeded in expanding the program of this fruitful literary project by including Hebrew and Yiddish books as well as English Judaica, and inaugurating the tri-lingual *Jewish Book Annual.* The Council, serving as a common platform, thereby strikingly achieved unity amidst colorful diversity in the realm of Jewish literature. This approach to the tri-lingual character of Jewish literature in America also found expression in the variety of programs sponsored by Jewish Community Centers.

The National Jewish Welfare Board, by furnishing the major portion of the Council's budget as well as sustained professional direction, has helped to revitalize and advance Jewish literary creativity through its constituent associations, conveying the message of Jewish books to an ever-widening audience and attracting increasing numbers to this literary enterprise. This fruitful relationship of the Board to the Jewish Book Council of America was a natural expression of the concern of the Jewish Community Center movement for Jewish literature.

This brief sketch of the literary contributions of Jewish Community Centers, Young Men's and Young Women's Hebrew Associations, and their national association, the National Jewish Welfare Board, might be summarized by quoting the following testimonial to the Board presented by the Jewish Book Council of America on the centennial of the Center movement:

"The National Jewish Welfare Board is observing the Centennial of the Jewish Community Center Movement which was founded in Baltimore, Maryland, in 1854. A direct outgrowth of the Young Men's Hebrew Literary Associations that were in existence in the middle of the nineteenth century, the Center Movement and the National Jewish Welfare Board continued the literary tradition. In many early YMHA's, the librarian was the first professional employed and throughout these one hundred years, YMHA's, YWHA's, and Jewish Community Centers have effectively shown an abiding interest in Jewish literary activities, such as establishing libraries, providing platforms for Jewish authors, and participating in Jewish book programs. They have thus served to enrich Jewish cultural life in America, especially under the stimulation and guidance of the National Jewish Welfare Board, the national association of Jewish Community Centers.

"This year also marks the tenth anniversary of the assumption by the National Jewish Welfare Board of the sponsorship of the Jewish Book Council of America which has entailed providing the means for the enhancement of the cultural resources of the American Jewish community.

"In this Centennial year, the National Committee of the Jewish Book Council of America, at its Annual Meeting on May 26, 1954, salutes the Jewish Community Centers of the nation and the National Jewish Welfare Board. It furthermore extends to its sponsor this expression of its warm appreciation of the invaluable auspices and services which it made available and which have served to strengthen and develop the best in Jewish life."

Books and the Holocaust

THE HEROIC ELEMENT IN JEWISH
LIFE AND LITERATURE

By Trude Weiss-Rosmarin

> We are so old a body that in our history,
> extending over thousands of years, every-
> thing has happened. Nothing new can
> occur to us. — Max Nordau.

WHEN Heinrich Graetz, master chronicler of the Jews, characterized Jewish history as *Leidens und Gelehrtensgeschichte*
(history of martyrdom and scholarship), he omitted the third
important strand of which Jewish history is woven: heroism. For
as Marvin Lowenthal has so well stated, "We shall never understand the survival of Israel if we imagine the medieval Jew weak
at soul and hunted in spirit. He felt himself to be a power, however fallen, and the warfare unremittingly waged upon his person
proved him as such." (*A World Passed By*, p. 53).
. It is to be regretted that the heroic element in Jewish history
has been rather neglected by analysts who view the Jewish destiny,
from the fateful date of the Destruction to the present day, as
as interminable chain of *Leiden* and martyrdom, although the
sufferers themselves conceived of their roles differently. They
knew, save for an insignificant minority, that theirs was not a
passive martyrdom but a purposive and conscious battle against
the forces bent upon their religious-spiritual enslavement. The
vast legion of Jews who died for their faith and their convictions
did not fall as passive martyrs but perished as indomitable fighters
who would not lay down their arms — the declaration of their
belief — till their last breath was spent.

In order correctly to appraise the medieval Jew, who submitted
to the worst tortures and the most cruel forms of death, we must
remember that he did so *voluntarily*. On the other hand, the
millions who were butchered by the Nazis in their mass extermination camps of Maidanek, Treblinka and Oswiecim, had no
other choice. They were murdered because, according to the
Nazi racial doctrine, a Jew can't stop being a Jew; for, as one of
their "poets" phrased it, "in der Rasse liegt die Schweinerei"
(the swinishness is innate to their race).

In the Middle Ages, however, a Jew could save himself, provided he was willing to renounce his religion. Some did so and lived securely ever after. But the preponderant majority preferred death to baptism. They died as martyrs, to be sure, yet not as *passive* sufferers. Death was not inflicted upon them but chosen by them. Fully conscious of what awaited them, they rejected the easier alternative and walked "the last mile" as heroes unafraid.

THE BIBLE

Jewish literature — from the Bible to the latest *Black Book* on the horrors of Nazi atrocities against Jews — is largely the record of Jewish heroism which is synonymous with Jewish martyrdom. Viewed thus, the Pentateuchal narrative of Israel's sufferings in Egypt is not a story of woe passively endured, but primarily an inspiring account of unflinching steadfastness and courage, which were ultimately rewarded by the liberation from the House of Bondage. Analogously, the biblical chapters describing the end of the Kingdom of Judah, the destruction of the Temple and the humiliation of the Babylonian Captivity are not so much a recital of national calamity as inspiring accounts of Jewish pride and perseverance. Just as their late descendants in the centuries to come refused to humble their spirits before the temporal rulers, so the captives by the rivers of Babylon declined to sing the songs of Zion on strange soil:

> "For there they that led us captive asked of us words of
>   song,
> And our tormentors asked of us mirth:
> 'Sing us one of the songs of Zion',
> How shall we sing the Lord's song in a foreign land?
> If I forget thee, O Jerusalem,
> Let my right hand forget her cunning.
> Let my tongue cleave to the roof of my mouth,
> If I remember thee not;
> If I set not Jerusalem above my chiefest joy."
>
> Psalm 137:3–6

Even in *Lamentations* and its harrowing recital of atrocities perpetrated by the Babylonians in vanquished Judea ("They have ravished the women in Zion, the maidens in the city of Judah. Princes are hanged up by their hands ... the young men have borne the mill, and the children have stumbled under the wood..." 5, 11 ff.), notes of courage, confidence and defiance of the enemy are not missing.

The first individual conscious and determined martyr-heroes

glorified in Hebrew literature were Daniel and his companions, who, in order to remain faithful to Jewish law, braved the terrors of the lions' den and the horrors of the fiery furnace.

Leopold Zunz, "Father of the Science of Judaism" and the first modern chronicler of Jewish suffering in the Middle Ages, pointed out that many post-exilic Psalms are, in fact, "martyrologies" in which the individual woe is suffused and identified with the heroic martyrdom of the Jewish people as a whole.

Last, but not least, there is the *Scroll of Esther*, which is the most perfect specimen of biblical "martyrology" with the accent on the heroic element.

THE APOCRYPHA

Among the apocryphical writings, the books of *Judith* and the two books of the *Maccabees* exemplify Jewish heroic martyrdom at its best. There is no need to recount the contents of these early narratives of Jewish heroism, especially the stories recording the bravery of the women — Judith, who slew the enemy of her people, and Hannah, "Mother of the Seven Sons," who urged them to die rather than become unfaithful to their religion.

JOSEPHUS

Josephus, who witnessed the Roman assault on Judea and the Second Destruction, is our chief source for the record of Jewish heroic martyrdom at the hands of the Roman legions under Vespasian and Titus. In his *History of the Jewish War*, Josephus records numerous instances of the type of Jewish valor and courage which have been unjustly subsumed under "Martyrdom" rather than being assigned to a special rubric, "Heroism." In his militant pamphlet *Against Apion*, Josephus ventured a rather interesting psychological theory of the cause of the Gentiles' eagerness to force the Jews to adopt their modes of worship. Writes Josephus: "I believe that our conquerors have subjected us to such torturesome deaths not because they hated us so bitterly after having defeated us, but rather out of their desire to witness the surprising phenomenon that there are men who believe that no evil is greater than to be compelled to do or to speak anything contrary to their own laws."

THE TALMUD AND THE MIDRASH

The Talmud and Midrashic literature contain numerous accounts of Jewish heroic martyrdom, especially of the time of the Hadrianic persecutions when the study of the Torah was proscribed on pain of death. The heroic stuff of which the "Doctors of the Talmud" were made is hauntingly pictured in the narrative describing how Rabbi Hanina met his death. When arrested by the Romans and questioned why he persisted in the unlawful endeavor of studying the Torah, he defiantly replied: "Because God commanded me to do so." He was sentenced to be burned alive and, in order to prolong the death agony, the Romans wrapped him in the Torah Scroll, the *corpus delicti*, placing tufts of wool soaked in water on his chest. But Rabbi Hanina ben Teradyon did not demean himself by betraying any fear or weakness. When he was about to be led onto the pyre, he consoled his daughter: "If I were to be burned alone, it would be hard to bear. But now that the Torah Scroll is to be burned with me, He who will avenge His own humiliation of the burning of the Scroll will also avenge my humiliation." And even when the flames had seared his flesh and he was about to die, the Rabbi remained a hero. His last words were: "Only the sheets of the Scroll are burned — the letters are soaring upwards." (Aboda Zara, 17b. f.)

Even greater heroism was shown by Rabbi Akiba, the enthusiastic supporter of the ill-fated Bar-Kochba revolt. The Talmud records that when Rabbi Akiba was executed, the Romans combed his flesh with iron combs, yet no complaint escaped his lips, as he recited the "Hear, O Israel." When his disciples, who witnessed the ghastly scene, asked him whether the Torah requires one to go that far in endurance, he replied: "All my days I worried that I did not fulfill the text 'And thou shalt love the Lord thy God with all thy soul,' that is to say, even when He take thy soul. I used to wonder: When shall I be able to fulfill it? And now that the opportunity has come, shall I not fulfill it?" (Berakhot 61b).

Thus dies a hero, unafraid of pain and death — a hero, we emphasize, and not a *mere* martyr. It is characteristic of this type of Jewish "heroism" that the quest for other-worldly reward was totally absent from it. A Midrashic elaboration of the story of the three valiant challengers of Babylonian idolatry, Hananiah, Mishael and Azariah, proves this rather forcefully. The Midrash has it that the three companions of Daniel would not accept the Prophet Ezekiel's advice to go into hiding to escape punishment for the refusal of worshipping the idol. Instead, they chided the Prophet, "Should people say that all nations worshipped the idol? ... We want to degrade it by not bowing to it, so that they shall say that all nations worshipped the idol, except Israel." Anxious, Ezekiel pleaded with them to wait at least until he would inquire of God regarding their fate. But the Lord refused to exert Himself on behalf of the three whose pious merit was eclipsed by the collective guilt of Israel.

When Ezekiel informed them that God would not help them, they exclaimed: "Whether He deliver us or not, we shall not worship the idol!" (Midrash Shir Hashirim, VII, 8).

MEDIEVAL LITERATURE

Medieval Hebrew literature is largely the record of Jewish *heroic* martyrdom. Local chronicles, the so-called *Memor-Books* (the name is derived either from the Latin *memoria*, or more likely, from the *Almemor* on which the scrolls or books were placed for public recitation), carefully kept in hundreds of communities have preserved the memory of the countless thousands who died for *Kiddush Hashem*, the Sanctification of the Name, in the scores upon scores of international, national and local waves of persecution which engulfed the Jews since the early Middle Ages and which grew to dreadful dimensions in the eras of the Crusades and of the Christian reconquest of Spain and Portugal.

Next to the *Memor-Books*, many of which have been rescued from certain doom and oblivion by the careful critical editions of competent scholars, (Salfeld, Stern, Adolph Neubauer, Aronius, M. Weinberg, and many more), medieval Hebrew liturgy is the richest single source of information on Jewish heroic martyrdom. In hundreds upon hundreds of *S'lichoth* (penitential prayers), *Kinot* (elegies) and *Yozroth* (liturgical martyrologies which were recited after the prayer *yotzer or* . . .), well-known and anonymous medieval liturgical poets commemorate the brave, heroic martyrdom of individuals — men, women and children — and of entire communities who died for the sake of *Kiddush Hashem*. Zunz, in his classic *Die Synagogale Poesie des Mittelalters* and in his *Literaturgeschichte der Synagogalen Poesie* (two volumes which since long have been overdue for an English translation!) was first to call attention to the vast historical significance of the liturgical poems scattered in the *Machzor* (festival prayer book) and in special collections of penitential and elegical poems. While the heroic martyrologies couched in poetic style are invaluable to the student of Jewish literature who would also understand its deeper undercurrents and motivations, the factual historian will be more attracted to the matter-of-fact chronicles, especially the three most comprehensive ones, the record of the persecutions of the *Second Crusade* by R. Ephraim ben Jacob of Bonn (born ca. 1132 died ca. 1200), Joseph ben Joshua Ha-Cohen's (born 1496 died ca. 1576) "Vale of Tears" (*Emek Habakhah*), a complete history of Jewish persecutions up to his time, and the celebrated *Shebet Yehudah* (the Rod of Judah) by three successive members of the Ibn Verga family (Solomon, Judah and Joseph, 15th and 16th centuries) with R. Judah Ibn Verga taking credit for the lion's share of the compilation and the writing of the most readable of this type of chronicles.

It is deplorable that, thus far, very little of the medieval heroic Hebrew literature has been made available to the English reader. Save for a limited number of excerpts in anthologies (see especially: Jacob R. Marcus, *The Jew in the Medieval World*; A. Millgram, *An Anthology of Medieval Hebrew Literature*; Leon I. Feuer, *Jewish Literature Since the Bible*, Vol. I.; J. Hoexter and M. Jung, *Sourcebook of Jewish History and Literature*), and George Alexander Kohut's translations of Zunz's German renditions of liturgical heroic martyrologies incorporated in his *The Sufferings of the Jews in the Middle Ages*, this rich and vast mine of Jewish information and, what is more important, inspiration is inaccessible to the English reader. And yet, it is precisely this type of literature which inspired Zunz's classic statement (quoted by George Eliot in the superscription to *Daniel Deronda*, Book VI, 42): "If there be an ascending scale of suffering, Israel has reached its highest degree. If duration of afflictions, and the patience with which they are borne ennoble, the Jews may vie with the aristocracy of any land. If a literature which owns a few classical tragedies is deemed rich, what place should be assigned to a tragedy which extends over fifteen centuries in which the poets and actors were also the heroes?"

Especially in our days of unprecedented Jewish heroic martyrdom on the vastest scale ever, it would be desirable that the comfort and pride to be derived from the ancient records of Jewish heroism be made available to the Jews — and to the world at large — who interpret Jewish sufferance as passive endurance rather than active and aggressive heroism. We should like to see an English *Anthology of Jewish Heroism* patterned along the lines of Simon Bernfeld's representative 3-volume Hebrew anthology *Sefer Ha-Demaoth* (The Book of Tears), where the heroic elements of Jewish existence and survival would be assigned their rightful place of importance.

The medieval Hebrew accounts of Jewish heroism, which are unjustly referred to as "martyrologies," hold treasures of wisdom, beauty and inspiration which deserve to be brought within reach of the "average Jew." Here is not the place for copious quotations but to convey an inkling, at least, of which riches are buried in the medieval Hebrew chronicles of heroism, we wish to cite one instance of unsurpassed heroism, which is recorded in the Ibn Vergas' "The Rod of Judah." There it is told that among those who were expelled from Spain in 1492, there was a Jewish family, consisting of father, mother and two sons, who suffered the well known hardships entailed by this expulsion. In the end, the mother and the

two children died of lack of food and general exhaustion. Lonely
and himself at the brink of death, the bereaved husband and
father addressed himself to God: "Master of the Universe! Indeed,
you are doing all and everything to make me desert my faith.
Know, then, for sure that, against the very will of Heaven, I am
a Jew and I shall remain a Jew — and all the sufferings You have
inflicted upon me and which you will inflict upon me cannot
change my mind . . . . "

It was this kind of Jewish "obstinacy" which made a prominent
Inquisitor complain to the King of Spain (the incident is likewise
recorded in "The Rod of Judah") that "Judaism belongs to the
incurable diseases . . . . "

MODERN LITERATURE

The German Jewish scholars who, in the half a century preceding the victory of Nazism, published critical editions of the medieval records of Jewish heroism, studied this type of literature as
part of a closed era in Jewish history. The events of the past
twelve years, however, have taught us that the measure of Jewish
martyrdom is not yet full . . . . . The time is not yet ripe for a
complete history of the worst Jewish massacre ever — the mass
murder of five million Jews at the hands of the most brutal and
depraved killers mankind has known thus far, but already a large
literature describing the unmentionable horrors endured by the
Nazis' most pitiful, because most helpless, victims has come to
the fore, ranging from carefully assembled and edited collections
of true and authenticated reports on the atrocities to personal
letters and impromptu accounts of individuals who miraculously
escaped from the Nazi charnel house.

The heroic note, which is so pronounced a feature in the Jewish
literary residue of the martyrdom of ages past, is not missing
from the latest Jewish tragedy either. The valiant "Revolt in
the Warsaw Ghetto," which already has inspired a large number
of creative works of literature besides having served as a theme
of factual accounts, proves that the modern Jew is in direct line
of succession to his ancestors, who braved "death in the waters
and in the fire" for the sake of their religious conviction.

Tracing the story of Jewish heroism from the Bible to the latest
magazine article on the tragedy of our time, one can feel with
pride with the medieval liturgical poet, who sang:

> *Throughout the kingdoms of the nations,*
> *Who can be equalled to Thy people?*
> *They followed Thee through flame and flood*
> *As none on earth have followed Thee.*

THE FATE OF THE JEWISH BOOK
DURING THE NAZI ERA

By Philip Friedman

JEWISH books often shared the persecutions inflicted upon Jews, the "People of the Book." The first recorded persecution of the Jewish book probably occurred about 2,100 years ago. Antiochus IV, King of Syria, in his zeal to Hellenize the Jews, ordered the Torah Scrolls to be torn to pieces and set on fire (I Macc. 1:56). Later, during the destruction of the Second Temple, Torah Scrolls and other Hebrew manuscripts were destroyed. The same happened during the Bar Kokhba uprising.

In the Middle Ages, the burning of Jewish books often preceded the extermination of "Jewish heretics." In 1242, twenty-four cartloads of Talmud manuscripts were publicly burned in Paris, and in 1288, ten Jewish martyrs and their books were burned in Troyes. Jewish books were publicly burned in Spain on various occasions; for example, in 1263, in Barcelona. Christian kings and ecclesiastical authorities in several countries ordered the burning of the Talmud and other Hebrew books. Thus, Pope Clement IV issued a bull decreeing the confiscation and destruction of the Talmud. In 1299, Jewish books were destroyed in England, and in 1415, after the famous dispute in Tortosa, Pope Benedict XIII condemned copies of the Talmud. An order including also the books of the Kabbalah and other Hebrew works was issued by Emperor Maximilian I in 1510. The last large-scale persecution of Jewish books prior to the Nazi period occurred 200 years ago. After a disputation between the Jews and the adherents of Jacob Frank, Dembowski, Catholic bishop of Kamenetz Podolski (Ukraine), ordered the confiscation and destruction of all Talmud copies in his diocese. None of these recorded confiscations and destructions, however, attained the gigantic dimensions of the Nazi crusade against the Jewish book.

In order to appreciate the magnitude of this greatest book pogrom in Jewish history, let us take stock of the Jewish books in libraries and private collections in Nazi-occupied Europe. Jewish libraries existed in almost every European country before 1939. They were founded and maintained by institutes of higher learning, rabbinical seminaries, educational and research institutes, synagogues, youth organizations, and the like. Jewish book stores, publishing houses, scholars, bibliophiles, and private families, were proud possessors of large collections or of innumerable small libraries. Valuable collections were also to be found in many non-Jewish municipal, state, university and ecclesiastical libraries, and in the possession of individuals. A complete computation of this vast wealth of printed treasures is patently impossible.

We made a checklist of Jewish book collections in twenty European countries occupied or controlled by the Nazis, or exposed to Nazi bombing. Our calculation included only Jewish and a few large non-Jewish collections like the Rosenthaliana in Amsterdam and the Simonsensiana in Copenhagen. Only libraries containing a minimum of 1,000 volumes were included in this survey.

There were 469 such libraries, with 3,307,000 volumes, in the twenty European countries. The largest collections were in Poland (251 libraries, 1,650,000 books), Germany (55 libraries, 422,000 books), the Nazi-occupied sections of the Soviet Union (7; 332,000), France (16; 146,000), Austria (19; 126,000), Hungary (5; 76,000), the Netherlands (17; 74,000), Roumania (25; 69,000), Lithuania (19; 67,000) and Czechoslovakia (8; 58,000). If the numerous small libraries and private collections could be added, the figures would probably aggregate five million or more books. It may be assumed that of the approximately 1,500,000 Jewish families comprising the 6,000,000 Jews killed during the Nazi period, at least several books, religious and profane, in Hebrew, Yiddish and other languages, were treasured in every Jewish home. There is, however, no way of making an accurate estimate of those stupendous cultural losses.

The diabolical forms of destruction inflicted by the Nazis were diverse. During the first phase of their domination in 1933–38, the Nazis were bent on outright destruction of Jewish books, preferably by spectacular *auto-da-fés*. After they had seized power in January, 1933, they initiated a savage campaign calling for the burning of all "non-German books." This included books by liberal, democratic and leftist authors, and, of course, all books written by Jews. The campaign culminated in raucous and barbarous celebrations which drew wide-spread attention in the free world and evoked severe condemnation in the press (*The New York Times*, June 11, 1933). Hayyim N. Bialik, who was still alive, articulated his lament in a touching poem entitled (כל כתבי ח. נ. ביאליק, תל־אביב, תש"ז, ע' 379) איכה יירא את האש.

The implacable warfare against the Jewish book entered a new phase in 1938, when several synagogues were wrecked in Munich, Nuremberg and Dortmund. These hostile acts were the precursor of the ominous Cristall Night of November 9–10, when one of the worst pogroms in modern history was carried out by SA and SS troops in every part of the country. In revenge for the assassination by Herschel Grynszpan of Ernst vom Rath, third assistant in the Nazi Embassy in Paris, numerous synagogues together with thousands of books, Torah Scrolls and manuscripts, were put to the torch and completely destroyed. Reinhard Heydrich, head of the Reich Security Chief Office, reported at a meeting of German ministers on November 12, 1938, that 101 synagogues had been destroyed by fire and seventy-six wrecked. Many more synagogues were seized between November, 1938, and September, 1939. These were converted into German schools, Hitler youth houses, sport clubs, and the like. Synagogues were blasted and burned also in Austria, Sudetenland and Danzig, although not yet incorporated into the Reich. A contemporaneous Jewish estimate puts the number of destroyed religious edifices between 413 and 520. This destructive pattern was continued during World War II. According to an authentic estimate (*Former Jewish Communal Property in Germany*, New York, 1947), there were approximately 1,300 synagogues in Germany in the beginning of 1938. Only a few of this number were still in existence in 1945. It is impossible to speculate on the number of books that were consigned to a fiery doom. In only a few instances were Jewish religious objects and books salvaged by courageous and well-meaning non-Jewish Germans. The commendable efforts of Cardinal Michael Faulhaber in 1938, on behalf of the Great Synagogue in Munich, are a noteworthy example.

After the outbreak of World War II and the invasion of Poland in September, 1939, the German armies embarked upon a wild spree of destruction, mainly of synagogues. German newspapers described these acts of vandalism with utter callousness. In this vein the *Krakauer Zeitung* of November 29, 1939, stated: "A few nights ago the synagogue and prayer-house in Tomaszow . . . went up in flames. The fire brigade succeeded in preventing the fire from spreading to neighboring buildings." The *Litzmannstädter Zeitung* of November 16, 1939, reported: "The synagogue on the Kosciuszko Alley went up in flames yesterday morning. The first and third fire brigades prevented the flames from spreading to adjoining buildings." At times, however, the Nazi correspondents shamelessly exhibited their flagrant glee in reporting the barbarous acts. Thus, the destruction of the famous library of the Lublin Yeshivah in 1939 elicited this arrogant statement: "For us it was a matter of special pride to destroy the Talmudic Academy which was known as the greatest in Poland . . . We threw the huge Talmudic library out of the building and carried the books to the market-place, where we set fire to them. The fire lasted twenty hours. The Lublin Jews assembled around and wept bitterly, almost silencing us with their cries. We summoned the military band, and with joyful shouts the soldiers drowned out the sounds of the Jewish cries" (*Frankfurter Zeitung*, March 28, 1941).

In several Polish cities, notably in Bedzin and in Poznan, special German "Brenn-Kommandos" (arson squads) were assigned to burn synagogues and Jewish books. Jews attempting to save Torah Scrolls or books from the burning buildings were shot or thrown into the flames. Similar brutalities were reported also in other countries, especially Holland and France, after their occupation by the Nazis. In the Nazi-occupied Soviet territories, 532 synagogues and 258 other buildings belonging to religious institutions whose denomination is not specified, were "burned, looted, destroyed and desecrated," according to General R. H. Rudenko, Chief Prosecutor for the U.S.S.R., before the Nuremberg International Military Tribunal (*IMT*, vol. VII, p. 189). Inasmuch as Jewish religious buildings had long since been nationalized in the Soviet Union proper, the U. S. S. R. prosecutor listed only the synagogues destroyed in the former Polish areas of the U. S. S. R. The Nazis put the torch not only to Jewish books, but also, in a limited degree, to non-Jewish books. In his book *Vilner Ghetto* (Paris, 1945), Abraham Sutzkever, the Jewish poet, asserts that Dr. Johannes Pohl, a high German official, ordered the burning of the books in the medical library of the Vilna University Hospital. Other non-Jewish libraries are also known to have been pillaged, but the vandalism never attained the dimensions directed against Jewish institutions.

Simultaneous with the destruction of Jewish books, the Nazis inaugurated a policy of saving a small number of rare and precious volumes for commercial and scholarly purposes. These looted items were offered for sale by agents in various European countries. The well-known Jewish historian, Cecil Roth, stated in an address in April, 1943: "More than once in pre-war days I was offered, through reputable agencies in this country [England], objects of art of German-Jewish provenance, sold by order of the Nazi Government; and in 1939 even the contents of the Jewish Museum in Berlin were hawked about the art world on the instruction of the Reich Minister of Finance." In the same address Dr. Roth stated also: "After the German occupation of Lithuania, new copies of the much-reviled Talmud, from the famous Rom Press in Vilna, were offered for sale in Amsterdam, in return for ready money." Copies of rare Jewish books and manuscripts were also offered for sale, according to unconfirmed reports, by Nazi agents in Switzerland.

A few "intellectuals" among the Nazi leaders came to realize that the captured Jewish book treasures might serve a useful purpose for founding specialized research libraries on the Jewish question. Upon the seizure of the Sudetenland in the autumn of 1938, Alfred Rosenberg, the Nazi top theoretician, requested the Reich Commissioner for the Sudeten area, Konrad Henlein, to confiscate all Jewish religious and secular literature. Henlein promptly delegated this undertaking to one of his aides, Dr. Suchy. In November, 1938, the Chief of the Security Policy, Reinhard Heydrich, accompanied his directives for the Cristall Night pogroms with this injunction: "The archives of the Jewish communities are to be confiscated by the police, so that they will not be destroyed [in the planned anti-Jewish riots] . . . Important in this respect is the historically valuable material." The following dispatch sent on November 15, 1938, by local SS and police leaders from Graz, Austria, reveals how Heydrich's orders were observed: "By order of the Special Police the valuable library of the Rabbi [D. Herzog] was placed under the seal of the Gestapo during the night of November 10th, [also] . . . large portions of the archives and the library [of the Synagogue] were removed by the Special Police from the burning office building to safe custody." The same line of action is indicated in a letter written by a high SS officer in Munich on March 18, 1939: "The Special Police . . . is designated as the official agency for the processing of the Jewish archives [and books] taken into custody during the *Judenaktion*.

Alfred Rosenberg, whom Hitler had charged with the Nazi indoctrination of the German people, was given the additional assignment of waging the "ideological and spiritual war against Jews and Judaism." This program included, among other things, the establishment of a *Hohe Schule* (Advanced Training Institute) of the NSDAP in Frankfurt to study the "ideological enemies of Nazism," particularly the Jews. On January 29, 1940, Hitler authorized Rosenberg to continue the preparations, already under way, for setting up the *Hohe Schule*, and to procure for its library all necessary items from Jewish libraries and collections. Rosenberg was also authorized to set up an adequate staff for the acquisition of Jewish property. Thus the infamous *Einsatzstab Reichsleiter Rosenberg* (task force Rosenberg, hereafter referred to as ERR) was created. The ERR engaged well trained German librarians familiar with Jewish books, archives, museums and art collections. Dr. Pohl, author of several vicious anti-Semitic books, was one of the chief collectors for the ERR. In 1933 he was sent by the Nazis to study in Palestine, and is purported to have attended the Hebrew University until 1936. On March 1, 1941, he became chief of the Hebraica collection in the library of the "Institute for Study of the Jewish Question," founded by A.

Rosenberg in Frankfurt-am-Main. Another German expert on Judaica, Professor Peter-Heinz Seraphim, compiled a bulky volume on East European Jewry (published in Essen, 1938), with the help of a staff from the *Ost Europa* Institute in Koenigsberg. He made several research trips to Eastern Europe, and also visited the YIVO library in Vilna in 1936. Dr. Volkmar Eichstädt, another Nazi expert on bibliography, compiled a survey of the literature on the Jewish question available in German libraries (*Forschungen zur Judenfrage*, vol. VI, 1941, pp. 253–264). The Nazis established an *Institut fuer deutsche Ostarbeit* in Cracow for the occupied Polish areas. Its Jewish department was headed by Dr. Joseph Sommerfeldt, who was conversant with Eastern European Jewish history and bibliography (cf. his article on Jewish historiography in Eastern Europe, published in the quarterly *Die Burg*, Cracow, 1940). The Hungarian Nazi, Mihail Kolozvary-Borcza, published a comprehensive bibliography of Jewish literature in Hungary. Also associated with Rosenberg's Institute was Dr. Wilhelm Grau, a Nazi specialist in Jewish history. He was succeeded in 1942 by Dr. Otto Paul, and, after Paul's death in 1944, by Dr. Klaus Schickert, author of a voluminous volume on the "Jewish Question in Roumania."

The ERR became active without delay. Its representatives arranged in July, 1940, with the SS and police in France and Belgium, for joint examination of Jewish libraries in those countries. August Schirmer, a former staff member of the anti-Semitic news agency, *Der Weltdienst*, became the ERR representative in Amsterdam. Up to March 1, 1942, the ERR had established offices in Paris, Amsterdam, Brussels, Belgrade, Riga, Minsk, Vilna, Kaunas, Dorpat, Liepawa, Bialystok, Kiev, Dniepropetrovsk, Kherson, Simferopol, Kharkov, Rostov, Lodz, Vitebsk, Smolensk, Mohilev, Orel, Stalino and Krasnodar. According to a post-war estimate by a high United States official, Colonel Seymour J. Pomerenze (*YIVO Bleter*, vol. XXIX, 1947, pp. 282–285), the Germans screened and looted in Eastern Europe alone 375 archives, 957 libraries, 531 research and educational institutes, and 402 museums. The widespread spoliation of Jewish libraries and collections in France was described and carefully documented in Jacques Sabille's *Le Pillage par les Allemands des oeuvres d'art et des bibliothèques* (Paris, 1947). The jurisdiction of the ERR was not limited to Nazi-occupied areas. On March 21, 1942, it was extended to the territory of the whole Reich.

Among the confiscated collections incorporated in Rosenberg's Frankfurt "Institute" were the libraries of the Berlin Jewish Community, of the *Rabbiner Seminar* in Breslau, and of the Jewish community and the *Rabbiner Seminar* in Vienna. Also seized were the Hebraica and Judaica departments of the Frankfurt Municipal Library, which had survived the bombings in March, 1941, and the library of the *Collegio Rabbinico* in Rome (part of the loot, approximately 6,600 books, was identified and returned after the War). The report of August Schirmer, ERR leader in the Netherlands, reveals the enormous extent of the confiscations in that area. The libraries and archives of various Masonic lodges were packed in 470 cases and transferred to Germany. The libraries of the *Societas Spinoziana* in the Hague and in the Spinoza Home in Rijnburg were packed in eighteen cases, and the libraries of the publishing houses Querido, Pegazus, Fischer-Berman and others, in seventeen cases. The library of the International Institute of Social History in Amsterdam (staffed mainly by Jewish refugee scholars from Germany) was packed in 776 cases. Also "acquired" in Amsterdam were the libraries of Beth Hamidrash Etz Hayim (4,000 volumes), of the Israelitic Seminary (6,300 volumes), of the Portuguese Israelitic Seminary (25,000 volumes and 600 incunabula), and of the Rosenthaliana (25,000 catalogued books, but actually, according to Schirmer, 100,000 volumes and 300 manuscripts). An ERR group, headed by Dr. Pohl, went to Salonica in 1941. After sealing off the collections of various yeshivas, they proceeded to Volo to seize the library of Rabbi Moshe Pessah. Most of the Greek loot, however, probably for lack of adequate transportation facilities, was never transferred to Germany.

Vilna, with its famous Jewish libraries, became an important hunting ground for the Nazi "book lovers." The Germans began in August, 1941, with the Strashun Library. They conscripted the services of the Gestapo prisoners: Noah Prylucki, the great Jewish scholar, Yiddish philologist and civic leader, and A. Y. Goldschmidt, writer and librarian of the Historic-Ethnographic Society. Mr. Strashun, grandson of the founder of the Library, committed suicide when ordered to assist in the cataloguing project.

In January, 1942, Dr. Johannes Pohl arrived in Vilna accompanied by four assistants: Dr. Miller, Dr. Wulf, Sparkett and Gimpel. Dr. Pohl ordered all important Jewish book collections to be concentrated in the building of the YIVO at 18 Wiwulski Street. He demanded twenty workers from the Judenrat of Vilna, five of them experts on Judaica, for the task of selecting, cataloguing and shipping the books. The number of the Jewish workers in this ERR enterprise was later increased to about forty. They included the great scholar and executive member of the YIVO, Zelig Kalmanovich (who described his ERR work in his diary, posthumously published in *YIVO Annual*, vol. VIII, 1953, pp.

9–81); the writer and civic leader, Dr. Herman Kruk; the poets, Abraham Sutzkever and Shmerke Kaczerginski (who reported his ERR work in his book *Partisaner geyen*, Buenos Aires, 1947); the teacher, Rachel Pupko-Krynski (see her article in *YIVO Bleter*, vol. XXX, 1947, no. 2, pp. 214 f.) and others. New books arrived from Kovno, Shavle, Mariampol, Volozhyn and many other localities. Books were also assembled from at least 300 synagogues and from various private collections. During his short stay, Dr. Pohl made the first selection of books suitable for transport to Germany. Out of 100,000 books he selected 20,000 for shipping, and ordered the rest to be sold for pulp to a paper mill for Reichsmark 19 per ton of paper. He disposed of the copper plates of the famous Rom publishing house in a similar commercial deal. Pohl's assistants were even more unscrupulous in their transactions. One of them, Sparkett, dumped five cases of rare books and manuscripts from a transport prepared for shipment to Berlin, in order to make room for a black market shipment of hogs.

The Jewish employees of the ERR, some of them connected with the Vilna underground, tried to save as many manuscripts and books as possible. Risking their lives, they concealed the most valuable items and smuggled them, one by one, out of the closely watched YIVO building. Many of the salvaged cultural treasures were buried in safe hideouts in the Ghetto. After the war some were restored to the Jewish Museum in Vilna and others were sent to Jewish institutions the world over.

Many libraries were destroyed and looted also in Kovno. Soon after the German invasion, the books in the famous Mapu Library were publicly burned. The ceremony was witnessed by high German officials, while a military band played and Storm Troopers danced around the fire. The vandalism of those early days, however, gave way to a lucrative business pattern. Dr. Gotthardt, aided by Dr. Giselher Wirsing and other experts, took charge of the ERR in Kovno and proclaimed a Jewish "book action" in February, 1942. The most valuable books were transported to Germany, and the remainder was turned over for pulp to a paper mill.

These exploits did not sate the avarice of the ERR. In May, 1941, Wilhelm Grau suggested in a memorandum to Alfred Rosenberg that the ERR activities ought to be extended to Spain, Italy, Roumania, Hungary and Slovakia. Three years later, after Hungary had come under the heel of the Nazis, Dr. Gerhard Utikal, ERR chief of staff and author of the slanderous *Der jüdische Ritualmord*, dispatched a special unit (Sonder-Kommando) headed by Dr. Zeiss to confiscate Jewish books, archives and art treasures in Hungary. The Jewish libraries suffered not only from these roving pillagers, but also from domestic Hungarian Nazi rogues and from periodic bombing. The Nazi sponsored "Institute for Study of the Jewish Question" amassed a considerable library from books looted in Transnistria, in the Carpathian Ukraine and in Budapest (among them the collection of Jehiel M. Gutman). The Institute was bombed during the siege of Budapest and most of its books were destroyed. The library of the Rabbinical Seminary was also hit, with a loss of half of its 40,000 books. Little was left of the libraries of the synagogues and the *batei-midrashim*, both in Budapest and in the country. Among others, the library of the late Rabbi Emanuel Löw in Seged was confiscated.

In June, 1944, Gerhard Utikal sent SS Colonel H. W. Eberling to carry out the seizure of Jewish books in Denmark and in Norway.

The libraries in occupied Poland were hard hit. The great library of the Synagogue and of the Institute of Jewish Studies on Tlomackie in Warsaw was carried away to Berlin by a special Commando unit headed by the SS Untersturmfuehrer, Professor Paulsen. Other Jewish libraries in Warsaw were removed to Vienna. What remained of the huge library of the Lublin Yeshiva after the auto-da-fé of 1939, was catalogued (about 24,000 volumes) and prepared for transportation together with 10,000 volumes from private collections (*Nowy Czas*, vol. 5, no, 81, July 14, 1943). Approximately 70% of all the libraries in Poland, Jewish and non-Jewish, were looted and destroyed. The percentage in Czechoslovakia was somewhat lower — about 50%. A considerable portion of Jewish books from Bohemia and Moravia was concentrated in Theresienstadt, where the Nazis had transferred part of the Berlin research library. In addition, a library called the Central Ghetto Library was established for the residents of the Ghetto. At least 200,000 Jewish books in Hebrew, Yiddish and other languages were assembled for this purpose. Both collections survived the end of World War II.

Another sizeable collection was established in Poznan (Posen), where the Germans founded a chair for Jewish history and languages. Some 400,000 books were confiscated from various Jewish libraries for this venture. The hastily gathered books were deposited in temporary storages — in churches, in damaged and abandoned buildings, and the like. Unfortunately, only a portion of these carelessly scattered treasures could be recovered after World War II. Other Nazi institutions were also equipped with looted Jewish books, notably the Jewish Department of the Reich Institute for the History of the New Germany in Munich. (Later, after the books had been recovered from the Institute and restored to the library of the Central Committee of the Liberated Jews in Germany, the writer saw in Munich part of the library of Professor Moshe Schorr of Warsaw.)

When the ERR selected books for shipment to Germany, the rejected books were usually destroyed on the spot. The following directives were issued in February, 1943, by Dr. Cruse, of the Section of Acquisition and Examination: Books in Hebrew script (Hebrew or Yiddish) of recent date, later than the year 1800, may be turned to pulping; this applies also to prayer books, *Memorbücher*, and other religious works in the German language. All writings, on the other hand, which deal with the history, culture and nature of Judaism, as well as books written by Jewish authors in languages other than Hebrew and Yiddish, must be shipped to Frankfurt.

The Frankfurt Institute apparently had no interest in acquiring Torah Scrolls. One ERR official suggested, "Perhaps the leather can be put to use for bookbinding." Many scrolls were in fact used in Nazi-occupied areas for binding books and for manufacturing shoes, pocket books, belts, and other leather products.

The coveted goal of establishing a great Judaic library for the Frankfurt Institute was nearing achievement. A comprehensive report stated that, as of April 1, 1943, more than a half million valuable Jewish volumes had already been assembled there, and many additional thousands were at various points awaiting transportation.

A serious competitor of the ERR in the collection of books was the Reich Chief Security Office in Berlin. Its first chief was the notorious Professor Franz Alfred Six. A prolific writer, SS general and head of the Department of Foreign Studies in the University of Berlin, he had been in charge of one of the murderous *Einsatzgruppen* (Nazi extermination squads) in Eastern Europe in 1941. S. S. Sturmfuehrer Dr. Guenther was head librarian, and Dr. Kellner, an unfrocked priest, controlled the Jewish collection. The library "collected" more than 2,000,000 books in the fields of religion, Marxism, Freemasonry, and Jewish studies. In the fall of 1941, the Reich Security Office ordered the Association of Jews in Germany (*Reichsvereinigung der Juden in Deutschland*) to produce eight scholars qualified to deal with the Jewish books. Headed by Dr. Ernst Grumach, this staff was eventually increased to twenty-five (all of whom survived). When the evacuation of Berlin was ordered in August, 1943, many of the books were transported to castles in Czechoslovakia; some 60,000 Hebrew and Yiddish books were sent to *Theresienstadt*. Here a group of Jewish Ghetto inmates led by Dr. Benjamin Murmelstein, the *Judenältester* of the Ghetto, was put in charge of cataloguing the collection. The principal contents of the Security Office Library, however, including the library of the *Hochschule für Wissenschaft des Judentums* (Berlin), and collections brought from Vienna and Warsaw, were left behind in Berlin and were largely destroyed by bombings.

After Germany's defeat in the spring of 1945, the Jewish collection at Frankfurt passed into the custody of the American authorities. A great cache of books, manuscripts and art treasures was subsequently discovered (about 100,000 items) in a cave near Hungen, thirty-two miles from Frankfurt. The Rothschild Library in Frankfurt was designated by the United States Army as the assembling point for Jewish cultural treasures recovered in the U. S. Zone of Occupation. Up to November 1946, 2,300,000 volumes were assembled in Frankfurt. This massive gathering contained approximately 400 collections from Poland, a like number from Lithuania, 582 from Germany, 141 from Latvia, 50 from Austria, 15 from Czechoslovakia, and smaller numbers from other countries. Eventually the collections were transferred to a large depot in Offenbach, where they were processed and returned to their legitimate owners. Since a number of institutions had gone out of existence, and many former owners were no longer alive, the ownerless property was distributed, with the aid of the Commission on European Cultural Reconstruction in New York, to Jewish libraries and to other institutions the world over.

Also semi-official libraries or private collections of German scholars or experts on the Jewish question were equipped with Jewish books. Thus, for instance, the editor of *Der Stuermer* acquired several thousand Hebrew books from every part of Europe and employed a Hebraist of little competence to organize the library and to indicate the importance of each book. The retributive pattern of history seems to have been vindicated by the ironic fate that overtook Julius Streicher, the ignominious editor of *Der Stuermer*. After the Liberation his villa, together with his farm and its valuable agricultural experimental equipment, was assigned by the United States military authorities to the Kibbutz NILI (*Netzah Yisroel lo yeshaker*). This kibbutz was composed of young halutzim who survived the Nazi holocaust. Thus, the treasures collected by the rapacious and ruthless *Judenfresser* eventually came to serve a noble purpose — the training of his victims, the youthful pioneers, for *hakhsharah* to Israel. This presage of a brighter tomorrow is a happy augury for the "People of the Book." It cannot obliterate the tragic past, but it will surely inspire a deeper rededication by the whole Jewish people to the spiritual and intellectual tasks that must be woven into the architecture of our future.

THE LITERATURE OF REMORSE*

By Richard Grunberger

I T IS A REMARKABLE COINCIDENCE that I should be dealing with the literature of remorse on this day of all days. Today is the 11th of March—and it was on the 11th of March 1938, exactly 26 years ago, that the Nazis annexed Austria and embarked on the road of foreign conquest ending in world war and genocide.

When I went out into the streets next morning I saw a transformed Vienna: the houses were swathed in swastika flags and bunting, and endless Wehrmacht columns were pouring into the city from the West. The stream of field-grey uniforms seemed to wash over me till I felt utterly naked and defenceless.

Fortunately the human mind has a tendency towards pushing memories of this nature into the background and with the passage of time the impact of that day lost its sharp outline, became blurred and almost dissolved into obliviousness.

Then, quite a few years after the war I picked up Rex Warner's novel *The Professor* and read the following passage:

> "So he stood and watched until he could distinguish clearly the bodies of cavalry, the beetle-shapes of tanks, the gun-carriages and lorries proceeding at regular intervals and behind them an indistinguishable grey mass of moving infantry. He saw the long column of grey boring like a caterpillar or grub into the entrails of the city. . . . The troops had now filled the main avenue and smaller bodies were branching off the larger stream and parading up the other roads. It was as though some fluid were being injected into the veins, altering totally the complexion of the city in which he had spent his life."

As I was reading this a long-buried memory thrust itself to the surface of my consciousness. When the shock of recognition had worn off I started to ask myself how it was possible for a

* This paper was presented on March 11, 1964, during the 12th annual celebration in London of Jewish Book Week under the auspices of the Jewish Book Council of England, during the session organized by the World Jewish Congress, British Section.

man living in a different country—and under totally different circumstances—to put himself so completely inside the skin of someone like myself.

The answer to this somewhat naive question is of course that Rex Warner possesses the faculty of imagination and sympathy which is the hallmark of all creative writers.

This gift, which for want of a better word I would call empathy, is something which the literature of remorse demands of its German practitioners to an unparalleled degree. These German writers are confronted with the task of extending their imaginative range and power of human insight in two totally divergent directions. In the first instance they have to get inside the skins of their Nazi compatriots—a difficulty permitting of no easy solution; how many English novelists, for instance, could give a valid account of the world as seen through the eyes of Colin Jordan or the mass-murderer Christie? Even more difficult must it be for German post-war writers to depict the Jewish victims of their compatriots authentically—since their knowledge of Jews and things Jewish must of necessity be mainly second-hand.

A case in point is Erwin Sylvanus, author of *Dr. Korczak and the Children,* a play about the head of the Jewish Orphanage at Warsaw who voluntarily entered the gas chamber ahead of his charges although the S.S. had offered to spare him if he would help them mislead the orphans about their fate. Sylvanus spent many months gaining background knowledge and establishing contact with rabbis of the small reconstituted Jewish communities in Westphalia prior to writing this play (which has, incidentally, been shown on British television).

The novelist Henning Meincke seems to have taken even more trouble to steep himself in Jewish knowledge and religious lore —yet the end-product of his academic as well as literary labors is hardly commensurate with the effort expended. Meincke's *Davids Harfe* (The Harp of David) seems to me to suffer from the same distortion of focus as Hannah Arendt's *Eichmann in Jerusalem*. It has been said of Miss Arendt that in a situation where A puts his gun to the head of B and threatens to shoot him unless he strangles C, she finds more fault with B for accepting A's orders than with A for issuing them in the first place. Meincke's novel is set in a Jewish ghetto in war-time Poland and deals mainly with the diverse personalities making up the Judenrat, their respective nostalgias, obsessions and recriminations on the eve of the liquidation of the ghetto. By overstressing the friction and antipathies existing among the Judenrat members and by focusing his readers' attention largely on the demoralization and disunity gripping the ghetto, Meincke is not merely guilty of a grievously sin of omission—I would go so far as to say that he is virtually desecrating the graves of millions who have no grave.

Meincke, however, is in no way typical of the authors coming under the general heading of this evening's talk. Every other German playwright or novelist whose work concerns itself with the holocaust and with whose writings I am familiar is quite free from Meincke's reprehensible distortion of focus. In fact there seems to be a remarkable unanimity of outlook among all of them—certainly as far as analyzing the constituent elements of German society in the Nazi era is concerned. At the risk of oversimplification I would say that all these writers postulate the existence of four numerically widely disparate groups, one of which—that of the Anti-Nazis—was so ineffectual (or politically insignificant) that some writers barely mention it. The other three, in ascending order of importance, are the philistines, the thugs and the demons. (It should be noted that within these three groups constituting the great bulk of the German population, numerical strength was inversely proportionate to power exercised, i.e. the philistines numbered tens of millions, the thugs tens of thousands and the demons just tens—or hundreds.)

To exemplify what it meant by these rather cryptic terms I am going to quote from a number of German writers. The first excerpt concerns itself with philistines and is taken from Heinrich Böll's *Wo warst Du, Adam?* (Where were you, Adam?) a collection of connected stories dealing with the retreat of the German Army through Hungary in 1944.

> The green furniture van had an excellent engine. The two men in the driver's cab who took turns at the wheel didn't say much to each other, but when they did speak they spoke of little but the engine. "Goes like a bomb," they said now and then, shook their heads in surprise and listened, as if hypnotized, to its strong, dark, very regular throbbing in which there was not a single false or disturbing sound. The night was warm and dark, and the road along which they drove continuously northwards was sometimes jammed with army vehicles and horse-drawn carts. Occasionally they had to brake sharply because they were too late in noticing the marching columns and almost drove into a shapeless mass of dark figures. The roads were narrow, too narrow to let the removal van, tanks and marching columns pass each other, but further north the road got emptier. Here they could let the furniture van run in top gear for long stretches at a time. The lightcones of their head-lamps illuminated trees and houses, occasionally picking out details from the fields stretching alongside: stalks of maize or tomatoes. They finally halted somewhere along a side street in a village; they unpacked their haversacks, sipped the hot

and very strong coffee from their flasks, they opened their butter-dishes, sniffed at the contents and spread the butter thick on the bread before putting large slabs of sausage on it. The sausage was red and moist and full of pepper-corns. The men were eating heartily. Their grey and tired faces became animated and the man who now sat on the left and had finished first lit a cigarette and took a letter out of his pocket; he unfolded it and produced a snapshot; on it was a delightful small child playing with a rabbit in the grass. He showed the photo to his companion and said "Have a gander, nice isn't it—my little one." He laughed. "Result of a week's leave." The other one was chewing. He stared at the photo and mumbled, "A leave-child, eh? Nice. How old is she?"

"Three years."

"Haven't you got a snapshot of the wife?"

"Oh yes."

The one sitting on the left took out his wallet, but stopped suddenly and said. "Listen; they must have gone mad. . . ." Out of the green furniture-van's interior came an insistent dark murmuring and the shrill screams of a woman.

"Go on, make them shut up," said the one sitting at the wheel.

The people inside the van were Hungarian Jews being transported to a camp where they were to be liquidated.

When they eventually arrived at this camp they encountered its commander, Filskeit, a typical example of the demoniac type— great intellectual or artistic ability coupled with total inhumanity —which has kept on recurring in German history from Luther to Goebbels.

> It was his ambition to carry out all orders correctly. He had soon discovered the immense innate musical talent of his prisoners; this rather surprised him in the case of Jews and he applied the principle of selection by giving every new prisoner a singing test. For this he awarded marks ranging from nought to ten which were entered on the prisoner's file. The few who got nought joined the camp-choir at once—those with ten had less than two days to live. When selecting transports he always arranged it so that a nucleus of good male and female voices remained intact. He was proud of the choir which was regularly supplemented by new arrivals, very proud. With this choir he could have held his own against any competitor but unfortunately the only remaining audiences consisted of dying prisoners and the camp-guards.

But orders were even more sacred than music to him and recently there had been many orders that had reduced his choir. The Hungarian ghettos and camps were being cleared and because the larger camps to which he had previously sent Jews had been dissolved and because his small camp had no rail-link he had to kill all inmates inside the camp. Even so there were still sufficient commandos—for the kitchen, the baths, the crematorium—left to preserve at least individual singers.

Filskeit did not like killing. He had never yet done any in person and the fact that he could not bring himself to do it was one of his abiding disappointments. He realized the necessity for it and he admired the killing-directives which he caused to be carried out to the letter. Obviously what mattered was not whether one liked carrying out the orders but whether one realized the necessity for them, honored them and put them into execution.

My last excerpt from Böll shows the dreadful confrontation between the demon Filskeit and one of his victims—a Hungarian Jewess converted to Catholicism, who had formerly taught music at a convent school.

In the room was a man who wore officer's uniform. He had a small impressive cross-shaped silver decoration on his chest. His face looked pale and suffering and when he raised his head to look at her she was startled to see his chin which was so heavy that it almost disfigured him. He put out his hand silently, she gave him the card and waited: fear had not yet come to her. The man read the card, looked at her and said quietly, "Sing something."

She hesitated. "Come on" he said impatiently "sing something—anything." She looked at him and opened her mouth. She sang the All Saints' Litany to a setting she had only recently come across and had wanted to rehearse with her pupils. She sang beautifully—without knowing that she smiled in spite of the fear which slowly rose inside her throat like nausea.

Since she had started to sing it had grown quiet, outside as well. Filskeit stared at her. She was beautiful, a woman—he had never had a woman yet—his whole life had been spent in lethal chasteness. His life had been acted out when he stood before the mirror, looking in vain for beauty, greatness and racial perfection. And here was beauty, greatness and racial perfection linked to something which completely paralyzed him: faith. He could not understand why he allowed her to continue. Maybe he was dreaming. In her expression—although he noticed that she was trembling

—there was something almost like love, or was it scorn? She sang: Fili, Redemptor Mundi, Deus—he had never before heard a woman sing like that.

"Spiritus Sancte, Deus," her voice was strong, warm and of extra-ordinary purity. He was obviously dreaming. In a moment she would sing "Sancta Trinitas, Unus Deus"—he still remembered it—and indeed she sang it now. "Sancta Trinitas. . . ." Catholic Jews, he thought; I am going mad. He ran to the window and tore it open. Outside no one moved; they were all standing and listening.

Filskeit felt a spasm. He tried to shout but only a hoarse groan broke from his throat. From outside came a breathless silence whilst the woman sang on.

"Sancta Dei Genetrix . . ." he picked up his gun with trembling fingers, swung round and blindly aimed at the woman who fell and started to scream. Now that her voice was no longer singing he found his again. He yelled "Kill them; all of them . . . the choir as well . . . out with them, out of the block. . . ." He emptied the whole magazine of his gun into the woman who was lying on the ground and vomiting with fear in agonies of pain.

Outside the massacre began.

Böll has drawn representative examples of the philistines and the demons—the bottom and top layers of Nazi society. Both groups' psyche exhibited a total dichotomy: the philistines combined the natural human attributes of family-affection and sentimentality with a stony indifference to the fate of others, and in the minds of the demons giftedness cohabited with total inhumanity.

The thugs, the medium-layer of Nazi society, were less complicated. Their *raison d'etre* was simply violence, torture and destruction for its own sake. A short, but infinitely telling example of this middle-category occurs in Günther Grass' best selling novel *Die Blechtrommel* (The Tin Drum). It refers to the events of the Kristallnacht (November 9, 1938), the day on which Germany reached—and passed—the point of no return.

There was once a grocer who closed his store one day in November because something was doing in town; taking his son Oscar by the hand he boarded a Number 5 streetcar and rode to the Langasser Gate, because there as in Zoppot and Langfuhr the synagogue was on fire. The synagogue had almost burned down and the firemen were looking on, taking care that the flames should not spread to other buildings. . . .

There was once a toystore owner; his name was Sigismund Markus and among other things he sold tin drums lacquered red and white. Oscar, above-mentioned, was the principal taker of these drums, because he was a drummer by profession and was neither able nor willing to live without a drum. . . .

They, the same firemen, whom I, Oscar, thought I had escaped, had visited Markus before me. . . . I found them still at play when I, also through the window, entered the shop. Some had taken their pants down and had deposited brown sausages in which half-digested peas were still discernible on sailing vessels, fiddling monkeys and on my drums. . . .

Outside, it was a November morning. Besides the Stadt-Theater, near the streetcar stop, some pious ladies and strikingly ugly young girls were handing out religious tracts, collecting money in collection boxes, and holding up between two poles, a banner with an inscription quoted from the 13th chapter of the First Epistle to the Corinthians "Faith . . . hope . . . love . . ."

He's coming, He's coming. Who is coming? The Christ child, the Saviour? Or is it the heavenly gasman with the gas meter under his arm, that always goes ticktock? And he said: I am the Saviour of this world, without me you can't cook. And he was not too demanding, he offered special rates, turned on the freshly polished gas cocks and let the Holy Ghost pour forth.

Whereas Grass makes a German dwarf who had stopped growing at the age of three his central character, Bruno Apitz in *Nackt unter Wölfen* (Naked Among Wolves) centers his plot around a three-year-old Jewish child. This pitiful creature has been smuggled into Buchenwald Concentration Camp in a suitcase by the inmate of a camp further East being evacuated in face of the Russian advance. The secreted Jewish child exists on two planes in Apitz's novel; on the action-plane its arrival confronts the members of the Buchenwald underground with many problems.

In the case, all twisted up the little hands pressed against his face, lay a child covered in rags. A boy, no older than about three years. Kropinski squatted down and stared at the child. It lay motionless. Pippig stroked the little body with tenderness. He wanted to turn the child round, but it seemed to resist. At last Kropinski thought of something. "Poor worm," he said in Polish, "where are you from?" At the sound of the Polish words the child pushed its little head forward like an insect that had retracted its feelers. The narrow face already had the seriousness of a knowing person and its eyes had a lustre which wasn't that of children.

Höfel cursed softly, "Small children get scared, and then they holler. The devil take it." He stared at the child for a long time. "Maybe . . . maybe he can't holler at all." He got hold of the child's shoulders and shook it gently. "You mustn't holler, d'you hear? Or else the SS will come." Suddenly the child's face contorted with fear. It wrenched itself free, threw itself back into the case and made itself as small as possible, hiding its face with its hands.

"He knows what's what," exclaimed Pippig. To test his assumptions he shut the case. They listened. Everything was quiet.

"Exactly," Pippig repeated, "he knows what's what."

He opened the case again. The child had not moved. Kropinski lifted it up and it hung between his hands like a twisted-up insect. The three looked at the creature in consternation. With its legs and head pulled in the child appeared as if it had just been torn from the womb or like a beetle feigning death.

But the Jewish child is not to be seen merely as an additional burden upon the underground—a further mouth to be fed and an appalling security-risk; its function in the story is also symbolic. At the end, when the prisoners liberate the camp ahead of the advancing Americans and stream out of the camp-gates they carry the child triumphantly above their heads. This I take to mean that they have managed to preserve the symbol of innocence and humanity inviolate under conditions of appalling degradation; had they failed to shoulder the additional burden presented by the child, had they let no other laws than those of expediency and survival govern them, the underground would have allowed themselves to be dragged down to the level of the system whose victims they were.

The imagery of the Jewish child occurs over and over again in the literature of remorse. In *Das Brandopfer* (The Burnt Offering) by Albrecht Goes the central character is a German woman who acts as the "Judenmetzge" (Jews' butcher) in a small town in 1942. Every Friday evening after the "normal" shoppers have all gone, wearers of the Yellow Star are allowed to purchase their meagre meat-ration. On one such occasion an SS thug bursts in accompanied by a "correct" Nazi official.

And now I see him smash the little parcel out of the old man's hand. "Mausche," he shouts, "don't over-eat. Otherwise you'll be too heavy to go up to heaven. You'll be off on the 15th—swish, like a bird through the air."

Everybody looked at Goliath. No, two or three customers pretended not to have heard anything, one came up to me and gave me his order. I could not listen to him right away. I had to look across to Frau Zalewsky; she had put her shopping bag down, her whole body was trembling. She was a musician's wife and was in an advanced state of pregnancy. I knew a few things about her. She had had the courage, when she was four months gone, to ask for supplementary maternity rations—for a quarter litre of milk and a few ounces of sugar and flour. The food-office had replied to her application. "A Jew brat has to be aborted. Contact the health office, department D." She had kept that letter in her bag and had shown it to me, once. I spoke to Frau Zalewski. The woman, who was as pale as death, replied: "Don't worry, I'll be all right soon." I turned back to the customer who repeated his order and the Goliath started afresh. "Swish, like birds through the air." He seemed to want to perform a dance. At this point his puny companion took a step towards him, stood to attention and said in a half-whisper "Untersturmführer, you are on duty."

The Goliath opened his eyes and raised his arm. It seemed incredible that anybody should dare tell him anything. He shouted: "Rubbish. Bloody stupid rubbish. I think it's positively bighearted of me to let these people know when they'll be going up the chimney. You don't believe me, Beck? Sarah here with the fat tummy—isn't that so, Sarah? —is altogether grateful to me for telling her she doesn't have to worry about baby-nappies anymore, those sweet little shitty nappies. . . ."

The unborn Jewish child inside the womb of the mother about to die—this most harrowing symbol of man's inhumanity to man—also occurs in Rolf Hochhuth's *Der Stellvertreter* (The Representative). The published version contains the interior monologues of three Auschwitz-bound detainees, of whom one has been rounded up, heavy with child, almost within sight of the Pope's Vatican apartment.

THE WOMAN. How happy we were with our daily life and being no one's enemy; we loved the narrow kitchen balcony, and sought the sun in the piazza besides the grapesellers, and the cool in the park. And on Sunday, relaxing at the cinema.

And now . . . never a family, never the three of us. Never to eat, to talk at our own table, no room to protect us . . . nor paths that are safe and dreams and daily milk and light by night and a bed and a man who loves his work, and gives me comfort and warmth in the night and a shield. We had forgotten the menace of the world.

In *The Representative* Hochhuth also presents two of the most unfathomable demoniac characters produced by the whole literature of remorse.

The first of these is a minor character in the play: the historically authentic figure of Professor Hirth of Strassburg. Hirth's scientific life-mission was the setting-up of a comprehensive collection of formalin-preserved skulls taken from Jewish corpses. Rationalizing his necrophilic obsession, he claimed that these exhibits would provide incontrovertible proof of the degeneracy and the necessity for the Final Solution—if future generations of Germans should ever doubt the wisdom of their forefathers' actions.

Going beyond the historically established facts, Hochhuth attributes a wish-fulfillment fantasy to Hirth which reveals tremendous poetic insight into the depths of the demonic psyche. Musing on the apparently not-too-distant day of Germany's final victory, Hirth has a vision of ecstatic bliss. On Victory Day he wants to hear Bach's Mass in B minor at Strassburg Cathedral and have the Fuehrer inspect his collection of skulls afterwards. Hochhuth heightens the impact of this monstrous juxtaposition of images by making Hirth add that his meeting with the solitary Hitler should take place in complete silence. No sound, no loud word should intrude itself to disturb the mystical rapport between visitor and host within sight of the last remains of an extinct race.

The other and far more important demonic character in *The Representative* is the "Doctor"—a composite figure combining Dr. Mengele's scientific fiendishness with Goebbel's nihilism and the philosophizing sadism of Camus' Caligula. This "Doctor" has been acknowledged by many critics as such an ingenious portrayal of total evil on the stage and so much has already been written about him that I shall not deal with him in any detail.

Another doctor playing a crucial role in a work touching upon the holocaust is the medical officer of Andorra, in Max Frisch's parable of the same name. (The fact that doctors and teachers figure so prominently—either as demons or as philistines —in this genre of literature arises from the view that their particular "trahison du clercs" made them even more culpable than other sections of the population.)

The doctor in *Andorra* is a totally believable creation—a garrulous, phrase-mongering philistine existing on quite a different level to his satanic counterpart in *The Representative*, but who is, nevertheless, just as lethal in his own more prosaic way. Having been a prime accessory to the murder of the alleged Jew Andri he subsequently tries to exculpate himself in a statement which reads like the distilled essence of all the specious alibis recorded in the files of the denazification tribunals.

> DOCTOR. I shall try to be brief, although there are a great many things being said today which ought to be corrected. It's always easy to know afterwards how one ought to have behaved at the time, quite apart from the fact that as far as I am personally concerned I really don't know why I should have behaved differently. What did I do? Nothing whatever; I was the local medical officer as I still am. I can't remember what I am supposed to have said at the time, but anyhow that's my way, an Andorran says what he thinks—but I shall be brief. . . . I admit that we were all mistaken at the time, which naturally I can only regret. How often do I have to say that? I'm not in favor of atrocities, I never have been. Anyway, I only saw the young man two or three times. I didn't see the beating-up that is supposed to have taken place later. Nevertheless I naturally condemn it. I can only say that it's not my fault, quite apart from the fact that his behavior (there is no point in concealing the fact) became (let us be quite frank) more and more Jewish, although the young man may really have been just as much of an Andorran as I am. I don't for one moment deny that we were somewhat influenced by the events of the period. It was, let us not forget, a turbulent period. As far as I am personally concerned I never took part in brutality or urged anyone to indulge in it. I can state that publicly. A tragic affair, undoubtedly. It wasn't my fault that things turned out as they did. I think I can speak in the name of everyone when, to conclude, I repeat that we can only regret the things that took place at that time.

This is the sort of unrepentant self-vindication the teacher Siegfried would have advanced in Paul Schallück's novel, *Engelbert Reineke*, if he had ever been asked to account for his part in causing the death of his colleague Lehmköster's wife. Early in 1942 their headmaster had called a staff-meeting for the purpose of putting pressure on the few remaining teachers who still made a distinction between teaching and indoctrination. During the verbal fencing that took the place of discussions in German staff-rooms Siegfried had jocularly suggested that Lehmköster must have a Jewish wife—how could his negative attitude to the strengthening of the homefront be explained otherwise?

Lehmköster, in fact, had a Jewish wife and had hitherto managed to safeguard her with the connivance of the local priest—but Siegfried's chance remark had caught him completely off guard and he concealed his confusion so ineptly that Siegfried's wild surmise soon gained credence among the others.

Siegfried merely had to mention Ella Lehmköster's name casually, make a joke or raise his brows. But that was sufficient to spawn a rumor. As soon as this rumor started circulating, it began to acquire a life of its own. Unguarded, it sneaked through the alleyways, sauntered through the streets, moved through living-rooms, public bars, cafes and shops, a barely audible whisper past people's ears and right through them; it was blown along by the wind and pushed forward by many tongues until grown into a hungry beast with an existence of its own; it came to rest in the appropriate desk. There Ella Lehmköster's name was written on a typewriter that was cleaned every day by a girl in a white blouse, with her hair in a bun. The name was typed on a list headed Secret Reich's matter and some time later a pencilled tick was placed against it.

An innocent rumor—that was all that was needed so that one night, probably just before dawn, a car with dimmed headlights pulled up noiselessly in front of Lehmköster's house. And a few minutes later, minutes which differed in no way from the preceding or subsequent ones, it left as quietly as it had come. Nothing more was required.

After that day Lehmköster never went to church again.

Many years later Engelbert Reineke, one of Lehmköster's former pupils, went to seek out the old teacher who had been retired soon after the deportation of his wife and had led the life of a recluse ever since.

The door of Lehmköster's house gave on to a gravelly path that ended at the river. I pressed the bell-button with slightly trembling fingers. I pressed it once, twice, three times. But there was no sound at all. Then I noticed a small glass container fastened to the doorpost; inside it was a yellow scroll of paper covered with an unfamiliar script, maybe Hebrew. Small urgent ciphers. Revelations to one who lacked comprehension, signals from an invisible star, messages from a ghostly twilight-zone.

Then I heard steps. The door opened and Herr Lehmköster stood before me. I noticed at once how he had changed, how terribly old he had become. His grey beard was streaked with white; over his shoulders he wore a rectangular shawl of dark-blue wool fringed with colored tassels. What seemed strangest to me were two narrow straps which he had tied round the left arm and across the forehead. From each strap dangled a small box.

In the ensuing, most poignantly-written passage Schallück shows how the trauma of his wife's death had made Lehmköster seek escape from reality by withdrawing from all human contacts and assuming a fictitious Jewish identity.

A fictitious Jew living on as mute witness to bygone horrors in the era of post-war amnesia and the economic miracle—such is the role of the awesome figure of Lehmköster; Woizele in Martin Walser's *The Rabbit Race* is an analogous survival, but this pathetic residue of what was once a human being differs from Lehmköster in two important respects. Whereas Lehmköster is an assumed Jew, Woizele is an archetypally authentic one—hunted, bewildered, rootless; the grief that has driven Lehmköster in on himself makes Woizele wander ceaselessly among strangers and inquire after the whereabouts of his three lost sons.

When *The Rabbit Race* was first performed in Berlin the heart-rending spectacle of the feeble-minded Woizele's persistent delusion that his sons were still alive proved too much for the nerves of the audience and Walser in consequence had to tone down the most harrowing sequences in his play.

This particular incident brings me to the most crucial—and controversial—aspect of my theme: the question of the degree to which the impact of the literature of remorse can be nullified by audience-reactions of embarrassment, indifference or downright hostility. This is a problem going to the very root of the foundations of post-war Germany; the reading and theatre-going public's response to the literature of remorse is a not-to-be-underestimated indicator of the viability of German democracy. In this connection the impressive number of performances of *The Representative* and *Andorra* in West German theatres can be accounted an encouraging sign—but the fact that the Andorran doctor's unrepentant self-justification occasionally drew applause from audiences carries a warning which should not be overlooked.

The problem confronting authors and playwrights is of the greatest complexity; how can the readers (or the audience) be made to accept moral strictures which in many cases are only thinly disguised indictments of their own past conduct?

One of the most obvious ways in which this obstacle can be circumvented is by the conscious linking of Jewish martyrdom with the war-time suffering of individual Germans. Walser uses this dramatic device in *The Rabbit Race* where Woizele's incoherent references to his lost sons are counterpointed by the broodings of a German woman condemned to permanent childlessness because her Communist husband had been castrated in a Nazi concentration camp.

An even closer parallel of Jewish and German suffering is drawn in Maria Mathi's *Wenn nur der Sperber nicht kommt* (If Only the Sparrow-hawk Doesn't Come). This novel, set in a rural backwater, spans three generations; its point of departure is the rivalry between the Jewess Fanny and the peasant-girl Rosa for the love of a young farmer. This farmer really loves Fanny but religious and family pressures on both ·sides compel him to marry Rosa. Increasingly realizing the hollowness at the heart of their marriage Rosa gradually becomes an embittered Jew-baiter. This anti-semitism turns to dementia when her own daughter defies her and marries Fanny's fully Jewish son. Shortly afterwards the Nazis come to power; the novel ends at the euthanasia centre of Hadamar where Fanny and Rosa, the lifelong rivals and enemies, are at long last united in a dreadful form of death—Fanny because she is Jewish and Rosa because of her mental condition.

Another approach to the problem of overcoming audiencereactions of embarrassed indifference (or worse), is the device common to many authors of including representatives of the other "good" Germany in their works, so that spectators or readers can identify with them. It is interesting to note what varied roles the anti-Nazis play in the creations of diverse writers. In Maria Mathi's novel, for instance, a handful of decent villagers abhor what is being done to their Jewish neighbors on the Kristallnacht and show their disapproval of the outrages by locking themselves in their own homes and praying.

Lehmköster in Schallück's novel carries resistance much further; he only turns to prayer after his efforts at saving a Jewish life had ended in tragic failure.

Gerstein in *The Representative* goes further still; he is shown joining the SS to save lives by working inside that murderous organization—yet in the end the efficacy of his efforts is no greater than that of the pathetic Lehmköster. The actions of the good Germans were of considerable symbolic significance—but in terms of actual lives saved their importance was practically nil.

It is a staggering paradox that—within the narrow compass of the works under review—the only occasion on which good Germans are seen taking effective action occurs in Apitz's novel

Naked Among Wolves, the entire action of which is set inside Buchenwald Concentration Camp. It would appear that the greatest freedom for acting humanely in Nazi Germany existed inside its prisons.

The very paradox of this conclusion seems to me proof of its validity—as well as proof of the integrity of the authors involved in the literature of remorse. (The contention may of course be advanced that Apitz, an East German cultural functionary, was bound to give his novel the obligatory "positive" slant, but I would hesitate to impute pure opportunism to a writer who himself lived through the hell of Buchenwald.)

Just as his West German colleagues lack Apitz's background so do they not share his "retrospective optimism." The continued underground existence of the good Germany, only temporarily obliterated by the Nazi eruption, is to them no deeply-held article of faith. Many are beset by grave doubts about the nature of the society in which they live and about the moral responsiveness of their fellow countrymen. This lack of rapport between themselves and their public also has its effect in a wide divergence of approach to the cathartic function of the literature of remorse.

Gunther Grass, for instance, distances himself from his audience and from the events he depicts by such alienation-devices as describing the firemen's feces as "brown sausages" and similar shock images.

At the opposite extreme to Grass's alienation is Walser's pathos-laden bid for audience-involvement—when both Woizele and the barren German woman ramble on about their dead or never-to-be-born children, as it were in unison.

Somewhere between these two lies the approach of the author of *The Burnt Offering,* Pastor Albrecht Goes, a man equally endowed with the gift of writing—and the gift of love.

> In those days at Offenbach I had Rebecca for a friend. It was the only time I really ever had a friend; usually I can't form friendships—the others always demand too much. Rebecca was the daughter of the cantor at the Synagogue and in truth she looked like Rebecca at the well. . . . When the manhunt began the cantor's family started hiding the child; always somewhere else. People were helpful. She also stayed with us a few times. We had long conversations at bed-time; I haven't forgotten them.
>
> And then, suddenly, Rebecca had vanished. "Where is Rebecca?" I asked every day; I asked morning, noon and night. I knew the world without Rebecca wasn't the world

any more. "She has gone away," said my mother, and that wasn't an untruth. She had gone away—to Auschwitz, I think, into the gas-chambers, but my mother didn't talk about that. One should tell the truth but I don't blame her for not telling me the whole truth at that time.

"Where is Rebecca?" I was alone with my father and asked for the twentieth, the thirtieth time. I asked, "Where is Rebecca?" And father replied, "In you!" That was all he said, as if he wanted to give me time to spell it out to myself—in you!

THE JEW IN POSTWAR
GERMAN LITERATURE

By Lothar Kahn

T HE JEW in postwar German literature is lacking in flesh and blood and is overendowed with symbols. He is of interest to Germans only as a factor in their own national past and future. He incarnates moral issues for those who like neither the rampant materialism and self-seeking individualism of the Bundesrepublik nor its convenient forgetfulness of past responsibility. Frequently the Jew serves as the opposite pole of spirituality to current materialist emphases. The Jew is so much symbol that he is often left nameless. This fleshless anonymity may be due to the fact that this generation of young German writers has known very few Jews. What they know about Jews they know from history—a history difficult to come by. By and large, the novels in which the Jew appears are works of national self-flagellation—in which the Jew as noble victim becomes a prime instrument of flagellation. This latter tendency has become especially pronounced in the last decade, the first post-Hitlerian decade having been marked also by attempts to shift the guilt from the individual to the leaders.

The combination of tool, symbol and abstract knowledge has produced, especially in recent years, an idealized Jew who has done no wrong, can do no wrong, and looks pallid if not inhuman in the process. Perhaps German imperfections required Jewish perfections. Such perfection is sometimes achieved by endowing the Jew with biblical and patriarchal dignity on the one hand and a Jesus-like noble suffering on the other. Some of the fictional Jews possess a supranatural wisdom and insights which lift them clearly above the human. An aura of mystery surrounds them which makes them nothing less than awesome.

A German critic recently wrote that chaotic times—such as the Nazi era—are marked by the dominance of extremes and the casting aside of all things moderate. Although twenty-one years have elapsed since the Nazi terror, the tendency of the period to split into extremes has survived in the literature concerning it. The Nazis are Caesar, the Jews are Jesus; the Nazis are matter, the Jews are spirit; the Nazis are beast, the Jews are civilization.

139

One could just as easily apply the polarities of Satan (Nazi) and God (Jew); even Thomas Mann's Drive or Instinct (Nazi) and Intellect (Jews). Invariably, the feminine or weaker element is defeated physically by the male element of power, drive, bestiality, only to triumph morally and spiritually in the long run. These polarities seem partly evident in the love-hate relationship between the German and half-Jew in Günther Grass' recent *Hundejahre* (Dog Years).

Few Convincing Characters

It may be interesting to note that, just as there are no convincing Jews in contemporary German fiction, there are also few convincing Nazis. The Nazis, too, tend to be symbol, though all negative symbol. They represent stupidity, opportunism, greed, evil psychological deviationism; in some cases, where they are Nazis in name only, they are the epitome of weakness, compromise and lack of character—the *Mitläufer*. Only one Nazi stands out as a truly terrifying and original creation, Judejahn, the erstwhile Nazi big-wig in Wolfgang Koeppen's powerful *Der Tod in Rom* (Death in Rome). Judejahn achieves the status of a full-fledged character, while retaining his symbolic value. He is indeed a unique, terrifying and original mixture of Satan, drive, deviation, instinct and maleness.

But if the Jew seldom rises above symbol status, he compensates by the frequency of his appearance. In novels and stories, plays, radio and TV plays, he appears in his noble but pallid way. In the words of one of the characters in Erwin Sylvanus' short play *Korczak und die Kinder* (Korczak and the Children), "Tears for the Jews—this is the vogue today." Whereupon another character responds, "And a good business." In many ways this also reflects the response of many American and Jewish critics of the recent German novel. They chastise German writers—and with good cause—for being monotonous in their criticism, their mea culpas, their critique of contemporary society, especially in terms of the past. They show their impatience with the dominant stance of tears for the Jews and anger at themselves. Yet what would happen if German writers were to ignore the past and dismissed it as mere past? These same critics would hardly be satisfied if contemporary writers were to concentrate on the present or universals, independent of Auschwitz and Theresienstadt. Yet frequent criticism levied against post-war German literature is partly justified, that its primary concern has been with social criticism and that it has not given itself to a single-minded pursuit of literary creativity. In their social criticism they have tried too hard, a tendency that has led some into bathos.

In overstepping this precarious balance, German authors have shared some of the problems of the Jewish writers on the holocaust; especially in relation to their work as art. With the exception of two or three efforts, notably Elie Wiesel's *Night* and Peter Weiss' as yet untranslated *Die Ermittlung* (The Investigation), the Jewish literature on Auschwitz has fallen far short of art, while yet maintaining power as humanized document and history. If these works have failed as art, it is for the same reasons as the German failure. Their authors did not maintain the proper distance from their subject which emotionally—and perhaps intellectually—overpowered them; they fell into the pitfalls of rhetoric, polemics or sentimentalism. Perhaps art in relation to subjects like Auschwitz or Hiroshima needs to be redefined or eliminated entirely as a consideration. Perhaps too, as Wiesel has suggested, only those indulging in silence are really the effective spokesmen.

Thus the heirs of executioner and victim shared, perhaps ironically, a similar difficulty in interpreting the experience. As yet many of the German fictional works on the Nazi past are recognizable more easily as social documents, moral proclamations and political exhortations. Few are convincing as novels. And even in terms of their social, moral and political importance, their acknowledgment of guilt and their prognosis of the German future, the novels are more sincere in intent than persuasive in effect.

The Vacuum in German Letters

When the Thousand Year Reich crumbled in 1945, there was a huge vacuum in German letters. The great men, many of them Jewish, had aged in exile and were reluctant to return; those who had become Hitler's literary tools stood discredited and fell into limbo. A handful who had resisted and suffered were broken old men. To compound the problem, there were now two Germanies, and Berlin which had so valiantly sought to become the cultural as well as political capital, lost both after an historically brief reign. Deprived of writers and also of a center, German letters made a slow recovery. Until the emergence of Günther Grass in the early sixties, and previously perhaps of Heinrich Böll, Germany had no writers of note. Brecht was in East Germany, engaging in experiments in stagecraft. What achievements there were in German language theatre had to be credited to two Swiss, Frisch and Dürrenmatt. The Germans were busy catching up with literary developments abroad, kept from them during the years of darkness.

German letters needed young men. But what had the young seen? They had seen and even participated in Nazism, often on

142   KAHN — THE JEW IN POSTWAR GERMAN LITERATURE

parental order. By and large they were too young to understand. They had also seen war into which this Nazism had thrust them and the ugliness of which became manifest on the Eastern front or in bombed out cities at home. Hence it was the war novel which unmistakably dominated German letters in the first ten years after Hitler. Philosophically the early war novel was often a reaction against the charge of German collective guilt. Among those defending the German people as such was Hans Werner Richter whose *Die Geschlagenen* (Beyond Defeat) and *Sie fielen aus Gottes Hand* (They Fell from God's Hand) advanced the thesis that leadership had been to blame on both sides and not the mass of people. German leadership, of course, had been especially guilty and Richter was hoping for a Nazi defeat. But he had wished for defeat for the sake of the German people who deserved better than Hitlerism with which they had saddled themselves. In "They Fell from God's Hands" the failure to distinguish between degrees becomes almost unintelligent. Richter compares Israel's attitude towards the Arabs with those of the Nazis toward Jews. Yet his Jew, Salomon Galporin, is the most sympathetically delineated character in the novel. Richter's own political position could not be questioned. As a founder of the *Feuerwehr,* an organization of intellectuals fighting the resurgence of Nazi ideals and co-founder of the socially liberal Group 47 to which nearly all significant West German writers belong, his own sympathies were clearly established.

Some war novels much less honestly devolved the bulk of guilt on Hitler, advancing the usual apologetics. What could the individual soldier do against a powerfully entrenched, ruthless party which terrified even generals and army? Nevertheless, their chief purpose was hardly a moral whitewashing job. Again, Jews are used as symbols and tools and are not generally identified with names. The war novelists concede frankly that soldiers and civilians usually accepted the war and Hitler while the war was going well. In *Wir werden weiter marschieren* (We Shall March Again) Gerhard Krämer offers a transition from the early apologetics to the later acceptance of guilt by expressing fears over the recrudescence of the spirit which had led Germans astray previously. He stresses that for many Germans, Hitler's crime had been the fact of failure.

In general, the war novel depicts the German soldier as a nonpolitical being. But in several novels of the Eastern front, they see the dead bodies of disfigured Jews on the streets of Polish cities. They turn away in shame and disgust and wonder about the sense of such actions committed in their name. But by 1943 they have witnessed enough such scenes to have become impervious to them. Wolfgang Ott's *Haie und Kleine Fische* (Sharks and Little Fish), a novel of submarine warfare, presents some

Germans as incredulous of Nazi crimes against Jews, but he refuses to condone their ignorance. He assails their feeble "We didn't persecute the Jews" as a typical German argument. "In Germany," writes Ott, "when the bakeries are on fire, the butchers stand looking on, and vice-versa."

Also published at the end of the first post-Nazi decade was *Am Grünen Strand der Spree* (All Through the Night), by Hans Scholz, an art critic. It revolved around the experiences of Jurgen Wilm, a non-political, small factory owner, now with the Army in Poland, who witnesses the maltreatment of Jewish women. "What right has anyone to humiliate a human being to this extent?" asks Wilm. When he is threatened for taking photographs he asks, "If we think we are justified in taking measures against the Jews, we shouldn't have to hide it. Or don't we think we are justified?" Though he stands by doing nothing, he is horrified and recognizes his own guilt and responsibility.

But some writers have their heroes take action on behalf of Jews, a situation that would add dramatic dimension to any fiction. In Heinrich Böll's *Wo Warst du Adam?* (Where Were You Adam?) his hero after a few quick and innocent encounters falls in love with a Jewess in Poland. They finally see each other carted off in trucks which lead them, in opposite direction, to a tragic and ironic death. Perhaps Böll sought to comment on the bond that unites victim to victimizer. In *Feuer und Asche* (Fire and Ashes) by Felix Lützendorf, a guilt-ridden anti-Nazi intellectual, unhappily serving in the East, saves a Jewess from certain death, sacrificing his own life in the process. Their acts of conscience are not designed to stress German nobility, but rather to accentuate the contrast between what might have been and what was.

Powerful Novel of German Guilt

Perhaps the most powerful novel joining German past and present in guilt is *Der Tod in Rom*. Here, long after the end of the war, Judejahn, an unrepentant Nazi leader who had escaped in the waning years of the Reich to become a military advisor with the Arabs, has come to Rome to plan his return to Germany. He has done so at the suggestion of his brother-in-law Pfaffrath, an upper middle-class German who once before had helped the Judejahns to power, only then to recede cautiously into the background. Pfaffrath was now in the clear after the war and has had no difficulty becoming the mayor of his town. Judejahn's wife also joins them. She is still morosely dedicated to her Führer and blames her husband for not following him into Walhalla. Present also is Judejahn's son, who has become a priest to atone for the father's sins. Koeppen's thesis is clear. The Pfaffraths are prepared to help the ruthless Judejahns again. Judejahn, who recognizes a Jewish woman from his home town, and shoots her in a Roman window, is prepared to kill the Jews again. The opposition, represented through the weak members of the family, are still no match for the shrewd Pfaffrath or the criminal Judejahn. Significantly Koeppen sees in the Pfaffraths the clue to the German past and present. Since they have not changed, Koeppen is not filled with pleasant forebodings.

In much of the above literature the Jew is anonymous victim, a tool for recognizing or devolving guilt, an instrument for appraising the German situation. In a few other novels, notably Walter Jens' excellent *Der Blinde* (The Blind Man) and Albrecht Goes' much discussed *Das Brandopfer* (The Burnt Offering) the Jew emerges as a statuesque, semi-biblical symbol, possessing deep moral awareness, patriarchal wisdom, born of suffering and persecution. In *Der Blinde* Jens uses a concentration camp graduate to help a German school teacher gone blind to return to spiritual health. "The Burnt Offering" has a saintly rabbi perpetuate an image well known in philo-semitic literature.

Like Böll and Jens, Stefan Andres is one of the better known German literary figures. His *Sperrzone* is a short drama of guilt. Dr. Schneider, recently returned from a P.O.W. camp in Russia, visits a small German town seeking to establish itself as a resort. All is well, except the controversy over the uncomfortable cemetery located on the site of a former concentration camp for women. The local bigwigs, some of them erstwhile Nazis, want to be rid of the ugly cemetery which mars the town and which, according to what a child has been told, has *only* Jewesses in its graves. But young Welch, a teacher at the Gymnasium, opposes this move, eager as he is to teach his charges about the criminal past. He himself had "reason taken away from him at sixteen," but "in the prisoner camps it had come back with a vengeance." To the town leadership Welch is a nuisance. They work with his principal, the politically active and compliant Dr. Kaiser. The latter, with the town officials, wants the past forgotten. But this morning Kaiser was visited by the former director of the concentration camp who, in the closing days of the war, had tried to create a good image by warning Kaiser the camp was to be blown up. Kaiser had taken no action to save the women. Here is his guilt—silence and acquiescence. But Kaiser, like most Germans, had been raised to regard duty to the state the highest duty. That night Kaiser, the issues finally made clear by Schneider and Welch, resolves to side with those who remember and assume the unpopular and dangerous responsibility. The cemetery will remain.

Heinrich Böll's *Billiard um halb zehn* (Billiards at Half Past Nine) and especially *Ansichten eines Clowns* (The Clown) stamp him as a decidedly angry man. He is merciless in exposing the hypocrisies of German life, especially as they relate to the past. In "The Clown," Catholic Böll's ire is vented at those who have made a quick changeover from calling the approaching Americans "Jewish Yankees" to becoming chairmen of the "League for the Reconciliation of Racial Differences." He has no illusions about the present. "I'm afraid," states his clown, "of being spoken to by half drunk Germans of a certain age, they always talk about war, think it was wonderful, and when they are quite drunk it turns out they are murderers and think it wasn't really 'all that bad.' " Böll is equally aghast that a prominent Nazi who had killed a boy, manhandled the hero, spouted anti-Jewish doctrines in the closing hours of the war, should have received the Federal Cross of Merit "for his services in spreading democratic ideas about the young."

A Portrait of German-Jewish Relations

The dishonesty of the erstwhile Nazis is only equalled by their impertinence. The following passage, in a way, summarizes the portrait of German-Jewish relations in the contemporary German novel:

> I recalled having met him (the Nazi youth leader) at one of my parents' At Homes; he had looked at me beseechingly and shaken his head, while he was talking to a rabbi about "Jewish spirituality." I felt sorry for the rabbi. He was a very old man, with a white beard and very kind, and innocent in a way that worried me. Of course, Herbert told everyone he met that he had been a Nazi and an anti-Semite, but that "history had opened his eyes." And yet the very day before the Americans marched into Bonn, he had been practicing with the boys in our grounds and had told them: "The first Jewish swine you see, let him have it." What upset me about these At Homes of my mother's was the innocence of the returned emigrants. They were so moved by all the remorse and loud protestations of democracy that they were forever embracing and radiating good fellowship.

Christian Geissler is not likely to achieve Böll's literary power, largely because he cannot keep adequate distance from his subject. But few have displayed greater fire, conscience and courage in facing the heinous crimes toward Jews. *Die Anfrage* (The Inquiry), a semi-documentary novel, keeps raising the question just how it was possible for the then adults not to prevent the crimes toward Jews, or why this generation would wish to shroud its record in silence. Using as his leitmotif the proverb "The pride of the children is their father," Geissler argues that the restoration of this pride demands the end of silence and the frank avowal of past responsibility. In his effort to understand this past—to establish facts—Geissler's research minded hero encounters once more all the myths which brought Hitler to power and enabled him to destroy the Jews. Geissler later adapted *Die Anfrage* to television. His other TV play, *Das Schlachtvieh* (Slaughter Cattle), deals very emotionally with the exterminations. The Jews, of course, are the cattle led to slaughter.

The role of German and Jew as executioner and victim, and the scrutiny of the German Zeitgeist forms the focal point of several better than average novels. They are explored in Kasimir Edschmid's *Drei Häuser am Meer* (Three Houses by the Sea), Paul Schallücks *Engelbert Reineke,* Kurtmartin Magiera's *Tag und Nacht* (Day and Night) or Martin Walser's play *Eiche und Angora* (Oak and Angora). Occasionally there is a variation of the theme, as in Hans Keilson's *Der Tod des Widersachers* (Death of the Opponent), which is less concerned with the hatred between victim and executioner than a polarity of repulsion and attraction, creating, as one critic put it, a suprapersonal solidarity between them.

As the most important German writer today Günther Grass has, of course, also dealt with this question. But the viewpoint and approach are similar with only Grass' highly distinctive style and manner to set him apart. In "Dog Years" he advanced what seemed to be the theory of a love-hate relationship between German and Jew, with each representing a pole of human values (see above). To put over his theory, Grass needed a Jewish character. But a Jew living openly in war time in Germany was not feasible and Grass had to content himself with a half-Jew. Grass' half-Jew, however, has very little of the Jew in him. On the whole, his treatment is not convincing because his half-Jew is just that, and the half that is supposedly Jewish is that only because Grass tells us it is.

Jews are again writing in German, though not in Germany. Jakob Lind wrote *Eine Seele aus Holz* (The Soul of Wood) in England; Peter Weiss wrote *Marat/Sade* and *Die Ermittlung* (The Invesigation), not to speak of *Abschied von den Eltern* (The Leave), in Sweden; Ilse Aichinger, a half-Jewess, at one time wrote out of Vienna. The ghost of Auschwitz and local persecutions loom large in the work of these most talented of Jewish writers employing the German tongue today. Other novels by Jewish writers, which so far have appeared in German only, are Soma Morgenstern's biblical novel of the Holocaust, *Die Blutsäule* (Statue of Blood), the late Nicholas Lothar's not very credible *Der Richter und die Söhne* (The Judge and His Sons), to name some of the more recent. These novels obviously are different in interest and tone and merit entirely separate consideration.

To sum up, the Jew is anonymous in contemporary German fiction; he is a symbol, devoid of flesh and blood, a victim before the German executioners and silent witnesses. The authors are aware that in the attitude toward the past, the tendency to be reticent on it or to find worthless, empty excuses, lies the key to the German future. In general, the writers are too full of their subject to treat it well in terms of art, but moral chaos lends itself little to artistic treatment. The authors appear further aware that the collective guilt with which some non-Germans have saddled Germany in postwar years is beyond comparison with the collective guilt which their leaders heaped upon Jews for the purpose of destroying them. German literature today tends to view the Jew with awe and reverence, as a non-human or supra-human figure. Increasingly there is evidence of little physical contact with Jews which is at least partly responsible for the symbolification. Whereas such popular media as comic strips, newspaper feuilletons, and the like, have not shown this tendency, the overwhelming majority of serious German writers wants to face the past, in justice to Jews, but even more for the sake of their own personal and national future.

MEANING AND DESPAIR IN THE LITERATURE OF THE SURVIVORS

By Irving Halperin

We stumbled on in the darkness, over big stones and through large puddles, along the one road leading from the camp. The accompanying guards kept shouting at us and driving us with the butts of their rifles. Anyone with very sore feet supported himself on his neighbor's arm. Hardly a word was spoken; the icy wind did not encourage talk. Hiding his mouth behind his upturned collar, the man marching next to me whispered suddenly: "If our wives could see us now! I do hope they are better off in their camps and don't know what is happening to us."

That brought thoughts of my own wife to mind. And as we stumbled on for miles, slipping on icy spots, supporting each other time and again, dragging one another up and onward, nothing was said, but we both knew: each of us was thinking of his wife. Occasionally I looked at the sky, where the stars were fading and the pink light of the morning was beginning to spread behind a dark bank of clouds. But my mind clung to my wife's image, imagining it with uncanny acuteness. I heard her answering me, saw her smile, her frank and encouraging look. Real or not, her look was then more luminous than the sun which was beginning to rise.

VIKTOR FRANKL, *From Death-Camp to Existentialism*

So our nights drag on. The dream of Tantalus and the dream of the story are woven into a texture of more indistinct images: the suffering of the day, composed of hunger, blows, cold, exhaustion, fear and promiscuity, turns at night-time into shapeless nightmares of unheard-of violence, which in free life would only occur during a fever. One wakes up at every moment, frozen with terror, shaking in every limb, under the impression of an order shouted out by a voice full of anger in a language not understood. The procession to the bucket and the thud of bare heels on the wooden floor turns into another symbolic procession: it is us again, grey and identical, small as ants, yet so huge as to reach up

148

to the stars, bound one against the other, countless, covering the plain as far as the horizon; sometimes melting into a single substance, a sorrowful turmoil in which we all feel ourselves trapped and suffocated; sometimes marching in a circle, without beginning or end, with a blinding giddiness and a sea of nausea rising from the praecordia to the gullet; until hunger or cold or the fullness of our bladders turn our dreams into their customary forms.

PRIMO LEVI, *If This Is a Man*

Felled to the ground, stunned with blows, the old man cried:

"Meir. Meir, my boy! Don't you recognize me? I'm your father . . . you're hurting me . . . you're killing your father! I've got some bread . . . for you too . . . for you too . . ."

He collapsed. His fist was still clenched around a small piece. He tried to carry it to his mouth. But the other one threw himself upon him and snatched it. The old man again whispered something, let out a rattle, and died amid the general indifference. His son searched him, took the bread, and began to devour it. He was not able to get very far. Two men had seen and hurled themselves upon him. Others joined in. When they withdrew, next to me were two corpses, side by side, the father and the son.

I was fifteen years old.

ELIE WIESEL, *Night*

I learnt that within me, as in others, the murderer and the humanitarian exist side by side; the weak child with the voracious male. That I am not in any way superior, that I am not different from others, that I am but a link in the great chain, was among the greatest discoveries of my life. From then on I resolved to support those who fell, even as I had been supported. When someone was despicable, greedy and selfish, I remembered all the occasions when I, too, had been despicable, greedy and selfish. Buchenwald taught me to be tolerant of myself, and by that means tolerant of others.

EUGENE HEIMLER, *Night of the Mist*

Four statements by four authors and two essential points of view: to survive as a prisoner in the camps one had to descend to the level of animals; and, conversely, despite the brutalizing conditions in the camps, it was possible for a prisoner to be impressively human. There is, of course, nothing unique about this two-sided observation. One would expect that there were as many different kinds of behavior among the prisoners as there were environmental differences from camp to camp; for example, it was generally easier for a prisoner in a so-called "model" camp like Sachsenhausen to maintain a semblance of composure than prisoners who were exposed to substantially greater hardships and pressures in Auschwitz. All this is to underscore the self-evident: so many prisoners, so many camps, so many conditions. Therefore it is not for us to assert cavalierly that this and this former prisoner conducted himself commendably whereas this and this prisoner carried on badly. Especially those of us who were spared the ordeal of being "there" have not earned the right to make such easy value judgments.

Then why the opening four quotations and the above statement about the two essential points of view they represent? For one, this arrangement is intended to provide a principle of organization for some key issues in the personal narratives. Also, the opposing views represented by the above quotations underscore the opposing evaluations of some survivor-writers as they look back at the past; those who, on the one hand, contend that in a time when men bestially defiled and disfigured the bodies and spirits of other men, suicide or madness or nihilism for any self-respecting person would have been understandable and who aver that there was no such thing as "transcending" one's suffering in the camps, that the Nazis were beasts and they made beasts of the prisoners. And, on the other hand, those survivor-writers who believe that many of the oppressed in the camps were ennobled by their suffering.

What follows, then, is an examination of some widely acclaimed personal narratives* (in this genre I include Elie Wiesel's autobiographical novel, *Night,* whose point of view is essentially that of personal narration).

A Depressing Body of Literature

Such an unbearably depressing body of literature! But are there any places in it which "lift up" the reader? In affirmative response to this question, we can look to *From Death Camp to Existentialism* (New York, 1964) by Viktor Frankl, a professor of psychiatry and neurology at the University of Vienna. A number of incidents in this important book point up the spiritual resources of some remarkable human beings. First, there is the unforgettable scene where Frankl buoys up the spirits of his fellow-prisoners. This happened at a time when the morale of the men in his hut was at a dangerously low point. Hungry and cold, plagued by lice, illnessess and severe depression, they despaired of going on; it seemed to them that their

---

* They are sometimes referred to as eye-witness accounts.

suffering was senseless, that it would be better to give up, die and be done with the daily torture. From such despair the next step downwards was to become a Mussulman, a member of the living-dead, they who were almost beyond pain. In this dark moment a senior block warden, knowing of Frankl's background as a psychiatrist, persuaded him to offer his disconsolate comrades a "medical care for their souls."

One evening after work, Frankl spoke to them. He sought to instill in them a justification, a moral sanction, for attempting to live through their unbearable circumstances. He encouraged them to bear their suffering with whatever dignity possible; to be, in short, as Dostoevsky used the phrase—and Frankl frequently alludes to it—*worthy* of their suffering. As the present was a nightmare, he began by speaking to them of the past and future.

Frankl himself is ailing, hungry, cold, despondent; so he is scarcely in a frame of mind to minister to others. Yet he says that their situation, though extremely grave, is not altogether futile; some of them will survive; they need to "hold on" and hope for the best. But it would not have taken an extraordinary man to say this much to them. Inmates of the camps frequently exhorted one another to hold on, to *iber-lebyn* (to remain alive). What makes Frankl's exhortation distinctive are the power and depth of his remarks. Even if they perish, he suggests, whatever they have experienced in the past is not lost.

> Again I quoted a poet—to avoid sounding like a preacher myself—who had written, *"Was Du erlebt, kann keine Macht der Welt Dir rauben."* (What you have experienced, no power on earth can take from you.) Not only our experiences, but all we have done, whatever great thoughts we may have had, and all we have suffered, all this is not lost, though it is past; we have brought it into being. Having been is also a kind of being, and perhaps the surest kind. (p. 131)

Then he turns to the present, to their situation in the camp. His comrades lay motionless, listening attentively, as he goes on to speak of the spiritual challenge before each man: the necessity to be "worthy" of one's suffering and to find some meaning in their seemingly senseless situation.

> I told my comrades . . . that human life, under any circumstances, never ceases to have a meaning, and that this infinite meaning of life includes suffering and dying, privation and death. I asked the poor creatures who listened to me attentively in the darkness of the hut to face up

to the seriousness of our position. They must not lose hope but should keep their courage in the certainty that the hopelessness of our struggle did not detract from its dignity and meaning. I said that someone looks down on each of us in difficult hours—a friend, a wife, somebody alive or dead, or a God—and he would not expect us to disappoint him. He would hope to find us suffering proudly—not miserably—knowing how to die. (pp.131-132)

"Knowing how to die . . ." How remarkable! To encourage one another to die with dignity in, of all places, an extermination camp! His words invoke accounts of observant Jews who went to their deaths in the gas chambers with heads high, backs straight, singing *Ani Maamin* ("I Believe"). So, too, in *The Holocaust Kingdom* (New York, 1965), Lena Donat recalls the way in which some Greek Jewish women went to the gas chambers (p. 306):

When they went to their deaths they sang the "Hatik-vah," the song of an old people which has always carried the vision of Zion in its heart. Since then every time I hear "Hatikvah" I always see them, the dregs of human misery, and I know that through mankind flows a stream of eternity greater and more powerful than individual deaths.

What was the immediate result of Frankl's remarks to his comrades? He remembers that at the conclusion of his words, he saw "the miserable figures of my friends limping toward me to thank me with tears in their eyes." With striking humility, Frankl does not consider this response an occasion for self-congratulations; for in the sentence directly following the one just cited, he adds: "But I have to confess here that only too rarely had I the inner strength to make contact with my companions in suffering and that I must have missed many opportunities for doing so."

How are we to view this incident? Men are ill, in pain; they need food, warmth. Frankl offers them only words—yet the words touch responsive chords in them, and they come forward to express their gratitude. In other parts of the camp, the SS are sadistically humiliating, torturing, murdering. Defenseless men and women are shot, Germans dispose of thousands with phenol injections, prisoners are hanged on the courtyard gallows, the infamous camp official, Boger, employs his "typewriter"* with zeal. These are the self-styled cultured and civilized Germans. In contrast, the conduct of Frankl and his

---

* A form of torture devised by this despicable camp official.

comrades; these "sub-humans" probe into the farthest reaches of the spirit while the "superior" Aryans lash out with truncheons and fists. In this perspective, then, when Frankl's comrades came toward him with tears of gratitude in their eyes, we can understand why there was a genuine release of spiritual elation in Auschwitz.

There are other equally moving incidents in the book. To dwell lovingly on the image of one's wife and to take immense pleasure from seeing the forms of Nature, these, too, were ways of giving meaning to one's wretched existence in the camps. For such reflection and observation helped him to find a *why* to live for—to recall Nietzsche's saying: "He who has a *why* to live for can bear almost any *how*."

One "why" was through love. Although he had no way of knowing where she was—or whether she was even still alive—Frankl often thought of his wife. Nothing, he avows, could diminish the strength of his love.

> Had I known then that my wife was dead, I think that I would still have given myself, undisturbed by that knowledge, to the contemplation of her image, and that my mental conversation with her would have been just as vivid and just as satisfying. "Set me like a seal upon thy heart, love is as strong as death." (p. 61)

In the camp men are proficient in the means of hate, Nazi-style, and yet Frankl wills to love! He is mercilessly beaten with the butts of rifles, forced to walk for miles through darkness and over ice; and yet, astonishingly, his mind clings to an image of his wife. Sometimes the intensity and radiance of this image makes it more real than the all too palpable landmarks of fences, huts, watchtowers, crematoria. And once, in a particularly black moment, Frankl feels he has grasped the deeper meaning of human love.

> A thought transfixed me: for the first time in my life I saw the truth as it is set into song by so many poets, proclaimed as the final wisdom by so many thinkers. The truth —that love is the ultimate and the highest goal to which man can aspire. Then I grasped the meaning of the greatest secret that human poetry and human thought and belief have to impart: *The salvation of man is through love and in love.*

The point is that it was in Auschwitz, in *annus mundi,* as the Nazis referred to it, he perceived this "truth"; before then it apparently had been for him only a theoretical generalization. Thus, in the greatest extermination center of recorded history,

Frankl experienced on his very pulses the validity of love as the "final wisdom."

A Mystical Experience

Furthermore, just as it is remarkable that his devotion transcended the physical absence of his wife, so, too, not even the coldest days nor the abuse of the guards could quash his feelings for her. He would recall her face, voice, and this would help to sustain him through cycles of exhaustion, hunger, depression. On one especially memorable occasion, a freezing winter dawn, as he was at work in a trench under the surveillance of a sadistic guard, he seems to have had a mystical experience.

> For hours I stood hacking at the icy ground. The guard passed by, insulting me, and once again I communed with my beloved. More and more I felt that she was present, that she was with me; I had the feeling that I was able to touch her, able to stretch out my hand and grasp hers. The feeling was very strong: she was *there*. Then, at that very moment, a bird flew down silently and perched just in front of me, on the heap of soil which I had dug up from the ditch, and looked steadily at me. (p. 64)

What is the value of one such "mystical" moment, it may properly be asked, against the twelve years of destruction? For every such transcendent experience there were thousands of banal ones. The day by day "banality" of men and women being reduced to Mussulmen, dehumanized and murdered. Is it "mystical" to expire in a gas chamber? Or to be shot down at the infamous Black Wall of Auschwitz? Or burned alive in a ditch?

And yet it would be unfortunate if the significance of this incident were minimized. For prior to its occurrence, Frankl had despaired that his suffering was meaningless. He and his fellow prisoners were clad in rags; they stood hacking away at the icy ground; gloom enveloped him, and he felt that death drew near. Altogether, the moment was no less grim than the one in which Camus' Sysyphus finds himself before his decision to keep rolling a stone up the hill. Precisely then, when his suffering was at a nadir, Frankl came to reflect on an image of his wife. And while he was "conversing silently" with her, he heard a "Yes," as though in response to the question—"Is there any meaning to all this?"

Just then, as though to indicate some sign under the "miserable grey" sky, a light went on in a distant farm house. The Yes and the light were immediately followed by the appearance of the bird. All these "responses" to Frankl's question served to shape his belief in an ultimate higher meaning of human existence; and he felt he had found a "why" to live for.

As Frankl's inner life became more intensely attuned to the memories of his wife and to the spiritual needs of his comrades, he apparently became more open to the beauty of the physical world beyond the barbed wire. On one occasion he was moved by a view of nearby mountains with their summits glowing in the distance. Another time he was arrested by an especially beautiful sunset. Here the sky was as a light shining through the darkness, and the peacefulness and beauty of Nature appeared to him as evidence of the essential health of the universe.

The astonishing capacity of human beings! The prisoners were hungry and cold, plagued by illness, harrassed by guards, and yet they would respond powerfully to a sunset, the song of a lark, a flowering meadow.*

Ultimately, then, Frankl came to see his ordeal in Auschwitz as a spiritual challenge which he wanted to be "worthy" of. Determined to "get through"** his suffering, he, in effect, said to himself: this apparently is how my lot must be for a time: meanwhile, it is important to be composed, inside and outside, and to be of good courage.

> When a man finds that it is his destiny to suffer, he will have to accept his suffering as his task; the fact that even in suffering he is unique and alone in the universe. No one can relieve him of his suffering or suffer in his place. His unique opportunity lies in the way in which he bears his burden. (pp. 123-124)

What Frankl learned in the camps was not to "go around" his suffering, nor to look at it as something abnormal, tangential to his existence but rather as a spiritual test—a test that had to be squarely confronted with toughness of mind, compassion for the anguish of one's comrades and trust in the ultimate meaning of the ordeal. In the face of all that was Auschwitz, the will to believe that something significant might be taking place within one's self was an extraordinary expression of spiritual freedom. Within this perspective, Frankl's experiences as a prisoner are instructive for contemporary readers who wish to probe the moral center of holocaust literature.

---

* Thus the response of another kind of prisoner in Holland, Anne Frank, to a blue sky and sunny day:
  "As long as this exists," I thought, "and I may live to see it, this sunshine, the cloudless skies, while this lasts, I cannot be unhappy."
** Here Frankl has reference to Rilke's saying—*"Wie viel ist aufzuleiden!"* (How much suffering there is to get through!). Rilke spoke of "getting through suffering" as others would talk of "getting through work."

How Men Remained Human

It is important to dwell on the spiritual resistance of survivors like Frankl. It is well to realize that there were men in the camps who lifted up their fellow-sufferers, who were moved by sunsets, the sight of flowers growing beside barbed wire. For although we have mountains of evidence documenting what was destroyed during the twelve Hitler years, we are far from glutted by accounts, like Frankl's, of the ways in which men remained impressively human.

But—and this is a big word here—just as it is important to know that some prisoners could not be spiritually broken by their imprisonment, so, too, it is important to realize that we have been discussing an exceptional man; few are capable of Frankl's iron-willed resolve—and ability—to conduct himself with pride and courage in Auschwitz. Hence almost at the poles from Frankl's affirmative, will-to-meaning perspective is a view which has been preeminently represented by Primo Levi, the celebrated Italian-Jewish writer, in *If This Is a Man* (New York, 1961).

We do not believe in the most obvious and facile deduction: that man is fundamentally brutal, egoistic and stupid in his conduct once every civilized institution is taken away, and that the Häftling is consequently nothing but a man without inhibitions. We believe, rather, that the only conclusion to be drawn is that in the face of driving necessity and physical disabilities many social habits and instincts are reduced to silence. (p. 79)

". . . many social habits and instincts are reduced to silence." What exactly is meant here? *What* social habits did Levi see "reduced to silence" in Auschwitz? His observations therein began with his arrival at the camp in early 1944; he was then 24. Overnight he found himself in a nether universe where blows, cold, hunger and death were the order of the day. A year later he took stock of his circumstances; and no writer on the Holocaust has written a more somber statement on how such an experience alters a man.

This time last year I was a free man: an outlaw but free, I had a name and a family, I had an eager and restless mind, an agile and healthy body. I used to think of many, far-away things: of my work, of the end of the war, of good and evil, of the nature of things and of the laws which govern human actions; and also of the mountains of singing and loving, of music, of poetry. I had an enormous, deep-rooted foolish faith in the benevolence of fate; to kill and to die seemed extraneous literary things to me. My days were both cheerful and sad, but I regretted them equally, they were all full and positive; the future stood before me as a great treasure. Today the only thing left of the life of these days is what one needs to suffer hunger and cold; I am not even alive enough to know how to kill myself. (p. 130)

Levi soon realized that to exist from day to day in Auschwitz, one had to make compromises with his usual standards of ethics and morality. Prisoners were encouraged by the German camp officials to feel that each man had to look after only Number One. Their captors had taken almost everything away from them—their clothing, hair, and even their names; the Nazis often referred to them merely by the numbers tattooed on their flesh. Indeed, the only thing the former could not take away from them was their resolve to hang on, as long as possible, to a sense of their own identity.*

In such circumstances survival often depended, Levi observed, on being cunning, selfish, ruthless; sometimes it depended, alas, on serving as an informer. Further, to resist the pressures which turned the resigned into Mussulmen, one had to wear an inner armor which was resistant to pity and, above all, hope; for hope could be still another source of disappointment and pain. Rather the imprisoned were constrained to become inwardly as hard as steel so that they would not break. The suffering of the prisoners did not make for saints; brutalized, starving men compromised their usual moral principles for a piece of bread.

Thus in the world of the Lager where men had to be "less than human," where aberration and compromise were the rule not the exception, where men found it wise not to try to "understand" what was happening to them, certain traditional social habits and values were, of necessity, "reduced to silence." Within this perspective, then, Levi poses the question, "Would it have made sense for a prisoner to adhere to a well-defined and structured system of ethics and morals? His answer is in the negative. What the world outside the camp considered "virtue" was not desirable from Levi's viewpoint or from that of his fellow-prisoners. In the Lager, the familiar meanings of the words "good," "evil," "just" and "unjust" were blurred. Auschwitz and Buchenwald were hardly ideal settings for maintaining moral

---

* For example, the resolve of Tania in Zdena Berger's novel *Tell Me Another Morning* (New York, 1961) :
The only thing that remains is the I in me. I find suddenly some strange pleasure in knowing that when I die I will die the same, unchanged, as when I was me. It matters very much. Yes, as I was.
Keep that last thing. Hang on to it as to the last wall. (p. 78)

absolutes. If ever there was a time and place when the practice of an ethical relativism or situational ethics could have been justified, it was in the Lager.

The question bitterly raised by Levi at the end of his narrative is—"Are these, the survivors of Auschwitz, actually men?" The last chapter describes the miserable conditions confronting Levi and his comrades after the Germans had fled and while they were waiting for the Russians to arrive. Everywhere, prisoners, "starving specters," "unshaven with hollow eyes, greyish skeleton bones in rags" lay dying from typhus, pneumonia, scarlet fever, dysentery and tuberculosis. Allied bombs had cut off the water and electricity supply. Latrines were overflowing, for no one had the strength to look after their maintenance. During below zero weather, the central heating system was inoperative and windows were broken in some of the huts. Even those who were comparatively well felt inert and helpless. Levi saw "ragged, decrepit, skeleton-like" prisoners dragging themselves over "the frozen soil, like an invasion of worms." Many corpses lay exposed in the snow; and others, "rigid as wood," rested on bunks in the huts. In the wards of the camp infirmary, lying in frozen excre-ment, patients continually cried out for help that could not be given to them. Some died slowly, torturously, and in the grip of delirium.

I have deliberately underscored the details of the misery which gripped Levi and his comrades as they waited some ten days for the Russians to arrive. Perhaps it would be well if these details were to be repeated again and again, like the words of a dirge, for they are emblematic of the anguish that men inflicted upon men in our time.

Death as a Merciful Deliverer

It is not surprising, then, that in such an inferno some would prefer death to life, like the former woman prisoner at Auschwitz who was found hiding among the bone piles of the dead in a barracks. When asked what she was doing there, she replied, "I prefer to be with the dead."* After having been witness to the most degrading scenes of the twentieth century, many prisoners did not want to return to the "civilized" world. "Enough!" they must have cried out from the depths and given up the fierce daily struggle for clinging to life. Untouchables in their own eyes and in the eyes of others, they may have eventually looked to death as a merciful deliverer.

* Bernard Naumann, *Auschwitz* (New York, 1966) , p. 132.

And yet here one recalls Frankl thinking lovingly of his wife while working on a winter dawn in a ditch. The ground is icy, the guard supervising the prisoners hurls insults at Frankl, but the latter is sustained by dwelling on an image of his wife. By comparison, it is a rare moment in Levi's *If This Is a Man* when prisoners are actually shown thinking of their loved ones. The most notable exception to this condition occurs once when Levi and his hut-mates have an unexpected windfall—an extra portion of rancid soup and turnips. They eat, feel content, stronger, and *then only* are "able to think of our mothers and wives, which usually does not happen." Did not often happen when a prisoner was starving, because then he might have only enough strength to think about one thing: bread.

Given the nature of his experiences, there is wisdom and courage in Levi's reluctance to reach for moral absolutes or "transcending" experiences. Not for him discourses on "love," "meaning," "beauty." Perhaps his morality is the stark honesty with which he documents the view that to survive in Auschwitz one had to become *less* than human. For we recognize the terrible clarity of what he says to us at the end of his book: there is no "meaning" to be gleaned from the story of this wanton destruction; it was all cruelly senseless. And because finally we were liberated does not mean that we won a victory over our oppressors. In the end, though freed, we were defeated; in reality the Germans, though vanquished, emerged the victors. They "won" because by the time the day of liberation came we had already been reduced to the state of animals. Hence the tone of what must be one of the most profoundly disquieting passages in holocaust literature.

> We lay in a world of death and phantoms. The last trace of civilization had vanished around and inside us. The work of bestial degradation, begun by the victorious Germans, had been carried to its conclusion by the Germans in defeat.

> It is man who kills, man who creates or suffers injustice; it is no longer man who, having lost all restraint, shares his bed with a corpse. Whoever waits for his neighbor to die in order to take his piece of bread is, albeit guiltless, further from the model of thinking man than the most primitive pigmy or the most vicious sadist. (p. 150)

There can be no more tragic commentary than Levi's on what was done by men to men in our time. When the prisoners pounced like beasts upon the bread which was given to them, their liberators could not have readily pictured that these half skeletons had once spoken of Truth and Beauty, Goodness and Justice? The liberated had come through cold, starvation, torture, and yet, in any ultimate reckoning, they had not really been freed. Many would long be enchained by recurring feelings of guilt and shame for having survived. Survived? In body, yes, but internally they were still back in the camps. Hence the next to last sentence of *Night* when Eliezer first looks at himself in a mirror, "a corpse gazed back at me."

Bodies in calcium chloride, infants killed by lethal injections and placed in bodies, prisoners sharing their bunks with corpses, prisoners stealing bread from the sick and dying—this is what some of the survivors remember looking back on their days in the camps. In contrast, Frankl remembers how his comrades and he responded to sunsets, to the singing of Italian arias. How, following his liberation, he walked through the country for miles, hearing the joyous sounds of larks; and that at some point during this walk he looked up at the sky and then went down on his knees, thinking: "I called to the Lord from my narrow prison and He answered me in the freedom of space." Granted, Frankl's "rebirth" in the fields needs to be valued for what it says about the capacity of human beings to weather despair and loss and still seek spiritual resurrection. But saying this much is not to stipulate that Frankl's religious experience ought to call forth from the reader an entirely affirmative response; his spiritual achievement here has to be seen in scale. For surely the center of holocaust literature is not concerned with a few remarkable men who may have transcended their suffering but rather with the millions who were destroyed. Resurrection may follow death, the phoenix may rise from the ashes, but paeans of praise to human endurance and spiritual resistance can not turn ashes back into warm living bodies.

Still, any balanced computation of the tragic facts must include recognition of some extraordinary ways in which the oppressed turned a human face to one another. Neither Primo Levi or Elie Wiesel, grim as their reports are, deny the crucial importance of human relationships in the camps; indeed, they point out that to the extent the prisoners helped one another their ordeal was given a semblance of meaning. True, not the kind of "meaning" which evolved from dwelling on an image of one's beloved or from being moved by a sunset or from giving a "pep talk" to one's despondent hut mates; rather the "meaning" derived from responding compassionately to the needs of one's comrades-in-suffering. Hence in *Night* the advice given by a Polish prisoner at Auschwitz to newly arrived inmates:

> . . . let there be comradeship among you. We are all brothers, and we are all suffering the same fate. The same smoke floats over all our heads. Help one another. (p. 50)

An when the veteran has finished speaking, Eliezer thinks: "The first human words." Similarly, Levi acknowledges the importance of his relationship with an Italian civilian:

> I believe that it was really due to Lorenzo that I am alive today; and not so much for his material aid, as for his having constantly reminded me by his presence, by his natural and plain manner of being good, that there still existed a just world outside our own, something and someone still pure and whole, not corrupt, not savage, extraneous to hatred and terror; something difficult to define, a remote possibility of good, but for which it was worth surviving. (p. 111)

In the last days of Auschwitz, Primo Levi, as we indicated earlier, existed in a "world of death and phantoms"; starving prisoners waited to steal a piece of bread from the weak and defenseless; in the dispensary, the sick and dying lay beside corpses; the bodies of the dead rose out of ditches, latrines overflowed . . . Even so, embittered as he is by the knowledge of what men did to men during that time, the last words of his book describe the healing influence of human friendship. We see Levi and his friends Arthur and Charles by a stove at night, smoking cigarettes made of herbs, and listening to gunfire sounds in the distance. "In the middle of this endless plain, frozen and full of war, we felt at peace with ourselves and with the world." Sitting with his friends by the stove, Levi felt that they were beginning to change from Häflinge (prisoners) to men again. In Levi's words:

> Part of our existence lies in the feelings of those near to us. This is why the experience of someone who has lived for days during which man was merely a thing in the eyes of man is non-human. We three were for the most part immune from it, and we owe each other mutual gratitude. (p. 156)

Giving to others—this, too, is the last word of Eugene Heimler's *Night of the Mist*. Heimler was twenty-one when the Germans invaded Hungary in the spring of 1944. His father was arrested and never seen again. His wife and family were deported to Auschwitz and died there. Heimler survived Buchenwald and other camps.

Before his imprisonment, Heimler felt—and apparently with good reason—that Hungarian Christians treated him as though he were a second-class citizen. Looked upon as an inferior person, he came to think of himself as one; in consequence, he was plagued by self-hatred and doubt. Perhaps in an attempt to compensate for his frequent sense of being rejected by others, he became very competitive and sought to "show the world" that he was "twice as good" as those who looked down at him.

In Buchenwald he outgrew this immature need. There he learned that he had to answer to no one but himself. From the beginning of his internment, he was thrown back upon his own resources; and the more these supported him the more he developed a sense of self-esteem. Gradually, as he came to see that he was being tested by Buchenwald, his inner strength was revealed to him. And—he discovered the deeper ways in which he was bound to other men.

> It was in Buchenwald that I learned, from Jews, Christians, Moslems and pagans, from Englishmen, Serbs, Rumanians, Czechs, Frenchmen, Belgians, Dutch, Russians, Greeks, Albanians, Poles and Italians that I was only one more suffering insignificant man . . . I learned that within me, as in others, the murderer and the humanitarian exist side by side; the weak child with the voracious male. That I am not in any way superior, that I am not different from others, that I am but a link in the great chain, was among the greatest discoveries of my life." (pp. 158-159)

In sum, having come to accept his own worth, he was able to accept the worth of others and to feel responsible for their welfare.

The most noteworthy example of his readiness to help others occurred when he was elected to be the protector of sixteen young boys who had been brought to Buchenwald. Heimler probably saved their lives—but for his intervention, they very likely would have gone to the gas chamber—by getting permission from an SS officer to let them peel potatoes in the camp's kitchen. Working with these children before the ovens, he would attempt to feed their inquiring minds. He would speak to them about "democracy, about the world we hoped for after the war—a world where one would have enough to eat and be able to roam the streets freely, where everybody would be able to think what he liked and say what he thought . . ."

At night in the barracks, they would ask him such questions as "whether there had ever lived another Hitler who had destroyed other people," about the "differences between Judaism and Christianity, and whether Jesus was really the Son of God." In being their teacher, Heimler felt the power of his humanity; and thus, by his actions, he had earned the right to respond to the question posed by a fellow-prisoner, Dr. Ekstein: "Tell me, on what does it depend whether a man remains a man?"

Frankl speaking to fellow-prisoners of his hut, attempting to lift up their morale; Heimler in Buchenwald ministering to sixteen children; Frankl kneeling in the fields and offering thanksgiving to God for his deliverance from the camps. Compare these scenes with the endings of *Night* and *If This Is a Man:* Eliezer's corpse-life face staring back at him in the mirror; the accumulating dead bodies in Levi's hut.

The Lessons To Be Learned

Given these differences, how should one conclude this investigation? It would be comforting to do so by paying tribute to those prisoners who apparently were "worthy" of their suffering. But ending here on a bright note would not be appropriate. Still, one need not go to the other extreme by asserting that there are no "lessons" to be derived from the reading of these accounts. Perhaps all that should be said is that almost any man, even those with exceptional inner strength, could be dehumanized. That resolution and courage did not necessarily prevail against starvation, cold, disease, beatings. That even thoughtful and intelligent men did not find meaning in the sufferings or find them spiritually "challenging." And that many who survived did so at considerable expense to their humanity.

There is perhaps one slim consolation: despite the general condition that each man was fiercely alone in the struggle for survival, some prisoners apparently drew sustenance from their kinship with others. Their captors had almost succeeded in turning them into animals but through the grace of those who ministered to their needs, or who were helped by them, they came to feel like men again. In so doing they recognized the value of Alyosha's words to the boys at the end of *The Brothers Karamazov*: Help one another.

And yet there can be no truly substantive consolation. We may assume the instances of human goodness during the Hitler era; nevertheless, a hard light needs to be focused and kept on the suffering and loss and brutality. Men died by the millions, and words in memorium to the spiritual achievements of a few remarkable men are as nothing against that indictment. Studies on the Holocaust cannot resurrect the dead. The communities they once comprised are destroyed. Many of the survivors are marked for life. Nothing can alter those tragic facts.

Love of Books

HEBREW AUTHORS AND HOLY WRITING

A Miscellany*

COMPILED BY SHMUEL YOSEF AGNON

TO EACH HIS OWN TORAH SCROLL

Rava said: Even one who inherits a Torah scroll from his parents should write a scroll of his own, as it is written, "Now therefore write this song for yourselves" (Deut. 31. 19).

THE TORAH LETTERS

The six hundred thousand letters in the Torah correspond to the six hundred thousand Israelites who stood at Mount Sinai; everyone of them was deemed worthy to have a letter inscribed in the Torah in his name. (Iggeret ha-Tiyul)

GOD—WEAVER OF CROWNS

When Moses ascended on high he found the Holy One, blessed be He, sitting and weaving crowns for the Torah letters. "Sovereign of the universe," said Moses, "who compels Thee to do this?" He replied: "After many generations a man will appear, Akiba ben Joseph by name, who will expound innumerable laws for each tip of every letter." (Menahot 29b)

A SCRIBE'S QUILL

Rabbi Moses Zabara, a noted ancient sage, copied Torah scrolls with dedicated fervor out of devotion to his Maker. His method was to write the entire Torah, leaving blank spaces for the ineffable Name. On completing the scroll he would engage in ablutions and fasting that whole day; after which he would insert

---

* Translated by Maurice T. Galpert and revised and prepared for publication by the editor.

Reprinted from S. Y. Agnon's *Sefer Sofer ve-Sipur,* Schocken Publishing House Ltd., Jerusalem, Tel Aviv. Copyright © 1967 by Schocken Books Inc., New York, New York.

the Divine Name with a special pen reserved for that purpose. When he was about to die, he directed that this pen be placed in his hand for the burial. His disciples forgot their master's request, and when the time came to carry his coffin they could not lift it. Recalling his request, they hastened to bring the pen and placed it in his hand, whereupon the coffin became light enough to be carried. (Malkhe Rabbanan)

PROPHECIES WITH A LESSON

Many prophets arose in Israel—twice the number of Israelites who went out of Egypt. However, only those prophecies were written down which contained significant lessons for future generations; the others were not reduced to writing. (Megillah 14a)

THE BOOK OF RAZIEL

Whosoever seeks to acquire wisdom should read each day the *Book of the Angel Raziel* from cover to cover. Any home possessing this volume will be protected from fire, loss, or destruction of any kind. (Sefer Raziel 40a)

BEGINNING AND END

The Mishnah begins with an open *mem* and concludes with a closed *mem,* to teach that when one begins to study he believes the whole spectrum of knowledge is open to him, but when he finishes he discovers that a great deal of knowledge is still a closed door to him. (Peer le-Yesharim 16)

THE SIX ORDERS OF THE MISHNAH

Whenever Rabbi Hanina and Rabbi Hiyya engaged in a dispute, Rabbi Hanina would say to Rabbi Hiyya, "Would you dispute with me? If, heaven forbid, the Torah were forgotten in Israel, I would restore it through the efficacy of my argumentation." Rabbi Hiyya replied, "Would you argue with me who made possible that the Torah should not be forgotten in Israel? What did I do? I began by sowing flax seeds from which I wove nets; then I trapped deer and gave their flesh to feed orphans, and from their hides I prepared scrolls on which I wrote the Pentateuch. Then I went to a town which had no teachers of children, where I taught five of them the Pentateuch and six of them the orders of the Mishnah. Finally, I bade them: 'Until I return teach one another the Pentateuch and the Mishnah,' and thus I preserved the Torah from being forgotten in Israel." (Ketubot 103b, Baba Metzia 85b)

THE TALMUD

When Mar bar Rav Ashi, who lived in Babylon, began to compile and arrange the Talmud, he set himself between two great mountains and summoned the clouds to witness; whereupon four clouds encompassed him from all sides. He then charged the winds to transport air from the Holy Land; and only when the entire vicinity was saturated with the holy atmosphere did he proceed to edit the Talmud. For this reason, anyone engaged in studying the Gemara, even though he resides outside the Holy Land, is regarded as though living in the Land of Israel. (Pitgamin Kadishin)

PROPER STUDY

A man who appeared before Rabbi Baruch of Medziboz (18th century) was asked by the master what was his occupation. "I occupy myself with the study of Torah," he replied, "and I've already gone through the entire Talmud." Said the rabbi, "Excellent, but tell me, has the Talmud gone through you?"

HALAKHAH AND AGGADAH

While Rav Ami and Rav Assi were sitting before Rabbi Isaac the Smith, one of them said to him, "Will the Master kindly instruct us in some halakhic point?" while the other said, "Will the Master please give us some aggadic instruction?" When Rabbi Isaac embarked upon an aggadic discourse, he was deterred by one; and when he began a halakhic presentation the other deterred him. Whereupon he said to them, "Let me cite you a parable. This is comparable to a man with two wives—one young and the other old; the young wife would pluck out his white hair and the old one his black hair. As a consequence, he became completely bald." (Baba Kamma 60b)

MIDRASH

The devout Rabbi Moses of Kobrin (19th century), of blessed memory, was known to say that only one man in each generation was able to understand the Zohar; but as for the Midrash, not even one could fathom its contents; it remained a tightly sealed book to all. This is explained by the fact that the holy Zohar was unsealed by the Ari (Rabbi Isaac Luria—16th century), of blessed memory, while the closed gate of the Midrash will not be opened until the advent of the Messiah—may he come speedily in our day! (Or le-Yesharim 12)

A DREAM INTERPRETER'S BOOK

Bar Hedya was an interpreter of dreams. He gave a favorable interpretation to any one who paid him, and an unfavorable one when he was not remunerated. . . . One day he dropped his book, and when Rava picked it up he noticed this maxim: "All dreams follow the mouth [of the interpreter]." (Berakhot 56a)

BOOKS FOR THE DEPARTED

Books are arrayed on tables for souls of the departed; from these they study as when they were alive. It is reported that a group of gentiles passed a cemetery on a Sabbath eve and saw a Jew seated by a table reading his book. (Sefer Hasidim)

RASHI'S COMMENTARY ON THE TORAH

I learned from a saintly rabbi who had heard it from his teacher, that Rashi (Rabbi Solomon ben Isaac, 11th century) fasted 613 times before he wrote his commentary on the Torah. His grandson, Rabbi Jacob ben Meir Tam, is said to have remarked: "I might have been able to duplicate my grandfather's commentary on the Talmud, but it is not within my competence to match his Torah commentary." (Shem Gedolim)

Rabbi Nahman of Bratzlav (18th century) declared that Rashi had established, as it were, a brother kinship with the Torah. (Sihot ha-Ran 74b)

THE TOSAFISTS

Rabbi Isaac ben Samuel ha-Zaken (12th century), together with sixty other Tosafists, studied one halakhah daily and in time each mastered an entire tractate of the Talmud. When Rabbi Isaac saw, after introducing the Tosafist writings into his school, that many of them were alternative interpretations, he was apprehensive that the dialectics might supplant the Torah. He therefore secreted many of them and intermittently produced those of impelling urgency. (Melekhet Mahshevet lehe-Rav Moshe Zerah Eidlets)

THE MISHNEH TORAH

In an ancient manuscript I chanced on Rabbi David ha-Nagid's observation that when Rabbi Moses ben Maimon (Maimonides —12th century) composed the Mishneh Torah, he began with the

Ineffable Name—"Foundation of all foundations and Pillar of all wisdom"—and concluded with an allusion to the Messiah—"And the earth shall be full of the knowledge of the Lord as the waters cover the sea" (Isaiah 11.19). He also said that Rabbi Moses remained secluded in his room for ten years and did not venture forth until the work was finished. On the night of its completion his father and another man appeared to him in a dream. When the father identified the other man as Moses, son of Amram, Maimonides trembled with awe. Moses said, "I have come to examine your work," and after perusing it he commended Maimonides, "Well done!" (Seder ha-Dorot)

GUIDE TO THE PERPLEXED

I heard it said in the name of Rabbi Hayyim of Krasnow (18th century), of sainted memory, that the son of Rabbi Pinhas of Koretz wanted to present a book to a poor man in need of security for a loan. Searching for a volume infrequently read, he decided to give him Maimonides' *Guide to the Perplexed*. He consulted his father who said, "Don't remove this holy book from our house, for the fear of the Lord pervades a house containing Maimonides' works." (Peer le-Yesharim)

NO WRITING ON THE KABBALAH

The pupils of the Ari, of blessed memory, asked him why he had never written a book on the Kabbalah. He replied it was impossible because as soon as he plunges into one subject a torrential stream of thoughts overwhelms him without surcease. One subject leads ineluctably to another, and even when he speaks to them he must strive to confine his thoughts to a limited area. (Shem ha-Gedolim)

BLESSED REMNANTS

The gaon Rabbi Ephraim Zalman Margolis, of blessed memory, wrote: I heard from my father and teacher, who in his youth had heard it from reliable folk, that owing to an epidemic or some other cause, my grandfather, Rabbi Moses Isserles (16th century), was forced to live for a time in a village near Cracow. Remnants of his writings found their way into the archives of the local prince, whose prestige began to soar steadily. He held on to these writings tenaciously and would not surrender them to anyone. He also left instructions for his heirs to treat them with utmost reverence. Each year the manuscripts were spread in the open air to prevent their perishing. (Shem ha-Gedolim he-Hadash)

THE MAHARSHA

All literary creations in Israel up to and including those of Maharsha (Rabbi Samuel Eliezer Edels, 16th-17th century) were written under Divine inspiration. Subsequent works were also divinely inspired, but even those that were not, attained an aura of sanctity if they were accepted by a single congregation. Every Jewish community, however small, is vested with the prerogative to endow with Divine sanction any work it accepts, provided the contents do not divert the Israelites' hearts from their Maker. (Sheerit Yisrael)

"SIFTE KOHEN"

I once heard from Rabbi Naftali Herz Simhoni, may he rest in peace, but I do not recall whether he said he had read it or had heard it from his grandfather, Rabbi Naftali Herz Bernstein, that the gaon Rabbi Aryeh Leib ben Asher (18th century), author of *Shaagat Aryeh,* was in vehement disagreement with the book *Sifte Kohen,* written by Rabbi Shabbetai ben Meir ha-Kohen (17th century). He vigorously disapproved this work and kept it out of reach on the highest shelf of his bookcase. One day a notion occurred to him which he thought would refute a statement in the book. He climbed on a ladder to check the relevant passage, but the ladder tumbled and the gaon fell, exclaiming, "Shabbetai, what a vile temper you have!" As a result of this fall, he is said to have contracted an illness from which he never recovered, and his soul ascended to heaven.

SHAMEFACEDNESS

Rabbi Simhah Bunam of Parsischa (18th-19th century) related: "As I sat before my master, the saintly Yehudi of blessed memory, he noticed that I appeared crestfallen. When he inquired as to the reason, I told him someone had shamed me with his words. He asked who had perpetrated such a hurt, but I would not disclose his identity. Although my master urged me strongly, intending to reprove the offender, I remained silent. However, when I finally revealed that I had kissed him twice, the saintly Yehudi was astounded and ordered me to expose the humiliator, which I could no longer refuse to do. I informed him that while reading the book *Shevet Musar,* the author's words shamed me into realizing how derelict I had been in not serving the Creator properly, and how deficient I was in those attributes which according to our sages, peace be unto them, every good Israelite is expected to cultivate. I was chagrined to the point where I almost despised myself; but I finally picked up the volume, kissed it with fervor, and gently set it down." (Ramataim Tsofim)

ENVY AMONG SCHOLARS

In a dispute between Rabbi Jacob Joshua ben Zvi Hirsch of Frankfort (18th century) and Rabbi Jonathan Eyebeschutz, the latter maintained that while Rabbi Joshua's forte lay in his proficiency in the Shulhan Arukh, he could never find his way in the Talmud. Rabbi Joshua countered that while his opponent possessed a modicum of knowledge of the Talmud, the Shulhan Arukh was a closed book to him. When the scholars got wind of what the other had said, a mutual jealousy was incurred between them. Subsequently, Rabbi Jonathan authored a book on the Shulhan Arukh, and Rabbi Joshua wrote a treatise on several tracts of the Talmud. Although the Talmud avers that envy among scholars enhances knowledge, contemporary savants maintain greater erudition is accumulated when each scholar concentrates on his specialty. (Ohel Avraham)

A NEW COMMENTARY

One Friday morning Rabbi Levi Isaac of Berditchev (18th century) stopped at an inn. Since he had not yet completed reading the weekly Torah portion, he asked the innkeeper to loan him a Humash. Unaware that it contained a commentary by an unbeliever, the saintly rabbi began perusing sundry segments of the commentary. When the rabbi returned to his home, his friends observed that his mien was gravely disturbed. They asked him the reason but he refused to answer. Thirty days later he arranged a banquet for his family and friends, and explaining his behavior told them how he had chanced upon a Torah interpretation which, unbeknown to him, had been composed by a heretic. After he had been attracted to read parts of it, a heavenly decree proclaimed that as punishment for his transgression no prayer of his would be received for thirty days. That is why he had been so deeply troubled; in fact, he feared a possible heart seizure. But now that the thirty days have expired and his prayers are again acceptable, he was celebrating with this feast. (Shaare he-Emunah be-Shem Darkhe Hayyim)

RABBI NATHAN'S PRODIGIOUS LEARNING

I heard from the gaon Rabbi Simon Sofer, of blessed memory, that he had once inquired of his father, Rabbi Moses Sofer (18th-19th century), concerning the merits of his teacher, Rabbi Nathan Adler; to which Rabbi Moses Sofer replied, "I am not a hasid nor am I given to exaggeration, but this I must tell you. My teacher was superior to an angel or seraph. Throughout his lifetime he never reduced a single matter of the Oral Law to writing, because our sages proscribed the writing of

Oral Tradition, save when a man's studies have become so onerous that he is fearful of forgetting them. In the case of my teacher who never forgot a single item he had learned, the sages' interdiction did apply to him." (Likkutim be-Sof Sefer Keset ha-Sofer).

RABBI KOOK'S PARABLE OF THE SIDDUR

A group of us, including Hayyim Nahman Bialik, Eliezer Meir Lifshitz, Rabbi Simhah Asaf and Reb Binyamin among others, once gathered in the study of the eminent Rabbi Abraham Isaac Kook (20th century), of blessed memory. We were discussing the serious breaches of tradition by the current generation, and what could be done about it. One of those present began to disparage the rabbis who over the centuries had instituted many innovations and fences which militated against the Torah. Rabbi Kook virtually leaped from his chair, pained and obviously irate; but as was his wont he immediately subdued his anger and said calmly, "I recall something I once heard." It seems, he went on to relate, that a noted scholar found himself at sundown in a small town where he was compelled to spend the night in the home of one of the townspeople. Desiring to study, he asked his host for a tractate of the Gemara, but he had none. Perhaps he had a copy of the Mishnah? No. An *Ain Yaakov*? No. How about a *siddur*? The villager brought him at once an old tattered *siddur*.

All night long the rabbi perused the commentaries in the *siddur*, and was fascinated by the many charming insights he found there. The next morning he offered a good price for the book, but the villager refused to sell it. "I'll give you in exchange a magificent, beautifully bound *siddur*." But the villager was adamant. When the rabbi asked him for an explanation he replied, "Rabbi, upon arising in the morning I usually have my glass of hot tea. Since I build the fire myself and want it to start quickly, I use a piece of paper to ignite the kindling wood. Paper being scarce in my house, I tear each day a page from my *siddur* with which to start the fire. I do the same whenever I want to light my pipe—out comes a page from the book. I am approaching seventy years and my *siddur* is still pretty much intact. This is because, while ripping out the pages, I have left the heart of the book untouched."

WHEN WILL THE MESSIAH COME?

In the book *Ben Porat Yosef* by Rabbi Jacob Joseph of Polnoye, it is stated that when the Baal Shem Tov (18th century), inquired of the Messiah when he was coming, he received the rejoinder: When your teachings will be fully revealed and your fountains of wisdom universally disseminated.

EFFICACY OF BOOKS

It is written in Mishnah Avot, "Know what is above you—a seeing eye, a hearing ear, and all your deeds are recorded in a book." "Know what is above you" refers to the days of the first and second Temples. "A seeing eye" pertains to the period of the first Temple when men consulted the Urim and Thumim and could foresee future events. "A hearing ear" refers to the days of the second Temple, when men hearkened to a Divine Voice (*Bat Kol*). "All your deeds are recorded in a book" has reference to our bitter Diaspora when any zaddik can become knowledgeable by reading a book, since it chronicles all events. In similar vein the Besht, of blessed memory, once remarked that by opening a book a zaddik can perceive everything. (Sifte Tsaddikim Parshat be-Har)

LIKE MASTER LIKE SERVANT

After Rabbi Jacob Joseph of Polnoye had issued his book *Toldot Yaakov Yosef,* he traveled from place to place endeavoring to sell it. Arriving in Berditchev, he set himself up in the town inn and waited for customers, but none came. This enraged him. At that moment Rabbi Zev, sitting in Zhitomir, sensed intuitively that charges were being preferred in the Heavenly Academy against the city of Berditchev, which might lead to her destruction. He hastened to Berditchev and purchased a hundred copies of the book, which pacified Rabbi Jacob Joseph considerably. When Rabbi Zev asked why he had become so incensed, Rabbi Jacob Joseph replied, "Because the teachings of my master, the Baal Shem, are included in my book." Rabbi Zev interjected, "But why all your sound and fury? After all, the Holy One, blessed be He, also went from nation to nation offering his Torah, but none desired it." (Sefer ha-Hasidut)

TORAH FROM EDEN

Rabbi Pinhas of Koretz (18th century), of blessed memory, always extolled the book by the rabbi of Polnoye. He was wont to declare that such a book had never appeared before, and that it was Torah direct from the Garden of Eden. (Nofet Tsufim)

ON GOSSIP

I have read that before the saintly Rabbi Menahem Mendel of Vitebsk (18th century), blessed be his memory, left for the

Holy Land, he called on Rabbi Pinhas of Koretz to bid him good-by. Several days preceding his honored guest's arrival Rabbi Pinhas, realizing that a veritable royal personage was coming, began to tidy up his home. When the guest arrived Rabbi Pinhas remarked whimsically, "How do rabbis act when they come together? They gossip a bit, and that's what I'll do. When the venerable Rabbi Jacob Joseph ha-Kohen of Polnoye wrote his book, he printed a thousand copies and sold them for a coin a piece. Why did he bother to do this? He should have printed one copy, and I would have given him a thousand coins for it." (Derekh Tsaddikim)

NOAM ELIMELEKH

The rabbi who headed the court of the Kosov community wrote: I learned from someone who heard it personally from Rabbi Abraham Joshua Heschel, head of the court in Tlust, that he was browsing through a copy of *Noam Elimelekh* at the home of his father-in-law, the *zaddik* Rabbi Hayyim of Kosov, may his merit shield us. His aged father-in-law entered and asked what book he was reading, and whether he understood it. Abraham Joshua replied, "How can I understand this book which, according to popular belief, is intelligible only to one who is capable of resurrecting the dead?" The venerable rabbi commented, "I state it differently: only one who can resurrect the dead can comprehend this book." (Ohel Elimelekh 191)

A WRITER'S DISPOSITION

When Rabbi Shneur Zalman of Ladi (18th century) visited a rabbi who was a leader of the *mitnagdim,* the *mitnaged* said to him: "Under my bench I keep a book *Noam Elimelekh* by Rabbi Elimelekh of Lizensk who, I understand, was a disciple of the Maggid of Mezerich. Perhaps you can tell me something about this man's disposition." Rabbi Shneur replied, "Such was his temperament that if he were placed under a bench, he would not utter a word." (Bet Rebbi 63,3)

THE POWER OF STORIES

Rabbi Nahman of Bratzlav (18th-19th century) averred that his awakening to serve the Holy One, blessed be He, was stimulated by the many hasidic stories he had heard in his childhood. His father's house in the town of Miedzyboz, center of the Baal Shem's followers, teemed with hasidim spinning their captivating tales. Listening to these fascinating stories stirred him to devote himself to the Holy One, blessed be He, and to attain his worthy achievements. (Sihot ha-Ran)

HOLY FUMES

Before Rabbi Nahman of Bratzlav departed from this world, he left instructions to burn all his writings which, secreted in a special box, no one had been permitted to read. Immediately after his soul left him and his clothes were being removed, Rabbi Simeon hastened to open the box, took out all the hidden manuscripts, carried them to the stove, built a fire, and consigned them to the flames. I followed after him, in order to snuff the sacred fumes of the awesome Torah whose enjoyment was denied to our generation. (Yeme Maharnat)

"LOVER OF ISRAEL"

When the book *Lover of Israel* appeared, a sigh was heard in the celestial Library, "Alas, how can this book enter, with all the bookcases crammed full?" Two books, *Noam Elimelekh* and *Kedushat Levi*, exclaimed: "We shall shrink ourselves to make room for the book of our colleague Rabbi Joshua Heschel, for he was a lover of Israel."

A BOOK OF CHARITIES

The devout Rabbi Isaac of Neshchiz, of blessed memory, was gifted with an elegant penmanship. Throughout his life he kept meticulous records of the amounts he gave to charity, but he never indicated the name of the recipients. (Zikhron Tov)

THE CELESTIAL DEPOSITORY

Said Rabbi Ishmael: Metatron, chief of all the angels, told me there is a prince-on-high, superior to all the ministering angels, who oversees the celestial depository of books and documents. It is his task to open the cases, remove the books and bring them to the Holy One, blessed be He, Who hands them to the scribes. They, in turn, read them in the Great Upper Court before the entire Heavenly Household. (Seder Ruhot, Bet ha-Midrash Heder Hamishi)

THE JUDGE OF NATIONS

Rabbi Abahu said in the name of Rabbi Eliezer: The Holy One, blessed be He, inscribes on His cloak of purple the names of all the righteous slain by gentile nations, as it is written (Psalms 110.6), "He will judge among the nations." When He confronts them, "Why did you slay My righteous ones such as Rabbi Hananya ben Teradyon and the countless others who died in sanctification of My Name?" the nations deny their guilt.

What does the Holy One do? He brings out His purple cloak with names of martyrs and renders His verdict, as it is written: "He will cast His judgment on the nations." (Midrash Tehillim 9, Yalkut Shimeoni 247)

THE BOOK OF WOES

Moses, our Master, peace be upon him, recorded all the wanderings of the Children of Israel, and from all this the Torah was fashioned. In our time it is the prophet Elijah who inscribes the roamings and vicissitudes of each and every Israelite. When the Messiah comes—may it be speedily in our day—Elijah's records will also be embodied in a book from which all men will glean knowledge. (Ohel Yitshak)

THE BOOK OF MIRACLES

Said the gaon Rabbi Abraham of Sachatzov (19th-20th century), of blessed memory: There isn't a person to whom a miracle does not occur every moment, but he is not aware of it. Rabbi Abraham also said in the name of his father-in-law, of blessed memory: There is a book of remembrance in which every miracle is recorded, and in the distant future it will be made clear to each person what miracles happened to him. (Siah Sarfe Kodesh)

THE JEWISH LOVE OF BOOKS

By Cecil Roth

The Koran speaks of both Jews and Christians as "Peoples of the Book"— that is, of the Bible. Subsequently, the title was arrogated to the Jews alone. But, based on error though this ascription may be, it is in fact fully justifiable. For the Jews are a People of the Book, very literally and unquestionably, in more senses than one. In the first place, they are no less the creators than the creation of the Book of Books — the Bible (itself none other than the Greek *biblia*, "little volumes"). Jewish history and Jewish literature — the most ancient history of any people of the world, and the longest continuous literature that the world can show — are indeed from beginning to end little more than a commentary on the Bible; and the Jew of to-day is the creation of the Bible and of that great religious literature that has received its inspiration from it.

This subject is one pre-eminently for a theologian or a philosopher. My intention here is to deal with another aspect of the question. For the Jews are a People of the Book in another sense as well. They have been, for the past 2,000 years, essentially a literary and an educated people. To an extent unequalled among any other section of humanity, they have been interested in books. In an unlettered world, when even kings could not sign their names, they had already developed a system of universal education, so that an illiterate Jew was even in the Dark Ages a contradiction in terms. Centuries before the modern idea of adult education was evolved, Jews regarded it as a religious duty to band themselves together for study every morning before the labors of the day began and every evening when the ghetto gates closed them off from association with the outside world.

In consequence, the Jew was, from early times, book-conscious. He copied books. He owned books. He patronized literature. He was interested in intellectual life and productions and movements. Thus, even in the most soul-destroying period of oppression, it might be assumed that almost every ghetto Jew, however humble his circumstances and however lowly his calling, was likely to have his modest library. A book was not to him, as to his neighbor, an object of veneration, of mystery, of distrust. It was a sheer necessity of every-day life.

We Jews, above all people, venerate the memory of our martyrs. But even among our martyrs the highest place is held by our literature. If anything excels the brutality with which Jews were treated during past ages, it is the brutality with which their lit-

179

erature was tracked down, condemned, burned, destroyed. From the thirteenth century down to the nineteenth, censors, ecclesiastical and lay, devoted their hateful attention to every work printed with Hebrew characters or dealing with Jews. From 1240 onwards, there was a long series of autos-da-fé, in which Jewish literature was the victim. There were periods when it was a crime for a man to possess any Jewish book whatsoever, excepting the Bible and censored editions of the prayer book; and sometimes even these reservations were overlooked. Down to the close of the eighteenth century, there were frequent searches in ghetto after ghetto, and the few volumes that, in spite of everything, the Jewish householder had been able to bring together were dragged out, submitted to ruthless examination, and in the end committed to the pyre. These holocausts were mourned by the Jews no less bitterly than the loss of their own kith and kin; for they realized that here it was the soul and not the body that was imperilled. This long persecution is largely responsible for the fact that so many Hebrew books once known to exist are now lost, that Hebrew incunabula (that is, works printed before 1500) are so few that the complete text of the Talmud, for example, is preserved in only one single ancient manuscript. Yet such was the tenacity of our fathers that more than this was needed to eradicate from their hearts the passion for their ancestral lore. The persecution served indeed only to strengthen their devotion. In the words of the ancient martyr-Rabbi who was burned wrapped in a Scroll of the Law: "The parchment is consumed in fire, but the characters inscribed on it form themselves together anew in the heavens."

The Redemption of Books

In that dark age (not so far past, alas, as one had once hoped), when the redemption of fellow-Jews enslaved by land and sea was considered to be among the prime good actions that a man could perform, there was associated with that Mitzvah, the Redemption of Captives, the allied one of the Redemption of Books — the repurchase of volumes of Hebrew literature carried off when corsairs raided some Synagogue, or captured a ship in which studious Jews were sailing peacefully from port to port. Document after document, of the Middle Ages and after, deals with this question. Let us quote one instance only, of special Anglo-Jewish interest. At the time of the terrible massacre in York Castle in 1190, we are told by the contemporary chronicler: "The enemy spoiled gold and silver and beautiful books, of which the Jews of York had written many — more precious than gold or fine gold, and not to be equalled in all the world for beauty. These they brought to Cologne and to other places in Germany, and sold to the Jews."

In what light did this persecution of literature appear to contemporaries? I should like to cite a couple of passages which illustrate it as vividly as is possible. The first instance comes from the time of the Expulsion from Spain at the end of the fifteenth century — the greatest tragedy in Jewish history until our own day. The following is from the introduction of an eye-witness, Rabbi Abraham Sebag to his unpublished exegetical work, "Zeror haKesef":

Now while I was in Portugal, after having come thither with those expelled from Castille, it came into my mind to compose a commentary on the Five Scrolls, which I did. At that time, the anger of the Lord was kindled against my people in the Second Expulsion, from Portugal. I therefore abandoned all my books, and determined to take with me to Lisbon (the port of embarkation) only the commentary I had composed on the Pentateuch and the commentary on the Five Scrolls, and a commentary on the Ethics of the Fathers, and the work "Hibbur haKasef" that I had composed in my youth. When I arrived in Lisbon, certain Jews came and told me that a proclamation had been issued, that any person in whose possession a Hebrew book was found should be put to death. Forthwith I went and concealed them beneath a certain olive tree, verdant and fruitful, but in my eyes bitter as wormwood: and I called it the Tree of Weeping, for there I had buried all that I held most dear. For my commentaries on the Pentateuch and the Precepts were precious to me more than gold and treasure. Therewith, indeed, I had comforted myself for my two sons, the very walls of my heart, who had been seized by force and baptised: and I saw them no more, for immediately they were thrown into prison. Therefore I said of my books, "Surely these are better for me than sons and daughters." So I remained there for nearly six months, until through the merits of my forefathers God enabled me to reach Fez, where I determined to restore the Chaplet and to attempt to recall a little at least of what was written in my books.

The reading of this text is doubtful, and it seems that there is some scribal confusion. The translation should perhaps run: "and I saw my books no more, for immediately afterwards they threw me into prison."

A New Year Holocaust

My second instance is slightly later than this. In the autumn of 1553, in consequence of the slanders of a couple of spiteful apostates, a search was made in the houses of all the Jews of Rome, and all copies of the Talmud and subsidiary works were seized. Shortly after, the New Year's day, Rosh Hashanah, the great solemnity of the Jewish religious year, was chosen by the arch-persecutors to commit these treasures of the Jewish spirit to the flames; and they were burned by the common executioner on the Campo dei Fiori at Rome. The example was followed all over Italy with a ridiculous lack of discrimination, copies of the Bible itself suffering because they happened to be printed in the sacred tongue. Hear, now, the words of an eye-witness taken from the introduction to R. Judah Lerma's "Lehem Jehudah" (Sabionetta, 1554):

This work of mine I published for the first time in Venice. Now on the New Year's Day of the year "For God hath dealt bitterly with me" (that is 1553) the Curia of Rome issued an edict in all the countries that owed it obedience and they burned the Talmud and all works allied thereto. In the month of Marheshvan, the Bitter Month, the edict was published in Venice, and they burned the Talmud and all like works on a Sabbath day, and among them were all the copies of my book which I had just printed, 1,500 volumes in all. Thus I lost everything that I had in Venice and I did not have even so much as a single leaf either from the original or from the printed work as a remembrance. So I was forced to begin all over again and to write it from memory from the very commencement. After I had written three chapters anew, I found one single copy of the printed work in the hands of a non-Jew who had snatched it from the blaze, and I purchased it at a very high price; and I found that by the providence of God I had made the second copy more complete than the first.

A work which represents so vast a sum of human suffering, over which a man labored and wept and yet, undaunted, labored again, surely acquires a sanctity of its own. The literature that was the object of these persecutions must be sacred for all time among the descendants of those who fought to produce it, and had to fight again to save it. That to-day it can be treated with neglect or contempt passes human understanding.

Quaint Illustrations of Book-Lore

The Jewish love of books is demonstrated time after time in the old literature. In the most unexpected sources, one finds quaint illustrations of book-lore, sometimes curiously in advance of their age. It is worth while to assemble a few instances. Let us begin with a charming instance from Hai Gaon. In his "Musar ha-Sekhel," a rhymed ethical treatise consisting of counsel for guidance in life ("Advice to a Young Man," we would call it to-day), we find (§§32–3) the following characteristic admonition:

If children thou shouldst bear at length
    Reprove them, but with tender thought.
Purchase them books with all thy strength,
    And by skilled teachers have them taught.

Or again (Ibid, §128):

To three possessions thou shouldst look:
Acquire a field, a friend, a book.

A similar attitude of mind is reflected in that typical, but in some ways unenlightened, book of godly anecdotes, the "Book of the Pious," composed in the twelfth century by Judah, the Saint of Regensburg. We are given much advice about the proper use of books, some of which throws interesting light on contemporary social habits — as, for example, when we are informed (§656) that a man should not kneel on a recalcitrant folio in order to fasten its clasp, or (§649) that pens or note-tablets should not be used as bookmarks, or (§662) that a book should not be used as a missile, a shield, or an instrument of chastisement. "If a man has two sons, one of whom is averse to lending his books while the other does so willingly, he should have no hesitation in leaving all his library to the second son, even though he be the younger," runs one recommendation (§875). A gruesome anecdote (§647) recounts how in time of persecution the body of a certain pious man was dug up from his grave and stripped of its shroud and treated with brutal indignity. No one could understand why a person of such exceptional piety should have deserved this post-humous maltreatment, until he appeared to an acquaintance in a dream and revealed that it was in punishment for the fact that he had neglected to have his books (sacred books, *bien entendu*) proper-ly bound when they became worn. Another pious man, we learn in §676, enjoined his sons on his death-bed that they should not refuse to lend books even to those with whom they had had a serious quarrel, as thereby the cause of learning would suffer. If a man is in reduced circumstances, and forced to sell his property he should (§1,741) dispose first of his gold and jewellery and houses and estates, and only at the very end, when no alternative is left, denude himself of his library.

Reverence for Volumes

When a man is travelling on business and finds books that are unknown in his own city, it is his duty to purchase them in pref-erence to anything else and bring them back with him, so that he may be an agent in the diffusion of knowledge (§664). When a man is buying a book, he should not try to reduce the price by saying "This is a bad book." All he should do is to state the price that he is prepared to pay without degrading the quality of the literature (§665). The whole is succinctly summed up in a pithy general injunction: "It is a man's duty to have an eye to the honor of his books."

This conception was carried beyond the present evanescent state: for otherwise Paradise would be deprived of the greatest of possible delights. The Jewish pietists pictured the future world as a vast library, where all the good books that had ever been written were treasured up for the posthumous delectation of the righteous. The souls of the blessed, the "Book of the Pious" in-forms us (§1,546), have books lying before them in decent array on tables, so that they study in death even as they studied in their lifetime. One Friday evening, we are told, a non-Jew passed through the Jewish cemetery after dark and there he actually saw a Jew, who had passed away some time before, sitting and conning a book which lay on a desk before him. A later fantasy informs us how the Heavenly librarian was the Archangel Metatron, who brought books from the shelves before the Holy One, Blessed be He, who in turn handed them for study to the Academy on High. When a certain work was written in the eighteenth century, when the shelves were already full, the books in the celestial library pressed themselves together of their own accord to make room for the newcomer.

As great merit is attached to the lending of books, it might be imagined that a man acquires vicarious righteousness by borrow-ing them, purchase being thus a superfluous extravagance. But this is by no means the case. A Spanish Rabbi, who lived a cen-tury before Christopher Columbus discovered America, deals with this question trenchantly. R. Judah Campanton, in his intro-duction to the Talmud (c. E.) 1400), wrote:

Of a truth, a man's wisdom goes only as far as his books go. Therefore, one should sell all he possesses and buy books; for, as the sages put it: "He who increases books increases wisdom."

Rashi, of blessed memory, speaks to the same effect in interpreting the injunction of the Rabbis: "Acquire thyself a companion." Some read, according to him: "Acquire thyself a book"; for a book is the best of all companions. If a man reads only borrowed books, he is thus in the category of those of whom the Bible speaks: "And thy life shall hang in doubt before thee" (Deuteronomy, xxviii, 66).

But the prince of medieval Jewish book-lovers was Judah ibn Tibbon, the great scholar, grammarian, and translator, who lived in Provence in the thirteenth century. His will, in the form of last injunctions to his son, deals to a large degree with the treatment of his library. It is worth while to quote one or two passages *in extenso* from the translation by Israel Abrahams:

> My son! Make thy books thy companions, let thy book-cases and shelves be thy pleasure grounds and gardens. Bask in their paradise, gather their fruit, pluck their roses, take their spices and their myrrh. If thy soul be satiate and weary, change from garden to garden, from furrow to furrow, from prospect to prospect
> . . .
> I have honored thee by providing an extensive library for thy use, and have thus relieved thee of the necessity to borrow books. Most students must bustle about to seek books, often without finding them. But thou, thanks be to God, lendest and borrowest not. Of many books, indeed, thou ownest two or three copies . . .
> Examine thy Hebrew books at every New Moon, the Arabic volumes once in two months, and the bound codices once every quarter. Arrange thy library in fair order, so as to avoid wearying thyself in searching for the book thou needest. Always know the case and the chest where the book should be. A good plan would be to set in each compartment a written list of the books therein contained. If, then, thou art looking for a book, thou canst see from the list the exact shelf it occupies without disarranging all the books in the search for one. And cast thine eye frequently over the catalogue so as to remember what books are in thy library.
> . . .
> Never refuse to lend books to anyone who has not the means to purchase books for himself, but only act thus to those who can be trusted to return the volumes. Thou knowest what our sages said in the Talmud, on the text: "Wealth and riches are in his house; and his merit endureth for ever." But, "Withhold not good from him to whom it is due," and take particular care of thy books. Cover the book-cases with rugs of fine quality; and preserve them from damp and mice, and from all manner of injury, for thy books are thy good treasure. If thou lendest a volume, make a memorandum before it leaves thy house, and when it is returned draw thy pen over the entry. Every Passover and Tabernacles call in all books out on loan.

Similarly, about 1400, the grammarian, chronicler, and wit, Profiat Duran, gave advice to the intelligent student in the introduction to his Hebrew grammar "Maaseh Ephod." Use works which are brief or systematic, he said — advice which would be fatal to many authors of the present day, especially in view of his further injunction to the reader to keep to one book at a time.

But he goes on with a really memorable piece of advice. Use only books that are beautifully written, on good paper, and well and handsomely bound. Read in a pretty, well-furnished room, and let your eye rest on beautiful objects the whilst, so that you will be brought to love what you read. What an advanced outlook for a provincial student of five centuries ago! It is only in our own day that schools and libraries have begun to catch up with this medieval Jewish point of view.

THE BOOK — GOD'S BLUEPRINT

By Bernard Heller

I

SOMEWHERE in the writings of Shalom Jacob Abramowitz better known as Mendele Mocher Sefarim, we are presented with a picture of a market place in a small Ghetto town in Russia. Between the rows of stands, on which there are sparing displays of wares, kerchiefed women and bearded men in long caftans wend their way eyeing the articles for sale and reflecting whether the coins in their pockets are sufficient to acquire these articles. If the answer is in the affirmative the bargaining then begins. The small pile of vegetables on one stand, the bit of dry goods on another, and the sundry pieces of crockery and hardware on a third stand, reveal the pathetic poverty of the population of the village. For from the sale of this meagre assemblage of goods these must eke out a living.

Between these stands with edible goods and various other articles there is a table on which are a few bound volumes and pamphlets. In front of the table there stands the Mocher Sefarim — seller of books, a bespectacled elderly man with a gentle mien and kindly eyes. He calls the attention of bypassers to his wares.

"Here are Pentateuchs with excellent type and paper like parchment, and with all the standard commentaries," he cries with a voice more of a teacher than a hawker. Now and then a woman stops and furtively scans the pamphlets. She seems to hesitate to tell the book dealer what she wishes. The elderly merchant of the works of the pen proffers, not without delicacy, the information about the brochures he imagines the woman is seeking. "If you wish a most transporting tale then read this romance. Its setting is in a large city and the persons belong to the most elegant people. Read this book and you need not make the costly trip to Berdichev or Kamenetz." If the sales talk does not evoke the expected response the bookseller ventures with a new line, as he selects another pamphlet. "If your husband has difficulty in earning "Parnoso" (a livelihood) then recite this

185

"Techina" (prayer) and he will find that those difficulties will melt away like the snows of the spring." If he still notices a reticence, he very likely tries another brochure and in a still lower voice assures the reserved and demure woman that if the prayers of this booklet will be piously read it will constitute a sure "segula" (relief) for childbearing. "I know of one woman who read this Techina and God blessed her with twins."

II

I have brought this portraiture to show that in the midst of want and poverty books were deemed by Jews to be an essential commodity and that to their contents was attributed a power which (despite the crust of superstition that gathered about them) displays a realization of the sovereignty of ideas. For what is a book if not the material representation of considered judgments and vital ideas? What is the Torah if not a Book in which there are crystallized the time-tested insights and experiences of the Seers and Sages of Israel?

The Torah is a Book to which there has been attached a matchless significance and sanctity. It is a Unique Book in the sense that it has a beginning but is without end. It is like one of those loose leaf encyclopedias which are constantly supplemented by new facts but which are so integrated with antecedent facts that the new data seem to be implied in or flow from the old truths.

Books are to thought what storage batteries are to electricity. From nowhere and everywhere that mysterious and dynamic essence is drawn and given a locale or habitat.

III

For centuries savants have been debating the question whether ideas come ahead of things or the reverse. Plato affirmed that ideas constitute the foundation and the very scaffold of the material world while such thinkers as Democritus and Lucretius asserted that thoughts and concepts are concomitant effects, shadowy projections of physical things and events. These men are the forebears of two schools, representatives of which were not lacking in recent decades. Haeckel and Watson stood arrayed against Green and Royce.

The spokesmen of Judaism while avoiding extreme positions, proclaim their belief in the paramouncy and priority of ideas. God, say they, created the Universe according to a Plan. A Book — the Torah — was God's Blueprint.

"The Holy One Blessed Be He looked into the Torah and created the Universe." "In the beginning was the Word and the Word was made Flesh," is the affirmation of the Apostles of the new faith who in the beginning were Jews.

IV

The Universe was not only created by the Book, but also for the Book. Spirit, vision are concepts of supreme import. They constitute the heart of the Cosmos. If ideas and ideals, values and visions were to be extirpated then nature would be inconceivable or sink into a state of disorder which would make its existence impossible. The Universe would be like a chart of an optometrist with lines of letters of various sizes, but which are totally devoid of meaning.

Do you know how an eminent philosopher countered the skeptic's contention that everything — even man's objective reality — is an illusion, a phantasmagoria? "Cogito ergo sum" — "I think therefore I am," was his answer. The presence, persistence and profoundness of thought is the surest index of reality. This is a truth which moderns must relearn. For we have been accustomed to deem a man alive who pampers his appetites and indulges in all emotional craving, even though he utterly neglects to develop the mental powers with which nature has endowed him.

V

Now one may say, "Why make such a fuss about books? You don't see people languishing and dying when they are deprived of books. Has it not been said that, 'Of making many books there is no end; and much study is a weariness of the flesh?' and is there not a maxim that 'ignorance is bliss'?"

Let us therefore examine the value and usefulness of books.

1 — Good books tend to make our minds keen and alert. One can through reading and the study of books develop an ability to see things as they are and distinguish between a mirage and what is actual. To an inexperienced desert traveller the inability to distinguish between the glint and sheen of an imaginary and an actual oasis with its life-sustaining spring or streamlet may prove to be a fatal error. The same is true of our appraisals of social situations.

2 — Books do not merely sharpen the mind, they cultivate one's imagination. One may be in body in one land and yet in spirit move in a distant country. One may live in the twentieth

century but through books transport himself to bygone periods and eras.

3 — The habitual reading of books, regardless of their content, trains the mind to be attentive and withstand distractions. It helps to enable the reader to concentrate, without which our characters would be undisciplined and life's problems could never be successfully faced.

4 — Books also help us to interpret events and place things in a setting which clarifies and illumines the whole. The pebble is not merely a discrete piece of stone attractive because of its shape and color. It is perceived as a part of a grand mosaic. Books therefore, tend to make the reader creative. For he is taught to coordinate and evaluate experiences. The reader becomes an amplifier as well as a purveyor of knowledge. The reader does not merely partake of the artist's insight. He deepens it and to that extent he, too, is an agent of revelation.

5 — Books, in a sense, may be said to bestow upon the reader as well as the author a form of immortality — not the immortality which expresses itself in the egotistical desire for self-perpetuation. The immortality which books give to reader and writer is one which comes from the imperishability of one's influence — an influence which leaves an ineradicable impress upon the minds of one's fellowmen, and therefore upon the very Universe itself.

This is also true in another sense. Great ideas are indestructible. They defy time and space. They are eternal as well as transcendent. To the extent that we identify ourselves with them and become possessed by them we share their fate and future.

Milton sensed the true essence of books when he wrote, "Books are not absolutely dead things but do contain a progeny of life in them to be as active as that soul was whose progeny they are; nay, they do preserve as in a vial the purest efficacy and extraction of that living intellect that bred them."

VI

Jewish Tradition, more than that of any other folk, reflects this noble estimate of the value and significance of books. When an ark containing The Book is placed in a room, humble as it may be, that room becomes a shrine. When good books become old and worn and their pages become loose and separated, it is deemed a sacrilege to discard them and subject them to the mercy of tramping feet or the whims of shifting winds. They are collected and deposited in the attic of the Synagogue, with a tenderness that a mother displays to an infirm child. When their multiplication taxes the available space, they are taken and buried with a ceremony and solemnity that is given to sages and heroes who served God and man.

All faiths were disposed to burn books which they stigmatized as heretical. The Dominican Monks assumed for themselves this assignment and termed it a holy task. The Jew shuddered about the thought of books, any books, being set to devouring flames. Zealous as he was for preserving the integrity of his faith, the worst punishment he could devise for heretical volumes was to brand them as Seforim Hitsonim, Apocryphal or Outside Books. These were to be kept in isolation and even hidden but not to be destroyed by acts of incendiarism.

The most shameless act of the Nazis was their consignment to flames of heaps of books of noble and revered authors. The failure of leaders of governments and heads of cultural institutions all over the world to perceive in this outburst of barbarism a tendency which was the antithesis to all that civilization stood for and which inevitably was bound to end in a titanic struggle, besides which all previous conflicts would seem mere skirmishes, and their failure then and there to terminate all relationships with such vandals — is a sin of myopia or moral apathy for which they and we are now making due expiation.

When the Roman tyrant ordered that the rabbi, who refused to abstain from the study of sacred lore as his decree prescribed, should be wrapped with the parchment of the Holy Scroll and be burnt, legend tells us that as the flames scorched his body, his soul was seen ascending, and as the flames consumed the parchment, the letters too became alive and winged their way toward heaven, where in the presence of the Divine Throne their vigor and strength were renewed. The tyrant is now dust and well-nigh forgotten. The spirit of the martyred rabbi and the words of the Scroll which he thought he destroyed continue to march on.

To the Jew the book was an impregnable fort, an insurmountable citadel which shielded him against all attacks. The Psalmist uttered a profound truth when in thankful appreciation of the saving quality of the book he cried out: "Had not Thy Torah been my delight then I would have perished in my affliction."

VII

Now this reverence of the Book was a characteristic of the Jew of olden days. Our problem is to induce him to continue in that tradition. That this anxiety is not without basis is evidenced in the query of a contemporary writer at the end of a description of a pushcart peddler on Allen Street. Reb Chaim was a middle-aged man with a blackish beard. He had a large forehead and black eyes that reflected a mystic and far-off look. He sat on an empty orange box near his cart, engrossed in reading a tome which disclosed age and excessive use. Occasionally Reb Chaim would forget that he was in the street and would intone his reading in the manner which was customary in the study hall of the synagogue.

When a customer approached and sought to purchase Reb Chaim's merchandise he seemed as if he were roused and unwillingly brought into a strange world. He wrapped the goods, accepted money and gave the change, but his thoughts continued to be engrossed with the discussion of the Talmudic doctors. When his wife, Hannah, came to relieve him in the afternoon, his recreation consisted in making a dash for the Synagogue where he recited Mincha (afternoon prayers) and for an hour sat listening to the Rabbi's reading and exposition of a chapter of the Mishna. He returned to his pushcart refreshed and invigorated. Our author concludes the description with a question, "What will Reb Chaim's sons and grandsons read, we shall not say during but after their business hours? Will it be the Mishna and Gemara, will it be Goethe and Schiller or will it be detective stories and articles of pulp magazines?"

VIII

The hopes of the originators and sponsors of the Jewish Book Month are to impress upon the children of these people the beauty and blessedness of preserving and continuing the noble tradition of their fathers. Theirs is not an easy job, free of difficulties. They must sail against the current and buck the wind. But I am convinced that their efforts will not be in vain.

The initiation of an intensive program by the Jewish Book Council at this time is a token of future achievements. For here was a titanic struggle the like of which the world has never seen, a struggle that has enveloped continents. The Jewish people found themselves in the very center of this hellish vortex. Upon the outcome of the Armageddon depended their continued life and existence. In the midst of such a scene, bruised and battered Jewry paused to pay homage to Books.

Does not this augur well for a revival of the spirit and a renaissance of loyalty to traditional visions and values? This is, to me, a sign that Jews will continue to be true to the Book.

HEARTBEATS OF BOOKS

By A. Alan Steinbach

THE earliest impact of a book upon a child of tender age has been portrayed by Jessie E. Sampter in "The First Lesson":

> When first, a little boy of three,
> I stood beside the Rabbi's knee;
> He gave me cake to make me see
> The sweetness of the Holy Book.
>
> "More sweet than honeycomb," he said,
> "When once the word of God you've read,
> You'll gladly live on crusts of bread
> That you may know the Holy Book."

This "first lesson" has passed into desuetude, certainly here in America. Regrettably, so has the second lesson—a father leading his son to *heder* for the first time.

The father takes his son's little hand and says, "Come, my child, let us go to the *heder* where you will learn how to become a good Jew." Before they depart, the mother places a *talit* around the child's shoulders and whispers with a smile, "Wear this holy garment, my sweet one, and take good care of it always." She kisses her child and her husband, and they are on their way.

Arriving at the teacher's home, the father places his son on the teacher's lap and the educative process begins. A tablet is brought and the *aleph bet* is written on it. Pointing to each letter, the teacher reads the *aleph bet* in its regular order and nods as the child repeats after him. The same procedure is enacted with the alphabet reversed. What a wonderful psychological pattern! Very early in his life the child's eyes, ears and mouth comprise a syndrome that introduces him to the sacred Hebrew letters.

But this is not all. Honey is brought and is poured over the letters on the tablet. The child licks the sweet honey on the letters so that thenceforward he will be conditioned to think of them with a "sweet taste" in his mouth.

191

Now comes the final action. What has happened is a *simhah* calling for a celebration. But it must be neither strident nor hilarious. The parents prepare a dinner for the poor in honor of their child's initiation into the ranks of religious education, and they distribute appropriate gifts among the poor.

This idyllic picture is intended as a backdrop for my subject, "Heartbeats of Books." We Jews have been the most literate group in history, not excepting the Greeks with their rich cultural heritage. Indeed, Judaism has translated religious education into an article of faith. In assessing the relative worth of the *mitzvot* our sages taught, "The study of Torah is equal in importance to all the other commandments combined." Maimonides paraphrased it succinctly, "The advancement of learning is the highest commandment."

It has rightly been said, "The centuries of Jewish history are centuries of study—millennia of study." I do not know of any other people in the annals of history whose religious calendar includes a festival like *Simhat Torah*, rejoicing over the Book. Jews the world over exult in their cherished religious and literary treasure, "the inheritance of the Congregation of Jacob." The sixth chapter in *Pirke Abot* is a paean of praise for the Torah and its study. There is a distillation of tenderness in the practice of reciting a blessing when the Torah is read.

The Book of Judges (1.11) speaks of a city in Judah which Joshua called *Kiryat Sefer*, Book Town. The library in the Hebrew University in Jerusalem today may well be called a modern *Kiryat Sefer*. In addition to its 1,000,000 volumes and more than 10,000 different periodicals, there are many collections catalogued separately; also incunabula, microfilms, manuscripts, and the like. I know of no other geographical spot in the world whose map listed a *Kiryat Sefer*.

Jewish history texts written for children regale them with the fascinating story of Rabbi Johanan ben Zakkai who, after the destruction by the Romans of Jewish national independence in 70 C. E., gained permission from Emperor Vespasian to found the school in Jabneh. Not so well known, however, even to adults, is the fact that in 1942, almost nineteen centuries later, one of the first acts of the Jews in the Jewish ghetto set apart in Shanghai by the Japanese was to establish a yeshiva and to reprint a full set of scholarly classics.

Reverence for study is paralleled in Judaism by reverence for books. When books were written the authors intended them not only for their contemporaries, but for future generations as well. They were contemplated hopefully as bequests to posterity. The ultimate hope was that the books might become uninterrupted carriers of the Hebrew religious and literary heritage; bridges extending in time from mind to mind; lamps to diffuse illumination for the gropings of future travelers. The analogy may seem somewhat indelicate, but this strange foresight purposing to link present with future thinking brings to mind certain types of insects that collect food before dying and store it away for the unborn they will never see.

This desire to link the present with the future was more than a temporal phenomenon. It involved also spatial considerations as well as language. For example, while Hebrew was the dominant conduit through which the Jew poured his sagas of joy and suffering, his hopes and his doubts, his realizations and his disappointments, other languages also became vehicles to transport the fruits of Jewish thinking. To illustrate, the Passover Haggadah has been translated into over twenty languages.

Jewish literature is not couched in a monolithic language. Philo wrote his expositions and philosophical treatises in Alexandria, Egypt, in the Greek tongue. Josephus' works were penned in Rome, also in Greek. Solomon ibn Gabirol wrote his principal philosophical work *Mekor Hayim* in Arabic, in Spain. A monk translated it into Latin under the title *Fons Vitae,* and for a while it exercised a considerable influence upon early scholasticism. Maimonides wrote his *More Nebuhim* in Cairo, in Arabic.

Judah Halevi's *Kusari* was written in Arabic, in Spain. Manasseh ben Israel, attempting to harmonize contradictions in the Bible and the Talmud, wrote his *El Concillador* in Spanish, in Amsterdam. Moses Mendelssohn's *Phaedon* was penned in Germany, in classical German. Glueckel von Hameln's *Memoirs* appeared in Hanover, Germany, in the Judeo-German of the time "interspersed with Hebrew and with many Latinisms and Gallicisms." Israel Zangwill wrote his *Voice of Jerusalem* and his novels in London, in English. Bialik's Hebrew poems were written in Odessa, Russia. H. Leivick wrote his collected poems "I Was Not in Treblinka" in New York City, in Yiddish. Edmund Fleg employed French for his poems like *Ecoute* and *Israel,* his plays like *Le Juif du Pape,* and his novels like *L'enfant Prophete.* In Canada we have the *Poems* by A. M. Klein, and it is hardly necessary to enumerate the galaxy of writers in Israel using the medium of Hebrew.

The Jewish literary map is indeed expansive—in time, in space, and in language.

Works That Do Not Die

Heinrich Heine wrote wistfully, "A book, like a child, needs time to be born." But unlike a child, a book need not necessarily anticipate inexorable oblivion. This year marks the 400th anniversary of Shakespeare's birth; after four centuries his writings are perhaps more vital and vibrant today than they were when the bard penned them. There *are* works that do not die with their authors.

Not only from the first book in the Bible, but from its very first word, *Braishit,* books have been the throbbing heartbeats of which the Jew was the understanding heart. However, unlike the little child licking the honey on the *aleph bet* tablet, the Jew throughout history was constrained to lick gall, bitter gall and wormwood.

For corroboration we need but mention two *tannaim* who were martyred during the Hadrianic persecutions—Rabbi Akiba ben Yosef and Rabbi Hananiah ben Teradyon. According to tradition the former, after three years of incarceration, was subjected to excruciating torture before he expired with the *Shema* on his lips. The latter was burned at the stake, draped with a Torah scroll the Romans had fiendishly wrapped around him. As the flames seared the flesh of their revered teacher, his anguished students rent the heavens with their wailing. His words comforted them: "I see the parchment burning but the letters are soaring heavenward." This outcry became a paradigm for the invincible faith the Jew somehow managed to muster in his darkest hours.

The truculence vented against Jewish martyrs was directed also against Jewish literature. Thus, both body and soul became the targets of the oppressors. For a period of six centuries, from the 13th to the 19th, frightful holocausts against Jewish books were the rule rather than the exception. Ghettos were raided, Jewish homes were pillaged, synagogues were plundered, libraries were looted; their books were consigned to the pyre. Precious Hebrew books and incunabula known to have been extant, were irrevocably lost.

A melancholy commentary on our modern period is reflected in an essay by the late Dr. Philip Friedman, erstwhile chief of the Bibliographic Division of Yad Vashem and YIVO, titled "The Fate of the Jewish Book during the Nazi Era" (*Jewish Book Annual,* Vol. 15). He discusses the Nazi auto-da-fé against Jewish books and other Jewish cultural treasures during World War 2.

After some 8,000,000 books went up in flames, there was a radical reversal in the Nazi policy. Hitler appointed the lecherous Alfred Rosenberg to confiscate all the books, archives, and collections still remaining in Nazi-occupied areas. These were to have been placed in a museum to house the "remains" of the Jewish people. Happily, thousands of volumes and some collections pilfered by the infamous *Einsatzstab Reichsleiter*

Rosenberg (Task Force Rosenberg) were recovered by the victorious Allies after Germany's defeat. A considerable portion, however, of the looted treasures did not survive the end of World War 2. Therein lies an incalculable catastrophe: the needless amputation of a valuable limb from the corpus of the future.

The Systole and Diastole of the Jewish Heart

The ancient Biblical injunction to Joshua, "This Book of the Law shall not depart from your mouth, but you shall meditate on it day and night," originally referred to the Eternal Book. But its import extended to the written word in its broadest sense. Books became the systole and diastole of the Jewish heart. The Jew burned with an insatiable yearning to probe for the creative spiritual and intellectual power lying coiled in their pages. To what private heavens they uplifted him! They therefore came to be appreciated not only as cultural nutriment, but also as mental embroidery to ornament the Jewish psyche. They infused Jewish thinking with a volatility and intoxication which dwarfed the tribulations that crowded into the life of the Jew.

To some people books were excess baggage; to others they were little more than rubbish. But to the Jew they were an infallible Baedecker for an expedition into a universe where the human mind and the human spirit need never be an impoverished, naked nomad. In dawns and in starshine, in mountain heights that must be climbed because they are there beckoning to man's hunger for "upwardness," in every plight and in all circumstances confronting man, the passion for books shows us the analogues of our own thoughts reaching out for confirmation and affirmation in literary testaments created through the ages. Books for the Jew became a survival value, a qualitative and inspiring efflux which was to Jewish life what blood is to the veins and to the arteries. This dedication to literary creativity so profoundly intrigued and fascinated Mohammed that he could not refrain from denominating the Jewish people *Ahl' ul kitab*—"The People of the Book."

This Jewish "book consciousness" extends over the longest continuous period in man's chequered history. To an extent unparalleled in the tortuous trek of civilization, the Jew has been a patron of literature. He always owned books; he copied manuscripts; he listened to their speech with a responsive "third ear." If perchance he inadvertently let a volume fall to the ground, he picked it up and kissed it. If he handed someone a book, he did so respectfully, and with his right hand. The *mitzvah* of *pidyon shevuim*, "ransoming human captives," was equated with *pidyon se'forim,* "redeeming books" purloined by bandits who periodically swooped down to plunder Jewish settlements. They learned from previous experiences that, no matter how indigent a community might be, its members would manage somehow to collect funds for the recovery of their literary treasures. A "buyer" of Jewish books was never wanting among Jews.

A Middle Age document which goes back to the bloody massacre in York Castle in 1190 contains the following entry dealing with a case of *pidyon se'forim:* "The enemy spoiled gold and silver and beautiful books, of which Jews of York had written many—more precious than gold or fine gold, and not to be equalled in all the world for beauty. These they brought to Cologne and to other places in Germany, and sold to the Jews."

Jewish Gallantry Toward Books

An admirable example of Jewish gallantry toward books is reflected in the declaration of the medieval poet and historian Moses ibn Ezra (1070-1138): "A book is the most delightful companion... An inanimate thing yet it talks... it stimulates your latent talents. There is in the world no friend more faithful and attentive, no teacher more proficient... it will join you in solitude, accompany you in exile, serve as a candle in the dark, and entertain you in your loneliness. It will do you good and ask no favor in return."

No less significant than the purport of this monition is the age in which it was promulgated—in the early twelfth century, when a large segment of humanity was steeped in ignorance and superstition. Ideas which vied for acceptance by the illiterate masses were frequently the offspring of chaos spawned in untutored minds. It is therefore all the more amazing that as many as five centuries after ibn Ezra's death, here in our country in 1656, two Quaker women were arrested and thrown into dungeon for reading books. It was probably this type of naive, immature mentality that later inspired Rabindranath Tagore's satirical epigram, "The worm thinks it strange that man does not eat his books."

This brings to mind Disraeli's caustic reply to a taunt by Daniel O'Connell in the British Parliament: "Yes, I am a Jew, and when the ancestors of the right honorable gentleman were brutal savages in an unknown island, mine were priests in the Temple of Solomon." I believe the analogy is relevant. Five centuries before English justice concerned itself with witches who dared to read books, Moses ibn Ezra enshrined books as altars for the human mind.

Another example of Jewish reverence for books is provided by the sublime utterance of Moses ibn Tibbon (1220-1283): "My son, make your books your companions. Your book cases and bookshelves shall be your garden and your paradise. Find your nourishment in their fertile fields, pluck their roses, gather their fruit, enjoy their flavor. When you tire, walk on; from garden to garden, from furrow to furrow. Then your zeal will be reawakened and your mind will be refreshed."

The two quotations cited above testify to the enlightened cultural status of Jews even in those backward eras. Despite humiliation, discrimination and persecution, notwithstanding physical and social barriers that restricted and inhibited them, the Jews radiated more light extracted from books than did their tormentors who swaggered and strutted under the chandeliered glitter of castles and pavilioned mansions. When only paltry crumbs could be their fare, they embraced their books and manuscripts as if they were miniature mines of phantom gold.

What literature can parallel the teachings propagated in the 13th century by Judah the Hasid of Regensburg, Germany, in his *Sefer Hasidim*: "If a drop of ink fell at the same time on your book and on your coat, clean the book first and then the garment." "If you drop gold and books, first pick up the books and then the gold." "If a man in straitened circumstances must sell his property, he should first dispose of his jewelry, his house and estate, and only when no other alternative is left should he strip himself of his library." In case of fire or flood, wrote this same Judah, books had to be rescued before all other possessions. "If a man has two sons, one of whom is averse to lending his books while the other does so willingly, he should have no hesitation in leaving all his library to the second son, even though he be the younger." Rabbi Jacob Moelin (14th century) wrote: "If two men are about to enter or leave a house and one is carrying a book, the man with the book should be permitted to proceed first."

Books are couriers sent forth, each to communicate its special mission. A book is the soul, the mind, the heart, the thirst, the sleeplessness, the solitude of a brain flaming like Vesuvius with a fire that must burn itself on page after page after page. There is much wisdom in Milton's declaration, "A good book is the precious lifeblood of a master spirit, embalmed and treasured up on purpose for a life beyond." And as if hurling a scornful condemnation against the barbaric practice of consigning books to the hellish flames of *autos-da-fé,* he thundered prophetically: "As good almost kill a man as kill a good book; who kills a man kills a reasonable creature, God's image; but he who destroys a good book kills reason itself."

Books are engaging companions—at times blithe and jocose, at times surly and morose; now amiable and lively, now critical and troublesome. Some weep, some laugh; some amuse, some accuse. There are books that have so much to give that we embrace them ardently; others, like ships that pass in the night, strike up a chance acquaintance and are soon forgotten. There are books that dispense the accumulated wisdom of the ages and become immortal. We cling to them as talismans that elevate us beyond the narrow circumference of our mundane existential span. They help us to comprehend the inscription over the library door of an Egyptian king: "Medicines for the soul."

A declaration by Charles Lamb will, I believe, serve as a final thought: "I own I am disposed to say grace upon twenty other occasions in the course of the day, besides my dinner. I want a form for setting out on a pleasant walk, for a friendly meeting, for a resolved problem, for spiritual repasts, for books, a grace before Milton, before Shakespeare, a devotional exercise proper to be read before the Faerie Queen."

LOVE OF BOOKS AS REVEALED IN
JEWISH BOOKPLATES

By Philip Goodman

LONG before man invented the printing press, the hand-produced book had been a cherished possession of Jews. The well-known exhortation of the famous translator of philosophical and ethical works, Judah ibn Tibbon, found in his ethical will (circa 1190) testifies to this: "Books shall be thy companions; bookcases and shelves, thy pleasure-nooks and gardens." It is understandable, therefore, why this exhortation, which appeared as a legend for several years on the official Jewish Book Month poster distributed by the Jewish Book Council of America, has found a place on modern bookplates, notably, on the one of Ann and Julian Jablin. The attachment to books expressed by ibn Tibbon is more vigorously phrased in this short poem of a Karaite, Moses ben Abraham Dari:

To One Who Asked for the Loan of a Book

Cease thine asking, thou borrower of books,
Since a request for the loan of books is an abomination to me.
My book is ever like my beloved.
Does a man lend his beloved to others?[1]

ON LENDING BOOKS

The viewpoint of the Karaite is not entirely consistent with the traditional Jewish attitude which considered the lending of books a meritorious act, a religious obligation. As much as the Jew loved his books, he was nevertheless ready to share his beloved volumes with those who did not have them. Thus, ibn Tibbon goes on in his will to admonish his son about the love and care that is due to books and the desirability of loaning them. "Never refuse to lend books to anyone who has not the means to purchase books for himself, but only lend to those who can be trusted to return the volumes ... When thou lendest a volume, make a memorandum before it leaves thy house, and when it

---

[1] *Karaite Anthology*, trans. by Leon Nemoy (New Haven, 1952), p. 139.

199

is returned, draw thy pen over the entry." Laudable as it is to lend books, it was deemed equally important to keep account of books on loan to assure their return. The bookplate, a device which was developed with mass production of books following the invention of printing, serves as a mark of ownership and as a gentle reminder to the borrower.

The sages applied the verse, "He who does righteousness at all times" (Psalms 106.3), to the one who writes books and loans them to others. This quotation with its commentary is found in Hebrew on the bookplate of the collection of Samson Toeplitz of Posen bearing the added warning that the book "is given on loan to everyone who desires to study in it but he should not consider it as his own for then he will violate the commandment 'Thou shalt not steal' [Exodus 20.15]; and 'the remnant of Israel shall not do iniquity' [Zephania 3.13]."

In the *Book of the Pious*, a Hebrew work published about the end of the twelfth century by Judah ben Samuel surnamed the Pious, there are found a number of references to the great virtue of lending books. For example: a pious man, who possessed books and loaned them to others so that they might study them, ordered his sons thus: " . . . be careful when you have a quarrel with people that you do not restrain yourselves from loaning books to them. If you suspect that they will not return the books, take security from them."

To remove an obstacle from the practice of loaning books and to assure the safe return of borrowed books, as early as the eleventh century a ban was issued prohibiting the withholding of borrowed books for any claim that the borrower may have against the lender, even if he owe him money.

Judah the Pious also urged that books should be loaned to the poor rather than to the rich. He further stated that if a man has two sons — one who takes pleasure in lending his books and one who does not — the son who loans graciously should inherit his father's books.

The *Book of the Pious* further recounts the story of an old man who died and whose library of beautiful books was sold by his heirs to strangers. When his townsmen expressed grief that the children had sold their father's books, the town's scholar remarked: "The previous owner refused to lend any of his books claiming that on account of his old age he would not be able to read the manuscript if the writing should fade. He also feared that the borrowers might destroy them. These books are now in strange hands as a punishment for his refusal to lend his books."

More noteworthy was the deed of Yekuthiel Zalman Lichtenfeld of Pressburg, Hungary. When he celebrated his eightieth birthday, his children presented him with a set of the Talmud and commentaries in thirty beautiful volumes as a remembrance of the day. He determined to donate these books to an academy of Jewish learning in memory of his wife and parents. The above story is found on an over-size bookplate, 8 x 9½ inches, especially printed in 1925 for the thirty volume gift. The legend also includes a warning which prohibits the removal of these books from the premises of the *Bet Ha-Midrash.* This is understandable as careless borrowers with an unquenchable thirst for knowledge may forget to return the books.

ON STEALING BOOKS

It has been reported that in every community of Russia and Galicia, no matter how small, where there was a Talmud Torah there was also a library. Of course, there was no librarian. The place was open to any Jew at any time. The only safeguard for the protection of the books was a large sign in Hebrew warning: "A ban will be placed on anyone who steals a book." Undoubtedly, this is a most primitive form of bookplate, yet it might be considered a universal *Ex-libris* in the fullest sense of the word.

What naivete and what grandeur lie in this simple approach to *Ex-libris.* Similar pious wishes and warnings against thieving borrowers are found on bookplates. Quite forthright is that of Meyer T. Lazar, depicting Moses with a rod in one hand and the two Tablets of the Law in the other. The ten commandments appear on the tablets in Hebrew, with the exception of the eighth — Thou shalt not steal — which is written in relatively large English letters. An intriguing Hebrew *Ex-libris* was made for Moses Aloni. Above a caricature of a thief in flight, dropping books from under his arms as he flees, is the assertion "In vain you run away!" and beneath the illustration is the warning "Moses Aloni will find you."

While not truly *Ex-libris*, the rhymed pleas, threats and protests that have been written as special messages to borrowers who may neglect to return books are interesting to note for they too reflect the owners' love of books. The following is an example of a doggerel that was found in many places of White Russia on the fly-leaves of Hassidic books:

השמים שמים לה' והארץ נתן לבני אדם.

חייב אדם לחתום שמו על הספר;

חייב למה? אלא חיישינן

מפני הרמאים:

שמא יבא איש ממצרים

ויקח הספר בשתי ידים

ויעשה פליטה על המים

ויקנה יי"ש ויאמר לחיים!

The words of the Psalm 115.16 begin the poem: "The heavens are the heavens of the Lord; But the earth hath He given to the children of men," indicating biblically that a man is entitled to the possession of books. The doggerel continues:

> Man is obligated to write his name on the book;
> Why is he so obliged? Because we fear the crook.
> Lest a man come from Egypt's lands,
> Take the book with his two hands,
> Make an escape upon the sea,
> And say "*Le-Hayyim!*," with whiskey.

ON PRIDE OF BOOK POSSESSION

This substitute formula for *Ex-libris* which won widespread popularity among Jewish school pupils in the Ukraine could have been found inscribed in many textbooks:

To whom does this book belong?	?למי שייך זה הספר
To whomever it belongs — it belongs.	.למי ששייך — שייך
Nevertheless, to whom does it belong?	?ואף על פי כן — למי שייך
It belongs to the owner of the book.	.הוא שייך לבעל הספר
And who is the owner of the book?	?ומי הוא בעל הספר
Whoever bought it.	.מי שקנה אותו
And who bought it?	?ומי קנה אותו
Whoever had money — he bought it.	.מי שהיה לו כסף — קנה אותו

And who had money?	?ולמי היה כסף
The one who bought the book.	.לזה שקנה את הספר
And who bought the book?	?ומי קנה את הספר
The owner of the book bought it.	.בעל הספר קנה אותו
And who is the owner of the book?	?ומי הוא בעל הספר
The one to whom the book belongs.	.זה שהספר שייך לו
And to whom does the book belong?	?ולמי שייך הספר

The signature which followed the above device further attested to the pride and joy of the book owner.

The proud possessor of books may also be discovered by portrait bookplates in which the likeness of the owner is fused with his books. This attestation of oneness is typical of many book-lovers. The legend on the portrait bookplate of an American rabbi reads: "From the library of J. Leonard Levy." A picture of the owner, seated at a table and reading a book, is the attraction of the *Ex-libris*. Rabbi Levy (1865–1917), author of a number of publications, was elected chaplain of "Keegan's Brigade of Pennsylvania Volunteers" during the Spanish-American War and later served as spiritual leader of Rodef Shalom Temple in Pittsburgh. Another example of a portrait *Ex-libris* is that of Dr. Samuel W. Boorstein, a veteran Zionist of the Bronx, N. Y. Within a frame of Jewish symbols copied from illustrations in Hebrew books, the bookplate portrays the owner's library where he and his father are seen reading. It was made just before Dr. Boorstein donated his collection of about five thousand Hebrew, Yiddish and English volumes to the public library of Nahariya, Israel.

A portrait bookplate sometimes depicts the owner's loved ones, thus associating his love of books with the persons most dear to him. The *Ex-libris* of Mitchell M. Kaplan (1882–1944), who donated an unusual collection of rare Hebraica and Judaica to the New York University Jewish Culture Foundation, shows an open scroll with the quotation in Hebrew: חבלים נפלו לי בנעימים "The lines [possessions] fell unto me in pleasant places" (Psalms 16.6). This verse symbolizes the owner's most cherished possessions: his wife, his books and a writing set. Thus, the bookplate also depicts a portrait of Kaplan's wife, piles of books, a quill and an ink-stand.

A similar theme dominates the bookplate that Ephraim Moses Lilien, whose numerous *Ex-libris* have gained for him universal recognition in this area of the graphic arts, etched for his wife, Helene. This exquisite bookplate consists of an open book at the bottom and, on top, in a beribboned oval, the head of his handsome son. In between is the inscription in German: My Child — My

Book — Helene Lilien. The child in the picture, now in full manhood, was recently in Israel as an expert of the United Nations.

These portrait *Ex-libris* declare the high esteem and affection in which the owner holds his books.

ON BOOK PRODUCTION

The scribe is honored in numerous bookplates for his many long centuries of book production. One of the relatively few *Ex-libris* with Yiddish was made in 1922 for S. Spero by the Russian-Jewish artist, S. Yudovim, a nephew of the Yiddish dramatist, S. An-Ski. A fine example of wood-cutting, the bookplate shows a skull-capped, bearded scribe writing with a quill on a roll of parchment. The legend is פון ש. שפירא׳ס ביכער.

A more pious scribe, wearing a prayer shawl and phylacteries and writing on a large sheet of parchment, dominates the *Ex-libris* made by Harry B. Goldberg of Buffalo, N. Y., for Rabbi Eli A. Bohnen of Providence, Rhode Island. On a streamer, above the background of shelves of books, is the Hebrew quotation: ואני אקרא בשם ה׳. מלכים א, יח.כד . . . "... And I will call on the name of the Lord." (I Kings 18.24). This passage, uttered by the prophet Elijah, which is the Hebrew name of the owner, is particularly appropriate for a rabbi.

Another bookplate, also expressive of the owner's calling, was used by an Austrian bookbinder, Franz Filipek. His trade is indicated by the press and other tools of a bookbinder which surround his name in the bottom part of the bookplate frame. A pair of shackled hands are longingly stretching upwards to reach an open book held by an angel, whose beautiful, large white wings make a sharp contrast against the dark sky. Filipek longs to read the book but, unfortunately, he is chained to his work so that he does not have the time to read the books he binds. This eloquent bookplate is the work of Lilien.

Presse de la Sagesse (Printing Press of Wisdom), a source of spiritual nourishment for mankind, is the theme of a wood-cut by Prof. S. Seidl made as a bookplate for Marco Birnholz. A printer's devil is shown pressing drops of knowledge from a book into a vat from which others are thirstily drinking. Dr. Birnholz of Long Island, N. Y., is one of the world's foremost *Ex-libris* collectors. Born in Austria, he has been active in this field since childhood and has served as president of the Oesterreichische Ex-libris-Gesellschaft. In this field the influence of the bookplate owner as co-creator of a work of art is very pronounced, for the *Ex-libris* is a reflection of the personality of the owner as the

artist attempts to portray it. It may, therefore, be justifiably asserted that Birnholz exerted wide-spread influence in this area of the graphic arts for he had nearly 350 different bookplates made for himself and members of his family by numerous artists. His collection of 40,000 *Ex-libris*, including many of the rarest as well as those of the foremost artists, was confiscated by the Nazis. Only in 1950, as a result of the intervention of the U. S. Department of State, was his collection restored to him, albeit with many items missing.

ON BOOKPLATES OF AUTHORS

That authors love books does not need underscoring. Their devotion is generally reflected in their bookplates. Professor Solomon Schechter (1847–1915), president of the Jewish Theological Seminary of America, made considerable contributions to Jewish scholarship and succeeded in making a deep impression on American Jewish life. He achieved outstanding recognition for his identification of a manuscript fragment from the Cairo Genizah as the lost Hebrew original of the *Book of Ecclesiasticus* or *Ben Sira*. This led him to discover in the same place thousands of valuable manuscripts. Using the manuscripts he uncovered, he published in cooperation with Charles Taylor the Hebrew text of the *Wisdom of Ben Sira* (Cambridge, 1899). It is therefore appropriate that Schechter's bookplate has the following quotation from *Ben Sira* 38.24: חכמת סופר תרבה חכמה (The wisdom of a writer increases wisdom). The symbols included in the *Ex-libris* are: two palms, each as part of the vertical borders; an open scroll with "Ex Libris Solomon Schechter" inscribed on it; a candelabrum standing on a closed book; and a Star of David in which are set a pair of hands in position for invoking the priestly benediction. The bookplate was designed by Joseph B. Abrahams who was Schechter's faithful secretary and "right hand" man all the years he lived in the United States. It was prepared under the personal direction of Schechter, following considerable discussion by the artist with him concerning what he desired to be included in the drawing. Unfortunately, it was not engraved until after his death.

Rabbi Isaac Landman (1880–1946) was for many years the guiding mind of the *American Hebrew*. His greatest scholarly contribution was undoubtedly his labor as the editor of the ten-volume *Universal Jewish Encyclopedia*. He wrote several books and numerous articles as well as a few plays. In 1927 he organized the Permanent Commission on Better Understanding among Catholics, Protestants and Jews. His bookplate, designed by Joseph Urban and presented to him by the staff of the *American*

Hebrew on his fiftieth birthday, October 24, 1930, shows his varied interests represented by symbols: Judaism, by the candelabrum; scholarship and editing, by the wise owl perched on two books and holding a quill; playwriting, by the mask; and the movement for better understanding between Christians and Jews, by clasped hands.

Dr. Joshua Loth Liebman (1907–1948) received world-wide recognition for his best-seller *Peace of Mind* (New York, 1946). Rabbi Liebman was an author, teacher and radio preacher. He occupied the pulpit of Temple Israel, Boston, from 1939 until his untimely death. His bookplate, effectively executed by Joanne Bauer-Mayer, is shaped similar to the windows of Temple Israel. In the center is the head of a bearded Jew, intended to portray Maimonides. Centered on the lower part is an open scroll with the words עץ חיים [Tree of Life] in Liebman's own handwriting. These Hebrew words symbolized for Liebman both the Torah and the subject of his doctoral thesis, a work with this title written by Aaron ben Elizah, a medieval Jewish philosopher. Beneath the scroll is the seal of his *alma mater*, the Hebrew Union College, and a bar of musical notes from "Hear, O Israel." To the left of the scroll are two books — *Talmud* and *Guide for the Perplexed* — and to the right the Bible. When Liebman passed away and his widow had to decide upon a monument for his grave, she selected part of the design of his bookplate which was carved into the tombstone.

Lazarus Goldschmidt (1871–1950) was noted as an orientalist and as the translator of the Talmud into German. His bookplate, designed by himself, shows a grove of fruit trees with a planter digging a hole for a new sapling. Each tree in it represents a work which Goldschmidt translated or edited. His famous book collection was acquired by the Royal Library of Copenhagen, Denmark.

ON BOOKPLATES OF BIBLIOPHILES

Nehemiah Samuel Libowitz (1861–1939), a businessman, was a Jewish book collector and authority on Jewish folklore. He was the author of a number of Hebrew works including *Tene Bikkurim* ("Basket of First Fruits," Newark, 1893) and *Sepher Shaashuim* ("Book of Delights," New York, 1927), an anthology of wit, humor, anecdotes and curiosities selected from Jewish literature. His love of books found expression in a Hebrew article entitled "Immortality of the Soul Through Books," written as a tribute to Abraham S. Freidus, late chief of the Jewish Division, New York Public Library. On the occasion of the seventieth anniversary of his birthday a booklet was issued in honor of Libowitz which included tributes from Hayyim Nahman Bialik, Israel Davidson and Menachem Ribalow. The booklet also contains a reproduction of one of his three bookplates. One is a bookpile with his name in Hebrew. More interesting is the one which shows King Solomon seated on his throne, flanked by lions. To the left of his face are the three books of the Bible ascribed to his authorship: Proverbs, Song of Songs and Ecclesiastes. In the lower foreground is the owl of wisdom. The names and symbols of the twelve tribes of Israel are found on the two side columns. On the bottom appear the Hebrew words: ויחכם מכל אדם ("and he [Solomon] was wiser than all men." I Kings 5.11). The third *Ex-libris* of Libowitz has at the top תו־ספר, the modern Hebrew equivalent for bookplate. Within a framework of flowers is a poem by Yehudah Halevi.

Louis I. Haber (1858–1947) was a collector of books, manuscripts and autographs. In 1885, the second year that the Grolier Club was in existence, he became an influential member of this society which is devoted to bibliography and graphic arts. He served as its treasurer from 1927 until 1941 when he became an honorary member and treasurer emeritus. Haber was a member of the board of directors of the 92nd Streed YM & YWHA, New York City, as far back as 1895. He was responsible for systematically organizing its library and headed its library committee for many years. Subsequently, he was elected vice-president of the Y. From 1906 to 1909, Haber served as president of Congregation Shaarey Tefila, New York City. Actual comfort and enjoyment are expressed in the bookplate of Haber. "In this interior, a fire is blazing on the andirons; the drowsy dog lies asleep before it; the hanging lamp sheds a brilliant light over the room, and furnishes the means of reading which the owner is enjoying, as he sits in an easy chair, in lounging-coat and slippers. The rows of books at the far end of the room add to the effect of comfort, and the motto which envelopes the whole design — *My silent but faithful friends are they* — disclose the attitude of the owner towards his volumes."[2]

ON BOOKISH QUOTATIONS

It is natural to expect that quotations on books culled from Jewish literature should be found on *Ex-libris* of Jews. These adages are often symbolic of the recognition by the owners of the important role that books play in life.

---

[2] Charles Dexter Allen, *American Bookplates* (New York, 1894), p. 349.

S. Spero

S. B. Freehof

"Oh that my words were now written! Oh that they were inscribed in a book!" (Job 19.23) appears on the bookplate for the library of Congregation Sinai, Los Angeles, Calif. In this verse Job expresses the fervent wish that his story be written in a book to serve as a record for future generations. On the other hand, Koheleth deplores the excessive production of books in his complaint "Of making many books there is no end" (Ecclesiastes 12.12). This quotation in Hebrew adorns the charming bookplate, designed by Sara Nusbaum Maisel for the Philadelphia, Pa., Congregation Rodeph Shalom, believed to be the oldest Ashkenazic congregation in continuous existence in the western hemisphere.

This Talmudic quotation in Hebrew graces the *Ex-libris* of Rabbi Arthur J. Lelyveld, national director of the B'nai B'rith Hillel Foundations: "And if the book will prevail, the sword will not" (Abodah Zara 17b). Designed by Meyer Singer and executed by Nelson Ronsheim, it is delicately illustrated with a scroll placed before a sword. The same sentiment is expressed in the bookplate of the Temple Beth El Library, Manhattan Beach, New York, executed by Serena Rothstein. This one depicts a sword whose point has turned into a pen, which severs a rope tied around a book. The source of the illustration is: "A book and a sword descended together from heaven. Said the Almighty, 'If you will abide by the moral law of the book, you will be saved from the sword'" (Sifre, 138, Ekeb).

ON *The Book*

An illustration by Ephraim Moses Lilien for Morris Rosenfeld's *Songs of the Ghetto* has become practically an universal *Ex-libris* for it has been adopted by numerous book-owners. Lilien himself used nearly the identical picture for the bookplate he made for Leo Winz, who was editor of *Ost und West*. The dominant feature of the *Ex-libris* is the head of an aged man, looking up from an open book and lovingly resting a hand on the open page. A shelf with burning candles behind the head as well as two tall flaming tapers in front which soon will be extinguished are expressive of a mood of impending danger and oppressive despair. Yet, in the face of approaching darkness, *The Book* will remain as the sole light and guide.

A similar theme is evident in the bookplate executed by the Chicago artist, Jacob Sander, for Dr. Solomon B. Freehof, spiritual leader of Rodef Shalom Temple in Pittsburgh, Pa., and author of a number of works, the latest being *The Responsa Literature*

(Philadelphia, 1954). Here, too, an old man is seen reading by the light of a candle. In the dark background is a case of books. Capping the bookcase is the reminder: והגית בו יומם ולילה, from God's charge to Joshua: "This book of the Law shall not depart out of thy mouth, but thou shalt meditate therein day and night, that thou mayest observe to do according to all that is written therein; for then thou shalt make thy ways prosperous, and then thou shalt have good success" (Joshua 1.8).

Striking is the bookplate, entitled "The Forsaken Nook," made by Dr. Solomon S. Levadi of Chicago, Ill., for his own use. In this piece of graphic art, the artist-owner successfully caught the idea which he also expressed in his three volume Yiddish novel, *Thresholds* (Chicago, 1948), dealing with the reconstruction of a life which began in Russia, continued in Israel, and concluded in Chicago. The illustration conveys the mood of the secluded corner of a student. A spider web in a corner denotes desolation. Penetrating a barred window, a wide ray of light illuminates the open pages of a volume of the Talmud, signifying the heritage of the Jewish people. The frame-work is an intricate composition of leafless branches, some barren (frustration) and some ready to bud (effort and promise).

"City of Books" is the title of an *Ex-libris* drawn by the famous Jewish artist, Uriel Birnbaum, now living in Holland, for Marco Birnholz. This depicts a road, winding up a mountain, surrounded by books. At the peak is a large volume of the Bible with the title on the spine: תורה, נביאים, כתובים. This same illustration, with the exception of *Ex-libris* and the name of the owner, was made by Birnbaum in full colors and, through the courtesy of Dr. Birnholz, was reproduced by the Jewish Book Council of America as the official poster for Jewish Book Month.

The examples of bookplates that we have been presenting are intended to reveal the love of books as portrayed through this graphic art. Although one may feel an obligation to treat with special care a volume that bears the *Ex-libris* of its owner, the bookplate is not intended merely as a protection; on the other hand, the bookplate may be construed as an expedient to facilitate the loaning of books. Furthermore, the bookplate testifies to the owner's artistic and aesthetic sense and his literary proclivity for it is a fusion of two personalities — the owner, who gives his own ideas reflecting his interests, and the artist, who executes the ideas in his own style. Carrying as it does a certificate of the master's love, the bookplate bestows upon the book an unusual status that it would not otherwise possess. Above all, the bookplate bears witness to that love of books which has sustained, inspired and protected the Jews from time immemorial.

N. S. LIBOWITZ

Makers of Books

THE RISE OF THE JEWISH BOOK
IN AMERICAN PUBLISHING*

By Charles A. Madison

ALTHOUGH THE FIRST BOOK printed in this country—*The Whole Booke of Psalmes* (Cambridge, Mass., 1640)— was of biblical origin, books of Jewish content were relative latecomers in American publishing. One obvious reason is that until late in the 19th century there were comparatively few Jews in the United States. Most Americans, having little or no contact with them, had only the haziest idea of their tragic history in Christian civilization or of their unhappy position in contemporary society. The Puritans in New England and their Brahmin progeny tended to think of Jews in the light of the Old Testament: as Hebrews who had established monotheism in the world and had brought forth the great ethical prophets as well as Jesus and his apostles. Many books published during the 19th century were studies— both scholarly and theological—of Judaism and Jewish ethics.

For all their high regard of these ancient Hebrew teachings, most Americans, many of them high-minded and liberal in outlook, were inclined to associate living Jews with international banking and money-grubbing. Men like Henry and Brooks Adams, Henry James, Henry Holt, George Santayana—to mention the first prominent intellectuals that come to mind who influenced publishing trends—did not hesitate to condemn Jews as undesirable human beings. Consequently American publishers manifested a negative attitude toward works of contemporary Jewish content.

Certain novelists occasionally included Jewish characters in their stories, but these had little relation to reality. Rebecca in Walter Scott's *Ivanhoe,* Fagan in Charles Dickens' *Oliver Twist,* and George Eliot's *Daniel Deronda,* three of the best-known characters, hardly mirror recognizable Jews. More true to life, if sentimentally romanticized, are the Jews in Grace Aguilar's popular novels. Born in London in 1816 of a Portuguese Jewish

---

* This article of necessity excludes consideration of books published by Jewish organizations or by publishers devoted to Jewish interests.

family, she wrote a series of stories concerned with Jewish-Marrano life, among them *The Vale of Cedars, The Jewish Faith,* and *A Mother's Recompense,* which were widely read. After her untimely death in 1847 her American publisher, D. Appleton and Company, brought out a collected edition of her writings, in itself an indication of her continued popularity.

No other Jewish books of particular significance, apart from those of a religious nature, appeared on the lists of American publishers for several decades. Bret Harte's stories were of course highly popular, but he was not known as a Jew and his books had no Jewish content. In the early 1880's Henry Harland, an American novelist strongly influenced by Felix Adler, published several books of Jewish content under the pseudonym of Sidney Luska; *As It Was Written* and *The Yoke of the Thorah,* to mention two of them, were praised by William Dean Howells and other reviewers and gained a modicum of popularity. Incidentally, Harland went to England in the 1890's and became the editor of the colorful *Yellow Book.*

The Modern Jew in American Publishing

The modern Jew entered American publishing with the books by Israel Zangwill. Macmillan, then still a branch of the British firm of that name, published *The Children of the Ghetto* (1892) and *The King of Schnorers* (1894); later Harper brought out *Dreamers of the Ghetto.* A number of other books of Jewish interest were issued by American firms during the 1890's: Richard Wheatley's *The Jews of New York* (1891), Joseph Pennell's *The Jews at Home* (in Austria-Hungary, 1892), Edward King's *Joseph Zalmonah* (1893), Ignatius Krajewski's *The Jew* (1893), Richard Voss's *Michael Cibula* (1893), Charles M. Slade's *The Jewish Question and the Mission of the Jews* (1894), Joseph Jacobs' *Jewish Ideals and Other Essays* and *The Jewish Race* (both in 1896), Israel Abrahams' *Jewish Life in the Middle Ages* (1896), Solomon Schechter's *Aspects of Rabbinic Theology* (1896), Maurice Jacobs' *Jewish Ethics* (1896), and Henry Iliowize's *In the Pale* (1900). It should be noted that the first six books are by non-Jews while the next five are by Jews and were included in Macmillan's Jewish Library, the first series of this kind.

A major undertaking by Funk and Wagnalls was *The Jewish Encyclopedia.* The firm invested much effort and capital to assure its general excellence both editorially and technically; its appearance in 12 volumes (1901-1906) made it a model for later works of this kind. The Jewish books published by American firms at the turn of the century continued to deal largely with

Jewish religion and ethics. By that time, however, there were enough immigrant Jews on New York's East Side to attract the attention of journalists and social workers, among them Jacob Riis and Lincoln Steffens. Articles about the sweatshop system and the grimy poverty of the workers began to appear in current periodicals, making Americans aware of the existence of these Jews. Abraham Cahan, the dynamic Yiddish journalist, published *Yekl, A Tale of the New York Ghetto* (1896), a collection of stories, *The Imported Bridegroom* (1898) and *White Terror and the Red* (1904). About that time Professor Leo Wiener of Harvard discovered the Yiddish poems of the sweatshop by Morris Rosenfeld, wrote about them in the influential *Nation*, and edited a two-language edition of *Songs of the Ghetto* (1898). Wiener's own important book, *The History of Yiddish Literature in the Nineteenth Century* (1899), gave Americans the first inkling of the existence of such a literature. Equally significant was the publication of Hutchins Hapgood's *The Spirit of the Ghetto* (1902), in that it was a sympathetic account of New York Jews by a prominent journalist. A new edition has just been issued by the Harvard University Press.

By this time several American publishers were sufficiently enterprising to venture into the field of current Jewish interest. They brought out F. C. Conybears' *The Dreyfus Case* (1899), B. Lazare's *Antisemitism: Its History and Causes* (1903), M. Davitt's book on the Kishinev pogrom, *Within the Pale* (1904), C. S. Bernheimer's *The Russian Jews in the United States* (1905), E. S. Brundo's *The Little Conscript* (1905), and Max Nordau's *The Dwarf's Spectacles* (1905). Nordau's *Degeneration* had earlier attracted several American publishers, among them Henry Holt. Although habitually prejudiced against Jews, he was an admirer of intellectual originality and wanted to publish the book, but suggested certain emendations to Nordau. Appleton, however, offered him a contract without conditions and obtained the book.

Of significance also is Holt's relation to Henri Bergson. When *Creative Evolution* (1911) was recommended to Holt by Paul Elmer More and other of his intellectual friends, he contracted for the book despite his own doubts about its philosophic validity. When Bergson came to New York in 1912 to lecture at Columbia University, Holt instructed his chief editor, a Columbia graduate, to ascertain that Bergson was a "gentleman" before inviting him to his house.

First Jewish General Publishers

The first Jew to enter general publishing, initially very modestly but soon impressively, was B. W. Huebsch, son of a rabbi and trained as a printer. He brought out his first book in 1902, and during the next two decades he established a reputation as the most sympathetic as well as the most liberal of American publishers. On his annual lists, relatively small but of good quality, were to be found new Jewish authors and books of Jewish content. He was the first American publisher to issue a Yiddish work in English translation—David Pinski's *The Treasure* (1915).

Alfred A. Knopf, son of a Polish Jew but fully assimilated, started his publishing firm in 1915. More conservative and a more astute businessman than Huebsch, he has for a half century maintained an exceptionally high literary standard and has issued a goodly number of Jewish books. In 1917 the flamboyant Horace Liveright joined Albert and Charles Boni in publishing the justly famous Modern Library; later, by himself, Liveright brought out a long list of books, many of outstanding merit and some definitely notorious. By this time a number of Jewish writers were actively engaged in the emerging literary renascence, and they naturally gravitated to the new and enterprising houses founded by Jews. Among Jewish publishers starting in the 1920's were Simon and Schuster, The Viking Press, and Random House, three of the currently successful firms. Subsequently a number of other Jews entered publishing, more or less flourishingly.

The old established publishers were at first hostile to their Jewish competitors, intimating that they were denigrating the profession with their loose standards, but in time they found it desirable to encourage authors of modern views and unconventional subject-matter. A good many of these authors were Jews who dealt with Jewish subjects. Thus Houghton Mifflin published Mary Antin's *The Promised Land* (1912), Longmans issued S. Joseph's *Jewish Immigration to the United States from 1881 to 1910* (1914), Putnam brought out Israel Friedlander's *Jews of Russia and Poland* (1914), Dodd, Mead added I. Cohen's *Jewish Life in Modern Times* (1914), and Harper made Jewish literary history with Abraham Cahan's *The Rise of David Levinsky* (1917). The market for these books was still small, but with the passing years they attracted more and more readers, and during the 1920's and 1930's quite a few Jewish books appeared on best seller lists. Some of the more popular works, if not best sellers, were Ludwig Lewisohn's *Upstream* (1922) and *The Island Within* (1928), Samuel Ornitz's *Haunch, Paunch and Jowl* (1923), Nat J. Ferber's *The Sidewalks of New York* (1927), Myron Brinig's *Singermann* (1929), Michael Gold's *Jews Without Money* (1930), and Meyer Levin's *The Old Bunch* (1937). Such Jewish writers as Montague Glass, Edna Ferber, and Fanny Hurst, while highly popular, wrote about Jews either only inferentially or in a humorous vein.

Among authors, novelists normally gain the widest recognition. By the end of the 1930's there were around sixty Jewish writers of fiction with some claim to prominence. Many of them were deliberately or subconsciously sloughing off their Jewishness, and a few suffered from a self-hatred that caused their Jewish characters to emerge as caricatures. Jewish writers also entered the field of literary criticism and the various academic disciplines, and their work made its impress upon American publishing.

A measure of the interest in Jewish books by American publishers is seen in their acceptance of Yiddish books in English translation. Pinski's *The Treasure* was followed by the sporadic publication of such books as Sholem Asch's *Mottke the Vagabond* (1917), Pinski's *King David and His Wives* (1923), *Arnold Levenberg* (1928), and *Generations of Noah Edon* (1931). In the 1930's Knopf undertook to bring out I. I. Singer's novels and issued four of them with considerable critical success. Also in the 1930's, and continuing until his death two decades later, Putnam published the works of Sholem Asch most profitably, several of the novels becoming top best-sellers. In the 1950's Farrar, Straus took over I. Bashevis Singer along with Noonday Press, and has brought out all his writings with notable enterprise. Other Yiddish writers, and of late Sholom Aleichem in particular, have also been published, as have several collections of Jewish stories and poems.

The Acceptance of the Jewish Book

The acceptance of the Jewish book as part of American literature has been considerably accelerated during the past quarter century. One need only examine the book lists of the *Jewish Book Annual* to note the increase in their annual publication. Equally notable is the growing number of Jewish writers in the lists of American publishers. Among them in the year 1942-43, for example, were such writers as Milton Steinberg, Joseph Klausner, O. S. Yanowsky, Solomon Zeitlin, Maurice Samuel, Albert Halper, G. B. Stern, Delmore Schwartz, André Maurois, S. S. Sassoon, Stefan Zweig, V. Jabotinsky, and S. A. Feinberg. Ten years later a sampling includes books by such writers as Joseph Gaer, Will Herberg, Abraham J. Heshel, Alfred Kazin, Michael Blankfort, Rufus Learsi, Hal Lehrman, A. M. Klein, Frederic Morton, Samuel Ornitz, Harold Robbins and Anne Frank. More recent lists are equally impressive, giving evidence of the prominence of Jewish books and Jewish authors in current American publishing.

As already intimated, the quality of these Jewish books varies according to the ability and attitude of their authors. Thus a good many of them are not only talented but highly serious, and their works serve to enhance the image of the Jewish people. Such authors of books published in the 1940's were Harry A. Wolfson, Koppel S. Pinson, Arthur Koestler, Louis Fischer, Philipp Frank, Max Brod, Mordecai M. Kaplan, Carlo Levi, Arthur Miller, Meyer Levin, Saul Bellow, Franz Werfel, Waldo Frank, Maurice Samuel, Martin Buber, and Louis Finkelstein. Unfortunately, a number of second generation writers of fiction are more glib than knowledgeable about Jewish history and Jewish character and consequently tended to distort and deride the Jews they wrote about. Their books in the 1940's and later, even as a few in the 1920's, are flawed by blurred vision and in a number of instances, by the effect of subconscious guilt—the inner struggle between the influences of assimilation and the forced dependence upon their Jewish experience for the material of their stories. Thus in novels by Norman Katkov, A. Bernstein, Harold Robbins, Irving Schulman, Daniel Taylor, Henry Denker, Jerome Weidner, Budd Schulberg, Herman Wouk, Daniel Fuchs, B. J. Friedman, and Jeremy Larner, Jews are depicted with little sympathy and less sensitivity—endowing them with neither reality nor dignity. By way of contrast with these books, which reveal the ignorance, irritation, or sheer maladroitness of their authors, one might mention several of the more truly felt and more creatively expressed recent novels of Jewish content: André Schwartz-Bart's *The Last of the Just,* the brief but poignant narratives by Elie Wiesel, Joanne Greenberg's *The King's Persons,* Saul Bellow's *Herzog,* and Bernard Malamud's *The Fixer.*

Of interest also are the multivolume Jewish histories and encyclopedias undertaken by such publishers as McGraw-Hill, Prentice-Hall, Holt, Rinehart and Winston, Rutgers University Press, and Random House. These works of cooperative scholarship, requiring a considerable outlay of capital and effort, are additional evidence that books of Jewish content are now finding a ready enough market to appeal to commercial publishers. Thus, while as late as a quarter century ago a Jewish book was still considered commercially unprofitable, today only the highly specialized Jewish books—but no more than any other work of restricted interest—will fail to attract an enterprising American publisher.

THE FIRST AMERICAN JEWISH
PUBLICATION SOCIETY

By Solomon Grayzel

The first American Jewish Publication Society was among the most promising and most shortlived projects initiated by Isaac Leeser. Since this first organized venture into the publication of popular books for the Jews of America was started just one hundred years ago, this is an appropriate occasion for recalling its aims and achievements.

The Society introduced itself in 1845 through an "Address of the Jewish Publication Committee to the Israelites of America." It promised to make it possible for Jews "to obtain a knowledge of the faith and proper weapons to defend it against the assaults of proselyte-makers on the one side and of infidels on the other." The need for self-defense against Christian proselytization was referred to again in statements by the Committee; it was also treated in several of its publications. But the annual Committee statements emphasized still another aim — "the placing of a mass of good reading within the reach of even the poorest families." The Society proudly pointed out that its publications were of the sort "which any parent can freely place in the hands of his children without the least danger of tainting their minds with ideas inimical to our holy religion."

The dues of the Society were set at one dollar a year, but no definite number of books was promised. The intention evidently was to publish four a year. The third report, however, regrets that failure of the financial resources to grow prevented the publication of more books. The Society actually published booklets rather than books. Each publication consisted of about 125 pages (4x6) in 8 point type.

Where the reports of the Publications Committee were signed, they carried the names of Isaac Leeser, Chairman, A. Hart and Solomon Solis. Leeser did the literary and editorial work and he sometimes took considerable liberties with the material. He eliminated a chapter, in one case, and substituted an introduction of his own; he warned the readers, in another instance, against the theological views of the author; the size of the publications sometimes compelled the excision of material. The works the Committee had to choose from were perforce limited in quality and quantity. The poverty of Jewish American literature at that time is illustrated by the fact that, with the exception of one brief

221

essay by Leeser himself, the authors were not American and in several instances not even Jews.

The projected series of publications was given the general title *The Jewish Miscellany*, and each item was numbered as follows:

I. *Caleb Asher*, the author's name not given, had appeared in England some years previously. It was offered (5605) as a sample of the work the Society aimed to do. It is a simple story, told in typical early Victorian style, of a Jewish boy whom poverty almost drives to conversion, since only thus could he find employment. He is deterred by the horrible remorse of another young man who had similarly gone astray. All turns out well in the end.

II. *Hebrew Tales* (selected and translated from the writings of the Ancient Hebrew Sages), by Hyman Hurwitz, had likewise already appeared in England. For American publication (5605) the Committee reduced the work in size. It consists of stories culled from Talmud and Midrash.

III. *The Prophet's Daughter*, by Mrs. Hartog (late Miss Marion Moss), was also a republished (5606) English story. The heroine is Mahla, daughter of the Prophet Micaiah who braved the wrath of King Ahab. The story itself is rather thin by modern standards, with the usual villain who kidnaps and hero who saves and marries.

IV. *Memoir of Moses Mendelssohn*, by M. Samuel, was republished (5606) from an earlier English edition. It is a biography of Mendelssohn, with the Lavater correspondence as the core.

V. *Mesillat Yisrael: The Path of Israel* (or an Abridgement of the Holy Scriptures for the Use of the Youth of our Nation), by J. Ennery, had originally been published in French under the title *Le Sentier d'Israel*. It was translated into English by A. I. H. Bernal, Hebrew teacher of congregation Mikveh Israel of Philadelphia. The work compares favorably with the many efforts which have been made since to retell the Bible in simpler language. Part I covers the Pentateuch (5607). [See nos. XI and XIV]

VI. Contained three items (5607): *Days of Old*, by Charlotte Elizabeth (Mrs. Tonna), retells the stories of the Egyptian enslavement, the Exodus and the Wandering by weaving them, not too skilfully, around imaginary characters. The story had appeared serially in a Jewish periodical in London. *Rachel Levy, or the Young Orphan: A Tale*, author not named, was also a reprint from an English edition. It is the story of a poor girl who insists on observing the Sabbath despite all hardships. *The Jews and their Religion*, by Isaac Leeser, seems to have been especially written to fill in the required number of pages. It mixes sacred history, apologetics, a statement of the fundamentals of Judaism with a resumé, in four pages, of the history of the Jews in the United States.

VII. *The Perez Family: A Tale*, by Grace Aguilar (5607), is a story about intermarriage. The Publications Committee, in a preface, agrees with the author that intermarriage cannot bring happiness, but is not so sure that a sinner of this sort should be treated leniently.

VIII, IX, X. *Patriarchal Times*, by Miss Adelaide O'Keeffe, contains biographies of Bible heroes told, with the aid of imaginary characters, in romantic style. It, too, had already been published in England. Part 1 (5607) deals with Abraham, Ishmael and Isaac; Parts 2 and 3 apparently issued as one (5608), deal with Jacob, Esau, Joseph and Benjamin.

XI. *Mesillat Yisrael: The Path of Israel*, by J. Ennery (5608), covers Joshua, Judges (with Ruth following) and Samuel. [See above no. V].

XII, XIII. *Shemang Yisrael: The Spirit of Judaism*, by Grace Aguilar (5609), is a fervently written apologetic work in which the presumed success of Christian proselytization is blamed upon Jewish adherence to obscure traditions and burdensome observances as well as upon the failure of Jewish educational efforts. Leeser, in an introduction and in numerous footnotes, takes direct issue with the author on many points of her argument.

XIV. *Mesillat Yisrael: The Path of Israel*, by J. Ennery (5610), covers the Books of Kings and tells the story portions of Daniel, Esther, Ezra and Nehemiah, Jonah and Job. The prophetic books are not treated. A few psalms are given in an appendix, which also contains very brief discussions of other biblical and apocryphal books. [See nos. V and XI].

The publications here enumerated were all that the Society succeeded in publishing. A fire which broke out in December 1851 in the place where the property of the Society was stored is said to have given it its death blow. This could not have been the only cause for its failure to carry on. No publications had been issued for more than a year previous to the fire. The Society had met with little encouragement, partly perhaps because of its choice of material and partly because of the general and Jewish environment. Yet the need for such an organization continued to be obvious and eventually resulted in the second American Jewish Publication Society (1873) which enjoyed an even briefer existence than the first. The third effort, in 1888, resulted in the establishment of the present Jewish Publication Society of America.

GENERATIONS OF JEWISH LITERARY LABOR

Sixty Years of The Jewish Publication Society of America

By MAURICE JACOBS

THE romance of Jewish book publishing in America affords an interesting sidelight on American-Jewish history. Jewish book publishing has been, however, more than a mere concomitant of the community's physical growth; it has reflected the intellectual needs of the emerging American Jewry and attempted to guide its spiritual development. In colonial days, our Jewish communities were small and scattered, and the demand for Jewish books was slight and easily satisfied by importation from abroad. As the immigration of Jews from Germany grew, and as the children of these newcomers accepted the English language as their mother tongue, the need for books in English dealing with Jewish religion, history and literature began to be felt, less perhaps by the average American Jew than by the rabbis and those concerned with religious education.

THE FIRST TWO ATTEMPTS

The first attempt to fill the need for Jewish books was made by the Reverend Isaac Leeser, the *hazan* of the Sephardic Congregation Mikveh Israel in Philadelphia, who practically unaided, established the American Jewish Publication Society on November 8, 1845. The impulse which brought this organization into being grew out of a genuine fear of the Christian missionary and his free literature. The Jewish religion was in danger because there were no Jewish books in English. Leeser, therefore, felt it necessary to confound the missionaries, save the younger Jewish generation, develop a group of American Jewish writers, and try to bring unity to a religiously discordant Jewish world through the creation and development of common literary interests. Isaac Leeser, in all probability, patterned his American Jewish Publication Society after one of the missionary and tract societies which existed in London at the time.*

But the Society's life was comparatively brief. It met with severe losses from a fire in Philadelphia, December 27, 1851, which destroyed the building where nearly all the Society's published

*An article on the "First American Jewish Publication Society" by Solomon Grayzel appeared in the *Jewish Book Annual* III (1944–45).

works were stored. Since the stock had been left uninsured, the loss was total and the Society could not survive it. The need for such an organization continued to be recognized. In 1868, soon after Leeser's death, Judge Mayer Sulzberger, of Philadelphia, editing the final issues of *The Occident*, again urged the organization of a publication society: but nothing more came of it than editorial comment. In 1869, Rabbi Isaac Mayer Wise began an active campaign to the same end. He entertained a grandiose scheme which envisioned the translation into English of every rabbinic and medieval Jewish classic, but out of this, too, no new publication society was born.

Two years later, however, in 1871, a second American Jewish Publication Society was founded in New York under the sponsorship of Leopold Bamberger, Benjamin I. Hart, Myer Stern, Edward Morrison, William B. Hackenburg and Simon Wolf. It died in the panic of 1875, after having published several books and laid plans for several ambitious projects, its managers having concluded that the measure of support received did not justify their efforts to continue the work.

Among this Society's publications was a translation from the German of the fourth volume of Professor Heinrich Graetz's *History of the Jews*. Rev. James K. Gutheim, a Jewish minister and scholar at New Orleans, Louisiana, was the translator of this volume, which embraced the period "From the downfall of the Jewish State to the conclusion of the Talmud." This was followed by *Jewish Family Papers; or Letters of a Missionary*, translated by Rev. Dr. Frederic de Sola Mendes of New York City from the German of Dr. Wilhelm Herzberg; and *Hebrew Characteristics*, a volume of miscellaneous papers, in translation by William Lewis; *Extracts from Jewish Moralists* by Dr. Leopold Zunz; *Jewish Marriage in Post-Biblical Times*, and *On Interment of the Dead in Post-Biblical Judaism — a Study in Archaeology*, both by Dr. Joseph Perles.

From 1875 until 1888, no publication society existed among the Jews of America, and those persons who produced works of instruction and entertainment of interest especially to Jews were more than once discouraged by financial losses or by an insignificant return for their labor.

THE THIRD AND SUCCESSFUL EFFORT

On December 11th, 1887, Hanukkah Sunday, Doctor Joseph Krauskopf, a young man but recently called to the pulpit of Reform Congregation Keneseth Israel in Philadelphia, preached his first published Sunday discourse, entitled "The Need of the

Hour," in which he urged the establishment of a publication society.

Soon thereafter, in January 1888, the Society of Knowledge Seekers, a group organized by Krauskopf, issued a call to the presidents of the Jewish congregations and to the Young Men's Hebrew Association, asking them to appoint delegates to meet them at the rooms of the Association for the purpose of effecting the organization of a Jewish publication society. The meeting took place, and a special committee was appointed, subject to the call of the chairman, to draft the constitution and by-laws. After several meetings of this committee, the general committee, on March 29th, took a vote and reached a decision, by a majority of one, to proceed with the immediate organization of a publication society on a national instead of a local basis. A call for a national convention was to be issued.

In 1888, therefore, Doctor Krauskopf and Dr. Solomon Solis-Cohen issued the call "to the Jewish community of America." On June 3, 1888, the organization meeting took place. One hundred people attended and Mr. Morris Newburger, a member of the Society of Knowledge Seekers, was elected President, and served for four years. Doctor Krauskopf was elected Secretary and served in that capacity for ten years, bringing to the new venture his great organizing genius. The other officers were: Jacob H. Schiff, the Rev. Dr. Gustav Gottheil, both of New York City, Bernhard Bettman of Cincinnati, and Leo N. Levi, of Galveston, Texas, Vice-Presidents; Herman S. Friedman, of Philadelphia, Treasurer; Miss Mary M. Cohen of Philadelphia, Corresponding Secretary; Ephraim Lederer of Philadelphia, Assistant Secretary; and an Executive Committee of twenty, and a Publication Committee of nine. The Society met in convention biennially; its second meeting was held at Mercantile Hall (on Franklin Street above Parrish Street) on Sunday afternoon, June 8, 1890; the third at the same hall on Sunday afternoon, June 5, 1892; and the fourth, also at the same hall, on Sunday afternoon, May 15, 1894.

The purpose of The Jewish Publication Society of America was declared definitely at the first meeting to be: "The publication and dissemination of literature, scientific and religious works, and also the giving of instruction in practices of the Jewish religion, history and literature." The first pledge of funds to this new Jewish Publication Society of America was a subscription of one hundred dollars from the "Knowledge Seekers." Mr. Jacob H. Schiff, who was abroad at the time of the organization meeting, cabled his greetings and five thousand dollars. Mr. Meyer Guggenheim subsequently gave the Society five thousand dollars. These two large gifts made it possible for the Jewish Publication Society actually to begin its work. Mr. and Mrs. Morris Newburger donated $500.00 in memory of their son Morton M. Judge Simon Rosendale, of Albany, presided at the first meeting, and continued active in the affairs of the Society as an Honorary Vice-President until his death in the spring of 1937.

The original seal of The Jewish Publication Society of America, stamped on its works, was designed by Moses Ezekiel, the celebrated American Jewish sculptor, at Rome, Italy. It represented the fulfillment of the glorious prophecy of Isaiah — the lion and the lamb lying down together and a little boy leading them. The two Hebrew letters (*Yod*, twice), representing the Name of The Lord, are emblazoned above, and within the seal are these words: "Israel's mission is peace." The second seal, adopted in 1906, and still in use, represents the Tree of Knowledge or of Torah, in accordance with the biblical sentiment that learning is "a tree of life to those who hold on to it. . . . . "

PUBLICATIONS

The first book to be published appeared two years after the founding of the Society — *Outlines of Jewish History* by Lady Magnus. This book, published 58 years ago, and revised and brought up to date in 1929 by Dr. Solomon Grayzel, is reprinted periodically and is still being used as a textbook by some religious schools. The second venture of the Society was the publication of Prof. Heinrich Graetz's abridged *History of the Jews*, the first volume of which was published in 1891. This splendid history still remains one of the Society's outstanding publications. A supplementary volume, by the late Professor Ismar Elbogen, called *A Century of Jewish Life*, was published in 1940. A new translation of the 12-volume, unabridged, Graetz's *History of the Jews* is under way; it will contain the original text and Graetz's notes, as well as additional bibliographies to be added by the foremost Jewish historians in America.

THE BIBLE TRANSLATION

Steps leading to the preparation of a new translation of the Bible into English were taken by the Society in 1892. It was intended to secure, through the cooperation of scholars in the United States and Great Britain, a new translation of each book, which an editorial committee, in constant correspondence with the translators, would then coordinate. This method was followed until 1901, under the general direction of Dr. Marcus Jastrow, Editor-in-Chief, with Doctor Kaufmann Kohler and Doctor

Frederick de Sola Mendes as the other members of the Editorial Committee. It became apparent, in 1901, that the procedure would indefinitely delay the project. The death of Doctor Jastrow in 1903 led to the formation of a new committee under the chairmanship of Dr. Solomon Schechter. This committe, however, soon found that the method adopted was too complex, and that it was impossible to accomplish by correspondence the extensive work required.

In 1908, The Jewish Publication Society of America and the Central Conference of American Rabbis reached an agreement to cooperate in the preparation of the new translation. The old plan was now abandoned in favor of a new plan whereby all the work would be done jointly by a Board of Editors. Such a Board was constituted; it was composed of Dr. Solomon Schechter, Dr. Cyrus Adler and Dr. Joseph Jacobs, representing The Jewish Publication Society of America, and Dr. Kaufmann Kohler, Dr. David Philipson and Dr. Samuel Schulman, representing the Central Conference of American Rabbis. By common agreement, Prof. Max L. Margolis was chosen as the seventh member, to be the Editor-in-Chief of the work and Secretary to the Editorial Board of which Dr. Cyrus Adler was elected Chairman. Incidentally, the Board contained an equal representation of the Jewish Theological Seminary, the Hebrew Union College, and the Dropsie College for Hebrew and Cognate Learning. For one year, Prof. Israel Friedlaender acted as a member of the Board instead of Dr. Schechter.

Through the generosity of Mr. Jacob H. Schiff, who in 1908 presented the sum of $50,000.00 to the Society to enable it to carry out this project, the translation was finally completed. The last meeting of the Board of Editors of the Bible was held in November, 1915, and closed with a prayer of thanks to God that the great task was finished and that the group which, for seven years, had toiled together, was intact. On January 30, 1917, the Bible was formally published, both in America and in Great Britain. In consideration of his interest in the work and his beneficence which made it possible, the Society presented the first copy of the Bible, printed on India paper, elegantly bound and suitably inscribed, to Mr. Jacob H. Schiff, at the memorable dinner given at the Hotel Astor in New York City on January 22, 1917. Twenty-two printings attest to the popularity of the Society's translation, and over 400,000 copies have already been printed.

An abridgment of the Bible, edited by Emily Solis-Cohen, Jr., was published in 1931. The publication of this volume was made possible by the Hebrew Sunday School Society of Philadelphia, which was represented on the Committee with which Miss Solis-Cohen worked.

In 1946, to satisfy a long-felt need for a preparatory volume to the reading of *The Holy Scriptures*, the Society published *Pathways Through the Bible*, by Mortimer J. Cohen. It provides a minimum of background information and interpretation by which alone the Bible's spiritual meaning becomes clear and vital. This volume has had a tremendous success and 33,000 copies of it have been distributed in two years.

An agreement was completed in 1946 with the Hebrew University in Palestine, whereby the University and the Society joined their forces in the preparation and eventual publication of a Hebrew text based on a 9th and 10th century manuscript. The manuscript was edited under the direction of the University's Professor Umberto Cassuto. The text of the Hebrew Bible is to be set in the Society's plant and the University will restrict itself to the distribution of an all-Hebrew Bible, while the Society will publish a Hebrew-English version, using the University's Hebrew text, and an improved J. P. S. translation. Publication of this Bible is expected in 1952.

ISRAEL ZANGWILL

The publication of Israel Zangwill's *Children of the Ghetto* in 1892, was the Society's first great popular success and vastly stimulated the publication of Jewish books in America. A commercial edition was published by Macmillan and Company. Commercial publishers were amazed by the popular success of this book, and from then on Jewish authors found it much easier to have their books published, while the publishers found an easier market for Jewish books. The popularizing of books of Jewish interest in America can thus really be traced back to Zangwill's immortal works sponsored by the Society. During its Golden Jubilee Year (1938) the Society published a *Zangwill Omnibus Book*, containing the *Children of the Ghetto, Grandchildren of the Ghetto, Ghetto Comedies*, and *Ghetto Tragedies*. In 1939 the Society repurchased the rights to *Dreamers of the Ghetto*, which was immediately republished. Subsequently, all of the plates and copyrights of the Zangwill books were purchased by the Society and are to be reprinted in a uniform binding.

THE YEAR BOOK

In 1899, the Society published its first *American Jewish Year Book* the outstanding source for current history and American Jewish affairs. Dr. Cyrus Adler was its first editor, and it was edited subsequently by Miss Henrietta Szold, Herman Bernstein,

Herbert Friedenwald, H. G. Friedman, Dr. Joseph Jacobs, Samson D. Oppenheim and Harry Schneiderman, who has been its editor for the past twenty-seven years. Morris Fine became co-editor in 1947. Its pages are invaluable for the student of Jewish life in America, and its statistics a necessity for every communal worker. Since 1909, *The Year Book* has been published jointly by the Society and the American Jewish Committee.

All branches of Jewish literature were essayed by the Society in its first few years. In its first 25 years of existence, it published eighty-seven books and distributed half a million volumes.

GINZBERG'S LEGENDS OF THE JEWS

The first volume of Prof. Louis Ginzberg's *Legends of the Jews* was printed in 1909. This monumental and epoch-making work on the Agadah is the greatest single contribution to the study of the subject within a century, and easily ranks as the most significant work on Jewish lore thus far published in the English language. The first four volumes carry the story from the Creation through the Book of Esther. Since Dr. Ginzberg's grasp is encyclopaedic, no tale left in tiniest literary crevice or hidden in obscurest midrashic corner is omitted. Volumes V and VI contain the notes and references, which open up the richest material for further study, not only in the legendary lore of the Jews, but in allied fields of theology, folklore and customs. The seventh volume, a complete index prepared by Dr. Boaz Cohen, was published in 1938.

SCHIFF LIBRARY OF JEWISH CLASSICS

In 1914, Mr. Jacob H. Schiff again manifested his interest in the work of the Society when he announced his intention to make further provision for the publication of Jewish literature, both in the original and in translation. For this purpose he gave another fund of $50,000.00 for the publication of a selection of the Jewish Classics. The Schiff Library of Jewish Classics was intended to represent the entire range of Jewish literature since the close of the Bible canon, and was designed to demonstrate that Jewish literary genius did not end with the Bible, but continued and was active throughout the ages in all branches of literature.

Nine titles, in seventeen volumes, have already been published, as follows: *Selected Religious Poems of Solomon Ibn Gabirol; Selected Poems of Jehudah Halevi; Poems of Moses Ibn Ezra; Mesillat Yesharim*, by Luzzatto; *Treatise Ta'anit of the Babylonian Talmud;* Albo's *Sefer Ha-Ikkarim* (five volumes); *Mekilta de Rabbi Ishmael* (three volumes); *Hebrew Ethical Wills* (two volumes); and the *Ma'aseh Book* (two volumes). Future additions to the Classics Series depend on the raising of additional funds, the original fund having been exhausted.

JUVENILES

Knowing of the great need for Jewish juveniles, the Society has printed twenty-two excellent children's books. *The Breakfast of the Birds*, translated from the Hebrew of Judah Steinberg by Emily Solis-Cohen, Jr., is a beautiful classic, on which several generations of Jewish children have been reared. Three recent juvenile books have become very popular: *What the Moon Brought*, the story of the Jewish holidays for children; and its sequel *Little New Angel*, both by Sadie Rose Weilerstein; and *The Aleph-Bet Story Book* by Deborah Pessin.

HISTORIES

An historical Jewish Community Series, containing the history of old-world Jewish communities, was projected many years ago. The first book in the series, *The History of the Jews in Frankfort* appeared in 1929 and additional volumes have since been published: *London, Venice, Vienna, Augsburg and Regensburg, Cologne, Rome,* and *Vilna.*

A start has been made on Jewish history by countries: *The History of the Jews of Italy; Germany;* and *Spain.* Others are under way, as well as a series of histories on American-Jewish communities.

In 1928, a one-volume Jewish history was published under the joint authorship of Alexander Marx and Max L. Margolis. This is the most authorative one-volume Jewish history ever printed; 50,000 copies have been sold, and translations made into Spanish and French. In 1946 a briefer one-volume history, profusely illustrated, written by the Society's Editor, Dr. Solomon Grayzel, was an immediate success. Two printings were sold out in less than one year.

BIBLE COMMENTARIES

A series of commentaries on the *Bible* has been started. *Micah* by Max L. Margolis was published in 1908; *Deuteronomy* by Joseph Reider, in 1937; and *Numbers* by Julius H. Greenstone in 1939. *Proverbs*, by the same author, will be published in 1949.

LOEB SERIES

Professor Morris Loeb, of New York, the distinguished chemist, scholar and public worker, who died on October 8, 1912, by his Last Will and Testament, created a Fund under the following terms: "I give and bequeath to The Jewish Publication Society of America the sum of Ten Thousand Dollars as a permanent fund, the income of which alone shall, from time to time, be utilized for and applied to the preparation and publication of a scholarly work devoted to the interests of Judaism." The books published under this imprint are: *Saadia Gaon — His Life and Works*, by Henry Malter, published in 1921; *The Pharisees — The Sociological Background of Their Faith* (two volumes), by Louis Finkelstein, published in 1938; *The Jewish Community — Its History and Structure to The American Revolution* (three volumes), by Salo Wittmayer Baron, published in 1942; and *The Jews in Spain — Their Social, Political and Cultural Life During the Middle Ages* (two volumes), by Abraham A. Neuman, published in 1942.

REPRINT LIBRARY

In order to make some of the titles available at a lower price, the Society created a Reprint Library, in a uniform binding, which makes it possible for every Jewish home to have a Jewish library. Approximately a hundred titles are available at the present time in this collection. All in all, the Society has published 250 titles, including books on ethics, history, essays, Bible study, fiction, juveniles, poetry, and biography. Over four million copies of the Society's publications have been distributed.

THE PRESS

The need for a Hebrew Press in America was first brought to the attention of the Society in 1914 by Dr. Cyrus Adler, whose vision as regards the needs of the Jews in America, in fact throughout the world, was remarkable. His associates on the Board of Trustees agreed with him, but thought the plan too ambitious because of the capital expenditures necessary to cut the type and provide the mechanical equipment. However, Dr. Adler, with the courage and enthusiasm which he devoted unselfishly to so many activities of The Society, and with the assistance of Simon Miller, then President, worked very quietly and, by 1920, secured a fund of $100,000.00 to establish the Press. Half of this sum was a gift by Jacob H. Schiff, the greatest benefactor the Society has ever had; $25,000.00 was given by Louis Marshall, the great Jewish leader, and the balance secured by Mr. Miller from among other friends of The Society. For the first time in the history of American Jewish scholarship it was not longer necessary to go to Europe to set Hebrew texts with vowels, by machine, instead of by hand. The growth of the Press from its humble beginnings to the finest foreign language press in the country, with the largest assortment of Hebrew type faces in the world, is one of the outstanding achievements of The Publication Society. During the war the Press also produced a tremendous number of Prayer Books and Haggadahs for the National Jewish Welfare Board, totaling approximately 2,500,000 volumes.

While the Press was originally designed for the printing of the Schiff Library of Jewish Classics, it has used machinery and processes which revolutionized the art of Hebrew printing. For the first time in the history of Hebrew printing, vowel-points as well as biblical texts with musical accents, were set by machine. The original Hebrew type used was designed by Joseph B. Abrahams, then Secretary of the Jewish Theological Seminary, under the guidance of Dr. Cyrus Adler. It was designed after the 17th-century type from the presses of Menasseh ben Israel. It has been much admired by scholars in Europe, Palestine and America.

Gradually other types in Semitic languages, as well as five beautiful English faces, were added. Today the Press does composition in Hebrew, Syriac, Greek, Arabic, Yiddish, Judeo-Arabic, Babylonian, Latin, Spanish, German, French, Russian and other Slavic languages, as well as English. Grown to ten keyboard machines and five casting machines, The Society's equipment has a present value of $250,000.00. The present staff includes twenty high-grade craftsmen, many of them trained during the past ten years.

In addition to setting the type for the J. P. S. publications, as well as various scientific magazines, such as *The Jewish Quarterly Review*, and the *Journal of Biblical Literature*, the Press now has for customers almost every educational institution and learned society in the country publishing books or articles in Semitic languages. The list is impressive and includes Yale, Harvard, Pennsylvania, Columbia, Princeton, and Johns Hopkins universities, the Jewish Theological Seminary, American Oriental Society, American Academy for Jewish Research, the Central Conference of American Rabbis, the Rabbinical Assembly, Hebrew Union College and Dropsie College. For the American Bible Society, the *Bible* in the Russian language and other works in Serbian were completed. Almost all of the new Jewish Prayer Books in America were set by the J. P. S. The Press now owns a complete composition plant, which will soon move to the new J. P. S. building.

PERSONALITIES

Morris Newburger served as President of the Society from 1888 until 1902, and was succeeded by Edwin Wolf, who served until 1913. The longest service as President was that of Simon Miller, who served for twenty consecutive years, retiring in 1933, so that an energetic younger man, J. Solis-Cohen, Jr., could assume the direction of the Society. Mr. Solis-Cohen has served for fifteen years.

The original Chairman of the Publication Committee was Judge Mayer Sulzberger, who served until his death in 1923. He was succeeded by Dr. Cyrus Adler, who was very active in the affairs of the Society from its very inception, and who served for ten years as Chairman of the Publication Committee. The President of the Society, Mr. J. Solis-Cohen, Jr., served as Acting Chairman from 1933 to 1938 and was succeeded by the present Chairman, Judge Louis E. Levinthal.

Miss Henrietta Szold, later the founder of Hadassah, attended the organizational meeting of the Society in 1888 and immediately became part of the official family. She served as Editor and Secretary of the Publication Committee from the organizational meeting in 1888 until January 16, 1916. She helped to write the concluding chapter, which dealt with the Jews in America, of the Society's first publication, Lady Magnus' *Outlines of Jewish History*. For Graetz' *History of The Jews*, she compiled the comprehensive and valuable index. She translated from the German Lazarus' *The Ethics of Judaism*. The first four volumes of *The Legends of the Jews* were also translated from the German by Miss Szold. From the French, she translated Slouschz' *The Renascence of Hebrew Literature*. She was co-editor of the *American Jewish Yearbook* in 1904 and editor in 1906 and 1907. She was elected an Honorary Vice-President in 1940 and served in that capacity until her death in 1945.

The roll of editors who followed Henrietta Szold has also contained distinguished personalities: Benzion Halper, who served from 1916 until 1924; Isaac Husik, who served from 1926 until 1939; and Dr. Solomon Grayzel, who is the Society's first fulltime editor.

REJUVENATION

In 1936 the Society underwent a rejuvenation, when an entirely new attitude was adopted on the type of manuscript printed, the number of books distributed, etc. From three books and no reprints in 1936, the program was moved up until, in 1947, seven new books were printed and thirty titles reprinted. In that 12-year period, eighty new titles were printed and one hundred and fifty of the older titles were printed one or more times. The volume of the Society's business has increased over five-fold in this 12-year period, under the direction of the writer as Executive Vice-President. In 1946 the Society purchased its own building in Philadelphia, where physical facilities are available for a large expansion of the Society's program and for the work of the Press.

PLANS FOR FUTURE

The history of the first sixty years of the Jewish Publication Society has indeed been an honorable contribution to the cultural wealth of the American and world Jewish community. The measure of the Society's future activity is entirely dependent on the support which the Society will receive.

JUDAICA PRODUCTION OF UNIVERSITY PRESSES

By Salamon Faber

PUBLISHING ACTIVITIES of university presses represent an important factor of academic endeavor in America. They began in 1878 at Johns Hopkins University to meet the need "to diffuse knowledge not merely among those who can attend the daily lectures but far and wide."[1] In the course of the years university presses were established on more and more campuses. Their objectives were expanded, (1) to provide an outlet for publication of research for the faculty members of its own and other universities; (2) to extend the instructional function of the parent institution by publishing and disseminating knowledge and scholarship as widely and as economically as possible to both scholars and educated laymen; (3) to publish learned books of small sale potential and limited possibility of financial return, which commercial publishers cannot profitably undertake; (4) to gain favorable publicity and prestige for the university of which it is part.[2] Their publishing program covers the entire spectrum of knowledge, e.g. agriculture and animal science, art and architecture, anthropology and archeology, biology, business and economics, chemistry, communication arts, education, engineering and mathematics, folklore, geography and geology, history, law, language and literature, linguistics, literary criticism, medicine, music, philosophy and religion . . . and even such specialized publications as reference books and works on Chinese paintings.[3] Their importance to the academic community can be gauged by the fact that in 1965 every 12th book issued in the United States had a university press imprint.[4] Equally significant is the fact that booksales of university presses grossed in 1966 over 30% of the total.[5]

The term "Judaica," according to the definition in *Webster's International* (3rd edition), covers "literary and historical materials relating to Jews and Judaism." Many such materials have been published by university presses.[6] The selection and number

---

[1] Gene R. Hawes, *To Advance Knowledge,* University Press Service (N.Y., 1967), p. 30.

[2] Chester Kerr, *A Report on American University Presses* (Chapel Hill, 1949).

[3] *America,* Jan. 9, 1965, p. 49.

[4] Charles A. Madison, *Book Publishing in America* (N.Y., 1966), p. 385.

[5] *Publishers Weekly,* Jan. 29, 1968, p. 49 ff.

[6] For purposes of this article only books are considered. Judaica materials in scholarly journals published by university presses were not included in the preparatory studies.

of titles published in a given period depend largely upon the sponsoring university's interest in a Jewish Studies Program. Where such programs exist, with faculties and students pursuing research in the various disciplines of Jewish learning, e.g. history, philosophy, contemporary Israel, art, linguistics, Jewish law, etc., more Judaica materials are included for publication by that university's press. Since departments and chairs in Jewish studies are of relatively recent origin on most campuses,[7] the Judaica production is rather limited in comparison with the press' total output. This is invariably confirmed by *Publishers Trade List Annuals.*

Some presses, especially those sponsored by older established universities, list series in Judaica. We describe these series alphabetically, without making judgments as to the value or impact of the published works upon Jewish scholarship. Sample works will be singled out, wherever logical, to indicate the publisher's orientation or special interest in the selection of subject matter.

1. Cornell University Press lists a series "Studies in Modern Hebrew Literature." Only two titles were published as of this year: *Abraham Mapu* by David Patterson (1964), and *Saul Tschernichowsky* by Eisig Silberschlag (1968). The name of the series describes its specific limited scope.

2. Harvard University Press lists among its 79 series the "Philip W. Lown Institute of Advanced Jewish Studies." Four titles in Jewish thought and history were thus far published under its aegis: *Biblical and Other Studies* (1963), *Studies in Nineteenth-Century Jewish Intellectual History* (1964); *Biblical Motifs: Origins and Transformations* (1966); and *Jewish Medieval and Renaissance Studies* (1967). All four volumes were edited by Alexander Altmann.

3. Oxford University Press[8] is known for its "Scripta Judaica." Among its heretofore published titles are *The Emergence and Linguistic Background of Judeo-Arabic* by Joshua Blau (1965); *Jewish Matrimonial Law in the Middle Ages* by Zeev W. Falk (1966); *Isaac Israeli's Works, Translated with Comments and Outline of His Philosophy* by Alexander Altmann and S. M. Stern (1958); *Exclusiveness and Tolerance: Studies in Jewish Gentile Relations* by Jacob Katz (1961); *Qamran Studies* by Chaim Rabin (1959); *Joseph Karo: Lawyer and Mystic* by R. J. Werblowsky (1962). Apparently, the interest and program of this series are all

---

[7] Comp. Jacob Neusner, "Everybody but the Jew," *Jewish Spectator,* Jan. 1970, p. 16 ff.

[8] Though Oxford and Cambridge Universities began their presses early in the 16th century, their programs of Judaica are apparently guided by the same criteria as those of the American university presses.

inclusive, without special preference for a particular branch of Jewish scholarship.

Oxford University Press lists Judaica materials in four other series: "Clarendon Bible"—three titles dealing with Biblical and post-exilic Jewish history; "New Clarendon Bible"—three more titles on the early pre-common era period of Jewish history; "Histories of Nations"—two titles, and "London Oriental Series"— four titles on Jewish history and Jewish law during the Second Commonwealth.

4. Princeton University Press has a special series "Jewish Symbols in the Greco-Roman Period"—a massive work in 13 volumes by E. R. Goodenough, whose publication took many years. Three titles on Old Testament studies by J. Pritchard are listed in the series "Princeton Studies on the Near East."

5. Rutgers University Press has a series in "The World History of the Jewish People." The following three works were brought out as of now: *At the Dawn of Civilization: A Background of Biblical History* edited by Ephraim A. Speiser (1965); *The Dark Ages: 700-1096* edited by Cecil Roth (1966); *The Patriarchs* edited by Benjamin Mazar (1969).

It is noteworthy that *Library Journal* reported that a special panel of librarians selected Speiser's work as "of particular interest to high school and public libraries." [9] For that matter, many other Judaica materials produced by university presses are of wide public interest and would undoubtedly be published by profit seeking commercial publishers.

6. Wayne State University Press has a series "The Morris and Emma Shaver Publications Fund for Jewish Studies." The following eight titles were published by this fund: *Onions and Cucumbers and Plums: 46 Yiddish Poems in English* by Sarah Z. Betsky (1958); *Ancient Jewish Philosophy* by Israel I. Efros (1964); *Profiles of Eleven* by Melech Epstein (1965); *The Sacred Portal: A Primary Symbol of Ancient Judaic Art* by Bernard Goldman (1966); *The Political World of American Zionism,* by Samuel Halperin (1961); *Hayim Greenberg Anthology* edited by Marie Syrkin (1968); *Louis Marshall, Defender of Jewish Rights* by Morton Rosenstoch (1966); *The Jew Within American Society: A Study in Ethnic Individuality* by Bezalel C. Sherman (1965). The special preference for works on Labor Zionism by this series may have been stipulated by its founder.

7. Yale University Press lists eighteen titles in "Yale Judaica Series." Eleven are translations of the Code of Maimonides. Four are Rabbinic and Midrashic texts: *The Fathers According to*

---

[9] *Library Journal,* June 15, 1965, p. 2766 ff.

Rabbi Nathan, translated by Judah Goldin (1955); *Pesikta Rab-bati* (1968) and *The Midrash on Psalms* (1959), both translated by William G. Braude; *The Tractate Mourning,* translated by Dov Zlotnick. The remaining three titles are: *Saadia Gaon, the Book of Beliefs and Opinions,* translated by Samuel Rosenblatt (1948); *Falasha Anthology,* translated by Wolf Leslau (1951); *Karaite Anthology,* translated by Leo Nemoy (1952).

Of these seven presses only Yale published all the Judaica mate-rials as part of its Judaica series. The others produced works in addition to the ones listed in the respective series. Cornell's catalog includes *Ancient Israel* by Harry M. Orlinsky (1954 and 1960); *Studies in Religious Philosophy and Mysticism* by Alexander Alt-mann (1969); two titles on the Middle East by George Lenchow-ski; *Franz Kafka: Parable and Paradox* by Heinz Politzer (1962 and 1967); *The Dead Sea Psalms Scroll,* by J. A. Sanders (1967); *Israel on the Road to Sinai, 1949-1956* by Ernest Stock (1967); *Moshava, Kibbutz and Moshav* by D. M. Weintraub (1969).

Harvard's "Loeb Classical Library" which is renowned for its specialization in translations of the Greek and Latin classics, produced *Josephus, with an English Translation,* translated by Ralph Marcus, in nine volumes. Harvard University Press pub-lished a number of other important works which enriched Jewish scholarship, e.g. Harry A. Wolfson's *Crescas' Critique of Aristotle: Problems of Aristotle's Physics in Jewish and Arabic Philosophy* (1929); *Philo: Foundations of Religious Philosophy in Judaism, Christianity and Islam* (1947 and 1962). This press also published *The Idea of the Jewish State* by Ben Halpern (1961); *Studies in History of the Sanhedrin* by Hugo Mantel (1962); *Judaism in the First Century of the Christian Era* by George F. Moore (1927-30); *Corpus Papyrorum Judaicorum* by V. A. Tchernikover (1957-64); and many titles in Biblical research.

The presses of Princeton, Rutgers and Wayne State also pro-duced more materials in the fields of archeology, Biblical theology, history and philosophy.

A number of university presses publish Judaica materials, either in related monographic series, Near or Middle East, History, Religion, etc., or as individual titles not part of a specific academic program of the sponsoring university. The series in a given instance may be of incidental significance, but the number and subject matter of published titles are of interest.

Cambridge University Press has been specializing for a long time in the printing of Bibles. Texts were produced in various formats, whole Bibles or single books, with or without commen-taries, for pulpit use, home use, etc. Cambridge press also estab-lished a record in book production covering all areas of knowledge, research and literary activity. Thousands of titles are listed in its catalog. Yet in the field of Judaica, this record is about the smallest of any of the large university presses. Only about half a dozen enumerated titles can be classed in Judaica.[10]

The University of Chicago Press lists a dozen titles in Jewish philosophy and religion, folklore and Bible. It has not published heretofore any works in Jewish history, nor in Jewish law. This press began in 1891 with three scholarly journals, one devoted to Near Eastern studies, originally named *Hebraica*. In its Judaica group belong *Patterns in the Early Poetry of Israel* by S. Gevirtz (1963); *American Judaism* by Nathan Glazer (1957); *The Ten Commandments* by Solomon Goldman (1958); *The Root and the Branch* by Robert Gordis (1965); *The Religion of Israel* by Yehezkel Kaufmann (1960); *Guide of the Perplexed* by Maimonides, translated with introduction and notes by Shlomo Pines (1963); *Legends of the Hasidim* by Jerome Mintz (1968); *Folktales of Israel* by Dov Noy (1963); *Major Trends in Modern Hebrew Fiction* by I. Rabinovich (1968); *The Challenge of Israel's Faith* by G. E. Wright (1944) and a number of other notable works. They total only a small fraction of the press' latest catalog of some 1500 titles.

Columbia University Press offers a more diversified range of Judaica in history, literature, literary criticism, philosophy and sociology. Among its notable contributions are *A Social and Religious History of the Jews,* by Salo W. Baron (1952-60); *The Jews of the United States, 1790-1840: A Documentary History,* co-edited by Joseph L. Blau and Salo W. Baron (1964); *The Book of Delight* by Joseph Ben Meir Zabara, translated by Moses Hadas (1960); *Macabees, Zealots and Josephus* by W. R. Farmer (1956); *Agenda for American Jews* by Eli Ginzberg (1950); *The French Enlightenment and the Jews* by Arthur Hertzberg (1968); *Israel Zangwill* by Maurice Wohlgelernter (1964). Its latest offering lists *Isaac Cardozo: A Study in 17th Century Marranism and Jewish Apologetics* by Y. H. Yerushalmi, and *A Vassal Jewish Principality in Carolingian Frankland* by A. J. Zuckerman (both titles in 1969).

The University of California Press was organized in 1893, the same year Columbia's came into existence. Both list in their catalogs for 1969 about 1000 titles. But while the latter includes some 20 titles in Judaica subjects, the former has less than half a dozen. Obviously these figures are related to the university's pro-

---

[10] However, George R. Barnes in *Cambridge University Press: List of Books 1521-1800* (Cambridge, 1935) lists a substantial number of Judaica titles, e.g. *De Legibus Hebraeorum* by J. Spencer (1685); *Hebrew Grammar* by I. Lyons (1735, 1738, 1757); *The Ancient History of the Hebrews,* by S. Squire (1741), etc.

gram in Jewish studies. Columbia has had this program for many years. California only recently began to develop one. The California press recently brought out *Mediterranean Society: The Jewish Community of the Arab World as Portrayed in the Documents of the Cairo Geniza* by Solomon D. Goitein (1968), and *Archives from Elephantine: The Life of an Ancient Jewish Military Colony* by Bezalel Porten (1968).

Johns Hopkins University Press lists only four Judaica titles: two in archeology by William F. Albright; *Covenant: The History of a Biblical Idea* by Delbert R. Hillers (1969); and *Britain's Moment in the Middle East, 1914-1956* by Elizabeth Monroe (1963).

The New York University Press lists six Judaica titles among a total of about 400 in its last catalog. Included are *Judaism and Islam* by Abraham I. Katsh (1953); *Jews in 19th Century Egypt* by Jacob M. Landau (1969); *Jewish Education in a Pluralistic Society* by Nathan S. Winter (1966); and two works on Isaac Bashevis Singer which will be discussed later. Of very special interest, however, is *Birth Control in Jewish Law* by David M. Feldman (1969), one of the few books in Jewish law published with the imprint of a university press.

University of Toronto Press lists works in archeology, Hebrew and Near East studies in the "Near and Middle East Series." In addition to a number of guides and outlines of Palestinian archeological collections in the Royal Ontarion Museum, this press published *Hebrew Opinions* by Theophile J. Meek (1950); *Hebrew Texts and Palestinian Vocalization* by E. J. Revell (in preparation); *Hebrew Syntax: An Outline* by R. J. Williams (1867); *Mosaic Tradition* by Frederick V. Winnett (1949).

Our discussion up to this point centered on large presses, those producing a score or even scores of titles in the course of the year. What of the smaller press, which publishes annually only five to ten titles? Are Judaica materials included in its program? The answer is in the affirmative. Its acceptance for publication of a Judaica title depends upon many factors, not all related to an interest in Jewish learning. For example, Indiana University Press published in 1960 *Studies in Biblical and Jewish Folklore,* edited by Raphael Patai and others. This was due only to the fact that Dov Noy, one of the co-editors, happened to be at the time associated with that university. But generally speaking, an author's standing in the world of scholarship will influence a press to be identified as publisher of his work.

Some interesting conclusions emerge from an analysis of the types of Judaica materials frequently selected by university presses, especially the smaller ones.

A. Studies in literature and literary criticism lead the list of publications. Isaac Bashevis Singer seems to receive considerable attention. As a matter of fact, he seems to be the only Yiddish writer whose novels are read (in translation, of course) and written about in literature classes. This is confirmed by the publication of at least four books about him in recent years by university presses: *The Achievement of Isaac B. Singer* by Marcia Allentuck, Southern Illinois University Press (1969); *Isaac B. Singer and the Eternal Past* by Irving Buchen, New York University Press (1968); *Critical Views of Isaac B. Singer* by Irving Malin, New York University Press (1968); *Isaac Bashevis Singer* by Ben Siegel, University of Minnesota Press ("Pamphlets of American Writers," 1969). Hardly any other contemporary writer in Yiddish, nor any of the classics, Mendele, Peretz, etc., commanded sufficient interest to produce a book by a university press. Franz Kafka is also widely studied. At least three works about him and his literary influence should be noted: *Franz Kafka: Parable and Paradox* by Heinz Politzer, Cornell University Press (1962 and rev. 1967); *Franz Kafka* by Walter Sokel, Columbia University Press (1966); *There Goes Kafka* by Johannes Urzidil, Wayne State University (1969).

B. Closely related to the above subject, the impact of a "Jewish" or "Jewishly motivated" theme upon English and world literature received due attention in scholarly works. Foremost in this category is *The Legend of the Wandering Jew* by George K. Anderson, Brown University Press (1965). The publisher recommended this title to be included among those which "have made the strongest impact on contemporary society or most enriched our culture" in the last quarter century.[11] The theme of Shylock was dealt with anew in recent years in at least two works: *Shylock on the Stage* by Toby Lelyveld, The Press of Case Western Reserve University (1960); *From Shylock to Svengali: Jewish Stereotypes in English Fiction* by Edgar Rosenberg, Stanford University Press (1965).

C. Anthologies and translations from Hebrew and Yiddish belong in the area of literary activity. Two books should be noted: *Onions and Cucumbers and Plums: 46 Yiddish Poems in English* by Sarah Z. Betsky, Wayne State University Press (1958); *Modern Hebrew Poetry: A Bilingual Anthology* by Ruth F. Mintz, University of California Press (1966).

D. Some university presses specialize in the production of materials which highlight regional problems and the heritage of the region. This is especially the case with state university presses.[12]

---

[11] *Saturday Review*, June 10, 1967, "A Quarter-Century of Milestones," pp. 31 ff.

Correspondingly, a number of Judaica with a distinctive regional flavor or regional interest were published in different parts of the country, e.g. *The Jewish Soldiers from Michigan in the Civil War* by Irving I. Katz, Wayne State University Press (1962); *Colonia Baron Hirsch: A Jewish Agricultural Colony in Argentina* by Morton D. Winsberg, University of Florida Press (1964); somewhat related to regional orientation is Don Halpern's *The Ancient Synagogues of the Iberian Peninsula,* University of Florida Press (1969).

E. A number of works were produced by university presses on Jews and Jewish endeavor in American society. We already mentioned Bezalel C. Sherman's *The Jew Within American Society.* Irving Malin's *Jews and Americans,* Southern Illinois University Press (1965), is of special interest since the author "analyzes the significance of contemporary Jewish writing and the subtle conflict in Jews writing in a Gentile society, and suggests solutions and rationalizations being produced by these writers." Nathan Glazer's *Beyond the Melting Pot,* MIT Press (1963), devotes an entire section to the Jewish minority.

Some works, though not entirely related to Jews or Judaism, include important studies in Jewish history, philosophy, religion, etc. As illustrations, we single out the following three titles: *The King is Dead: Studies in Near Eastern Resistance to Hellenism, 334-31 B.C.E.* by Samuel Eddy, University of Nebraska Press (1961); *Athens and Jerusalem* by Lev Shestov, Ohio University Press (1966); *Order and History,* by Eric Voegelin, in six volumes of which the first deals with Israel and Revelation, Louisiana State University Press (1956/57). Incidentally, these last two titles were also selected by their respective publishers as having made the strongest impact in the last quarter of a century.

Works dealing with social and political developments in the Middle East in this century, irrespective of an author's political orientation concerning the Arab-Israel struggles, must include valuable materials on Jewish history, colonization in Palestine, the emergence of Israel, etc. In this group belong *Middle East in Crisis* by Carol Fisher, Syracuse University Press (1969); *The Arab Israeli Dilemma* by Fred Khouri, Syracuse University Press (1968); and a number of other titles.

F. University presses consider among their primary responsibilities the production of esoteric works of interest to a limited group of specialists in a given field. Some Judaica titles fit the description, e.g. *Jewish Proselytizing in the First Five Centuries of the Common Era* by William G. Braude, Brown University Press

---

[12] Comp. *Directory of the Association of American University Presses* (N.Y., 1969/70).

(1940); *Immigrants From India in Israel: Planned Change in an Administrated Community* by Gilbert Kushner, University of Arizona Press (in press); *Guide to Jewish References in the Mexican Colonial Era* by Seymour B. Liebman, University of Pennsylvania Press (1964); *Ras Shamra Discoveries and the Old Testament* by Arvid S. Kopelard, University of Oklahoma Press (1963); *The Origin of the Modern Jew: Jewish Identity and European Culture in Germany, 1749-1824,* by Michael A. Meyer, Wayne State University Press (1967); *The Dead Sea Scrolls and the Early Church* by Lucetta Mowry, University of Notre Dame Press (1966); *A Biographical Dictionary of Early American Jews: Colonial Times Through 1800* by Joseph R. Rosenbloom, University of Kentucky Press (1960).

We may sum up our observations as follows:

The motivations and purposes which guide university presses in their general publishing policies apply also to Judaica materials. The scope of Judaica includes Bible, Jewish history and archeology, religion and philosophy, literature, linguistics, sociology and Jewish law. Selections of Judaica titles by various presses reflect an interest in subject matter in the above order, Bible appearing at the top of the list and Jewish law at the bottom.

A university's interest in a program of Jewish learning is usually attested by a larger offering of Judaica in the press' catalog. In view of the growing tendency on American campuses to develop such programs, more Judaica materials can be expected from university presses. This last hopeful assumption is, of course, predicated upon the availability of creative scholars in the many disciplines of Jewish learning.

OLD FRIENDS REVISITED

A Review of Judaica Reprints

By Sefton David Temkin

"BOOKS ARE NOT absolutely dead things," wrote Milton, "but do contain a potency of life in them to be as active as that soul was whose progeny they are." It might be an exaggeration to describe as "absolutely dead" a book that is merely out of print, but it is likely to be little more than comatose. Milton goes on to observe that: "A good book is the precious life blood of a master spirit." Very well; but circulation is the life blood of authors (not to say publishers), and it coagulates when the book receives peaceful burial in the stacks of the older libraries.

A phenomenon of the present age is the release of that which had been interred through the reprinting of hundreds of classical works which had become largely inaccessible. So great has been this movement that one wondered whether it has been caused by some development in printing technique which makes it easier and cheaper to copy existing works. Apparently not: the college population has leaped upward, and with it the demand for textbooks. It is not that earlier generations did not see the reissue of whole series of books on which the copyright had expired: witness "Everyman's Library" and the "Harvard Classics." Then the books were reset and redesigned to a new uniform format. Now conditions in the printing trade make this very expensive, so resort is had to simple photography of the original edition. We have every reason to be grateful that such processes exist, though in a few cases, e.g., Jastrow's *Talmudic Dictionary*, where they cannot or have not been applied so as to give a clear image, the strain on the eyes can be great.

The field of Jewish studies also has been irrigated by this stream. We may ask here whether the Holocaust has anything to do with the need to draw on the products of our grandparents' time; but even if due to the cutting off of the well springs of scholarly inspiration, the desire to know what the past produced is encouraging.

In this branch of publishing Ktav has projected "The Library of Jewish Classics" under the editorship of Gerson D. Cohen and "The Library of Biblical Studies" under the editorship of Harry M. Orlinsky. Schocken Books have made their contribution, and now Gregg International Publishers make Judaica an important section of its expanding list.

In the field of Judaica, the reprinting of *The Jewish Encyclopedia* is surely the greatest *tour de force*. Its appearance at the beginning of the century was a tribute to the capacity of American Jewry to think big even in its formative years. Naturally it is out of date in a number of respects, but despite its unevenness represents the fruits of a Golden Age of Jewish learning and is an indispensable adjunct to Jewish research. That the color plates disappeared from the reprint was no great diminution of the usefulness of the Encyclopedia. It was a pity that the publishers did not make use of the 1925 edition which contained the minimum of additional facts bringing the main body of the work up to date; it was even more of a pity that they did not project a supplementary volume which could have encompassed all the necessary additional information, but reprinting is a mechanical affair, and no doubt publishers look upon a diversion from mechanical simplicity as an unnecessary expense.

A little religious zeal can easily overcome the limitations of mechanics, and even, it seems, respect for the original author. Forty years ago Arthur Marmorstein wrote a learned volume under the title *The Old Rabbinic Doctrine of God*. Jew' College, London, where he was an honored teacher, now responds to different influences, and the reprint has been announced as *The Old Rabbinic Doctrine of G-d*. One awaits the book itself to ascertain whether the not inconsiderable labor of replacing "God" by "G-d" has been undertaken throughout the text.

It has become the common practice to furnish the reprint with an introductory discourse by a contemporary scholar in the same field as the writer of the original. In many of those issued by Ktav this is called the "Prolegomenon." We may boggle at these five syllables, but there is no reason to believe that the unknown genius who lighted on it was merely trying to show forth his learning; he had to find a word which had the same meaning as "Foreword," "Introduction," or "Preface" but which, since one or other of them was likely to be present already, was different.

These prolegomena are often different from the traditional *haskamot*—commendations from the great—with which rabbinical works were traditionally furnished. Sometimes (and this is healthy) they take a critical attitude to the work of the earlier scholar; the later scholar feels that he has the advantage of perspective, so that collectively they take on something of the character of an alumni reunion, with the class of 1970 inclined to eye disdainfully the old fogies of 1900.

Readers of *The Jewish Quarterly Review* will not be surprised to discover that in Dr. Solomon Zeitlin's "Prolegomenon" to

Gerald Friedlander's *Jewish Sources of the Sermon on the Mount*
the critical note comes over with vigor, excluding almost completely information as to who the original author was. On the
other hand, Professor Orlinsky's "Prolegomenon" to the three
volumes of Arnold B. Ehrlich's *Mikra Ki-Peshuto* provides an
incisive account of the personality and labors of the author and
also information not generally available as to the progress of
Bible studies.

In Moses Gaster's *Exempla of the Rabbis,* William G. Braude
furnishes not only instances of the shortcomings of Gaster's interpretations but—important with that careless scholar—a list of
corrigenda. A preface by Gaster often yields something that is
excitingly irrelevant. In the present work he resurrected quite
gratuitously a scandal that had been laid to rest nearly thirty
years earlier (". . . the memory alone is sufficient to deepen the
bitterness from year to year . . ."). Gaster was loved for his foibles,
and a sense of having been wronged seems to have fortified him
as he lived to a vigorous old age.

A reprint of a selective kind sponsored by Ktav is *The Jewish
Experience in America,* edited by Rabbi Abraham J. Karp. He
has combed the fifty-seven volumes of the *Publications of the
American Jewish Historical Society,* latterly known as the *American Jewish Historical Quarterly,* and he has chosen contributions
illustrative of a particular period in American Jewish history.
To each volume Rabbi Karp has written an introduction reviewing the period in question. Perhaps this was a case in which
something more than a reprint was called for. The field of
American Jewish history is one in which materials and expertise
have increased with the years, and probably some of the earlier
writings stand in need of correction.

Whole series of learned periodicals have been reprinted. The
*Monatsschrift fuer die Geschichte and Wissenschaft des Juden-
thums,* for more than eighty years the fountainhead of Jewish
scientific scholarship in Europe, has reappeared in Germany itself. The very last issue of the *Monatsschrift* was confiscated and
destroyed by the Nazis; only the chance survival of two copies
enabled the complete reprint to be made.

The *Monatsschrift* appeared first in 1851; its English counterpart, *The Jewish Quarterly Review,* which also has been reprinted,
first saw the light of day in 1888. For twenty years it was edited
by Israel Abrahams and Claude Montefiore. The latter footed
the bill. Montefiore had the delightful practice not only of paying
contributors—never the invariable practice in the case of learned
journals—but of building up the fee if he thought that an indigent
scholar needed support. It was Israel Zangwill who characterized
Montefiore in the couplet:

Of men like you earth holds but few:

An angel—with a revenue.

But perhaps this tenderness for the needs of others accounts for the unevenness of many of the volumes of the JQR.

When Abrahams and Montefiore tired of running the JQR in the face of the apathy of the Jews of England, it was taken over by Dropsie College. There followed thirty years of the impassive scholarship of Cyrus Adler, since when Solomon Zeitlin has impressed upon its pages the stamp of his own unshakeable convictions.

New York is a city of surprises, but even those who have trained themselves not to be "thrown" by anything it offers might be astonished to find that in a real estate office near one of the city's best known business intersections time is being devoted to the reprinting of works of Jewish scholarship. Such is the situation of Hermon Press. Of its productions I will mention only an old favorite of my own, Israel Abrahams' *Companion to the Authorised Daily Prayer Book*. More compact than the better known annotations by Chief Rabbi Hertz, the *Companion* has a decided literary flavor, and it led one child at least to begin to wander into the garden of Jewish literature instead of fidgeting through an incomprehensible service. Again, the original publication was financed by Claude Montefiore, with the result that two Reform Jews provided the English Orthodox Jews with the first commentary on their prayer book. And now through the concern of a couple of American Orthodox Jews the work has been rescued from oblivion.

Pirke Avot has had a special fascination for Christian scholars, and two of their editions have been reprinted—Travers Herford's and Charles Taylor's. The former is noteworthy because it appears to have been the only occasion on which that respected contemporary teacher of Talmud, John J. Tepfer, has been tempted into print. The latter may tempt the student of Talmud into contemplating the spacious life of an English university teacher of the nineteenth century, because of the excellent sketch of the life of Charles Taylor, Master of St. Johns College, Cambridge, provided by Professor Judah Goldin.

The two foregoing are of course entirely different editions of the same Hebrew text, and half a century lay between Taylor's edition and Herford's. An instance of the identical work attracting three separate publishers is Schechter's *Seminary Addresses*. Their photography is the same; only the price tag differs—one asks $1.45, a second $9.00 and a third $12.00. Clearly the maxim *caveat emptor* has not lost its meaning.

Is it all worth while? There are exceptions. It is difficult to believe that Sokolow's *History of Zionism* ever enjoyed the status which rendered it worthy of being disinterred. A contemporary once told me that Sokolow kept a sack under the bed of the London hotel in which he stayed during the First World War, into which he consigned a few pages of his history whenever he had a spare moment to dash them off. The result is a tribute to the flair of a vanished breed of *maskilim,* but hardly organized history. Besides, the Zionist movement went on to innumerable fresh achievements in the years after 1918, when Sokolow wrote, and a great deal of archival material is accessible which then was unknown. Here is an obvious task awaiting Jewish historians of the present day. For the most part, however, an unqualified welcome can be given to these offerings from the past. The present century has seen one of the sharpest breaks that Jewish history has known. The fact that, working on a purely commercial basis, publishers have felt the need to supply the post-Holocaust generation with the works of pre-Holocaust scholars, shows that continuity still exists. We do not have to begin again. We do have friends from the past and can visit them if we will.

From One Language to Another

AMERICAN JEWISH TRANSLATIONS OF THE BIBLE

By Bernard J. Bamberger

THERE are, to my knowledge, only two American Jewish translations of the Bible. We possess admirable renderings of individual books of the Bible by American Jewish scholars,[1] but a complete English version of the Bible made by Jews for Jews has been accomplished just twice in this country. The first, by Isaac Leeser, was published in 1853; the second, sponsored by the Jewish Publication Society of America, appeared in 1917.

I

We do not, unfortunately, possess an adequate biography of Isaac Leeser. He was perhaps the most gifted of the "chazan ministers" who provided spiritual leadership for American Jewry prior to the arrival of ordained rabbis. Leeser served most of his life in Philadelphia. An excellent preacher and conscientious pastor, he was one of the few leaders of his time whose vision extended beyond the confines of his own community. To rouse the scattered Jews óf the United States to a sense of unity and joint purpose, Leeser traveled extensively; to the same end, he established the pioneer periodical, *The Occident*. Yet he still found time to produce a good translation of the prayer book — in both Sefardic and Ashkenazic versions — and to carry through the great project of translating the Bible.

---

[1] For example, Psalms and Job by Moses Buttenwieser; Job, Song of Songs, and Ecclesiastes, by Morris Jastrow; Amos by Julian Morgenstern; Ecclesiastes by Robert Gordis. Mortimer J. Cohen's *Pathways Through the Bible* covers only selected portions.

In 1916, the Hebrew Publishing Co. (a privately owned enterprise) brought out an edition of the Hebrew Bible, frequently reprinted, with an English translation "revised by Alexander Harkavy." This was essentially the Authorized Version, modified to eliminate Christological interpretations and occasional obscurities. Harkavy himself, famous for his work as a Yiddish lexicographer, seems to have regarded this Bible revision as no more than a routine job. It can hardly be considered an independent translation.

The great Yiddish translation of the Bible by Yehoash was largely done in this country, and may therefore be regarded as an American Jewish translation. But, obviously, it must be studied in a different framework.

His introduction makes his purpose clear. He wants to protect his fellow-Jews against misinterpretations which have been utilized "to assail Israel's hope and faith." But his aim is not only the negative one of correcting the tendentious renderings of Christian translators. He wants also to make available both to Jewish and non-Jewish readers the rich fruits of Jewish biblical scholarship, past and present. Here he names the great medieval Hebrew exegetes, as well as the German scholars from Mendelssohn to Herxheimer, on whom he has drawn.

Leeser never made pretensions to great scholarship, and some of his contemporaries liked to dwell, with far from innocent delight, on the limitations of his Hebrew knowledge. In any case, he was a diligent and thorough student, who made excellent use of the available resources, and chose among them with discretion. His Bible translation is generally accurate and sound. In many passages it marks an advance in clarity and precision over the Authorized Version (hereafter AV) — and not only in those places where Christian presuppositions influenced the earlier translators.

In the very first chapter of Genesis, Leeser discards the traditional "firmament" and tells of God creating an "expansion." The word is perhaps not quite precise, but at least it conveys some meaning to the reader, whereas "firmament" means nothing at all. Again, in Exodus 15.21, where Miriam leads the Israelite women in song, the older versions read, "And Miriam answered them." Leeser, however, translates, "And Miriam began her song to them," recognizing that the verb *'anah* often means to start an utterance rather than to answer. (Cf. II Kings, 1.11, I Chronicles 12.18).

Externally, Leeser's translation differs from the Christian versions by following the order of books in the Hebrew Bible, not that of the Septuagint. The weekly readings from the Torah and prophets are likewise indicated. The English style, Leeser himself states, is modeled on that of King James' translators; but despite its many merits, his translation lacks the majesty and melody of AV. A few lines are sufficient proof:

"In pastures of tender grass he causeth me to lie down: beside still waters he leadeth me. My soul he refresheth: he guideth me in the tracks of righteousness for the sake of his name . . . Surely, only goodness and kindness shall follow me all the days of my life: and I shall dwell in the house of the Lord to the utmost length of days."

II

Leeser's translation met a real need. It was an English Bible that could be read in the Synagogue without embarrassment, and placed in the Jewish home without apprehensiveness. For the student it was doubly useful because Leeser appended numerous notes, referring to the authorities whom he followed, and giving alternative renderings of difficult and uncertain passages. American Jews regarded it as a standard work; and even in England, where two independent Jewish translations had been published, Leeser's version was widely read.

Nevertheless, in the course of a few decades the need for a new rendering was voiced, at least by scholars and rabbis. Two events served to underscore this demand. The Jewish Publication Society of America was established in 1888, and its leaders not unnaturally felt that a main undertaking of the Society ought to be the publication of the supreme Jewish classic. The second event was the appearance in 1885 of the Revised Version (hereafter RV), in which the leading Protestant scholars of England modified the King James translation to make it more accurate and understandable. (In 1901, the American Revised Version appeared, incorporating many hundreds of further changes.) The fact that the Anglican Church, for all its traditionalism, had not hesitated to modify the hallowed wording of AV, must have been an encouragement and stimulus to the Jews of the United States to attempt a similar enterprise.

The undertaking was launched in 1892. The various books of the Bible were assigned to a number of scholars; the renderings they were to prepare would be reviewed by an editorial board which was to give them uniformity of style. The procedure did not work out well. Not all the assignments were completed — indeed many were not even begun — and consequently the editors could not make much progress. In 1903, a tangible result was finally achieved: the Book of Psalms appeared in a translation by Dr. Kaufmann Kohler. Shortly thereafter, Dr. Marcus Jastrow, the chairman of the Editorial Committee, died. A new committee, headed by Dr. Solomon Schechter, tried to continue the work by correspondence and found it was making little headway.

In 1906, a fresh start was made. Negotiations between the Jewish Publication Society and the Central Conference of American Rabbis led to the establishment of a joint committee, headed by Dr. Cyrus Adler, a man with a knack for getting things done. In addition to Kohler and Schechter,[2] the committee included

---

[2] For one year, Dr. Israel Friedlaender served instead of Dr. Schechter.

Joseph Jacobs and Rabbis Samuel Schulman and David Philip-son. As Editor-in-chief the group unanimously chose Dr. Max L. Margolis, a Bible scholar of fabulous knowledge and brilliant acumen.

Dr. Margolis in his little book, *The Story of Bible Translations*, has told how the work was carried out. He himself prepared a draft text, on which the committee worked during sixteen meetings, each lasting from ten days to three weeks. If the committee was not satisfied with a passage in the first draft, other suggestions were considered, and a final decision was made by majority vote. Dr. Adler's reminiscences, entitled *I Have Considered the Days*, contain a few amusing anecdotes about the committee meetings, but do not tell much about the undertaking itself. But we still possess Max Margolis's notes, and these shed considerable light on the final result.

The Jewish Publication Society translation (hereafter JPS) may be considered a Jewish recension of RV.

The English revisers of 1881–1885, as well as the American revisers who supplemented their work, regarded the AV of 1611 as standard and classic. Their task was not to produce a new translation, but to make AV more accessible to the modern reader. The grandiose English style of the Elizabethans was to remain. But words that had become completely obsolete, or which had acquired an entirely different meaning, were changed to make the text more understandable. Other changes were introduced to correct errors and inaccuracies which were due to the scholarly limitations or theological preconceptions of the earlier translators. But while the English and American revisers thus modified or re-translated hundreds of passages, they worked within the frame-work of the Elizabethan vocabulary; and where AV was correct and reasonably clear, they retained it without change.

This, by and large, was the approach of the JPS committee. The notes of Margolis indicate that he would have preferred a more independent line, had not the committee ruled otherwise. Professor Harry M. Orlinsky, who has made a detailed study of the various renderings, thinks the committee was somewhat awed by the prestige of RV and so followed it in many places where (for ex-ample) Leeser had reproduced the sense of the Hebrew more exactly. Surprisingly, too, JPS retained Anglicisms — such as the use of "corn" in the sense of "grain" and the spellings "honour" and "labour" — which the American revisers discarded.

But the merits of JPS are real enough; they explain why this translation has been almost universally adopted by English-speaking Jews and has been consulted with respect by the Christian world. The style is noble and melodious, not only when it retains, but also when it departs from, the wording of AV. For instance, in Psalm 23, where Leeser had "he guideth me in the tracks of righteousness," and RV renders, "He guideth me in the paths of righteousness," JPS translates — more correctly and no less beautifully — "He guideth me in straight paths."

JPS, like Leeser, follows the arrangement of books in the Hebrew Bible and corrects Christological mistranslations. Isaiah 7.14 reads, "Behold, the young woman (not, a virgin) shall conceive and bear a son." Christian versions render Psalm 2.12, "Kiss the son" — a tendentious reading not justified by the Hebrew. The actual meaning of the passage is uncertain, due probably to textual corruption; JPS renders, "Do homage with purity."

The new Jewish translation was the first to make sense of I Samuel 13.21, which had long been the despair of exegetes. The passage reports the policy of the Philistines, who had removed all smiths from the land of Israel, lest the Israelites make weapons. Consequently, the latter had to take their farm-implements to the Philistines to be sharpened. At this point the difficulty occurs, chiefly because of the enigmatic Hebrew word *pim*. This difficulty was suddenly relieved when archeologists discovered a weight inscribed with this word; and JPS renders accordingly, "The price of the filing was a pim (that is, two thirds of a shekel) for the mattocks and for the coulters," etc. The "American Translation" and the Revised Standard Version have since adopted this rendering.

Earlier translations of the Bible had been printed according to the verse-divisions, with each verse a separate paragraph. But these divisions are altogether arbitrary; they often break up sentences that belong together, and the reverse. RV marked a new epoch in that prose passages were printed in paragraphs organized according to sense, and poetic passages were printed as poetry. For some reason, however, the revisers printed the prophetic books as if they were prose, though a great part of their contents is not only poetic but metrical. JPS followed the procedure more consistently; all sections recognizable as poetry were printed as such.

III

The last few decades have seen a greatly increased popular interest in the Bible. This interest has been stimulated in part by the advances in biblical archeology and by the publicity that has attended some of the discoveries. In part, the interest reflects the new attitude of the American public toward religion. It is doubtful whether there was a widespread demand among American Jews for a translation to replace that of Leeser — not because they were well satisfied with Leeser, but because nineteenth century American Jews were more likely to respect the Bible than to read it. The expense of producing the 1917 translation was borne by just a few persons, chiefly by Jacob H. Schiff. The situation today is somewhat different. At least a substantial minority of American Jews who cannot read the Bible in Hebrew are trying to read it in English, and are attending study courses for this purpose. For them, JPS has become increasingly unsatisfactory.

The present writer has been teaching Bible to adolescents and adults for many years. He has found — and the experience is typical — that a good part of the teacher's time is spent, not in explaining the Bible, but in explaining the English. Admittedly, the Elizabethan manner has a magnificence and grandeur which our plainer contemporary style does not possess. But the average reader does not read Tudor English with assurance. This may be regrettable; no doubt we should make the effort to read Shakespeare's plays as Shakespeare wrote them. The Bible, however, is not a product of the English Renaissance period. The translators of 1611 were simply trying to make the Bible accessible to their contemporaries. Ought not the scholars of every age do the same?

It was to meet this challenge that, under the auspices of the University of Chicago, a group of scholars produced a new "American Translation" (AT) in 1927. Later, the leading Protestant groups in the United States sponsored the Revised Standard Version (RSV), which was completed in 1952, and was hailed with much enthusiasm despite dissenting voices. In both these translations the effort was made — it could not perhaps be carried out with complete consistency — to render the Bible accurately in the speech of our time. The Catholic Church is likewise engaged in a similar project.

Many persons feel that a good deal was lost by modernizing the language of the English Bible. The archaisms impart a certain awesome tone which is dissipated when they are replaced by more commonplace diction. The Bible, however, does not remain constantly on a sublime level. It contains many a prosaic page. "Thou shalt not seethe a kid in its mother's milk" sounds unduly solemn to the modern reader, when all it means is, "You must not boil a kid," etc.

All the earlier translations adhered far too slavishly to the word order, sentence structure, and idiom of the Hebrew original. Many Hebraisms, in fact, have been naturalized in English. But this mechanical literalism has continued to cause confusion. Exodus 35.25 reads in JPS, "And all the women that were wise-hearted did spin with their hands." To us, the expression "wise-hearted" suggests intellectual and emotional maturity. But all the sentence means is that the women who were skilled spinners contributed their services.

The demand for a more adequate Jewish translation has been reinforced by the success of the RSV; and the Jewish Publication Society has acceded to this demand. It is characteristic of the change in the times that the funds for this new undertaking are being secured, not from a few wealthy benefactors, but from a large segment of the American Jewish public.

IV

The company of scholars who produced the RSV "Old Testament" included a professing Jew — something new in the history of Christian Bible translations. Dr. Harry M. Orlinsky, Professor of Bible at the Hebrew Union College - Jewish Institute of Religion occupied this novel role. Thereby he not only gained experience in the practical problems of translation, but also reached the conviction that there is both room and need for a revised Jewish version. It was most fitting, therefore, that he be given the major responsibility for preparing the new JPS translation.

Dr. Orlinsky, be it noted, was a pupil of Max Margolis. Unlike his predecessor, however, he has been provided with more expert assistance.[3] The translation committee includes two other eminent specialists in Bible, Professor Ephraim A. Speiser of the University of Pennsylvania (likewise a disciple of Margolis, and also a teacher of Dr. Orlinsky), and Professor H. L. Ginsberg of the Jewish Theological Seminary of America. In addition, the Jewish Publication Society coopted the services of Rabbi Max Arzt (conservative), Rabbi Harry Freedman (orthodox), and the writer (reform) — not, however, as official representatives of their "denominations." Dr. Solomon Grayzel, the learned and genial editor of the

---

[3] This is said without slight to the 1917 committee, all of whom were scholarly men. Schechter was a great master of Rabbinics; Kohler (who had published some biblical studies in his younger days) was a distinguished theologian. But Margolis was the only professional Bible-scholar in the group. Incidentally, this committee, though three of its members officially represented the Central Conference of American Rabbis (reform), carefully avoided any sectarian positions. It should be noted that a number of orthodox scholars undertook to prepare the translation of individual books for this version.

Society, is the seventh member of the committee. Dr. Freedman has now moved to Melbourne, Australia, but continues to participate actively in the work by correspondence.

The committee proceeds as follows: A draft text, with notes, is prepared by Dr. Orlinsky and circulated to all the members. Each then sends in written suggestions for improving the draft, and these are circulated also. When the committee meets, all opinions are considered fully. Often discussion leads to unanimous agreement; if not, a majority vote decides. Progress is slow; yet experience shows that discussion often produces a rendering superior to any of those available in print or suggested prior to the meeting.

AT and RSV frequently offer a translation not of the received Hebrew text, but of emended readings based on the ancient versions or on free conjecture. Such deviations from the Masoretic text are usually, but not invariably, noted. (Even JPS, which supposedly adhered to the received text, makes occasional tacit emendations). The new version will adhere to the traditional text with rare exceptions; in the few instances where emendation appears absolutely necessary or at least highly desirable, the modified reading will appear in the margin. The notes will not be as numerous or extensive as Leeser's, but will be less sparse than those of JPS, which are devoted chiefly to explanations of Hebrew word-plays. The new version will also indicate every instance where the meaning of a Hebrew word or phrase is uncertain or obscure. Thus the innocent reader need not blame himself if he finds these passages incomprehensible.

When will the new Bible translation be available to the reading public? I wish a definite answer could be given. Obviously there is no point in publishing another translation unless it represents a substantial improvement over what is already available. The committee hopes, through long, hard work, to meet that requirement.

HEBREW LITERATURE

The Art of the Translator[1]

By David Patterson

Therefore is the name of it called Babel; because the Lord did there confound the language of all the earth. (Genesis XI, 9).

IT IS all a question of communication. There is so much to tell, and so much to listen to. History unfolds her pages, mankind lays bare its soul—and we cannot read. Ideas come racing out of the brain, great poetry is fashioned, epics are sung—and we do not understand. The past remains a closed book, the present is surrounded by a wall, both equally impenetrable until the translator comes along to lift a corner of the veil and reveal a glimpse of the reality beyond.

That any organized society is utterly dependent upon language is too self-evident a fact to require further exposition. But the full extent of our dependence upon translation is perhaps less generally understood. From every nation there is a constant radiation of information and ideas that must pass through a process of translation. Indeed, the translator stands as the great transformer in the power house of the world, and all the various currents must inevitably flow through the channels of his mind. What happens in the process requires considerable analysis. But one factor, at least, becomes immediately manifest. The transformer, in this instance, is not an automaton but a human being, so that the element of subjectivity is always present.

Inevitably the great mass of translation, upon which society daily depends, is of a prosaic nature. For the purposes of commerce, law, news agencies, science and international relations, the qualities desired are those of literalness and precision. Where factual information is paramount the keynote of translation becomes an exact and accurate rendering in the new medium. But even where the subjective element is reduced to a minimum, the very nature of language makes its complete elimination an impossibility.

There is another sort of translation which is of a different character and subject to radically different techniques, namely, the translation of a literary work from one language into an-

[1] This paper grew out of a short article by the author published in the *Jewish Quarterly*, Spring 1957, entitled *Some Problems of Translation from Hebrew*. A longer version, given as a public lecture in London on February 3, 1958, was published separately by the Jewish Book Council, London, 1958.

other. Here the criterion of success or failure is no longer measured in terms of literalness or lack of ambiguity, but the
transference of literary values from the original into a foreign
medium. And here the translator must face the challenge of
those two most baffling and elusive qualities—the style and spirit
of the original. It is not merely a question of pouring wine from
one cask into another, but of preserving the richness and the
flavor into the bargain.

Two elements conspire to form the difficulties inherent in
literary translation. The first comprises the very nature of individual words, while the second lurks in the compounding of
words to create that overall effect called style. Both elements are
clearly, inextricably related, but each is fraught with its own
specific problems. The significant words in any language are
almost impossible to pinpoint, because, they frequently comprise
not one single, strictly limited connotation, but rather encompass
an area of meaning. That area may expand, contract or suffer
other changes according to context, association, or some particular tradition. Not only human beings have their histories. Words,
too, are subject to the vicissitudes of time, in the course of which
they acquire all kinds of subtle nuances and fine additional shades
of sense. In consequence, the values, character, experience and
civilization of any particular people are often reflected in the
words they use. As a result, many words in various languages
which at first sight appear equivalent, may well be found on
closer examination to straddle differing areas of meaning. Thus
it frequently occurs that a single word in one language may require several words or even sentences to translate it into another. There are, indeed, many instances of words which defy any
attempt at satisfactory translation—a theme that will recur. Certainly the fact that words have *overtones* presents the translator
with one of the most obstinate of problems.

This fluidity of meaning inherent in the very nature of individual words finds its counterpart in the equally elusive quality
of words in composition. There is an element of magic in language, but the potency of its spell depends upon the skill and
subtlety with which the individual fragments are bound together.
The very sequence of words, the order in which they appear, is
all-important for the power and efficacy of the magic spell. Every
language contains its own natural rhythms and its own specific
charms; every language speaks in its own particular music. Indeed, the secret of great literature, and especially of great poetry,
lies in the tapping of those hidden springs and in the harnessing
of their natural powers. The greatest writers, in fact, are those
who succeed in weaving words together—and frequently the
simplest of words—so as to invest them with a fresh significance
which inflames the imagination, quickens the mind or strikes a
chord in the emotions. Not individual words, but words in
composition, denote the essence of an author's style, a quality

which, for all its apparent simplicity, is as highly individual and difficult to imitate as is a signature. But even more difficult is the fact that once the various sentences are analyzed for the purposes of translation, the magic spell is broken. How to bind the spell again, if only in part, within the framework of a foreign medium presents the translator with a second problem no less obstinate than the first.

Divergences of Hebrew and English

This twofold difficulty of words and style becomes immediately apparent at the first attempt to translate a piece of literature from one language into another, even in the case of sister languages belonging to one family. But the difficulty is far more complex when the two languages are radically different in structure. The translation of a work from Hebrew into English implies a change from a Semitic to an Indo-European language. Each possesses its own distinctive grammar, morphology, syntax and vocabulary, quite apart from its own particular philosophy, spirit and tradition. Indeed, so sharply do the two languages diverge that literal translation is frequently misleading and sometimes incomprehensible. As a result, the actual words of the original must often be ignored entirely in the search for a comparable *effect* in English idiom. In consequence of the different emphasis which the two languages have come to lay on the various parts of speech in the course of evolution, the entire structure of a sentence must normally be broken down and remodelled in the process of translation from one to the other.

English is a language which lays particular importance on the noun. Indeed, in extreme cases the verb may be dispensed with almost entirely, as the following illustration from the *Pickwick Papers*[2] may serve to demonstrate:

> "Oh", said Mr. Pickwick, much relieved by this explanation, "I understand you. You have pawned your wardrobe."
> "Everything—Job's too—all shirts gone—never mind—saves washing. Nothing soon—lie in bed—starve—die—inquest—little bone house—poor prisoner—common necessaries—hush it up—gentlemen of the jury—warder's tradesmen—keep it snug—natural death—coroner's order—workhouse funeral—serve him right—all over—drop the curtain."

In the structure of Hebrew it is the verb which must be given pride of place. The Hebrew verb, in fact, possesses characteristics quite different from the English verb, and is capable of expansion, development, and the expression of a wide variety of meaning to an extent unfeasible in English. This phenomenon in itself confronts the translator with a number of formidable obstacles, of which two almost peripheral examples may suffice to show some of the difficulties involved. The dominant role of the verb allows Hebrew to make use of pronouns—he, she,

[2] C. Dickens, *Pickwick Papers*, Macdonald, London, 1948, p. 673.

him, her, etc.—to an extent which English will not tolerate for
fear of ambiguity. Again Hebrew shows a marked fondness for a
construction known as the cognate accusative, which English—
apart from one or two instances such as "he dreamed a dream,"
drawn in any case from Biblical sources—finds abhorrent. On the
other hand, the English verb has developed a complex and very
subtle series of tenses which serve as admirable instruments for
the fine resolution of time—a factor which the Hebrew verb seems
to find almost irrelevant within the same terms of reference.

Disparities in structure, however, are by no means confined to
the verb. English, for example, enjoys a great wealth and variety
of adjectives, which in Hebrew are comparatively scarce. This
deficiency has to be made good partly by a greater reliance on
verbal forms, and partly by the compounding of nouns to yield
an adjectival sense—"the wooden horse," for instance, is expressed
in Hebrew as "the horse of wood." Now description obviously
constitutes a vital element in literature, and description equally
depends upon the adjective, or at least the adjectival form. It
may readily be imagined, therefore, that such disparity in the
use of adjectives time and again obtrudes into the process of
translation.

Moreover, the differences of syntax between the two languages
are no less radical. The word order in both languages is quite
different—and not only the word order, but the sequence of
clauses, too, as we shall have occasion to observe later on. Again
the subordination of sentences favored in English is largely
replaced by their co-ordination in Hebrew, where a far more
important function is assigned to the conjunction "and" than
English would normally allow. Hebrew, moreover, is capable
of a remarkable economy and conciseness of expression, whereas
English tends to be expansive—a fact which even a cursory comparison of a Hebrew original with an English translation will
verify at once.

Thought Structure and Idiom

These are the mechanical difficulties of translation, arising
merely from the structure of the two languages in question. But
over and above all such factors is the difficulty of the translation
of words, which can be properly understood only in the light of
the significance attached to them by centuries of tradition. Even
familiar words such as *Israel, sacrifice, temple, holiness, Sabbath,
piety* and *exile*—to name a mere handful of the more obvious
examples—reflect but little of the meaning and connotation attached to the Hebrew originals. The following example from
Lask's translation of Agnon's *In the Heart of the Seas* may serve
to illustrate the point:

> "These children are not subject to any prince or ruler, neither to
> the king of Edom nor to the king of Ishmael, nor to any flesh-and-
> blood monarch; but they stand in the shadow of the Holy One, blessed

be he, and call him Father and he calls them my children. And all their lives long they speak of the glory of Jerusalem and the glory of the House and the glory of the High Priests and the altar, and of those who offered the sacrifices and those who prepared the incense and those who made the shew-bread.

"And whenever the Holy One, blessed be he, remembers his sons who have been exiled among the nations, who have neither Temple nor altar of atonement, nor High Priests nor Levites at their stations, nor kings and princes, he at once is filled with pity and takes those boys and girls in his arm and holds them to his heart and says to them, Sons and daughters mine, do you remember the glory of Jerusalem and the glory of Israel when the Temple still stood, and Israel still possessed its splendour?"[3]

The translation of this extract represents a brave attempt. The English reads well, the style is smooth and natural. But any reader who is acquainted with the corpus of traditional Hebrew literature will sense immediately the depth of association and idea frequently reposing in a single word of the original, with the English translation reflecting a mere shadow of the real substance. Such problems are among the most difficult in the whole field of translation, and may well defy any attempt at adequate solution.

But no less obstinate are the mental attitudes which both languages reflect. Hebrew and English each employs a fundamentally different idiom for the expression of its concepts. This factor is the result partly of the particular *milieu* out of which each language developed, partly of the philosophy of the language, which reflects but also helps to mould the character of the people that uses it, and partly of the historical consciousness inextricably embedded in any language. In other words, the attempts which Hebrew and English make to express reality are largely conditioned by the thought patterns which emerge from their very nature. For that reason modes of expression which sound quite natural in the one language frequently appear grotesque in the other. Consider, for example, the following passage from Lask's translation of an historical story by Hazaz:

"He (the robber) turned his face towards him as he stood, then lowered his voice and whispered to him angrily: 'Ruin of the world! Let me see your back, may tempest brand you! For otherwise, with this very sword I'll get down to you and in two breaths you'll find yourself in the bosom of the righteous! Scatter your legs! Fly away to Abaddon and don't let your smell spread here! Get down to the Jordan and wag your thighs there to better the world with the Kingdom of the Almighty and in your beard fetch up some stinking fish to feed some of the miserable and humble-spirited before they start their fast! Go, you standard piece of piety, you perfection and vast righteousness'."[4]

Now the translation of this fragment is both vivid and powerful, but it is not English—or rather, the words are English but the

[3] S. J. Agnon, *In the Heart of the Seas,* translated by I. M. Lask, New York, 1948, p. 65 f.
[4] The *Jewish Quarterly,* Spring, 1957, p. 15.

thought structure and idiom are not. The translator has attempted to preserve something of the spirit of the original at the expense of English idiom. The root of the difficulty lies in the fact that in any literature form and content are so closely interwoven, that neither can be reasonably extracted from the other without grievous loss to both. But if the content must undergo change side by side with the change in form in the process of translation, the question remains—and this perhaps is the most enigmatic question in the whole subject under discussion—how much of the original is it possible to preserve at all once the idiom has been radically altered? In other words, what is the real relationship of the translation to the original?

The Creativity of the Translator

Some slight conception of the ramifications of this question may perhaps be derived from a more detailed consideration of a few examples of one particular type of idiom. Hebrew displays a fondness for a somewhat primitive but very graphic use of parts of the body in a wide range of expressions. A comparison of the literal translation of some such phrases with their English idiomatic equivalent may serve to demonstrate the nature of the change demanded in translation, always remembering that the original of the literal translation represents good Hebrew style:

Literal Translation	Idiomatic Equivalent
He was caught in the hands of a woman.	He was tied to her apron strings.
He brightened his face against evil.	He made the best of a bad job.
He looked with seven eyes.	He examined the matter closely.
He gave his eye to the cup.	He applied himself to the bottle.
He could not find his hands and feet.	He was entirely at a loss.

Two points of interest emerge from a brief consideration of these examples. In the first place, the actual change of words required to render the literal translation into idiomatic English is very considerable. More importantly, that very change of words produces a meaning, which while approximating closely to the original, is not in fact the same. But if even a slight change of meaning is involved in the translation of each single phrase, the sum total of such shades of difference must inevitably be of great significance. In other words, the very nature of the idiom effects the quality of meaning.

The problem, therefore, remains that whereas the translation of literature from one language to another within the same linguistic group may be accomplished by a process of first selecting the words most nearly equivalent to those of the original—with due allowance for differences of idiom—and then stringing the words together on rhythmic principles best calculated to reproduce the spirit of the original, the translation of literature from

Hebrew into English is of a very different order. In the latter case the process becomes more of a transmutation than a translation, in which such fixatives as exist can only be the elusive qualities of the style and spirit of the original. Such elements as vocabulary, idiom and sentence structure must be poured wholesale into the crucible, melted down and then re-cast into an entirely different mould.

In order to accomplish this far from easy task, the translator must first steep himself thoroughly in the original. He must attempt an intuitive identification with the purpose and methods of the author, and with the style and spirit of his writing. Only when the original has been utterly absorbed into his being can the translator begin the process of squeezing his material into its new form. But by then two important changes will have taken place. In the first case the difference in language structure will have left its imprint on the form and content along the lines outlined above. And perhaps even more importantly, the material will have passed through the prism of the translator's own mind and acquired an additional element in the process.

All translation is commentary to some extent. Just as an original work of art is a product of the artist's attitude to his experience, so any translation of a literary work inevitably acquires a new perspective and a fresh coloring from the translator's own mind. There is, in fact, a common element in the process of original writing and in that of translation. The difference lies in the fact that creativity in translation is limited to the field of language, while the other ingredients, such as plot, drama, characters, ideas, background and so on, are predetermined. Nevertheless, what finally emerges is a new creation whose literary value will depend almost as much upon the translator as upon the author of the original.

The Real Test of a Translation

That a translation ought not to read like a translation is a generally accepted criterion which, although correct as far as it goes, is only part of the story—and even this criterion is all too often woefully ignored. The real test of a translation of a literary work lies in its capacity to evoke a mental and emotional reaction which approximates that aroused by the original itself. The verbal closeness of the translation is less important than the atmosphere it creates. What really matters is the ability to recapture the essential spirit of the original.

On such criteria, the painstaking and deliberate attempt to render each individual detail may well defeat the ultimate purpose. Indeed, translations from Hebrew into English are frequently marred by an over-conscious cleverness in the translation of particular words or phrases, which interrupt the smoothness of the flow. Far from heightening the overall effect, they serve rather to emphasize the fact that the work is after all merely a translation. The following example from Lask's very fine translation of Bialik's *Safiah,* one of the most sensitive and delightful works in modern Hebrew literature, may illustrate the point:[5]

> "I do not remember how often summer and winter went by from the time I became aware of myself in my native village till we all left for the suburb of the neighbouring town. I was still nothing more than a child playing in the dirt, not yet five full years old, it would seem; and what sense of time or sequence can an infant have? In my native village, presumably, the course of Nature around me was not other than normal; season came and season went at the appointed time, and the world made its customary round. Yet that primal, archetypal Universe which I brought out of the village with me, and which still lies hid in some especial nook of my heart's secret places—that strange, wondrous, singular world can never, it would seem, have known autumn or winter."

The point at issue is the *primal, archetypal Universe,* which sticks out of the narrative like a sore thumb. The overall effect might well have been greatly improved by using some simple, less self-conscious translation such as "that first, early world." Similar examples occur frequently in translation from Hebrew literature.

The sheer difficulty of translation is not, of course, of any absolute nature, but varies with the style and language of the original. Some works of literature naturally lend themselves more easily to translation than others. Indeed, there are moments—unfortunately rare—when a passage almost seems to be translating itself, so comfortably does it nestle in its new mould. It might be stated as a very general principle that the closer a piece of literature lies to the basic idiom of any language, and the more it reflects the history, traditions and thought forms of the people to which it belongs, the more awkward and obstinate does it become for the purposes of translation. For this reason such Hebrew writers as Agnon and Hazaz present the translator with the most difficult type of problems.

To state categorically that certain kinds of writing defy any attempt at adequate translation would be presumptuous, for given sufficient talent quite extraordinary feats can be accomplished. Even so unlikely a poem as Lewis Carroll's "Twas brillig and the slithy toves did gyre and gimble in the wabe . . ." has been translated quite delightfully into German in a version that evokes an almost identical response. But there are times when a piece of literature comprises many complex and sustained difficulties, as the following passage from Halpern's translation of *Mori Sa'id* by Hazaz may illustrate.[6]

---

[5] H. N. Bialik, *Aftergrowth and Other Stories,* translated by I. M. Lask, Philadelphia, 1939, p. 39.

[6] H. Hazaz, *Mori Sa'id,* translated by B. Halpern, New York, 1956 (London 1957), p. 26 f.

"Yoo-ooh, woe to your head!" Mori Sa'id clapped his two hands together in grief. "You are already famous for your speaking. Muddled from mind, mouth and tongue! Ba, ba, ba, ba ... Lo, the King of Kings hears your speech and sees you, how you are already queer beyond all the multitudes..."

"O me, O my, O father." Sion rolled his eyes and stood in various postures. "He who suspecteth the innocent. . ."

"Yoo-ooh, may your tongue be frozen! Are you still talking?"

"But you suspect me, O my eyes, but you suspect me! It is forbidden, *forbidden* you by the laws of Heaven, O light of my eyes. I am a poor wretch, with children clinging to my neck, and period, dot and be dashed for a slice of bread, the slime has climbed to the neckline, with nowhere to stand. A little more bitter than death, may darkness and death redeem it!"

As the greater part of Hazaz's novel is equally difficult to translate, the sum total of the English version evokes a reaction which bears little relation to the effect exerted by the original. Nor does it afford the English reader any real insight into the quality of Hazaz's work. And yet the following fragment of Lask's version of an equally difficult work, Agnon's *Bridal Canopy*, illustrates quite how successful a translation can be:[7]

"I'd shifted all the earthenware and the flax could be seen. Along came a robber, hit me over the head and knocked my hat off. But he didn't want me to go bareheaded and have a sin on my conscience, God forbid, for he immediately clapped a pot over my napper; what's more, he slipped a cord between its two handles so as it shouldn't tumble off, and tied both my hands to a tree. To finish off he landed me another blow as a parting gift and went his way; and it goes without saying that he took my horses with him, for horses are useful when you're in a hurry."

The striking difference in quality between the two passages just quoted lies in the fact that whereas the latter has both captured the spirit of the original Hebrew and transfused it into idiomatic and pleasing English, the former has accomplished neither. Lask's rendering might well pass for a piece of original English writing, but scarcely a single phrase of the passage quoted from Halpern's version reads naturally in English. Much of it, indeed, is hardly comprehensible at all. The failure lies inherent in the technique. The component elements of the Hebrew have not been adequately broken down nor made sufficiently pliable to be re-fashioned within a radically different framework.

In cases where the material is so difficult to remould, far greater liberties must be taken with the ingredients. The basic ideas must be allowed to range over a far wider linguistic area to produce a comparable effect in the new conditions. Nothing is more emasculating than to restrict the entry of the original to literal equivalents of its idiom, which the language of translation does not naturally possess. It is easy enough to squeeze tooth-

---

[7] New York, 1937, p. 25.

paste out of a tube, but virtually impossible to inject it into an-other tube without first removing the nozzle. Any attempt to force an entrance without first widening the area of entry must inevitably result in a formless, squelchy mess, unrecognizable and unattractive.

Translated Hebrew Novels

The most successful exponents of translation are those who have come to understand such basic laws. But as far as the trans-lation of Hebrew literature into English is concerned the number, as yet, is lamentably small. This paper is not concerned with the translations of the great Hebrew classics, such as the Bible, the Mishnah, the Talmud, or the Midrash, all of which have been rendered admirably into English. But then—with the exception of the first-named—the literary and aesthetic character of these works is less a prime consideration. The main purpose of this sketch is to survey the field of modern Hebrew literature in English translation, and here the horizons are sadly circum-scribed.

The novels previously mentioned account—so far as I am aware—for almost half the sum total of Hebrew novels translated into English. Of the remainder, two are by Ibn Zahav—*Jessica, My Daughter*, translated by I. Meltzer, and *David and Bathsheba*, translated by I. M. Lask; a third is Yehudah Yaari's *When the Candle was Burning*, translated by M. Hurwitz, and finally David Maletz's *Young Hearts*—as the English version is called—trans-lated by S. N. Richards. One further novel, Moshe Shamir's *The King of Flesh and Blood*, has been translated by the author of this paper. Five or six volumes of poetry, two or three dozen short stories and a handful of books of essays complete the sum total of modern Hebrew literature as yet translated into English or at least readily available. Of Hebrew authors—apart from Ahad Ha'am, who falls into a different category—only Bialik, Agnon and Ibn Zahav are represented in any adequate measure. It is scarcely surprising, therefore, that the English-speaking world is hardly aware of the very existence of modern Hebrew literature. Fortunately, the overall picture is not entirely devoid of hope. Certain sporadic channels remain, through which a trickle of Hebrew literature finds its way into English translation. From time to time the *Jewish Quarterly* presents translated fragments of modern Hebrew works, a procedure which is continued by the English periodical *Sifrut*, whose avowed aim is to acquaint the English reader with the trends and currents of modern Hebrew literature. Moreover, the admirable *Israel Argosy*, of which five volumes have appeared to date, is entirely devoted to the presenta-tion of Hebrew literature in English translation. This latter journal performs the additional useful function of providing a platform for a growing panel of translators. The selections published are carefully chosen to give a broad cross-section of representative Hebrew writing, and the quality of many of the translations is commendable.

But here, again, the standard varies considerably, and much remains to be learned in the broad field of technique. In the discussion, for example, on the differences in syntax between Hebrew and English, it was pointed out that not only does the word order differ in both languages, but the sequence of clauses is almost equally subject to re-arrangement. A disregard of this one single facet is responsible for much of the unnaturalness so frequently encountered in these translations. But even with such reservations, the overall quality of translation to be found in *Israel Argosy* is sufficiently high to deserve a far, far wider circle of readers than it enjoys at present.

Hebrew Poetry in English

Thus far the lion's share of attention has been reserved for the translation of Hebrew prose—and fiction at that. But the art of translating Hebrew poetry into English is equally worthy of consideration, brief though it be. For, in addition to the literary abilities so essential for the translator of prose, the translator of poetry must himself possess a highly developed poetic faculty. Ideally, only a great poet can translate great poetry, for the ultimate test is whether the version is accepted into the literary heritage of its new medium. Few translations from any one language into another win that distinction. In English literature, Fitzgerald's superb transmutation of the *Rubaiyat* of Omar Khayyam stands as a lone monument. No translation of any modern Hebrew poetry can rival that achievement; yet a considerable number of Hebrew poems have been rendered so successfully into English as to retain much of the spirit of the original. Perhaps the very nature of poetry has forced the translators into a more complete transfusion of the elements of Hebrew, thereby escaping the penalties of the slavish adherence to phrase sequence which so frequently mars the prose. Again, the fact that a number of poems have appeared in more than one English version makes it possible, by a process of comparison, for the English reader to attain a better appreciation of the originals.

In poetry, as in prose, Bialik has once again attracted the finest talent, and his translators include some of the best exponents of the art. Leonard Snowman, Jessie Sampter, H. H. Fein, R. V. Feldman, A. M. Klein and particularly Maurice Samuel and Helena Frank, have all produced excellent versions of his poems which catch much of the depth and spirit of the originals, no easy task considering the power of Bialik's poetry.

Although not nearly so well represented, the poetry of Tchernichovski, too, has inspired a number of fine versions. Most interesting, perhaps, are the very brave attempts to translate his two extraordinarily difficult sonnet cycles. The first, "To the Sun," translated by Shalom J. Kahn, appeared in the third volume of *Israel Argosy* in 1954, while the second, "On the Blood," translated by L. Bernard, was published in the second volume of *Sifrut* in 1956. Both versions show great dexterity in overcoming the formidable technical problems involved although neither attains the quality of Maurice Samuel's version of Tchernichovski's magnificent historical poem, "Baruch of Mayence."

The third great Hebrew poet, Shneur, is also represented by a number of forceful translations, mainly by L. V. Snowman and L. Bernard. But perhaps the most successful single line occurs in a version of "Dawn," a poem by Rachel, translated by Maurice Samuel. Rachel's poetry, by virtue of its very simplicity, is amongst the most difficult to translate; but the last line of the following stanza comes nearer to the ultimate goal, perhaps, than any Hebrew poetry as yet translated:

> "Upon my right the green hills fling
> Protecting arms; before me—the wide fields!
> And in my heart my twenty Aprils sing . . .'"

That line, at least, has captured something of the magic and rhythm of the English language.

The Need for Translations

No treatment of the art of translating modern Hebrew literature into English can be complete without reference to what is, perhaps, the finest and best sustained achievement in the whole field—namely, the three volumes of selected essays by Ahad Ha'am, translated by Sir Leon Simon. Those very qualities of clarity, precision and architectural balance which distinguish the original have been admirably captured by the translation. Like the Hebrew, the English version is characterized by a cold, compelling logic, mellowed every now and then by a charming literary turn of phrase, a ripple of humor or an illuminating metaphor. The flow of language, the natural continuity of phrase, the easy rhythm of the style all denote that intuitive identification which constitutes the very essence of successful translation.

The art of translating modern Hebrew literature into English is only in its infancy, as even a brief examination of the process in reverse shows only too well. The standard of Hebrew translations of English classics, where the difficulties are equally formidable, is far higher; and no English translators have as yet appeared who may be compared with such exponents of the art as Shlonsky, Alterman, Halkin or Leah Goldberg. The explanation, perhaps, lies in the fact that the importance of translating English into Hebrew is immediately obvious, while the need for English versions of Hebrew works may seem less urgent. Yet any strengthening of ties between Israel and the Jewries of the

Diaspora, and any impact which the renaissance of Hebrew may be expected to exert upon the outside world, will largely depend upon the medium of translation. The need, in fact, to train translators capable of producing English versions of Hebrew literature at the highest level is immediate; but no less important is it that such translations be read. Indeed, only a wide circle of interested readers can ensure the success of any such project. One can only hope that such a change may come about before, as Hebrew would say, "the grass starts sprouting out of our cheeks," or to use a more familiar idiom, before all of us are "kicking up daisies."

ISRAELI LITERATURE IN
ENGLISH GARB

By Jacob Kabakoff

DURING the first decade of Israeli statehood greater impetus than ever before was given to translation from Hebrew letters. During this period some of Israel's creative literary spirits were introduced to the English-reading public for the first time. A number of significant books were made available not only in Israel but also through publishers in America and England. By now it has become amply evident that good literary works from Israel are perhaps the most effective means of propaganda and education.

In some measure the modest accomplishments of the past decade represent a breakthrough for Israeli letters. Heretofore such translations as appeared were issued chiefly under Zionist institutional auspices. The Israeli literary product was limited for the most part to those Zionist circles which were already in contact with the land. The publication, however, of Israeli works in translation by private publishers has opened up a new field for this literature and has tapped a new reading public.

It is difficult to draw a clear line of demarcation between Hebrew literature generally and Israeli literature as such. After all, Hebrew literature preceded the State of Israel, and Hebrew writers were creating on Palestinian themes long before the dream of statehood became a reality. For the purpose of this article we shall consider chiefly Hebrew authors of the post-Bialik period. We shall, however, also include some writers of the Bialik period who wrote about the land.

In Volume 8 of the *Jewish Book Annual* (1949-1950), Maurice T. Galpert published a survey entitled "Modern Hebrew Literature in English Translation," in which he dealt with the writings of our Hebrew authors available up to that time. I shall evaluate this field further with special emphasis on the Israeli output, and shall point to the authors and areas of this literature that still await translation. It stands to reason that more volumes and studies, such as Itzhak Ben-Zvi's *The Exiled and the Redeemed* and Joseph Klausner's works on Christianity and on Messianism, will continue to find their way into the book market. Our concern here, however, will be with *belles-lettres*.

274

Zion Motifs

The Palestine ideal served as the main inspiration for our Hebrew writers throughout the period of rebirth. After many of our major authors settled in Palestine, their writing assumed new vitality and many new facets were added to their creativity. Thus, Shmuel Yosef Agnon, whose forte had been the interpretation of the hasidic world of Galicia, gave us a novel of the second aliyah and stories of Jerusalem life. Hayim Hazaz, who had been immersed in the ferment of revolutionary Russia, became our foremost interpreter of Yemenite life and folkways. All our prose writers became imbued with the spirit of the land, and in the period of Zionist realization the themes of pioneering and attachment to the soil became basic to their writing.

The poets, too, reacted vividly to the homeland. David Shimoni, Yaakov Fichman and Yehuda Karni became infatuated with the new landscape. Uri Zvi Greenberg, Yitzhak Lamdan and Avraham Shlonsky, the outstanding poetic figures of the post-Bialik era, all joined in giving modern expression to age-old Messianic hopes and dreams.

At the same time, a new school of indigenous Israeli writers emerged. In the novel, short story and poem the new relation between the individual and society has been explored. The kibbutz and city life have been subjected to analysis and even to criticism and satire. For the first time in our history there grew up a war literature based on the struggle for independence and on the heroic exploits of the Palmach. The various immigrant groups have begun to receive attention and to be given artistic portrayal. The Bible, too, has come in for literary reinterpretation, and not only the older writers but even some of the younger ones have turned to historical themes.

While much remains to be done in the area of translation, a sizable literature has already appeared. First mention should go to the *Israel Argosy*, published since 1952 under the editorship of I. Halevy-Levin and now in its fifth volume. Whereas the first three numbers in this series appeared in paperback editions in Israel and reached only a limited reading group in this country, the last two volumes have been released here through Thomas Yoseloff in hard cover editions. Similarly, few copies of I. M. Lask's anthology entitled *Palestine Stories* (Jerusalem, Tarshish, 1942) reached these shores, but the recent collection *Tehilla and Other Israeli Tales*, published as a Ram's Horn Book (N.Y., Abelard-Schuman, 1956), elicited a far wider response.

Early Translation Efforts

Before reviewing the various samples of Israeli literature in English translation, a word should be said concerning the initial efforts in this field. Perhaps the most outstanding contribution has been made by I. M. Lask, whose name figures so prominently as a translator. Already in the 30's Lask regularly contributed translations of short stories and poetry to the *Palestine Review* and to other journals. His work appears in the anthology *Yisroel* (London, John Heritage, 1933), edited by Joseph Leftwich, as well as in the two anthologies *The Jewish Caravan* (N.Y., Farrar and Rinehart, 1935) and *A Golden Treasury of Jewish Literature* (N.Y., Farrar and Rinehart, 1937), edited by Leo W. Schwarz. Other prominent translators whose work saw publication during the 30's were Maurice Samuel, A. M. Klein and A. H. Friedland in this country, and L. V. Snowman in England.

During the 40's the World Zionist Organization began systematically to sponsor translation. The initial efforts were issued in mimeographed form in such organs as the *Information Service* of the Zionist Organization Youth Department, as well as in various printed youth journals. In addition to I. M. Lask's regular contributions during these years, we find also those of Dov Vardi, Israel Schen, Sylvia Satten and others.

Among the early efforts of the Youth Department were the slim paperbacks published under the general title of *Palestine Pioneer Library*, of which a few were translations. A forerunner of the *Israel Argosy* was the *Palestine Miscellany I* (Tel Aviv, Zionist Organization Youth Department, 1948), which was envisaged as the first in a series of quarterly publications devoted to Hebrew prose and poetry. Among the authors represented were the veteran poets Saul Tchernichowsky and Yaakov Fichman and the short-story writers Yehuda Yaari, Yitzhak Shenberg, Israel Zarchi and Yigal Mossinson. Yaari's *The Three-Fold Covenant*, dealing with the struggles of the German immigrants of the third aliya, as well as Shenberg's *Israel Zvi*, based on kibbutz life, have since been reprinted in various anthologies.

Still another modest effort to bring some of the writing of Hebrew authors to the attention of the English reader was made by the *Artzi Palestine Almanac* for 5708 (1947-48) and 5710 (1949-50), respectively, published also by the Palestine Pioneer Library. These had their precursor in the Palestine almanac *Moledet* for 5707 (1946-47), published in Tel Aviv by Lion the Printer, who also produced the Palestine Pioneer Library. A similar purpose was served in England by the publication of *The Living Rampart* (London, Zionist Youth Council, 1948), dedicated to the popularization of literary pieces dealing with the Israeli struggle for independence.

Writing of Shmuel Yosef Agnon

Undoubtedly, the author who has most often been translated into other languages is Shmuel Yosef Agnon, the dean of Hebrew story writers, whose 70th birthday was marked this past summer. Agnon was first introduced to the English-reading public through the novel *The Bridal Canopy* (N.Y., Literary Guild, 1937), which paints a folk portrait of small town hasidic life in Galicia. In his introduction, the translator, I. M. Lask, dwells on the difficulties of rendering into English the studied and ornate style of this master of Hebrew prose. Although here and there some of Agnon's nuances eluded him, on the whole the translation reads well.

We are also indebted to Lask for his translation of Agnon's novelette *In the Heart of the Seas* (N.Y., Schocken Books, 1948), which deals with the pilgrimage of a group of 19th-century Polish Hasidim to Palestine. The story, which breathes love of the land and is replete with symbolic overtones, reveals Agnon as a master weaver of the folk tale. Agnon has also been presented to English readers through his High Holyday anthology *Days of Awe* (N.Y., Schocken Books, 1948), translated by Maurice T. Galpert and revised by Jacob Sloan, and through short stories in various anthologies.

Of particular beauty is Agnon's story "Tehilla", which opens the volume *Tehilla and Other Israeli Tales*. In addition to this version by Lask we find another translation of the same tale by Walter Lever in *Israel Argosy 4* (Jerusalem, Youth and Hechalutz Department of the Zionist Organization, 1956; N.Y., Yoseloff, 1956). One is tempted to dwell on the symbolism of this tale about an old Jerusalem woman who seeks atonement for breaking her betrothal vows in her youth at the insistence of her father. Elsewhere in this volume, however, an article appears which subjects Agnon's writings to critical analysis. Agnon is also the author of the story from which the recent collection of short stories in translation, *A Whole Loaf* (Tel Aviv, Karni, 1957), edited by Sholom J. Kahn, has taken its name. To this Kafkaesque story, translated here by Lask, our editor has added a short note on its probable allegorical significance. The same collection brings us still another story by Agnon, entitled *Metamorphosis,* a tale of divorce and reconciliation, in the translation of I. Schen.

It is thus evident that a good beginning has been made so far as the translation of Agnon is concerned. There is still room, however, for translations of his other novels, particularly *T'mol Shilshom* (Days Gone By), which deals with the second aliya, and for a volume of his collected short stories.

Works of Hayim Hazaz

Although the various published samples of the work of Hayim Hazaz, who last year celebrated his 60th birthday, revealed him as a fine craftsman, it was not until the appearance of *Mori Sa'id* (N.Y., Abelard-Schuman, 1956) that he became known as a major novelist. The novel, translated by Ben Halpern, presents three generations in the life of a Yemenite family and chronicles the story of its adjustment to the homeland. Halpern also published a translation of Hazaz' story *The Sermon* in the Spring 1956 issue of the *Partisan Review*. (Another translation of the same story by Lask appeared previously in *Artzi* 5708.) The story is significant from the ideological point of view, for it represents an extremely negative outlook on Jewish life outside Israel, an outlook which has been reflected in the writings of several of the younger writers.

A number of other short stories by Hazaz are included in various anthologies, particularly *Tehilla and Other Israeli Tales, A Whole Loaf* and Leo W. Schwarz' works. A sample from Hazaz' latest book *Copper Doors*, dealing with a Jewish town in revolutionary Russia, appeared in the original together with a parallel translation in the February 1958 issue of *Oroth*, a publication of the Department for Education and Culture in the Diaspora of the World Zionist Organization in Jerusalem. Only a few selections from Hazaz' epic four-volume novel of Yemenite life entitled *Ya'ish* have appeared in periodicals, but the work as a whole still awaits translation.

Among Other Novelists

Space permits only brief mention of the other novelists who have been translated. Ari Ibn-Zahav is represented by two historical novels. *Jessica, My Daughter* (N.Y., Crown, 1948), translated by Julian Meltzer, is a Jewish retelling of the Shylock story, while *David and Bathsheba*, translated by Lask (N.Y., Crown, 1951), is an enlargement upon the biblical theme. Previously there appeared as a paperback Ibn-Zahav's *A ' Gharry Driver in Jerusalem* (Tel Aviv, Lion the Printer, 1947), translated by Sylvia Satten and recounting a chapter in the growth and development of life in the capital city of Israel.

Another type of subject matter is dealt with in Avigdor Hameiri's *The Great Madness* (N.Y., Vantage Press, 1952), translated by Jacob Freedman. This is a vivid story of the maelstrom of World War I and of the Jewish soldiers caught up in it. A novel depicting the horrors of the Nazi concentration camps in Poland is *House of Dolls* (N.Y., Simon and Schuster, 1955) by Ka-tzetnick 135633, translated by Moshe M. Kohn.

Yehuda Yaari has recorded in his novel *When the Candle Was Burning* (London, Gollancz, 1947), translated by Menahem Horowitz, the struggles and hopes of members of the third aliya. The theme of identification with the land stressed here is underscored also in Yaari's short stories. A collection of ten of these, including extracts from his above-mentioned novel, appeared in Israel under the title *Prisoners of Hope* (Tel Aviv, Zionist Organization Youth Department, 1945). Some of these stories have become standard items in anthologies. A novel of kibbutz life, which attracted considerable attention in Israel not so much for its artistic form as for its critical evaluation of subject matter, was *Young Hearts* (N.Y., Schocken Books, 1950) by David Maletz, translated by Solomon N. Richards.

As is evident from this survey, a good deal remains to be done before the Israeli novel will be adequately presented to the English reader. Until there are made available the writings of such veteran novelists as Yehuda Burla, Asher Barash and Yehoshua Bar-Yosef, among others, as well as those of some of the younger writers like Nathan Shaham, Aaron Meged and S. Yizhar, the picture will necessarily be incomplete. Of the writings by Meged there is now available his *Hedvah And I* (Jerusalem, Youth and Hechalutz Department, 1957), a dramatization by the author of his novel by the same name dealing in humorous fashion with the adjustment of a kibbutz member to life in the "big city."

Moshe Shamir's King of Flesh and Blood

It is good to be able to report on the recent publication in English of the outstanding popular novel by Moshe Shamir, *The King of Flesh and Blood* (London, East and West Library, 1958), expertly translated by David Patterson, lecturer in post-biblical Hebrew at the University of Oxford. Shamir's novel won the highest literary award in Israel, the Bialik Prize, and has gone into several editions. It represents a veering away from the usual novelistic material drawn by the younger writers from kibbutz life or war experiences, and bespeaks a serious attempt to interpret the Jewish past.

Shamir, a native Israeli, has not given us a romantic historical tale but one infused with sharp realism. In dealing with the life and times of the power-thirsty King Alexander Jannai (103-76 B.C.E.), he has painted a wide and colorful canvas. Vivid descriptions of the land, bloody war scenes, an analysis of the "geopolitics" of the time, a re-enactment of the Yom Kippur Temple ritual, an interpretation of the issues that were at stake in the struggle between the Pharisees and Sadducees—all this and much more is masterfully encompassed here. And towering over all stands the tragic figure of Alexander Jannai, with whom the greatness of the Hasmonean dynasty came to an end. His relations with his wife, Queen Salome, and his constant conniving to gain power, are delineated with understanding and keen psychological insight.

Shamir's work, which appeared in Hebrew in 1954, represents the most vital full-length novel of the post-war generation in Israel, and marks a turning point in Israeli letters. In the words of the translator, it "may fairly claim to be the most significant historical novel in modern Hebrew literature." Despite tendencious elements which have crept in here and there, the novel bodes well for the future of Israeli writing. Some of Shamir's work has also appeared in the *Israel Argosy* and in anthologies.

Anthologies and Short Stories

Of the various types of literature being produced in Israel, the short story form is best represented in translation. This is due to the fact that a number of excellent collections have culled selections from this branch of writing and that various anthologies have sought this type of material.

Mention has already been made of the collection *Palestine Stories* (1942), selected and translated by I. M. Lask. This volume, which presented for the first time an interesting panorama of Palestinian life and which contains a dozen stories, deserves to be wider known. The more recent *Tehilla and Other Israeli Tales* (1956) has met with widespread critical acclaim. It should be noted that the book was prepared with the assistance of a committee of Israeli writers, established by the Jewish Agency and headed by the late Yitzhak Shenhar. The favorable response elicited by the book should serve as a stimulus for further efforts to bring to English readers not only the work of the veteran writers but also of the younger ones.

Reference has been made above to the most recent addition to short story collections, *A Whole Loaf* (1957), edited by Sholom J. Kahn, the American-born member of the English faculty of the Hebrew University. The main contribution of this collection, subtitled *Stories from Israel,* consists in bringing to the fore the work of several members of the younger guard of contemporary writers. Side by side with Smilansky, Agnon and Hazaz, we find the war stories of S. Yizhar and Nathan Shaham and the sensitive pieces of Aaron Meged, Moshe Shamir, Binyamin Tammuz and others. Biographical and critical notes by the editor serve to introduce the material to the reader.

The fifteen stories in the volume have been chosen primarily for their "literary value and universal human interest" rather than for their specific Israeli content. Thus, many aspects of present-day Israel which might have been reflected here have gone untouched. The War and the kibbutz figure in a number of the stories, but by and large the emphasis of the authors is on character portrayal.

In compiling this volume Kahn has leaned heavily on I. M. Lask, five of whose renditions appear here. The book also presents, however, the efforts of nine additional translators, many of whom are new to the field. The editor himself has translated a Yemenite story by Hazaz, and in order to transmit the flavor of the Yemenite speech he has utilized the Negro dialect. Whether the translation has achieved the desired effect, however, is debatable.

As is pointed out in the editor's introduction, only a fragment of the Israeli short story output is incorporated here. We need additional volumes whose short stories will be so chosen as to carefully delineate various central Israeli themes that have been given artistic expression.

To the works cited above must be added the excellent sections of Palestinian stories in *Yisroel, The Jewish Caravan* and *A Golden Treasury*. Leo W. Schwarz, editor of the last named two anthologies, has made still another fine contribution by including in his most recent compilation, *Feast of Leviathan* (N.Y., Rinehart, 1956), a section of stories entitled Israelian Fruit. Here one meets not only several of the established Hebrew writers but also a few of the younger ones.

In *Sound the Great Trumpet* (N.Y., Whittier, 1955), M. Z. Frank has essayed the difficult task of piecing together the dramatic story of the development of the Yishuv and its transformation into independent statehood. While not intended as a literary anthology, the book makes a unique contribution to the field, particularly because of its condensations and translations of Israeli novels. Among the names one meets here for the first time are those of Shlomo Reichenstein, Yonat and Alexander Sened, Yigal Mossinsohn and Shlomo Nitzan. In addition, our editor has drawn upon the writings of many of the established writers like Moshe Smilansky, Avraham Reuveni, S. J. Agnon, Yehuda Burla and others.

Deserving of mention in this connection are also Azriel Eisenberg's anthologies, *Modern Jewish Life in Literature* (N.Y., United Synagogue, 1948) and *The Bar Mitzvah Treasury* (N.Y., Behrman, 1952), in which Israeli authors are amply drawn upon. A few stories by Israeli writers are included also in *World Over Story Book* (N.Y., Bloch, 1952), edited by Norton Belth.

One of the earliest settlers in Palestine was Moshe Smilansky who arrived in 1890 at the age of 16 and was privileged to see the establishment of the Jewish State. His stories struck a new note in Hebrew literature; in addition to writing about the early settlers, he was the first to describe Arab life with all its passion and primitiveness. It was Lask who introduced Smilansky to the English reader with the collection *Palestine Caravan* (London, Methuen, 1935), containing 11 stories. Of these, *Latifa*, dealing with the attachment a young Arab girl feels for a Jewish settler, is most often found in anthologies. Among other volumes in which it is included is *Jewish Short Stories of Today* (London, Faber and Faber, 1938), edited by Morris Kreitman.

With the passing last year of Yitzhak Shenhar (Shenberg), Israeli letters lost not only a gifted short story writer and translator from world literature into Hebrew, but also one who helped guide translation efforts into English. As a member of the middle generation of Israeli writers, he is among those whose work served as a literary bridge between the old and new worlds. A number of his stories have been included in anthologies, and a collection entitled *Under the Fig Tree* (N.Y., Schocken Books, 1948), was published in Lask's translation. Shenberg, who lived through the problems of adjustment to the land, has permitted us to share his experiences. While not abounding in action, his stories probe the inner workings of their characters and describe various types, particularly settlement workers.

Perhaps the finest contribution of the *Israel Argosy* volumes to translation has been in the field of the short story. Among its stories of lasting value special mention should be made of *Yossy's Fiddle* (Volume 5, 1957), by Mordecai Tabib, in which a Yemenite mother poignantly recounts the story of the life of her fallen son, and *The Swimming Race* (Volume 2, 1953), by Binyamin Tammuz, a member of the younger school of writers who delves searchingly into the problem of Arab-Jewish relations.

Poetry Translations

One need not elaborate the problems of translating Hebrew poetry. In addition to the usual pitfalls awaiting the translator of verse, there is in Hebrew the additional factor of conveying the nuances of an old-new language. The new Israeli poetry has undergone much development. True, it still bears the influences of Bialik and particularly of Tchernichowsky, but more often than not it reveals a tendency to modernism and is less senti-mental than the poetry of a generation ago. It is in poetry that Hebrew literature has most distinguished itself, and the challenge of transmitting this poetry to the English reader must be taken up.

While it does not quite meet the need of an anthology of Hebrew poetry, *A Treasury of Jewish Poetry* (N.Y., Crown, 1957), edited by Nathan and Marynn Ausubel, contains a fairly wide selection of verse by contemporary Hebrew poets. The work of several of the younger poets, like Binyamin Galai, Zerubavel Gal'ed and David Rokeach, appears for the first time between the covers of an English book. Even though the anthology omits a number of important poets (the most glaring omission is that of S. Shalom) and offers sparse representation to others, it does impart some idea of the continuity of Hebrew poetry and its new forms. A number of translations from modern Hebrew poets are to be found also in Schwarz' *A Golden Treasury*.

A general anthology which has given generous space to Hebrew poetry is *A Little Treasury of World Poetry* (N.Y., Scribners, 1952), edited by Hubert Creekmore. In addition to selections from biblical and medieval Hebrew poetry and from Bialik and Tchernichowsky, we find represented here the poets Jacob Fich-man, Avigdor Hameiri, Rachel and Nathan Alterman.

Various sources have already drawn upon Simon Halkin's sensitive renderings from Israeli poets in his *Modern Hebrew Literature* (N.Y., Schocken Books, 1947). These translations virtually make up a small anthology. A number of illustrative translations, some original and some culled from other sources, are to be found also in Reuben Wallenrod's *The Literature of*

Modern Israel (N.Y., Abelard-Schuman, 1956). Harry H. Fein has included contemporary Israeli poets in his *Gems of Hebrew Verse* (Boston, Bruce Humphries, 1949), as well as in his *Chapters in Modern Hebrew Literature* (N.Y., Hadassah, 1947), issued in lithographed form as a study course. A few competent renderings of popular Israeli poems by Shoshana Grayer are to be found in *Israel Independence Day* (N.Y., Youth and Chalutziut Department, 1952), a selection of program material.

The poetess Rachel, who died in 1931, has long become the modern symbol of longing for Zion and many of her poems have become folksongs. In addition to her poems in anthologies, a fine selection of her writings is included in *The Plough Woman* (N.Y., Nicholas L. Brown, 1932), in the excellent translation by Maurice Samuel. Three of her poems appear also in *A Treasury of Comfort* (N.Y., Crown, 1954), translated by Sidney Greenberg, editor.

Bi-Lingual Series

Most of the efforts described above are fragmentary; they do not begin to do justice to the full scope of the creativity of our authentic Israeli poets. Mindful of this, we welcome the first two in a new series of bi-lingual volumes published last year in Jerusalem by the Youth and Hechalutz Department of the Zionist Organization. These volumes, translated by the veteran I. M. Lask, are *Idylls* by David Shimoni and *Poems* by Avraham Ben Yitzhak (Sonne). The former is the more ambitious project. It brings in faithful translation three works of Shimoni which voice the strivings and aspirations of the halutzim and describe caressingly the landscape of Israel. A foremost representative of the second aliya, Shimoni caught its spirit admirably in his poem *In the Hedera Forest,* which is devoted to the woodcutters who labored there. Another work, *A Memorial,* dating from the third aliya, recounts the tragic tale of Katriel who reduced the essence of the Eretz-Israel Torah to three rules: "First, holding and growing on; second, contentment with little; third, keeping on, keeping on." The final piece, *Dewdrops of the Night,* has as its background the unsettled days of 1936, when the halutz was called upon to play a new role, that of watchman. In a sense, this idyll is a summary which surveys the entire pioneering effort beginning with the early days of the second aliya. It mingles memories of the past with steadfast hope in the sabra generation of the future.

Avraham Ben Yitzhak's *Poems* represent a more modest effort; in his lifetime only a dozen of his poetic pieces saw publication. In essence a modernist who wrote in a symbolic style bearing a strong European influence, he served as the model for many a representative of the younger guard. Both volumes in the bi-lingual series include literary appreciations—the one on Shimoni from the pen of Joseph Klausner, and that on Avraham Ben Yitzhak by Benzion Benshalom.

Other Contemporary Poets

Perhaps the strongest voice in contemporary Israeli poetry is that of Uri Zvi Greenberg, who most directly continues the line of prophetic exhortation so strongly characteristic of the verse of Bialik. It is all the more deplorable, therefore, that so little of Greenberg is available. His poem *Jerusalem* (N.Y., Blackstone Publishers, 1939), translated by Charles A. Cowen, dates from the period following World War I. In verse tinged with Messianic overtones, Greenberg sang of both the earthly and the spiritual Jerusalem that was being built by a pioneering generation. His glowing vision of Jerusalem the Eternal is mirrored in his poem *Tale of an Ancient Jerusalemite,* translated by Sholom J. Kahn in *Israel Argosy*, Autumn 1952.

A modest effort to introduce the poetry of S. Shalom, on the occasion of his cultural mission to this country in 1950, was made by Gabriel Preil and Jacob Kabakoff in *S. Shalom the Poet and His Work* (N.Y., Histadruth Ivrith and Jewish Education Committee, 1950). Even the small selection of poems presented here in the translations of Eisig Silberschlag, Gabriel Preil and others, suffices to reveal Shalom as a writer who absorbed the spirit of the Bialik era and also epitomized the new life and struggles of Israel.

An insight into the creativity of three outstanding contemporary Hebrew poets who constitute a "new school" of Israeli writing, was offered by Dov Vardi in his *New Hebrew Poetry* (Tel Aviv, Wizo, 1947). Foremost among these poets is Avraham Shlonsky, whom the author characterizes as "a complete child of the twentieth century." A modern poet in the full sense of the world, Shlonsky has brought many innovations to Israeli letters and has profoundly influenced the younger writers. The other two poets represented in the volume are Leah Goldberg and Nathan Alterman. They followed Shlonsky by more than a decade, and have continued in the path he blazed. Vardi has written introductory essays on each of the poets and has appended translations of several samplings of their poetry. A tangy taste of the writing of the popular poet Nathan Alterman, who last year was awarded the Bialik Prize for poetry, can be enjoyed in selections from his *Joy of the Poor,* translated by Sholom J. Kahn in *Israel Argosy* 5 (1957).

It is clear from this rapid survey of Israeli poetry in translation that a considerable quantity has been made available in recent years. The time is patently ripe for an anthology of Israeli poetry in English translation which should contain representative selections from the poets of both the old and new guards. Moreover, we need special volumes devoted to Uri Zvi Greenberg,

Avraham Shlonsky and Yitzhak Lamdan, the three central figures in the poetry of the post-Bialik era, and to S. Shalom. There is room for an English version of at least some of the moving themes in Greenberg's epochal book of poetry, *Rehovot Hanahar* (Paths of the River), which gives powerful expression to the Jewish mood of our generation. Nor can our appreciation of the values contributed by Israeli poetry be complete without a translation of Lamdan's classic poem of halutziut *Massada*. Until these and other works become available, the full extent of the contribution of Israeli poetry to our literature cannot be grasped.

Periodical Literature

Only in a few instances have we referred to translation in periodicals. A more comprehensive treatment will have to deal with this material as well. A partial listing of such translations, beginning with 1946, is included in *Palestine and Zionism,* the bibliographical index published by the Zionist Archives and Library in New York. But the time has arrived for the compilation of a full bibliography of all the works and individual stories and poems translated from the Hebrew and scattered in periodicals both here and abroad. Such a work will be of inestimable value to all who seek to follow the development of Israeli letters.

We wish to refer here to a few key periodicals that have fostered translation from Hebrew literature and have been especially hospitable to Israeli writing. In London a unique periodical for contemporary Hebrew literature, *Sifrut,* was produced by the Jewish Agency Department for Education and Culture, under the editorship of Chaim Rabin. Issues have appeared annually since 1955, and the three numbers published to date contain translations as well as essays and reviews. Last year the editor left England to join the faculty of the Hebrew University in Jerusalem. Listed along with him in the third number (1957), we find David Patterson as co-editor and L. Gertner as editorial secretary. The *Jewish Quarterly* in London has also given space to Israeli literature. Its Winter 1954-55 issue devoted an entire section to the new writing. The translations by Lask and Vardi give some idea of the work of the younger guard, some of whom appear here in translation for the first time.

In America various English-Jewish periodicals have given space from time to time to Israeli short stories and poems. The magazine *Israel Life and Letters,* published by the American-Israeli Cultural Foundation, has consistently kept Israeli literature in the forefront and has published many translations. *Commentary,* the monthly sponsored by the American Jewish Committee, has brought Israeli poetry to the attention of its readers on several occasions and has printed in its columns competent translations by

Herbert Howarth, Robert Friend, Gabriel Preil and Jacob Sloan, among others.

On the occasion of the tenth anniversary of Israel, the new quarterly magazine, *The Literary Review,* an international journal of contemporary writing, devoted its entire Spring 1958 issue to Israeli letters. This magazine, edited by Clarence R. Decker and Charles Angoff for Farleigh Dickinson University, contains several short stories by well-known authors such as Agnon, Hazaz and Burla, and a section of poetry representing thirteen poets. Special features of the issue are the survey article, "An Old-New Literature in an Old-New Land," by Joseph Klausner, and a full-length biblical play by A. Ashman. It is regrettable that more members of the younger guard are not represented here and that the names of the translators of the various contributions are not indicated. Nevertheless, this Israeli number is to be welcomed as the first of its kind to be sponsored by a general literary review. It is highly desirable to focus the attention of non-Jewish literary circles on the literary creativity of Israel.

In Israel itself the latest periodical to foster translation is *Focus,* a journal for youth leaders edited by I. Halevy-Levin for the Youth and Hechalutz Department of the Zionist Organization. In volume I, number 2 (1957), we find several poems in the original and in parallel translation.

Another outstanding periodical which saw fit to devote an entire issue to Israeli literary creativity was *Poetry,* edited by Henry Rago. Its July 1958 issue consists entirely of a selection of contemporary Israeli verse, edited in consultation with Simon Halkin, professor of Hebrew literature at the Hebrew University. This is by far the finest sampling to date. We have represented the work of 21 poets whose "poetry either began or grew with the sense of Palestine as a place and a destiny." An insight will be gained here into the writings of such poets as Greenberg, Lamdan and Shlonsky, as well as of many of the younger men. Most of the translations are the work of Ruth Finer Mintz of Los Angeles, who is now in Israel. Professor Halkin himself has contributed an article entitled "Postscript: The Younger Poets," in which he sees a line of continuity stretching from the classic Hebrew poets to the younger writers.

On the basis of what has already been accomplished in the field of translation, we may look forward in the next decade of Israeli statehood to the unfolding in English of still more areas of Israeli life and experience. It is not too much to hope that some of the values cultivated in this literature will help nurture and sustain the Jewish spirit everywhere.

AMERICAN CLASSICS IN
HEBREW TRANSLATION

By Eisig Silberschlag

For the past two hundred years four literatures—German, Russian, English, American—effected a sea-change in Hebrew literature. Since the first center of enlightenment happened to be in Germany, German models confronted the Hebrew writer between the middle of the eighteenth and the middle of the nineteenth century. As late as 1859 Abraham Mapu, the father of the Hebrew novel, published a French primer under the German title *Der Hausfrancose* (sic)! And through German transliteration of French words in Hebrew script he endeavored to teach correct French pronunciation.

With the accession of Alexander II to the throne of Russia, the Russian factor predominated in Hebrew literature. The liberalizing reforms of the czar, especially the emancipation of the serfs, created a receptive mood for Russian culture. The great writers who flourished during his reign and the reign of his son Alexander III—Turgenev, Dostoyevsky, Tolstoy—exerted a powerful influence on contemporary Hebrew writers.

From the beginning of the twentieth century English and American literatures played a significant role in Hebrew literature. The reasons are self-evident: the establishment of a minor center of Hebrew literature in America and the re-establishment of a major center of Hebrew literature in former Palestine under the mandatory government. But English as well as American classics—and the word is used loosely to denote works of conceded excellence or established fame—exercised a powerful pull on Hebrew writers before the present century. Already toward the end of the eighteenth century Mendel Lefin of Satanov (1749-1826) was attracted to the writings of Benjamin Franklin. Like all Hebrew writers in the period of enlightenment, he had a passion for ethics. And Franklin was not only a statesman but an author with a moral stance and with an international reputation.

Mendel Lefin must have heard about Franklin in Berlin where he spent two years of his life: from 1780 to 1782. In 1780

287

the works of the great American appeared in a German translation. Franklin's *Autobiography—Memoirs* he called them—was published in French in 1791 and, together with some other writings, in 1798. Since Lefin finished his unpublished German work *Nachlass eines Sonderlings zu Abdera* in 1806, he utilized his knowledge of Franklin. It is probable that his German book contained, among other subjects, the essentials of his popular treatise *Ḥeshbon ha-Nefesh* (*Soul-Searching*) which was regarded by the author as the means to attain moral perfection.

The dependence of Lefin on Franklin has never been properly researched. A comparison of *Ḥeshbon ha-Nefesh* with the American source material yields the inevitable conclusion that Lefin's treatise is neither a translation in the proper sense of the word nor a paraphrase, but an independent work. What is paraphrased is a number of Franklin's proverbs from the issues of *Poor Richard's Almanac;* what is translated is Franklin's famous list of thirteen virtues: temperance, silence, order, resolution, frugality, industry, sincerity, justice, moderation, cleanliness, tranquility, chastity, humility. It is remarkable, in view of the lingual resources of the time, how precisely some of them—six to be exact—are rendered into Hebrew: silence into *Shetiḳah,* order into *Seder,* industry into *Ḥarizut,* justice into *Zedek,* cleanliness into *Neḳiyyut,* humility into *'Anabah.* The other virtues are merely approximated or adumbrated in Hebrew. While Franklin used the English idiom of the eighteenth century, Lefin had to invent an idiom of his own. Like his contemporaries, he favored the Bible as a source of lingual inspiration. But unlike his contemporaries, he did not hesitate to use a strong admixture of rabbinic Hebrew. And when the resources of Hebrew failed him, he boldly tapped the Aramaic language. Thus he translated one of Franklin's virtues, temperance, into the Aramaic *Niḥuta.* In his *Autobiography* Franklin is concise in the description of the thirteen virtues; Lefin devotes a chapter to each of them in his *Ḥeshbon ha-Nefesh.* Franklin's is a subtle, indirect, didacticism, Lefin's is an unabashed, direct didacticism.

Under Lefin's influence Nahman Krochmal, the Jewish philosopher in the period of enlightenment, was drawn into Franklin's orbit. He translated a tale of Franklin which appeared under the guise of an apocryphal chapter LXII of *Genesis:* a tale about Abraham, about the patriarch's initial impatience with an unbelieving guest and his ultimate hospitality in spite of the guest's religious shortcomings.

First Translations from American Literature

These first contacts between American and Hebrew culture led to an ever-increasing fertilization of an old literature by an emerging literature which was destined to fulfill a focal function in the world. The translations from American literature increased in number and in quality toward the end of the nineteenth century and, in our own day, they have become sources for new techniques and far-reaching insights in Hebrew literature. Even the basic documents of American democracy—the Declaration of Independence and the Constitution of the United States—were translated as early as 1891. Of the older American authors Washington Irving, James Fenimore Cooper and Harriet Beecher Stowe found capable translators. Cooper's *The Last of the Mohicans* was translated at the end of the nineteenth century but *The Pathfinder* and *The Pioneers* were translated only in the twenties of this century. Irving's "Rip van Winkle" was translated in 1928 while Stowe's *Uncle Tom's Cabin* reached four editions in Hebrew by 1903. The Hebrew title *Ohel Tom* bore connotations and allusions which were unintended in the American title. The obvious reference to Jacob who is described in Genesis 25:27 as *Tom* (simple or innocent) and *Yosheb Ohalim* (dwelling in tents) must have immediately created the illusion that the hero of the novel is a patriarchal type of biblical simplicity. Even the later translation of *Uncle Tom's Cabin* by Asher Barash (Jerusalem, 1926) retained some elements of the older title: *Ohel ha-Dod Tom*. None of the translators used for "cabin" the rabbinic equivalent *Zerif* which is current in modern Hebrew.

Jews were always capable of laughing at their own misfortunes. Since they fathered an enviable literature of wit and mordant humor, they could not bypass a Mark Twain. His major works, *The Adventures of Tom Sawyer* and *The Adventures of Huckleberry Finn*, were translated several times by several hands. The translation of *The Prince and the Pauper* by Judah Grazovsky was published in Warsaw in 1898. Two other translations of the historical novel by A. D. Markson and A. L. Jacobowitz appeared in the twenties.

Henry Wadsworth Longfellow, who was regarded as a distinguished poet in the nineteenth century, found a congenial translator in Saul Tschernichowsky. The Hebrew poet not only equaled but exceeded the range of interests, the epic gifts, the scope and originality of the American poet. Since Hebrew writers in general and Tschernichowsky in particular did not translate for money, their translations tended to be superior to the commercial products of profit-hungry publishers all over the world. *The Song of Hiawatha* especially, and *Evangeline* to a certain extent, had a salutary influence on Hebrew letters. The Hebrew version of *The Song of Hiawatha* affected the meter and rhythm of Lisitzky's Indian epic *Medurot Doakot* (Burning Campfires).

And the hexameter of *Evangeline* in Tschernichowsky's version gave rise to a plethora of hexametric poems in Hebrew.

Jack London was another favorite with the Hebrew public. Three Hebrew poets—Simon Halkin, Reuben Avinoam, Isaac Lamdan—translated most of his novels and stories. There were also other less-known translators. This partiality to the crude and adventurous story-teller can only be explained by the great reputation he enjoyed in Europe at the beginning of the century.

But the great renascence of American literature in New England—the complementary brands of transcendentalism represented by Emerson and Thoreau, the dark and stark realism of Hawthorne, the powerful symbolism of Melville—was not as thoroughly assimilated in Hebrew literature as it could have been. It is true that Emerson's *Representative Men* and *Essays* were translated by Isaac Leb Baruch, Thoreau's *Walden* by the American-born Hebrew poet Reuben Avinoam, Hawthorne's *The Scarlet Letter* by David Yehieli, Melville's *Billy Budd* by Abraham Regelson and *Moby Dick* by Elijah Bortniker. Still, with the possible exception of Emerson, the writers in the period of the American renascence made a slight impact on Hebrew literature. Ironically, Emerson was translated in the twenties when his influence in America was on the wane. The recent publication of a definitive edition of Emerson's *Journals* —five volumes have been published so far—may revive interest in the sage of Concord. But his nobility of thought has scant appeal to modern sensibilities.

Flood of Translations

The generosity of Abraham Joseph Stybel, patron and publisher in the first half of our century, inundated Hebrew literature with translations from many literatures including English and American. Other publishers emulated his example and engaged Hebrew writers to translate American authors. Between the two world wars the chief translators of American classics were Hebrew writers who lived or had lived in America. They were conscious of the heady atmosphere of their environment. In 1925, an *annus mirabilis* of American fiction, they witnessed the publication of Theodore's Dreiser's *An American Tragedy*, F. Scott Fitzgerald's *The Great Gatsby*, and Ernest Hemingway's *In Our Time*.

As immigrants, and most of them were immigrants, they were also fascinated by the novels of Upton Sinclair and Sinclair Lewis, Sherwood Anderson and Robert Penn Warren, Thomas Wolfe and William Faulkner, John Dos Passos and John Steinbeck, Pearl Buck and Eudora Welty. These novelists conquered

the American continent from Massachusetts to California on a
spiritual level as surely as their ancestors had subdued it on
a geographical level. The Hebrew writers of America felt the
dilemma of American poets like Frost and Sandburg in a non-
poetic or even antipoetic age; the anxiety of American dramatists
like O'Neill and Cauldwell and Arthur Miller, Thornton
Wilder, Clifford Odets and Tennessee Williams in a milieu
which was hostile to tragedy in the classic sense. They translated
American novelists and poets, sometimes brilliantly, mostly
adequately, rarely shoddily. For a reason difficult to fathom they
avoided to a certain extent Henry James—though not his brother
William—and they neglected George Santayana. Perhaps these
introspective authors presented difficulties for translators, perhaps
they did not find congenial translators.

Since most Hebrew writers of America were lyrical poets, they
were somewhat immune to the essays of John Crowe Ransom
and other representatives of the New Criticism. The analytical
dissection of poetry was less prized by them than the singing
line or the singing strength of the lyrical poets. That is why
they were drawn to the musical sonorities of Edgar Allan Poe,
Edna St. Vincent Millay and Edwin Arlington Robinson rather
than to the flat tonalities of Pound and Eliot and Auden. Only
the younger poets in Israel are fascinated by the poet of "The
Waste Land," which was rendered *in toto* by Noah Stern who
lived a number of years in this country.

The poet of Jewish pioneers, Uri Zevi Gruenberg, was inspired
by the poet of American pioneers, Walt Whitman, who revealed
a democratic vision of the world in free verse and in long,
majestic lines. He modeled himself on Walt Whitman to such an
extent that he was ready to adopt him as a Hebrew poet. In his
booklet *Kelape Tish'im we-Tish'ah (Against Ninety-Nine)*, which
attacked all contemporary Hebrew writers, Gruenberg said among
other things, "I think Whitman should have written in Hebrew.
What a pity that he didn't!" Small wonder that Simon Halkin's
translation of Walt Whitman's *Leaves of Grass* was warmly
received by writers in Israel. The virile rhythms of the untamed
American furnished a young generation of Hebrew writers with
a major text of poetic inspiration.

The rich vein of Negro poetry was diligently mined by Hebrew
poets in America. Hillel Bavli, a Hebrew poet of note in America,
was among the first to interpret their folk-songs and folk-poetry.
Stimulated by James Weldon Johnson's *The Book of American
Negro Poetry*, he studied individual Negro poets. In the transla-
tion of "The Negro Poet," a sonnet by James D. Corrothers,
"The Prayer from Atlanta" by W. Burghardt Du Bois, and
"Blood for Blood" by Claude McKay, he found emotional equiv-

alents in Hebrew for the exotic style of the Negro. It was not the Negro *per se* who interested Bavli but the Negro as symbol of Jewish destiny. The response to injustice and to rootlessness differed in Hebrew and in Negro poetry, but the basic feelings showed an indubitable identity.

Other Hebrew poets in America emulated Bavli's example. Reuben Avinoam translated Negro spirituals, Ephraim E. Lisitzky adapted Negro sermons, Negro folk-tales and Negro spirituals to Hebrew rhythms. He has projected and developed Negro themes in his book *bo-Ohale Kush (In Negro Tents)*. As a resident of New Orleans, he had unusual opportunities to observe colored people: "I have gone to their meetings, their clubs and their get-togethers for many years. I have heard the speeches of their spokesmen and the sermons of their preachers in their churches; I have listened to their prayers and their spirituals which are sung by their congregations and choirs with the enthusiasm and absorption of *Hasidim*. When I understood the life of the Negro, as much as a man who is not a member of their church and their race can understand it, I said to myself: here is poetic stuff that can have a beneficent influence on Hebrew poetry in America."

He used that poetic stuff with abandon. He translated beautifully part of the famous spiritual "Swing Low Sweet Chariot"; he imitated the folk-songs of the Negroes, especially songs with biblical overtones; he tried, in a burst of empathy, to feel as they feel and to write as they write. In contradistinction to other Hebrew poets, he let the Negro speak for himself and he let the reader draw an implicit analogy to his own fate. Thus he achieved a subtler integration of the Negro into Hebrew poetry. It was because of his preoccupation with the Negro and because of the interest of other Hebrew poets that the Negro theme has become an important ingredient of contemporary Hebrew literature in America, even as it is a significant factor in the literatures of the world.

Hebrew Anthologies of American Literature

When America emerged after the Second World War as the world's most powerful nation, the country's achievements aroused an insatiable appetite in Europe, in Asia, in Africa. Books by American authors—good, bad or indifferent—were translated indiscriminately. Anthologies of American poetry and fiction in Hebrew translation sought to transmit the cultural riches of America to the Hebrew-reading public. Three books in particular must be singled out for their diligent efforts on behalf of American literature: *A Hebrew Anthology of American Verse,*

American Short Novels and *American Novelists. A Hebrew Anthology of American Verse,* mostly in Reuben Avinoam's translation, attests to love for American poetry: fifty-one American poets with an aggregate of two hundred and forty-nine poems are represented in the book. Minor and major poets, the earliest and the contemporary poets, were translated with sensitive care: Anne Bradstreet (1612-1678), the first American poet who was characterized as "the tenth muse, lately sprung up in America" and Emily Dickinson, the Sappho of New England; John Greenleaf Whittier and Edgar Allan Poe. Some memorable poems have been included in the *Anthology:* Edwin Markham's "The Man with the Hoe," Poe's "Annabel Lee," Sandburg's "Prairie," Robinson Jeffers's "Shine, Perishing Republic," Conrad Aiken's "Music I Heard with You," Edna St. Vincent Millay's "Renascence" and Langston Hughes's "The Negro." Another Hebrew poet, Hillel Bavli, has done much to popularize American poetry in a series of essays. He not only wrote engagingly about poets like Robert Frost and Carl Sandburg, Amy Lowell and Edgar Lee Masters, but illustrated his literary evaluations with translations from their works.

American prose was well served with Solomon Wiseman's *Mesapperim Amerikaiyyim.* The title-page in English—*American Short Novels*—lacks precision: the book is an anthology of American short stories. Somewhat less ambitious than Avinoam's *A Hebrew Anthology of American Verse,* it contains twenty-eight stories by American writers and it ranges, chronologically and geographically, over a wide area of literary endeavor. Early writers are represented: Washington Irving and Hawthorne, Poe and Henry James. But the emphasis is on twentieth century writers: Sherwood Anderson, F. Scott Fitzgerald, James Thurber, William Faulkner, Thomas Wolfe, John Steinbeck and Ernest Hemingway. The stories are sensitively selected and translated. Such American classics as Washington Irving's "Rip van Winkle," Eudora Welty's "A Worn Path," and Faulkner's "A Rose for Emily," have found their way into the anthology. Wallenrod's book *Mesappere Amerikah (American Novelists)* is an evaluation of the chief representatives of American prose from Washington Irving to John Steinbeck. Together with Wiseman's anthology, it surveys the field of American fiction for the Hebrew reader.

There is an increasing preoccupation in Israel with the so-called Jewish writers in America: Bellow, Malamud and Philip Roth, Mailer and Fiedler. Even a Wouk and a Schulberg have aroused interest in Israel. They are being translated, dissected, evaluated. Their Jewishness and un-Jewishness are puzzling factors: their faint aspirations toward Jewish identity as well as their pattern of estrangement and alienation from the Jewish community. Their types and characters, often men and women without ideas and ideals, point up the nihilistic malaise of the age, not uncommon among contemporary writers of Israel. But it is a welcome sign of the times that the poet Karl Shapiro has found a sympathetic readership in Israel. For in his *Poems of a Jew* he emphasizes a new freedom:

> When I think of the liberation of Palestine,
> When my eye conceives the great black English line
> Spanning the world news of two thousand years,
> My heart leaps forward like a hungry dog,
> My heart is thrown back on its tangled chain,
> My soul is hangdog in a Western chair.

Curiously, Ludwig Lewisohn who made an impact on American literature a generation ago and who had closer ties of identity with Judaism was not as eagerly translated as contemporary writers of Jewish origin.

The progressive commercialization of literature all over the world has also affected Hebrew literature. While some writers still translate *con amore,* many heed the call of a publisher and turn out a product at a price. The American best-seller has a much better chance to be translated than the unpopular work of a genuine poet, dramatist or novelist. And translation in Israel is slowly becoming an industry rather than an art.

SHAKESPEARE IN HEBREW GARB

By Joshua Bloch

WHATEVER position Shakespeare's writings have attained in the literatures of the nations into which they have found their way in the form of translations, one thing is certain, these translations have gained for themselves an indigenous status. They have become well entrenched, and serve as models for writers seeking fame and recognition in many a literature and language. Most of Shakespeare's writings were available in practically every European language before any portion of them was presented to the Hebrew reader. It was not until the middle of the nineteenth century that Hebrew readers were afforded the opportunity to read Shakespeare in the Holy Tongue. It was only then that Hebrew translations first made their appearance. Unlike most other languages, Hebrew could not claim a rich dramatic literature of its own; it could not yet point to its own prolific and highly gifted dramatists whose contributions to twentieth century Hebrew literature are notable.

Some of the subjects which Shakespeare made his own and treated so masterfully in his writings are not of the kind which drew the interest of Hebrew writers prior to the present century. With but few isolated exceptions, Hebrew literature, until the turn of the century, seemed determined to tolerate nothing which referred to the sensual relation between the sexes. Regard for decency may have hindered any effort to introduce some of Shakespeare's writings to the Hebrew reader. Consider, for example, Shakespeare's sonnets. They have exerted a profound influence on Saul Tchernichovski and on some of his later contemporaries whose own sonnets are among the finest in Hebrew literature. No doubt, directly or indirectly, they influenced other Hebrew poets as well. They enable one to trace specific circumstances in Shakespeare's life. They vividly portray the actual situation and sentiments of the poet; they acquaint the reader with his passions and contain remarkable disclosures of his youthful errors. Indeed, they offer a basis, albeit a meager one, for gossip as to some of his personal experiences with men and with women.

There are other obstacles, but they are encountered not only by Hebrew translators of Shakespeare. The translation of his works into any language presents peculiar problems. Shakespeare's classical style and the great difficulty of translating him with fidelity present an insuperable obstacle to his widespread circulation. (It must not, however, be supposed that a literal translation can ever be a faithful one.) A comparative examination of translations of *Julius Caesar, Hamlet, Macbeth,* and *Antony and Cleopatra,* each of which is represented by three different Hebrew versions, reveals the extent of the inherent difficulties which confronted their respective translators. Each translator presents a version so different from the other as to betray a measure of inadequacy in the performance of his task. This accounts partly for the fact that translations of Shakespeare's writings in Hebrew and, for that matter, also in Yiddish, were made first from German versions which seemed less formidable to the translators than the original English texts. It is a noteworthy phenomenon in the history of German literature that warm hospitality was accorded all of Shakespeare's writings in translation. They were, so to speak, enthusiastically adopted in the literature of the German people. There was yet another reason which may, at least partly, account for the scant interest in Shakespeare on the part of Hebrew writers. It was the fact that translators, who introduced into Hebrew literature versions of classical writings in various western literatures, were often attracted to works containing biblical themes, episodes and characters. These could hardly be found in Shakespeare's writings, although biblical references are not altogether lacking.

If the Hebrew language can not yet boast of translations of everything the Shakespearean literary legacy bequeathed to English literature, it is because there has not yet appeared the gifted and dedicated translator who would undertake the entire task with the persistence, skill and talent required for its execution. Such an assignment is quite difficult. Many of Shakespeare's rhymes are faultless, ingenious with attractive ease and rich without false brilliancy. The songs interspersed in his plays are generally tuneful and altogether musical, and an awareness of their melody is evoked merely by reading them. All this presents a challenge to the translator. Most of the Hebrew translators of Shakespeare's works were poets. They were masters of the Hebrew tongue but could not always capture the original effect in the language they chose as their medium to reproduce the great poet's texts.

It is reported that August Wilhelm Schlegel once spoke of Shakespeare as "a correct poet." How true! No translation of his writings could be adequate unless executed by "a correct poet." It is for this reason that the most successful Hebrew versions of Shakespeare are those which have been produced by the gifted poets in the present century and especially by those who have

attained great fame in modern Hebrew literature. It is they who
have been instrumental in introducing Shakespeare to a constantly
growing audience of Hebrew readers. Such names as H. N. Bialik,
Saul Tchernichovski, Hillel Bavli, Israel Efros, David Frishman,
Reuben Grossman, Simon Halkin, Ephraim E. Lisitzky, Israel
Jacob Schwartz, Benjamin N. Silkiner, S. Shalom and others, are
among the creators of modern Hebrew verse. They are in the
forefront of the movement to accord Shakespeare the place he and
his writings justly merit in the literature of Hebrew translation.
While Hebrew literature has not yet felt sufficiently the impact of
Shakespeare's influence, there is abundant reason to look forward
to a not distant day, perhaps within a decade or so, when Shakespeare will become a major link in the chain that binds the Hebrew
reading public with English-speaking people everywhere.

In this survey no effort is made at interpreting any rendition of
Shakespeare's writings which have already reached the Hebrew
reader. Such a venture would be presumptuous on the part of one
who makes no special claim to mastery of the subject. Nor is
there any need for it, since the literature on Shakespeare is quite
extensive. There is a continuous flow of books and essays on every
aspect of the life and labors of the incomparable poet who occupies
a unique position in world literature. The present study is confined
merely to a rapid survey of the few portions of Shakespeare's
writings which have become accessible in Hebrew garb. Of his
plays, less than half are available to the Hebrew reader in one
form or another, and of his poems, an even smaller number are
extant in Hebrew translation.

It is reasonably safe to assume that this survey cannot purport
to be complete, for in a day when Hebrew writers are busily
engaged in enriching Hebrew literature with translations of the
great classics in all literatures, Shakespeare's works are not being
neglected. Whatever few translations have already made their
way into Hebrew literature indicate an unmistakable trend to
habilitate the greatest of English authors into our Hebrew literary
treasure-trove. While the beginnings were modest and stemmed
from the middle of the last century, the bulk of the output is the
product of the post World War I days. If the translations continue
at their present pace, we may look forward to the felicitous arrival
of the day when Shakespeare's complete works will become available to the Hebrew reader, well-edited and attractive in form, and
worthy of a place alongside the finest literary productions written
in the Holy Tongue.

Much of Shakespearean lore is transmitted in quite a number of
works by writers who erected literary structures of their own with
materials drawn from Shakespeare's plays and poems. Few of

them were originally written in Hebrew; others represent Hebrew translations from other tongues. An original work of this kind is Ari Ibn-Zahav's Hebrew novel *Shylock, The Jew of Venice* (שיילוק, היהודי מויניציה. Tel-Aviv, 1947). Where Ibn Zahav leaves off, indeed where Shakespeare himself leaves off, Ludwig Lewisohn continues. In his work *The Last Days of Shylock* (ימי שילוק האחרונים) which was translated by Reuben Grossman (Tel-Aviv, 1932), he re-creates a measure of the Jewish atmosphere in which Shylock presumably moved.

Moses Ben-Eliezer, who at the beginning of this century lived in New York, where he edited *Shibalim*, a Hebrew monthly, undertook in his later years, while residing in Israel, the translation from English into Hebrew of Shakespearean stories for children. Among his many publications in this field are two collections of Shakespearean tales for children (Jerusalem, 1927, and Tel-Aviv, 1948), and tales of three plays, *A Midsummer Night's Dream, Winter's Tale* and *The Tempest* (Tel-Aviv, 1954).

A bibliography of the Hebrew translations of Shakespeare's plays is appended to this paper. These translations are arranged in the chronological order of their composition as presented in the one-volume edition of *The Works of William Shakespeare*, printed for the Shakespeare Head Press and published by Oxford University Press (New York, 1934). Obviously, no claim to finality is made in a subject so beset with difficulties, but the sequence may be taken as fairly representative of the general results of recent research. The time-honored division of the poet's writings into *comedies, histories* and *tragedies*, dating from the First Folio in 1623 and universally followed ever since, has been abandoned here. It seems more desirable that readers approach the body of Shakespeare's writings not as a static literary monument, but as a vital and growing organism revealing the evolution of the poet's personality and genius.

The present age is one of great expansion in good reading. Though Hebrew readers possess a vast and rich literature entirely their own, they are nevertheless eager to gain access to the best in other literatures and to make them available in the language they cherish. Their greatest literature, beginning with the Holy Scriptures, was created in that language. They view with pride the rise in the output of entertaining Hebrew works, both originals and translations. Never before were Hebrew readers so free as they are now to indulge in books for recreation. The enormous increase in Hebrew publishing at the arrival of the second half of the twentieth century indicates the enthusiastic response to the new demand. In this renascent upsurge, Shakespeare's works are eliciting greater interest and attention, and the evidence appears in the growing eagerness to absorb his writings in modern Hebrew literature. Moreover, it is vigorously supported by the frequent performances of Hebrew versions of Shakespearean plays on the Hebrew stage in Israel. In the circumstances, it is not too difficult to believe that the time is not distant when a "complete Shakespeare" will take its place on the Hebrew book-shelf along with the classics of the other literatures to which the Hebrew language has already extended hospitality.

HEBREW VERSIONS OF SHAKESPEAREAN WRITINGS

The Comedy of Errors

תאומים המשמשים בערבוביה. Translated by E. Ben Jehuda. Reprinted from הצבי, Jerusalem, 5664 (1904).

Romeo and Juliet

רם ויעל. Translated from the English by Isaac Edward Salkinson. Vienna, 1878.

Reviewed by P. Smolenskin, in השחר, Vienna, 1877, vol. 9, pp. 287–288, 346–351 and 406–408. Cf. Israel Cohen, זלקינסון כאמן התרגום, in מאזנים, Tel Aviv, 5701 (1941), vol. 12, pp. 63–71.

A Midsummer Night's Dream

חלום ליל קיץ. Translated by Harry S. Davidowitz. Jerusalem, 1943.

King John

חיי המלך יוחנן ומותו. Translated and provided with an Introduction by Simon Halkin. Jerusalem, 1947.

The Taming of the Shrew

אלוף הסוררת. Translated by Raphael Eliaz. Merhavia, 1954.

מוסר סוררה. Translated from the English by Jacob Hillel Elkind. Berditchev, 1892.

On the production of this play, see A. A. Mendilow, "על אילוף הסוררת לשקספיר" in במות, Tel Aviv, July, 1952, pp. 154–158.

King Richard the Second

על המדינה. Translation of Act III, Scene 4, by Meir Gartner. In תרבות, London, 5714, vol. 8, nos. 5–6, pp. 51–56.

The Merchant of Venice

הסוחר מונציה. Translated from the English by Simon Halkin.
Berlin-Charlottenburg (Printed in Wilna), 1929.

The play was first performed by Habimah, Tel Aviv,
May 14, 1936.

Cf. Joshua Bloch, הסוחר מויניציה, in התרן, New York,
September, 1922, vol. 9, pp. 26–42; A. Z. Aescoli, מעשה שילוק,
in מאזנים, Tel Aviv, 5695 (1935), vol. 4, pp. 63–70; Gustav
Landauer, הסוחר מונציה, in במה, Tel Aviv, February, 1936,
pp. 14–21 and the articles by Leopold Jessner, S. Gronemann,
Reuben Grossman and K. Rathhaus, in במה, Tel Aviv, May,
1936.

The Merry Wives of Windsor

נשי ווינדזור העליזות. Translated by Nathan Alterman. Tel
Aviv, 5706 (1946).

Reviewed in מאזנים, 5706, vol. 22, pp. 378–380.

Julius Caesar

יוליוס קיסר. Translation of the first, second and third acts by
Ḥayyim Naḥman Bialik. In מאזנים, Hebrew weekly, Tel Aviv,
1929, vol. 1, nos. 3 and 7. Reprinted in כתבי חיים נחמן ביאליק,
Tel Aviv, 1935, vol. 3.

יוליוס קיסר. Translated by Ephraim E. Lisitzky. Tel Aviv,
1933.

יוליוס קיסר. Translated by Joseph G. Libes. Tel Aviv, 1951.

Twelfth Night; or What You will

הלילה השנים עשר או כרצונכם. Translated by Saul Tchernichovski.
Tel Aviv, 1931.

For review of performance of this play by Habimah, see
J. Lichtenbaum, in מאזנים, Feb. 26, 1931, vol. 2, nos. 42–43,
pp. 15–16.

Hamlet, Prince of Denmark

המלט, נסיך דניה. Translated and provided with an Introduction
and notes by Ḥayyim Yeḥiel Bornstein. Warsaw, 1926.

First published in הצפירה, Warsaw, 1900–1901, vols. 27–28.

המלט, נסיך דנמרק. Translated by Harry S. Davidowitz.
Jerusalem, 1942. Second edition, 1954.

המלט, נסיך דנמרק. Translated by Israel Isaac Efros. New
York, 1944. Cf. A. Fels (א. פלס), המלט" לשקספיר בלשון.

העברית, in מאזנים, Tel Aviv, 5705 (1945), vol. 20, pp. 367–371.

מרי שיח. Hamlet's Soliloquy "To be or not to be" (Act III, Scene 1). Translated from the German by Naphtali Poper Krassensohn. In כוכבי יצחק, Wien, 1867, no. 22, p. 55.

המתאונן. Another translation of Hamlet's soliloquy "To be or not to be" (Act III, Scene 1), likewise from the German, by Fabius Mieses. In his קבצת שירים, Cracow, 1891, pp. 1–2.

Othello, the Moor of Venice

איתיאל הכושי מוינעציא. Translated by Isaac Edward Salkinson. Preface by Perez Smolenskin. Vienna, 1874.

Republished with a new preface and under the title, אותלו הכושי מויניציה, Tel Aviv, 1929. Reviewed in מאזנים, June 26, 1930, vol. 2, no. 8, pp. 15–16. Act V, Scene 2 is reprinted in הסגנון העברי by Meir Krynski, Warsaw, 1910, vol. 1, cols. 873–878.

אותלו. Translated by Nathan Alterman. Merhavia, 1950.

Macbeth

מקבט חזות קשה. A Hebrew translation of Schiller's German version by Isaac Barb. Drohobycz, 1883.

מקבת. Translated and provided with a Hebrew version of William Hazlitt's essay on *Macbeth* by Harry S. Davidowitz. Jerusalem, 1946.

מקבת. Translated and provided with an Introduction and notes by Ephraim Brauda. Jerusalem and Tel-Aviv, 1954.

שירת המכשפות. Translation of the Song of the Witches (Act IV, Scene 1) by Benjamin N. Silk[iner]. In הדאר, New York, May 14, 1926, vol. 6, no. 24, pp. 454–455.

קטע ממקבת. Translation of Act V, Scene 5, by Benjamin N. Silk[iner]. In כתובים, Tel Aviv, 1927, vol. 1, no. 31, p. 3.

מקבת. Translation of Act IV, by Saul Tchernichovski. In בוסתנאי, Rechovoth, 1931, vol. 3, pp. 12–14.

King Lear

המלך ליר. Translated by Samuel Loeb Gordon. Warsaw, 1899. (ביבליותיקה עברית, vols. 61–62). Act III, Scene 2, republished in Meir Krynski's הסגנון העברי, Warsaw, 1910, vol. 1, col. 878–881.

ליר המלך. Translated and provided with an Introduction and notes by Reuben Grossman. Tel Aviv, 1944.

והמלך ליר זקן .... Translation of Act I, Scene 1, by Reuben Grossman. In במה, Tel Aviv, January, 1939, pp. 30–36.

Antony and Cleopatra

אנטוניוס וקליאופטרה. Translated and provided with an Introduction and notes by Reuben Grossman. Tel Aviv, 1947.

אנטוניוס וקליאופטרה. Translated and provided with an Introduction by Hillel Bavli. Tel Aviv, 1952. It was originally published in התקופה, vols. 32–33, New York, 1947, pp. 315–392 and vols. 34–35, New York, 1950, pp. 395–494.

אנטוניוס וקלאופטרה. Translated by Joseph G. Libes, Tel Aviv, 5712 (1952).

Coriolanus

קוריולנוס. Translated by David Frishman. Warsaw, 1924.

Cymbeline

שיר הקוברים על קבורת עובד האדמה. Song of the gravediggers in Act IV, Scene 2. Translated from Herder's German version. In כוכבי יצחק, Wien, 1862, no. 27, pp. 63–64.

The Winter's Tale

אגדת החרף. Translated by Harry S. Davidowitz. Jerusalem, 1945.

The Tempest

הסערה. Translated by Ephraim E. Lisitzky. New York, 1941.

קטע מן "הסערה". Translated by Ephraim E. Lisitzky. In הדאר, New York, 1928, vol. 9, no. 19, p. 320.

Sonnets

סונטות. Translated by S. Shalom (pseud. of Shalom Joseph Schapira). Tel Aviv, 1943.

מסוניטות שקספיר. Translated by Israel J. Schwartz. In התרן, New York, 1916, vol. 3, no. 4, p. 8.

סונטות שקספיר. Translated by Israel J. Schwartz. In התקופה, Warsaw, 1923, vol. 18, pp. 142–148.

עולם. Translation of Sonnet 66. In כתובים, Tel Aviv, 1929, vol. 3, no. 30, p. 1.

הסונטות אל הגברת השחורה. Translated by S. Shalom (pseud. of Shalom Joseph Schapira). Tel Aviv, 1941.

הסונטות אל העלם הרוק. Translated by S. Shalom (pseud. of Shalom Joseph Schapira). In מאזנים, Tel Aviv, Kislev, 5703 (1943), vol. 15, No. 3, pp. 143–147.

See משהו על סונטות שקספיר ועל המלט by Emanuel Bin-Goryon, in מאזנים, Tel Aviv, 5704 (1943), vol. 17, pp. 63–69.

Miscellaneous

מתורתו של שקספיר by Samuel Hurwitz, New York, 1935. A free rendering of gleanings from Shakespeare's *Sonnets*, *Rape of Lucrece* and *Venus and Adonis*.

Pseudo-Shakespearean writings are represented in Hebrew literature by a translation of *A Yorkshire Tragedy*, a one act drama.

טראגעדיה ביארקשיר או מחזה תוגה...העתק לשפת הקדש ע"י זאב בן ליבער סמאליענסקי. גראיעווא, בדפום חיים פיורקא, תרס"א (1901).

Some scholars maintain that it is very unlike Shakespeare, but it has a few passages of extraordinary vivid prose, which might conceivably owe something to him.

SHAKESPEARE TRANSLATIONS IN YIDDISH

By Adah Boraisha-Fogel

A TRANSLATION enriches the treasure-trove of a nation's literature, and we must judge it by the same high standards as we do an original piece. An ideal translation requires faithful rendition of form and content, and maximum utilization of its own language potential. Thus it evolves into an independent artistic creation.

In dealing with Shakespeare, the aim of the translator is to transport his reader back to the milieu of Elizabethan England, introducing him, on the one hand, to its unique ideology, and helping him to recognize, on the other, as Shakespeare did so profoundly, the permanent and universal truths of its people and the nature of their problems.

The retention of the balance of form and content, which is the essence of Shakespeare's mastery, is a formidable undertaking for any translator. It is needless to dwell upon the multiple technical problems of Shakespeare's versification, with all its rare and exacting tonality: the subtle nuances and shadings, word and sound play, compressed lines and unswerving pentameter. A further obstacle is the archaic expressions — 16th century idiom and humor. For this the translator has commentaries to help him, but not all puns are translatable, nor can a synonym be found for all archaisms.

The Yiddish translator has to cope with an additional hardship — a natural limitation of his language — which does not beset the Russian or German writer. The storehouse of Yiddish is far less abundant than that of English. The dearth of Yiddish adjectives and word shadings makes it, in many instances, impossible for the Yiddish translator to reproduce the hues and resonance of Shakespeare's ingenious and varied literary usages.

In view, therefore, of the extraordinary demands evoked by the original text, and of the limitations of Yiddish to satisfy those demands, the translator's work should, by adhering meticulously to the English version, strive to duplicate the original as closely as is possible under the circumstances.

We find that all the translators use modern Yiddish, transposing the archaic expressions into contemporary idiom, so that the basic meaning of the archaic word is blended into the text. This provides smoother passage for the Yiddish reader, but the reader of the original has the advantage of being able to savor the flavor of the archaisms, plus their interpretation in the glossary.

Joseph Bovshover's translation of the *Merchant of Venice*, which he calls *Shylock*, is an outstanding event in Yiddish literature, because it is the first Yiddish translation of a Shakespearean drama. In addition, it is a literary work of high calibre that can stand alone as a drama in Yiddish.

Bovshover and his predecessors, David Edelstadt and Morris Rosenfeld, were the first important Yiddish writers to function on American soil. They appeared at the close of the 19th century, when the major Yiddish literary centers were still in Poland and in Russia. Bovshover was born in Poland in 1872 and emigrated to America in 1890. Highly gifted and versatile, he wrote both in Yiddish and in English. He would have become one of our foremost poets; but in 1899, the year *Shylock* was published, he was committed to an institution for the mentally ill. There he remained, completely withdrawn, his pen forever silenced, until his death in 1916.

In a preface, which is an eloquent tribute to Shakespeare's compassion and humaneness, Bovshover denies Shakespeare's alleged malevolence towards Jews. He avers that it was Shakespeare's intent to paint Shylock as a tragic portraiture, not as the harsh and intolerant caricature seen by 16th century England: the pitiless money-lender, fawning and wily. Shakespeare understood whence came the stooped back, the seeming cringing meekness, and the proud and anguished spirit which revolted against its tormentors. Reacting to his own profound concern for the oppressed, Bovshover sees the main theme of *Shylock* as a vigorous condemnation of tyranny. Having himself suffered degradation and disappointment in public and private life, Shakespeare invents Shylock's revolt as a literary instrument to give vent to his poignant heartache and to his personal feeling of bitterness.

Bovshover's Yiddish version is an absorbing, swiftly-moving drama. Although it was never produced, one can readily imagine it on the boards.

The orthography and many expressions are German: words such as *herz, diesen*, and the like, which were freely used in Bovshover's time. This orthography is, however, hardly an impediment to the modern reader. The eye and the mind skim past it, mainly because Bovshover's general sentence structure is modern and not distorted. One might demand here and there a whit more tautness in phrasing and a bit more subtlety in nuance, for the Germanic influence creates a looseness and floridity which modern Yiddish style has abandoned. But this is the manner in which Bovshover wrote his own poetry. It is not a case of carelessness or indifference.

For Bovshover maintains close contact with the original, meticulously and ingeniously following the imagery, without forfeiting the pliability of his own language. The pentameter is retained throughout the verse passages — a feat which redounds greatly to the translator's credit. The dialogues are so forceful, so sparked with animation, that one can almost hear the characters breathing.

Possessing an agile wit indispensable in a Shakespeare translation, Bovshover skillfully transposes the puns and word-play. His prose passages prove, in this play as well as in the Halkin and Goldberg translations discussed later on, that Yiddish lends itself admirably to communicating Elizabethan lustiness and humor. Yet Bovshover never crosses the boundary to over-simplification.

The archaic expressions have, on the whole, with very few lapses, been translated into correct modern Yiddish. In a few instances, certain minor idioms with which Bovshover could not cope have been omitted, with no loss to the over-all action.

Bovshover's Yiddish translation of *Shylock* fulfils the chief aims of a translation in that it illuminates for the Yiddish reader the general world in which Shakespeare lived and the private domain of his genius.

The bulk of Shakespeare translations into Yiddish appeared in the United States and in the Soviet Union. S. Halkin and J. Goldberg produced their works in the 1930's, during a highly fruitful era of Jewish cultural activity in Russia. This activity embraced all the arts in the final decade before its tragic decline.

Halkin's translation of *King Lear* was performed by the Moscow Yiddish State Theatre, and was dedicated to Solomon Michoels, who played the title role. The book is handsomely published and contains illustrations of scenes taken from the production.

The translation was written to order for production. There is a rearranging and loosening of lines, and explanation rather than direct imagery. This bold treatment is for the purpose of fluidity of action and dramatic clarity which modern staging demands. But the deletion of passages and the omission of adjectives and phrases sacrifice poetic imagery and impoverish the content, particularly when the play is read and not seen on the stage. Halkin's boldness becomes sheer temerity when he adds his own pictures to the original text.

In the blank verse passages there is frequent and disconcerting inversion of subject and predicate, and general misplacement of phrases, causing a twisted and awkward sentence structure. Since this defect is not found in the prose portions, we assume it was employed to maintain the pentameter verse form which is assiduously adhered to throughout the play. One cannot, however, help but feel that with a little more effort Halkin, an authentic poet, could have avoided these inversions and produced a more coherent and logical grammatical sequence.

The prose portions of the play are picturesque, being both good Yiddish and faithful in reproducing Shakespeare. Here the translator is in full command. The rhymes sung by the Fool give evidence of Halkin's mastery of verse and his keen sense of humor.

On the whole, Halkin has succeeded in conveying the tragic power of the play. He was particularly effective in depicting such important scenes as that in which Lear curses Goneril and Regan, and in the storm scene. Lear emerges in his full stature as King, as a frightened old man, and as a tormented father.

Goldberg, a specialist in folklore, mastered ten languages. His penetrating study of Mendele Mocher Seforim's *Fishke der Krumer* is one of the best works of its kind extant in Yiddish literary critique.

He is the most productive of all, having completed eight translations between 1933 and 1937. This brief space allows for a survey of only one of these — *Hamlet*, but it can be used as a guidepost to Goldberg's methodology in all his other translations.

Every translation is supplemented with literary and historical data, and with an exhaustive glossary explaining the archaisms which are numbered in the text. Goldberg states that he based his translations on the Cambridge Edition of Shakespeare, but his comprehensive footnotes indicate that he also availed himself of additional, more extensive commentaries. He has "Russified" the names of the *dramatis personnae*, but this is inconsequential, since he translated not into Russian but into Yiddish.

Goldberg's Yiddish version of *Hamlet* is undeniably powerful and compelling. Many of the verse passages are brilliantly executed, reflecting the thunder and tragedy of the original text. The prose passages, the rhymed portions and the humorous sections are incisive and sparkling. For the Yiddish reader it is an exciting experience.

However, when we compare it with the original, we find that a deal of the poetic splendor has been dimmed and diluted. This is partly due to Goldberg's lack of natural perception and sensibility in this area, which is forgivable, and partly to his carelessness, which is not. The tender, exquisitely phrased monologue in which the Queen describes Ophelia's death, "There is a willow grows aslant a brook," points up both of these defections. Some of the descriptive words are entirely deleted; others are incorrectly interpreted. When words — which are the key to poetry — are tampered with in any way, the content is emasculated. There are many irritating inaccuracies throughout the Yiddish text: the phrase, "frailty thy name is woman," emerges in a completely antithetical meaning. Where the King uses "we," Goldberg uses "I." Twisted, inverted sentences and phrases, which Halkin used to maintain the pentameter, are entirely pointless here, because Goldberg does not retain the rhythm at all, except in the "Play within the Play" and in the couplets. All this not only renders the Yiddish text inferior, but reveals the translator's lack of control of his own medium, and what is worse, his poetic callousness.

Goldberg can be painstaking, as is evidenced by the prose passages. The conversation between the two grave-diggers in Act 5 is a perfect Yiddish parallel of the English text. Here Goldberg utilized to a maximum degree the lustiness and folk-wit of Yiddish. He is a skillful rhymester, transposing with a facile pen the "Play within the Play," and Ophelia's charming songs whose structure is so closely akin to the Yiddish folk-song. He even made an attempt at acoustical duplication by consonant repetition in the King's drinking-song.

The rapid rate at which Goldberg produced his translations may have precipitated undue haste, marring the calibre of his work. His natural affinity for direct, plain talk, which stands him in good stead in the rhetorical and folk-genre passages, fails him in the more demanding poetical portions. As a result, there is a coarsening or marked blotting out of their lyrical quality. A little more polishing and painstaking care would have rendered his translation of *Hamlet* not only more faithful Shakespeare, but also much better Yiddish.

Only two Yiddish writers have ventured to translate the sonnets.

Dr. Abraham Asen, in addition to his Shakespearean translations, has contributed to Yiddish literature translations of Byron, Shelley, Tennyson and the *Rubaiyat*. In dealing with the sonnets, he set for himself the modest aim of popularizing them. There is minimal effort to reproduce their vivid imagery. Each sonnet emerges as a synopsis in rhyme, followed by a prose explanation of the "plot." For the Yiddish reader who is unable to read the sonnets in the original, such treatment offers at best a surface acquaintanceship with Shakespeare and his ideas.

On the other hand, the late B. Lapin, a well-known Yiddish poet, made an earnest effort to transpoetize the sonnets. He scrupulously followed the poetic imagery, the rhyme and rhythm pattern, and for this he is to be commended. But he does not always vindicate the high standard he set for himself.

Lapin's attempt to duplicate the compressed architecture of the English text produces at times an uncomfortable constriction, at others a stretching out and contortion of phrase. His choice of words is not always felicitous. Poetry woos the reader through his mind and ear. When words are woven together in a poetic verse, they not only formulate a lucid meaning, but also produce distinct musical overtones. Both meaning and music are inextricable from each other. Lapin's language is not mellifluous. He has not effectively utilized the potential tonality of Yiddish. Nevertheless, he has adhered to the original content, and in this sense places his readers in intimate contact with Shakespeare.

Opposite each sonnet appears its English counterpart, for those readers who wish to study and compare.

Lapin labored at his ambitious project for eight years, but did not live to see the book appear in print. It was published posthumously by his widow and son.

BIBLIOGRAPHY

Shylock. Warsaw, 1898. Story based on Shakespeare's comedy.

Shylock. Translated by Joseph Bovshover. New York, Hebrew Publishing Co., 1899.

Content of Shakespeare's Selected Works and Biography. By D. Hermalin. New York, Drukerman, 1912.

Hamlet; Julius Caesar. Translated by I. J. Schwartz. New York, Forward Publishing Co., 1918.

Julius Caesar. Translated by J. Goldberg. Minsk, 1933.

Hamlet. Translated by J. Goldberg. Minsk, 1934.

Othello. Translated by J. Goldberg. Minsk, 1935.

Romeo and Juliet. Translated by J. Goldberg. Minsk, 1935.

Richard III. Translated by J. Goldberg. Minsk, 1936.

Henry IV: Parts One and Two. Translated by J. Goldberg. Minsk, 1936.

The Tempest. Translated by J. Goldberg. Minsk, 1937.

King Lear. Translated by S. Halkin. Moscow, Farlag Emes, 1937.

The Tempest. Translated by Aaron Zeitlin. Unpublished manuscript. Performed in Lodz by The Yiddish Folk Theatre in 1937. Later performed in Warsaw and throughout the Polish provinces.

Shakespeare's Sonnets. Translated by Abraham Asen. N. Y., 1944.

King Lear. Translated by Abraham Asen. New York, 1947.

William Shakespeare: A Monograph. By Abraham Teitelbaum. N. Y., 1946. The only monograph on the Bard in Yiddish.

Shakespeare's Sonnets. Translated by B. Lapin. New York, 1953.

HASSIDIC INFLUENCES IN IMAGINATIVE ENGLISH LITERATURE

By Joseph Leftwich

IF ONE is asked, as I was, about Hassidic influences in imaginative English literature, one's first impulse is to say there is no such influence, or there is very little, and it came recently through the spread of Buber's influence to the English-speaking world. There is, for instance, one of my boyhood friends, the poet Lazarus Aaronson, whose work prompted Edouard Roditi to write a quarter century ago about "Aaronson's spiritual waverings between Judaism and Catholicism, the beliefs and doubts of his tortured mind." Not long ago Aaronson wrote me, "Judaism in the religious sense meant less to me when I was sixteen than it does now. As I grow older I stand nearer to the Rabbis. Buber means a great deal to me." This has gone into his poetry. "My verse," he added, "speaks for itself."

Meyer Levin, who wrote a book of Hassidic tales, *The Golden Mountain,* has confessed, "Godless though I may profess myself, I have responded with more than warmth to the mystical elements of Hassidism. As a writer I have considered that I accept this material as folklore. But in my soul I know that I take more than this from these legends." When Marek Szwarc, the artist, spoke to him first of the Baal Shem, "these stories sang right home to me. It seemed to me that my affinity for Hassidic legendry was a mental heritage. Had my parents never come to America, had I been born near Vilna, I might have become a Hassid."

"At this time," he says, "Hassidic material was unknown in English literature, though Buber had already published much of his German material. In recent times," he adds, "philosophers and poets and literary men have discovered the legends for their meaning and their beauty." As recently as 1931, Lucy Cohen, a member of one of the leading Anglo-Jewish families, admitted that when someone gave her a copy of Buber's Hassidic tales in German, she found it new and so "striking to interest the general reader" that with the help of her kinsman, the scholar Claude Montefiore, she translated the book into English under the title *Jewish Mysticism.*

310

Buber's influence has not gone unquestioned in Jewish religious circles, which complain that Hassidic tales alone do not give the essence of Hassidic religious teaching, and that religiously Buber seeks overmuch to synthesise Judaism with Christianity. One critic has called him "a self-appointed Apostle to the Gentiles, carrying to them a metamorphosed message of Hassidism." There may be justification for that judgment when one considers how a Christianised Jew like Victor Gollancz, under Buber's influence, jumbles together in one of his books bits from the Apostles' Creed, from St. Thomas Aquinas, Kierkegaard, the Mass, the Lord's Prayer, the Shema and a great deal from the Hassidic Rabbis. According to a review in a Jewish magazine, the Jewish-Christian missionaries have started publishing in their "Judeo-Christian Studies" long essays on "The Hassidic Movement" and on "Buber's I-Thou Philosophy." Buber himself has said, "I consider Hassidic truth vitally important for Jews, Christians and others."

There can be no doubt that Buber's writings have played a great role in spreading the knowledge of Hassidism, and above all, of the Hassidic tales. But there have been other writings in the field. Jacob Minkin says in his *The Romance of Hassidism,* published in 1935, "Hassidism has an accumulated literature that may fairly be described as stupendous." Yet when he mentions some of it, we find it is not creative literature, but scholarly work like "Dubnow, Horodetzky, Buber, Kahana."

Influences other than the scholarly have of course contributed to the knowledge of Hassidism. There was, for example, the tremendous impact the production of An-sky's *The Dybbuk* by the Vilna Troupe and the Habimah made on the English stage. Not only Anglo-Jewish theatre groups, but also non-Jewish companies, were impressed by the play's dramatic possibilities and by the novelty of the Hassidic dances. Rabbi Azrael's speech from *The Dybbuk* found its way into Victor Gollancz's anthology. Maurice Schwartz's production of Singer's *Yoshe Kalb* brought more Hassidism to the English stage. Wolf Mankowitz and Sam Wanamaker recently produced *The World. of Shalom Aleichem,* making a point to stage the Hassidic features.

As far back as 1904, Helena Frank's early translations of Peretz's Hassidic tales, like *If Not Higher,* had roused interest among English-speaking Jews and non-Jews. It is noteworthy that Helena Frank's translation is the one Chief Rabbi Hertz incorporated in his *Book of Jewish Thoughts.* Other Yiddish and Hebrew writers who pictured Hassidic life did not get into the stream of English translation until Sholom Asch and Zalman Schneor brought the Hassidic world to English readers with such works as *Salvation (Tehilim Yid)* and *The Emperor and the Rabbi* (the Rabbi being the Hassidic Rabbi Schneor

Zalman, Schneor's ancestor). Asch embodied Hassidism also in some of his other books. In *Three Cities,* "Berl Krongold had been brought up in the traditional Hassidic fashion," and when Mirkin left Lodz he went to "the Hassidic prayer house at his door." Schneor pictured in *Noah Pandre* a saintly Hassidic Rabbi, some of the life in a Jewish town where Hassidism played a great part, and even a simple coach driver who went every Saturday night to hear the Rabbi expound Hassidic lore. There is Joseph Opatoshu's novel, *In Polish Woods,* published in English translation, about the Hassidim of the great Rabbi Mendel of Kotzk.

Chagall's rise to international fame as a painter revealed the fact emphasized by almost everyone writing about him, both non-Jews and Jews, that it is impossible to understand him without some knowledge of his Hassidic background. That is true, too, of another internationally famous Jewish artist, Yankel Adler.

Interest in Franz Kafka's writings has led to some extent to a consideration not only of his Jewish thought, but also of his attraction to the Hassidic outlook. "Writing is a form of prayer," said Kafka, entirely in the Hassidic tradition. It is a phrase that might have been used by Rabbi Nachman of Bratzlav. Buber had been in Kafka's circle, and Max Brod mentions among Kafka's influences Dora Dymant who, he says, came from "a good East European Hassidic family." Speaking of Hassidic influences of background and heredity reminds me of Dr. Roback's reference in his *Jewish Influence in Modern Thought* to "the Hassidic strain which probably runs in the families of both Freud and Bergson."

A Product of Time and Place

Why did Hassidic influence come into English literature so late? Hassidism arose in the eighteenth century out of the special conditions prevalent among the Jewish masses in Eastern Europe. It was a product of the time and the place. The Frankist heresy had made great inroads, and Rabbinism was above the heads of the ordinary folk. The new doctrine of joy and ecstasy spread from Podolia and Volhynia along the Rivers Pruth and Dniester, through the Ukraine and Poland, Galicia, Lithuania, Hungary and Roumania. It did not extend into Germany, France and England, where conditions were different.

Those who came to Germany from the Hassidic environment, like Solomon Maimon, sneered at it. He spoke of the Baal Shem as a Cabbalist who effected "some lucky cures by means of his medical knowledge and his jugglery." That was the Germany of the Mendelssohnian period, which Graetz calls

"The Age of Regeneration," while referring to Hassidism as "disintegration in Judaism." Graetz described the Hassidim as "miracle-maniacs who promulgated the wildest superstitions, and undermined the foundations of Talmudic and Rabbinic Judaism." Yet even Graetz conceded that "serious men too felt drawn to Hassidism in the hope of filling the void in their souls."

The Jews of the West had not been left untouched by mysticism. The Sabbataian heresy had invaded England too. The Messianic speculations of the Puritan millenarians had helped Manasseh ben Israel in his efforts to bring the Jews back to England. Hyamson, in his history of the London Sephardic community, speaks of "a Sabbataian undercurrent that had to be fought." It existed also in Germany. Eybeschuetz, a German Rabbi, was brought by Feuchtwanger into his *Jew Suess*: "Our teacher Rabbi Jonathan Eybeschuetz, Rabbi of Hamburg. Did he really believe in the teaching of the Cabbalah and practise it, the secret pupil and disciple of Sabbatai Zevi?" Feuchtwanger also brings in Jew Suess' kinsman, Rabbi Gabriel Oppenheimer the Cabbalist, who buried Jew Suess after his execution and said Kaddish for him. Jacob Frank himself, with some of his followers, had found refuge in Germany, in Offenbach.

But the Sabbataian collapse had not plunged the Jews of the West into such despair as in Eastern Europe. In Western Europe it was for the most part the Age of Emancipation. The Jews of these countries, unlike those in Eastern Europe, had prospered economically, and were accepted socially. Their next aim was political equality, on which they had set their minds. It was the time when Lord George Gordon had become a convert to Judaism (1787). Zangwill speaks of it in his *King of Schnorrers*. "In the days when Lord George Gordon became a Jew, there had been a special service of prayer and thanksgiving for the happy restoration of his Majesty's health, and the cantor had interceded tunefully on behalf of Royal George. The congregation was large and fashionable—far more so than when only a heavenly sovereign was concerned."

True, Anglo-Jewry had at that time, as Zangwill recalls in the same paragraph, "Dr. Falk, the Baal Shem of London, saint and Cabbalistic conjurer." But Falk was a different kind of Cabbalist. "He seems to have persuaded his superstitious contemporaries, Christian and Jewish, that he could discover hidden treasure and work other marvels, such as the transmutation of metals."

Cabbalistic Mysticism

The pre-Hassidic Cabbalistic mysticism on which Falk based himself had influenced English literature in his time and even earlier. One of Falk's contemporaries was the great English poet,

William Blake. As Professor Denis Saurat tells us in his *Occultism and Literature*, "Blake mentions the Cabbalah in his 'Address to the Jews.' He drew from the Cabbalah two of the leading ideas of his mythology." Milton, a hundred years before Blake, had also drawn on Hebrew lore and on the Cabbalah. "It cannot be maintained," says Saurat, "that all our poets borrowed straight from the Cabbalah. But even when they borrowed elsewhere the traditions which reached them were either the offspring or the poor and sometimes despised relations of the Cabbalah. In most cases the ideas must have reached our poets through conversation rather than through reading. The intellectual life of cultured Europeans was to some extent pervaded by an enormous mass of occult traditions which derived from the Cabbalah." Among the poets in whom Saurat traces this influence he includes, besides Milton and Blake, Shelley, Emerson and Whitman. Dr. S. A. Hirsch, of Jews' College, asserted in a lecture delivered there in 1901, that from some of the things Dickens said about Fagin, he wondered "if that great novelist had ever studied the Rambam."

That is not, however, the Hassidic influence which came into existence in Eastern Europe about the time William Blake was writing. There was, of course, a connection; the Cabbalah and Jewish mystic teaching linked them together. An article by Ariel Bension, who belonged to a Sephardic Hassidic group in Jerusalem, complains that "of the Sephardic Hassidim in Jerusalem the western world knows little. It has heard many intriguing tales of the Hassidim of Eastern Europe, how it flamed through the ghettos of Russia. Baal Shem and other great Hassidic names have become familiar, and the stories of their wonder-working are told in many tongues. But few know of its sister in Jerusalem—daughter of the same parents, the Zohar and Cabbalah." When I was in Israel and visited Safad, what I thought about Luria and Vital who had lived and worked there, was what I had remembered hearing from East European Hassidim.

The Hassidism founded by the Baal Shem came to the West—to England, Germany and France, and to America—with the Jewish immigrants from Eastern Europe. Some writers, not only Jews but also anti-Semites like the French brothers Tharaud, went to the homes of Hassidim to describe Hassidic life as they saw and depicted it in their novel, *The Shadow of the Cross.* They went to Belz and witnessed the Belzer Rabbi presiding at a table of more than two thousand Hassidim. Today, forty years after the brothers Tharaud published their book, French literature (and in translation, as the Tharaud book, English literature as well) has had added to it a novel, *The Sons of Avrom,* by Roger Ikor. There old Avrom, "a shrewd and energetic Hassid," emigrates from Russia to France, where his son shakes off the traditions of his Hassidic upbringing and his grandchildren assimilate and intermarry.

Polish and Russian Jews started coming to England very early after the Resettlement. In the British Museum there is a letter written by Thomas Crumpton to a Christian clergyman, the Rev. J. Greenhalgh. Describing his visit in 1662 to the first London Synagogue, before our oldest existing Synagogue in Bevis Marks was built, Crumpton tells of meeting a Rabbi named Samuel Levi, a learned Jew with a bushy beard who had come from Cracow, "the chief city of Poland." There was a continuous flow of Polish and Russian Jews to England, but until the 1880's their numbers were small. There were contacts, however, and legends arose in connection with them. Anglo-Jewry was concerned about the ill-treatment of the Jews in Russia, and it was decided that Sir Moses Montefiore should go to Russia to intervene with the Czar. He was in Russia in 1846, and the Jewish masses received him like a king and saviour. In the spirit of the legend the Jews of Russia wove around Montefiore's visit, An-sky, the author of *The Dybbuk*, wrote a story which I included in my anthology, *Yisroel*, about Moses Montefiore bringing back to England a Rabbi whose exposition of Torah was richer and greater than all of Moses Montefiore's wealth. It is noteworthy, since I am dealing with Hassidic influences in *imaginative* English Literature, that an Anglo-Jewish paper, in an article entitled *Queen Victoria and the Jews*, found it necessary to point out "that An-sky's story in *Yisroel* is a mere fantasy." The reference is to the story's conclusion that the Crimean War began because Moses Montefiore complained to Queen Victoria that the Czar of Russia had ill-treated his Jews and had tried to poison Moses Montefiore himself. Of course, no one had said it was history; it was the stuff of legend.

Zangwill on Hassidism

Zangwill was the first writer in English literature who brought Hassidism into his work. In *Dreamers of the Ghetto* he paints a picture of the Baal Shem. A dying man tells of his encounters with the Besht, "the ever-glorious and luminous Israel Baal Shem." The narrator had been a follower of Sabbatai Zevi, "nourished by the study of the Cabbalah." Then he heard of the Besht, met him and became his follower. He relates the Besht's life and miracles. "It is now many years since I first saw the Baal Shem, and as many years since I laid him in his grave, yet every word he spoke to me is treasured in my heart."

The subject remained in Zangwill's mind. When he died he left the unfinished manuscript of a "Cabbalistic Romance," about the pseudo-Messiah Frank whose degeneration had been one of the impulses which had brought the Hassidic revival into existence. In *Children of the Ghetto,* too, which appeared in 1892, Zangwill pictured the Hassidim who by that time, the 1890's, had made their home in London. In their little Synagogue, "they prayed metaphysics, angelology, Cabbalah." One of their number, Karlkammer, "was a great authority on Cabbalah."

The Hassidim began to interest London Jewish artists. Alfred Wolmark, who is now over 80, went as a young man to Cracow to paint Hassidim. Sir William Rothenstein became a member of the Mahsike Hadas Synagogue in Whitechapel, so that he could paint some of its orthodox and Hassidic Jews. They went also to the *Hevra Shaas,* known as the *Kahal Hassidim,* and to other Hassidic *shtibels.*

Zangwill was a friend of Schechter's and spoke of himself as his pupil. Schechter's writing was not imaginative literature, but he seems to have been the first to bring Hassidism to the attention of Anglo-Jewry. In his essay *The Hassidim,* republished in 1896 in his *Studies in Judaism,* Schechter referred to writers who have used the Hassidim in imaginative literature. "Some account of the sect is the more necessary," he wrote, "because although the Hassidim have not been wholly ignored by historians or novelists, the references to them have generally, for perfectly intelligible reasons, been either biased or inaccurate. The historians have been almost exclusively men saturated with Western culture and rationalism. To them Hassidism was a movement to be dismissed as unaesthetic and irrational. To the purposes of fiction the romantic side of Hassidism lends itself readily, but the novelists who have used this material have confined themselves to its externals. Thus Franzos in his references to the Jews of Barnow describes faithfully the outer signs of the man, his long coat and tangled curls, but the inner life, the world in which the Hassid moved and had his being, was unknown to him."

"As to my treatment of the subject," Schechter explained, "I confess that there was a time when I loved the Hassidim as there was a time when I hated them. And even now I am not able to suppress these feelings. I have tried to guide my feelings in such a way as to love in Hassidism what is ideal and noble, and to hate in it what turned out bad and pernicious for Judaism."

Dr. Moses Gaster was another Anglo-Jewish scholar interested in Hassidism. He introduced the English translation of Horodetzky's *Leaders of Hassidism.* "It (Hassidism) came," he wrote, "from the lowly, the poor, the ignorant, but it spoke with a tongue of fiery conviction, of deep enthusiasm. It brought hope and joy to the downtrodden." Rabbi Dr. Abelson, in his book, *Jewish Mysticism,* published in London in 1913, spoke of the

Hassidic movement as a "force that deserves an abiding place in the history of Jewish theology."

Afte Zangwill the mantle of Anglo-Jewish writing fell largely on Louis Golding. In *Day of Atonement* he has a group of Hassidim in Galicia, and one of them, Eli, who had come to Manchester, prayed "with a fervour typical of the Hassidim." In his book about the Warsaw Ghetto rising, *The Glory of Elsie Silver,* Golding pictured a Hassidic wonder-Rabbi telling the Jews to fight—"the last court the Rabbi held in Poland or anywhere on earth, and the most glorious, lit up as it were by the light of the Shechina." Hersey in his book about the Warsaw Ghetto, *The Wall,* speaks of "romantic Hassidism." There were, of course, Hassidim among the other Jews in the Warsaw Ghetto. Hersey gives us the picture of a Rabbi in *tallit* and *tephilin* going to his execution, saying: "Why do you mourn and tremble, Jews? We are going to the Messiah! Be glad! Be glad!"

Their spirit rose above persecution, torture and death. Almost as marvelous a survival as in Warsaw is that of persecuted religious Jews and of groups of Hassidim in the Soviet Union, pictured in a novel by one of them, Sabatyon. Lucy Dawidowicz, in *Commentary,* November, 1956, speaks of the way Sabatyon describes Hassidim who "surreptitiously maintained kosher kitchens and used the period allocated to Communist indoctrination for prayer and religious study."

Hassidic Numbers and Influence

Hassidic numbers and influence have grown greatly in England during the last few years, as they have also in America. Last September the *Jewish Chronicle* wrote about "a good many more *shtreimlach* worn by worshippers in London on Rosh Hashonah. In the streets with orthodox prayer-houses there were dozens of little boys with *pyot* and *shtreimlach* beside their fathers with silk *kapotes* and white stockings that made them seem to have come straight from a Galician *shtetl* or from Meah Shearim. The Hassidic congregations in North London were full to overflowing. Not even in pre-war Poland could one see a Synagogue more crowded or worshippers more devout."

The numbers are larger, but the phenomenon is not new in London. Izaak Goller in his novel, *Moses,* pictured Reb Zalman, the Rabbi, in his Whitechapel Hassidic *shtibel,* and Mr. Moses, the English-born Jew under his influence, resigning his post as a teacher in the Jews' Free School, growing a beard and becoming a Hassid. The enhanced Hassidic life in London today will surely find expression in the printed page. Henry Cohen, who writes as Roland Camberton and is a product of a North

London Yeshibah, naturally writes about that kind of Jewish life which is his background. Abraham Abrahams, who also was a Yeshibah student, has a characteristic poem called *To a Yeshibah Student* in his volume of poems published in 1932. Another London-born Yeshibah student is Hyman Lewis, who writes poetry largely on themes that derive from his religious upbringing and outlook. I picked up a fairly recent copy of the London *Jewish Quarterly,* and my eye was caught by the title of a poem, *Baal Shem in the Suburbs.* It begins, "I stood in the buff-washed Synagogue hall." He heard "the Chazan's tremolos dance about his head." The author is Alex Keller, 22, born in London, who "studied history at Cambridge, now doing post-graduate research at Oxford."

Young people are coming forward, with the new religious and Hassidic life around them. Hassidism came to England late but is becoming a force. "Twenty years ago," writes the Agudas Israel Bulletin, "no one would have imagined that a transplantation of traditional Jewish life as we know it would be possible in England. It was not only possible, but it was done. Jewish life in North London has undergone a tremendous change. The old ways of Yiddishkeit with all its outward manifestations are roaming the streets of North London. Nor have the other parts of London been unaffected. Everywhere are products of the change that Anglo-Jewish life has undergone. It has been shown that the streets of London could well digest a *shtreimel.*"

Hassidism has built a stronghold in London. Since literature is the mirror held up to life, in another decade we should find Hassidism reflected to a considerable extent in our continuing Anglo-Jewish literature.

Treasure Houses of Books

ON COMMUNITY LIBRARIES*

By Marvin Lowenthal

I WILL feel more at ease, and perhaps you will too, when I make it clear at the outset that I am not and never have been a professional librarian. I say this with neither satisfaction nor regret, for I have no prejudice in the matter: some of my best friends have been librarians.

I state it simply as an item of fact that I am not a caretaker or dispenser of books. I am merely a consumer of books. I have been —shall I say afflicted?—that way for nearly my whole life; and as a result I have had, it is true, long and varied and rather close acquaintance with libraries, not only in American towns and universities, but in a half-dozen countries of Europe as well as in other parts of the world.

Dr. Johnson once said: "A man will turn over half a library to make one book." In the course of the years I have been guilty of making about a dozen books, not one of which could have been written without extensive raids upon public and private libraries. If my audience were all librarians I could spend the evening telling about the amusing hurdles I have had to leap, the baffling regulations I have had to circumvent, the eccentric yet often charming librarians I have cultivated in order to add to their burdens by producing still another volume for their stacks.

But my deep interest in libraries, their strong attraction for me, and my ardent love for them, do not come from the professional use I have made of them. "A great library," it has been said, "contains the diary of the human race"; and I never tire of reading in that diary—of reliving, in all their drama, pathos and glory, the adventures of mankind. If I am not wise, I can at least, in a library, consort with the wisest men of all time, and hope, perhaps fondly, that a bit of their wisdom will brush off on me. If I cannot sing, I can at least listen and thrill to the songs of the supreme poets. When we come to think of it, most of us, in our daily business, lead prosaic and parochial lives; most of us, in the actual flesh, have virtually been nowhere, seen nothing,

* An address delivered at the inauguration of the Henry Meyers Memorial Library of the Jewish Community Center, Detroit (November 21, 1959) and at the annual meeting in New York of the Jewish Book Council of America (May 11, 1960).

and met nobody; but through the magic performed by a library we can live in any century or in any land we choose, we can share in any enterprise, exploit, and excitement we please, and we can hobnob with the best and—sometimes it is more fascinating— with the worst men who ever walked the face of the earth. Nothing human—no knowledge, no experience, no aspiration, no dream, and no reality—need be alien to us, so long as the doors of a library stand open for us.

But there is a wider view, one that leaves out of account any particular individual, even someone of such personal interest to us as our own self. There recently appeared in *Life* an account of the library of Harvard University—of Widener and its associated collections. A president of Harvard was quoted as saying that if all the buildings on the campus burned to the ground but if the library were spared, the university was still in business; whereas if the library alone burned down, that was the end of Harvard. More, however, than a university hangs on the fate of libraries. It should be apparent that without the knowledge and inspiration stored up and always on tap in our libraries, civilization itself would perish within a generation. Without books there could be no civilized administration of government or justice, no maintenance and progress of science. Not a single convenience of life that we now take for granted would survive: not a railroad would run, an airplane fly, or an auto move, without books; and not one of our darling gadgets—a deep freezer or a TV set—would exist. Moreover, to quote a famous phrase from the Danish scholar Bartholin, "without books God is silent, philosophy lame, letters dumb, and all things become shrouded in darkness." It is the library—what it contains and what it serves —that stands between us and primitive savagery.

The Long Chain of Jewish Libraries

Whenever, to come closer home, a Jewish community opens for general use a roomful of pertinent books, it constitutes the latest link in the long chain of Jewish libraries, public and private, which stretches back to a misty and dateless antiquity. No one any longer knows the nature or the precise origin of the first Jewish or, better said, Hebrew library. Ancient Israel, we do know, arose in a highly civilized region; and libraries, as I have indicated, are indispensable to civilzation. Vast collections of books, written to be sure on clay rather than on paper, have survived from the royal libraries of Nineveh and Babylon—collections whose earliest material, whose first editions, date from nearly five thousand years ago.

Of Israel itself, only hints are left us. There was a city in the territory of Judah, originally a Canaanite city, which Joshua called Kiriat-Sefer, that is, Book-Town—a name later changed to Debir, itself perhaps related to the Hebrew term for "word." When some three thousand years ago and more, the prophet Samuel wrote a book on the character of the kingdom which the Israelites insisted on adopting, he "laid" the book "up before the Lord"—that is to say, he put it into the safekeeping of a sacred, priestly library—possibly at Shiloh. To put a book in a sacred shrine-library was a way of preserving not only the document itself but the integrity of its text. The Greeks often employed the same safeguards; it was the ancient equivalent of taking out a copyright.

There must have been a library, a collection of archives at least, in the celebrated First Temple at Jerusalem. It was not any too well run—or so circumstantial evidence would imply. During the eighteenth year of his reign (621 B.C.E.) King Josiah ordered the Temple to undergo necessary repairs. While the repairs were in progress, probably in the stack room, a book was discovered which had long been lost to sight and mind. Tradition holds that it was the Book of the Law, or the Torah; modern scholarship identifies it as the presumably newly-written Book of Deuteronomy—in any case, either carelessness or a pious fraud, which one way or another speaks ill of the librarian, had been at work.

The first individual Jew credited with the creation of a public library was Nehemiah, one of the happy few who led in the restoration of Jerusalem after the return from the Babylonian captivity. The Second Book of the Maccabees tells how Nehemiah, "founding a library, gathered together the acts of the kings, and the prophets, and of David, and the epistles of the kings concerning the holy gifts" (2:13). Certainly the compilers of the two Books of Chronicles, the last historical writings included in the canonical Hebrew Scriptures, had at their disposal a rather extensive library, possibly the one founded by Nehemiah. The contents of its cupboards and shelves included all of the books now contained in the Hebrew Bible, except of course for such miscellaneous works as were not yet written. It also included a goodly number of books cited and sometimes tantalizingly described in Kings and Chronicles, but which—a sad testimony to the carelessness of the public—are lost forever. I may have overlooked a title or two, but I count twenty-one of these vanished treasures. Frankly, I would give the whole of Chronicles itself for the Thousand and Five Songs reputedly composed by Solomon, or for his Three Thousand Proverbs—not to mention what he had to say on trees, plants, beasts, birds, fishes, and "creeping things." And I would give all the Dead Sea Scrolls, with their enigmas wrapped in riddles, for the perished first-hand, contemporary account of "the acts of David the king, first and last . . . with all his reign and his might, and the times that went over him and over Israel, and over the kingdoms of the countries" (1 Chronicles 29:29-30); 1 have had my fill of the wearisome Teacher of Right-

eousness, whereas I could never have enough of David. But somebody at some time or another must have borrowed these fascinating books and, as borrowers will, disappeared with them into
oblivion. What says Ben Sirach? "Many persons, when a thing is
lent them, reckon it to be something they found" (Ecclesiasticus
29:4).

Yet, despite the depredations of borrowers, books multiplied
and libraries grew. Koheleth has an immortal word on this proliferation: "of making many books there is no end." Probably
the speediest and most copious output in the annals of the ancient
publication trade is recorded in the Second Book of Esdras (14:
44); in forty days five men under the dictation of Ezra wrote down
ninety-four different books composed on the spot. The last
seventy of them, incidentally, were placed under what librarians
today call restricted circulation; in this instance they were issued
only to such readers "as be wise among the people." But the account, I confess, smacks more of Talmudic midrash than of fact.

On Talking Books

In the period when the Talmud was in the process of composition—let us say, during the first two centuries before and after
the start of the Common Era—the rabbinical schools had at their
command, among more conventional library material, what might
be termed a talking book. For a long while the rabbis were loath
to commit to writing their prime source material, the Mishnah
or Oral Law, which was the basic subject of their studies, commentaries, opinions, and arguments. Writing down the Oral Law,
they felt, might impair the authoritative quality which derived
from its being *par excellence* the "unwritten" Law. They were
also afraid that scribes, who could not be checked up on the spot
and at once, might be led into making editorial changes or else
what we know as typographical errors. So they trained a band of
young men, usually not bright enough to think of anything
novel, to learn the Mishnah by heart; and when an assembly
of scholars wished to refer to this or that original Mishnah text,
about which there might be some dispute as to how it ran,
one of these young men would reel it off *verbatim*. As I have
remarked, these human parrots had powerful, well-developed
memories and not too much intelligence; they would have made
admirable contestants on a quiz show. Curiously enough, our
ultra-modern libraries are resorting to this old Talmudic method,
though for a different purpose; we have transformed the young
men into robots known as tape-recordings.

Independent of the scholarly or literary merit of their contents, the Dead Sea Scrolls, dating from just before the dawn of
the Common Era, have a dramatic interest which has captured
our imagination. The drama is multiple. The discovery and sub-

sequent adventures of the Scrolls is exciting enough, but it is more than matched by what must have been the dramatic scene and circumstance of their original entombment in the remote caves above the Wadi Qumran. Facing dire peril and perhaps extermination, the devout *yahad* or brotherhood, being a Jewish community, wrapped, double-wrapped, sealed in jars and hid away their most precious possession—their library. They showed in this a true and enviable sense of community values.

By its very nature, traditional Judaism is a religion, a view of life and a way of life, inextricably dependent upon books. With the passage of time and with the many varied and changing worlds to which the Jews found they had to adapt themselves, the necessary books grew more numerous and the dependence upon them more imperative. Mohammed called the Jews "the people of the book," meaning of course the Hebrew Bible, but "the people of books" would be more accurate. Besides the Bible, an adequate Jewish library had to possess the many-volumed Talmud, a whole arsenal of later digests, commentaries and casebooks, an array of prayer-books and other devotional literature, and, by the early Middle Ages, shelves of philosophic speculations, mystical and cabbalistic works, anthologies of fables, parables, and anecdotes (the *Midrashim*), moral disquisitions, as well as grammars, dictionaries, geographies, astronomies, travel accounts, and medical treatises.

Every Jewish community in the Middle Ages—which for most Jews lasted well into the 18th century—possessed a library, large or small, of this nature. It was usually housed in the synagogue, which was literally the community center, or else in the *Bet ha-Midrash* or House of Study. The community was dependent upon this library not only for recreation and for a fruitful way of investing one's time, but for the proper exercise of Judaism itself, for the maintenance of economic and social justice within the community's gates, for the adjustment of a thousand private, conflicting interests, and for the true worship of God. *Study, for the Jew, is also prayer.* May I quote you no less an authority than Hillel, in words you will find in your Sabbath prayer-book? "Do not say, When I have leisure I will study; perhaps you will have no leisure. An empty-headed man cannot be a sin-fearing man, nor can an ignorant person be pious, nor can a shamefaced man learn, nor a passionate man teach, nor anyone who is overmuch engaged in business grow wise." For centuries the Jews transferred these words from prayer-book precepts into daily practice in the synagogue library or at home by a book-laden, candle-lit table.

Besides the community libraries there were naturally certain fortunate individuals possessed of well-stocked book shelves. Lists and catalogues have survived of private medieval collections. Judah ben Saul Ibn Tibbon, a famous 12th century scholar and translator, has left us the injunctions he laid upon his son for the care of his library: keep the books, he enjoins, well covered against dust and damp and protected from mice; write a list of the books placed on each shelf, affix the list to the shelf, and arrange the books in the same order as on the list; check over the Hebrew books once every month, the Arabic books every two months, and the cases of unbound books every three months; restore and have restored all loaned books on Passover and on Succot. It was Ibn Tibbon who wrote some of the most gracious and inviting words ever applied to a library: "Let your cases and shelves be your pleasure-grounds and orchards." I would like to see this motto inscribed in every Jewish community library, which like all libraries should be enjoyed for both its delights and its fruits.

One of the great private collectors was the 17th-century court-Jew of Vienna, Samuel Oppenheimer. Eventually his 7000 printed volumes and 1000 manuscripts became the basis of the Bodleian Library's magnificent collection of Judaica (at Oxford). The earliest modern communal collection of which the precise origin can be dated was that of Mantua in Italy; it was founded in 1767 upon the acquisition of 4500 volumes from the private library of Raphael Emanuel Mendola.

Community Libraries in Far-off Places

I have visited some of these old traditional community libraries while they still flourished in far-off places. I recall being led by a youngster up an obscure back-alley in Tangiers, a town, by the way, far more cosmopolitan, experienced and wordly-wise than most American cities. Removed from this sophisticated bustle I found myself in a small dusty room—the neighborhood's House of Study. It was mid-afternoon. A half-dozen greybeards were squatted around a single large, worn and tattered tome, reading in a sing-song intonation and discussing what they read. They appeared to resent my intrusion, the more so because, despite my assurances, they did not believe I was a Jew. I had a hard time establishing my identity. My young guide could not understand my French and I could not understand the old greybeards' Arabic-sounding Hebrew. At last they thrust the big tome in my hands, its pages still open to where they had been reading in it, and asked me—as a sort of pass-word—if I could tell them what book it was. Luck was with me, for I am no Hebrew scholar; but a few words told me, and I in turn triumphantly told them that the book was the Zohar. I was *in*, and could examine their whole little collection at leisure. In the holy city of Sheshawan, a rocky eaglesnest built on top of a peak in the Riff mountains and long forbidden to foreigners, I found in the synagogue's book-cupboard a 16th century copy of an Aramaic translation

of the Pentateuch, the Onkelos version; but I had long ceased
to wonder that the people of the Book, in this case Arabic-speak-
ing Jews, should have fairly worn out the copy of a translation
in a language neither they nor any other Jews have spoken in
some fifteen hundred years.

I have even had the thrill of ordering a book to be written—
in manuscript, with fancy decorative flourishes—precisely as books
were ordered and written centuries ago. Up in the foothills of
the Atlas Mountains, at a picturesque town called Sefrou, I heard
of its famous native Hebrew poet, Rabbi Raphael Moses Elbaz,
famous at least in Sefrou and as far distant as Fez. Back in Fez,
I asked if a copy of his works could be had at a bookstore. They
had never, I was told, been printed. When I looked as dis-
appointed as I felt I should feel, I was bidden to cheer up; I
could arrange to have a volume of his poetry written out by a
local scribe. The scribe sat cross-legged before a low desk in his
his little shop, a den not much bigger than a dry-goods crate. We
agreed on a price per page, and since Rabbi Raphael Moses
Elbaz, who died toward the end of the 19th century, had been a
prolific genius, I contented myself with ordering two copies of
a hundred-page anthology, leaving it to the *Sopher* to select
characteristic specimens of Elbaz' religious, moral, and erotic
poems. Months later—during which time I could almost hear the
Sopher tell other customers, "Be patient, I'm busy with my Paris
trade"—the books reached me at my home in Paris. Anyone
hungering to read Elbaz will find one of my copies in the Hebrew
Union College library; and I can only warn him, apologetically,
that due to my inexperience in medieval ways, the paper, which I
neglected to discuss with the *Sopher*, is not so good as it could be.
I also warn him that the script is puzzling, suggestive of Arabic.
And the style is mediocre. But the lively flourishes or doodles
of the scribe carry on the Moghrebi pattern employed for generations.

In the communal libraries, the study halls, of old Jewish centers, whether in North Africa or in Poland, the very appearance
of the books piled on the shelves or scattered on the tables told a
story. For the most part they looked woe-begone, draggled, and
worm-eaten—not, however, because of neglect but because they
were used until they were virtually used up. The best books are
the worst preserved, because they are the best treated, for what
better treatment of a book can there be than to read it so often
that its pages fall apart? Speaking of some of these veteran
volumes, now retired among the treasures of Harvard's Widener
Library, Prof. Harry Wolfson has eloquently observed: "They
have broken their backs and worn out their covers in their noble
calling." While I am a lover of beautiful bindings and handsome pages, I could wish no better fate for the spick-and-span
volumes I see in so many of our present-day communal libraries
than distintegration through a passionate overuse.

I note that the Jewish Book Council of America has set forth eight minimum requirements which must be met by any communal library if it wishes to be accorded a "Citation of Merit" from the Council. I would urge and underline a ninth requirement: that a fair proportion of its books be read to shreds.

The Purpose of a Library

The purpose of a library is to be used; a library without readers, especially zealous readers, is just a cut above a library that doesn't exist. Regretfully, the analogous stricture need not be true of a modern synagogue. A new and luxurious structure fitted out in the latest style, with sliding partitions, a bizarre self-opening ark, a *Ner Tamid* hard to tell from a futuristic "mobile," and slit-panel windows draped like the show room of a *grand couturier,* will be an eye-catching advertisement for Judaism, a credit to the town, and will set up the morale of the Jewish community, even if it remains practically empty save for the high holidays and the annual UJA dinner.

A handsome, well-appointed, well-stocked library will not do the same trick. There is no public prestige or morale-boosting to be gained from the mere presence of a collection of books. A Jewish communal library has, we must keep in mind, a unique function of its own in relation to the community it serves. As things stand today, every Jewish community must look upon itself as a reservoir of forces devoted to the cultivation, enrichment and survival of Jewish life. Conceivably, it may not be a large reservoir, but it will be deep, and it will be fed by unfailing springs. These springs, I need hardly say, well up from within the books which contain the ever-living waters, the *Mayim Hayim,* of the Jewish tradition. Only to the degree that these waters are regularly imbibed by the individual members of our local communities will Jewish life thrive in America.

Some of us may feel too preoccupied, too old, intellectually too lazy or flabby, to resort in a serious way to Jewish learning. But fortunately, what we cannot always do ourselves we may induce our children to do—or else mankind would still be living in caves. Our children at least must be given, through the instrument of communal libraries and kindred institutions, a thorough, intensive Jewish education. By this I do not mean that we should fob off on our youngsters the obligations we shrink from taking upon ourselves. If the parents do not participate in acquiring or deepening their own Jewish education, the children, we may be almost sure, will have none of it, or will quickly discard what smattering they may have been led or compelled to learn. I would say to all Jewish parents: "Sit down and, if you do not know it, learn Hebrew with your children, and Jewish history and literature; and if they outstrip you, nobody loses and the future of the Jewish people stands everything to gain." Jewish libraries or Jewish schools without Jewish homes are not altogether wasted, but the cards are stacked against the permanence or value of an education that is confined to a school-house or a library reading-room.

As we know only too well, life in any Diaspora land sets up powerful currents and counter-attractions against the maintenance of an informed, vigorous Jewish culture. The Jewish library, the Jewish school, and the Jewish home, even when working together, will have a hard enough struggle to prevent the gradually complete evaporation of Jewish knowledge and values. Neither library, school nor home can afford to go it alone, and victory can be had only at the price of constant cooperation and effort. We can hope that some day this victory will be seen in the shabby, dog-eared, dilapidated condition of the books stacked in every communal library; these veterans will bear, like trophies, the scars of a triumphant campaign.

A book, after all, is chiefly an instrument for enabling us to master the art of living. David ben Gurion, the valiant prime minister of Israel, summed up three thousand years of history when he said, "We have preserved the Book and the Book has preserved us." He was referring to the Jewish people, but the thought and experience behind his words apply to all peoples— and indeed, in a profoundly intimate sense, to each and all of us individually. In books, as in all learning, we must constantly ask ourselves, not who knows the most things but who knows the best things. For only through assimilating the best things can we learn how to live; and, alas, as Montaigne reminds us, we usually learn how to live when life is fairly over. Still, it is never too late to advance one more step.

Remarks on libraries and books cannot be more aptly concluded than by another observation of Montaigne, who was in my judgment the wisest man in modern times. "If," said Montaigne, "you have known how to compose your life, you have accomplished a good deal more than the man who knows how to compose a book. Have you been able to take life at its stride? You have done more than the man who has taken cities and empires. The great and glorious masterpiece of man is to live to the point.

"It is," as he said in the final pages of his *Essays*, "an absolute and, as it were, divine perfection for a man to know how to enjoy loyally his own existence."

Whether we acquire it in a library or a class-room, education in the real sense seeks to impart, not so much by instruction as by infection, the means of enriching our existence and increasing our loyal enjoyment of it. If we can learn to do this we have become not merely educated men, but we have truly succeeded in life.

FAMOUS JEWISH BOOK COLLECTIONS AND COLLECTORS

By Cecil Roth

I AM NOT QUITE SURE who was the earliest known Jewish book-collector. King Solomon, I am inclined to think: for his aphorism in the Book of Ecclesiastes, "there is no end to collecting books," appears to me like the frank admission of the blasé collector rather than the sarcastic observation of the Philistine. Nor can I imagine that the remark of Hai Gaon in the eleventh century ("To three possessions that shalt look, Acquire a field, a friend, a book") could have been made by a person who thought in terms of a single bookshelf. Samuel haNagid, the Vizier to the King of Granada, Hai's great admirer, is known to have given books away lavishly to students, and it cannot be imagined that this eminent scholar-statesman did not have a choice library himself. But the recorded history of Jewish bibliophiles begins a trifle later than this. In the Cairo Genizah, there have been discovered several library catalogues, some of them made for the purpose of auction sales after the owner's death: the best known is that of R. Abraham the Pious, who probably had been an associate of Moses Maimonides. Of how books were kept and how they were regarded at this time, we know from the ethical will of Judah ibn Tibbon, in the most graphic detail. But somehow, I find it difficult to believe that a man who advised his son to go through his books every month or so could have had a really great library. In the Middle Ages the most remarkable Jewish book-collector of whom we know was the globe-trotting physician, Judah (Leon) Mosconi of Majorca, two inventories of whose library have been preserved: one of them for the auction sale after his death in 1377. It is not generally known that the King of Aragon ultimately cancelled the sale and seized the library for himself. In very many wills of Spanish Jews at this time we find records of the books they owned; and one is extant from Genoa in Italy in 1231—which is all the more remarkable because no Jews were supposed to live in that city at the time.

When we come to Italy, of course, we are in the land of bibliophiles, and the Jews, who managed to absorb so many of the characteristics of the Italians in the Renaissance period, fol-

330

lowed or preceded their neighbours in this. Everywhere in the
country there were enthusiastic book-collectors—not necessarily
scholars but also laymen, of whom we would know little or
nothing except their evident love of books: men like Menahem of Volterra in the 15th century, whose library is now
in the Vatican, or Baruch da Peschiera in the 16th, whose books
found their way to Turin and Parma. Solomon Finzi, son of the
Mantuan scientist Mordecai (Angelo) Finzi, had in his library
in the little township of Viadana, where he exercised the profession of loan-banker, a collection of 200 volumes, at that time
considered a number worthy of a great humanist. Another branch
of the Finzi family living in Bologna, however, were reputed to
own a couple of hundred manuscripts, besides a rich collection
of printed books.

The largest Jewish library in the Renaissance period was that
built up in successive generations by the family of Da Pisa,
friends of Don Isaac Abrabanel and patrons of David Reubeni.
They were, however, far outdone in the 17th century by Abraham Joseph Solomon Graziano (died in 1685), rabbi of Modena,
who wrote the initials of his name *ish ger* in vast numbers of
books now scattered in Jewish libraries throughout the world—
including the so-called "Golden Haggadah" in the British Museum, one of the most glorious Hebrew illuminated manuscripts
in existence. His contemporary, the physician Joseph Solomon
del Medigo (1591-1655), boasted that he owned no fewer than
4,000 volumes, on which he had expended the vast sum of 10,000
(florins?). Doubtless, in view of his wide intellectual interests,
many of these were in languages other than Hebrew. But the
same was true of many of his contemporaries in enlightened
communities, such as those of Italy or Holland. It is from this
last-named country, in the circle of the cultured ex-Marrano
communities, that the first printed sale catalogues of private
Hebrew libraries emerged—for example, those printed at the
time of the dispersal of the collections of Haham Moses Raphael
de Aguilar (1680), the earliest such publication known to Jewish booklore, and of Isaac Aboab da Fonseca, "the first American
rabbi" (1690), comprising about 500 volumes, many in Spanish,
French, even Greek and Latin.

The Great Library of David Oppenheim

By the time of Aboab's death, one of the greatest of all Jewish
book-collectors of all time had begun his activities. This was
David Oppenheim, Chief Rabbi of Prague and a close kinsman
of the notorious "Jew Suss," who compiled in 1688 the first
catalogue of his collection comprising at the time some 500 books.

Ultimately, he owned 5,000 works, apart from nearly 1,000 manuscripts, possibly the most important Jewish library that has ever been brought together in private hands. Others have exceeded it in bulk, but never in quality. But the tragic aspect of his collecting was that, owing to the ecclesiastical censorship prevalent at the time in Catholic countries, which imperilled the entire collection, he housed it not in Prague where he lived, but in the care of relatives in Hanover. After his death in 1736 the collection underwent all manner of vicissitudes. It was peddled from place to place without success (nothwithstanding the enthusiastic appraisal of Moses Mendelssohn), and was vainly offered to the Napoleonic Sanhedrin in Paris in 1806. It was finally purchased in 1829 by the Bodleian Library in Oxford at a price which would today be considered insignificant, thus elevating that great institution to a position of near primacy in the world of Jewish books and making the ancient university city a mecca of pilgrimage for Jewish scholars and students from all the world over. This it still is, thanks in part to further important additions to the collection in subsequent years and in part to the magnificent series of catalogues of its treasures that have been published. Hebrew bibliography, as an exact science, is to this day founded on the *Catalogue of Hebrew Books in the Bodleian Library*—mainly from the Oppenheim Collection—compiled over a century ago by the great Moritz Steinschneider.

Shortly after Chief Rabbi David Oppenheim built up his collection, an Italian Catholic Abbé Giovanni Bernardo de Rossi (1742-1831) followed on his path, with success almost equally striking. He was a Hebrew scholar of repute and a book-collector of genius; and in Italy, the land of Hebrew bibliophilism, he had opportunities which were equalled nowhere else. His great collection of Hebrew manuscripts, lovingly catalogued by him and comprising several superb illuminated codices, is now housed at the Palatine Library in Parma, having been acquired after his death by the Duke of that petty principality. What treasures are comprised among the printed book collection is still barely known, but they include, for example, the only known copy of the earliest Hebrew printed book, the Rashi, produced in Reggio di Calabria in 1475. Once De Rossi owned two copies of this book; one, however, was lost with other literary treasures when the barge conveying them was sunk en route in the River Po.

The next century produced a large number of more self-conscious collectors whose names are still remembered with reverence by Hebrew bibliophiles: men like Heimann Joseph Michael (1792-1846), a not very affluent Hamburg business man, but at the same time a considerable scholar. The learned catalogue composed by him and still a standard work of reference, lovingly describes no fewer than 860 MSS. and over 5,000 printed books, which in due course joined the Oppenheim Collection in Oxford. There were also Solomon Joachim Halberstamm (1832-1900), whose collection of MSS. (which he was compelled to dispose of owing to business vicissitudes) was purchased for the Montefiore Library and is now in Jews' College Library, London, and Eliakim Carmoly (1802-1875), rabbi of Brussels, who had the weakness of destroying the credit of anything he owned by embellishing it with ingenious, but sometimes transparent, forgeries. Italy still remained the mecca for Jewish collectors, as witness the great Almanzi collection which ultimately went partly to the British Museum and partly to New York.

In Russia, Baron David Gunzburg (1857-1910), in what was then called St. Petersburg, built up a magnificent MSS. collection which was to have been transferred to Jerusalem but was intercepted en route. It is now still in Russia, where it has been investigated by Professor Abraham I. Katsh of New York University, who has brought its treasures within reach of the scholarly world by means of microfilms. Meanwhile, in the United States the scholarly Judge Mayer Sulzberger (1843-1923), first president of the American Jewish Committee, built up a very considerable and important collection with the assistance of that remarkable globe-trotting dealer, Ephraim Deinard (1846-1930). He subsequently made it over to the library of the Jewish Theological Seminary of America—then beginning the dazzling period of progress it owed to the scholarship and enthusiasm of that great but somewhat unsystematic librarian Alexander Marx, whom so many of us remember still with affection and veneration. It is only proper to mention by his side Adolph S. Oko who, without the same background of profound Jewish scholarship but with an uncanny book-sense, made the library of the Hebrew Union College in Cincinnati into one of the great Jewish libraries of the world.

The Schocken Library in Jerusalem

Meanwhile, in Germany Salman Schocken was unobtrusively building up his great library, of which Judaica was only a part, but in which he concentrated on Hebrew poetry and rare printed books. This is now housed in a remarkably designed building in Jerusalem, the Schocken Library, under the aegis of the Jewish Theological Seminary of America: still a centre of research on Hebrew poetry in particular, and in recent years enriched by some remarkable illuminated manuscripts. A specialized library of another sort was that of David Montesinos of Amsterdam, who created a unique collection of works, largely in Spanish and Portuguese, illustrating the history of that community. He presented it to the Sephardi synagogue, and transferred himself thither to act as librarian until his death in 1916, in his eighty-eighth year. For a long while this has acted in friendly competition to the Bibliotheca Rosenthaliana in that city, consisting of the library of Rabbi Leser Rosenthal (1794-1868) which his son, Baron George Rosenthal, presented to the city of Amsterdam and is now a constituent of the University Library. Another outstanding rabbinical bibliophile who can hardly escape mention in this connection is the Hungarian David Kaufmann, eminent as a historian no less than as a philosopher, whose remarkable collection largely of Italian provenance, and including some splendid illuminated manuscripts on which he wrote with no less learning than charm, was also presented by his widow after his death to the Hungarian Academy of Sciences.

Outstanding Book-Collectors of England

In recent generations three of the greatest Hebrew book-collectors, with all of whom I was on familiar terms, resided in England. One was Elkan Adler, son and brother of English Chief Rabbis and a lawyer by profession, who travelled around the world in the course of his business affairs, with ideal presentations and recommendations. He visited most out-of-the-way spots and built up a library which for bulk if not for quality was perhaps the greatest assembled in private possession. No place, time or situation was in his eyes unsuitable for the acquisition of books. He purchased a copy of the *Mashal ha-Kadmoni* of 1491—the earliest Hebrew illustrated book—from a road mender in Morocco, and from a hill-monastery in Peru a copy of Columbus' famous letter announcing his discovery to the Marrano Luis de Santangel (it turned out to be a fabrication). I myself once saw him "swopping" books with another collector at a funeral. In order to make good the defalcations of a business associate, he was compelled to sell his library just after World War I to the Jewish Theological Seminary, thus elevating it to a foremost place among the Jewish libraries of the world. Another section of it went, however, to the Hebrew Union College. But he immediately set about collecting again, and the library which he left behind on his death in 1946 was of formidable proportions.

Adler's collection was the envy in particular of Rabbi Moses Gaster, the Roumanian born Haham of the Spanish and Portuguese community in London—an incredibly versatile scholar whose position, contacts and enthusiasm gave him unusual opportunities. Many stories were told of how he built up his collection by judicious "borrowing," apart from earnest soliciting, of which I have particular reason to be aware, since he thus acquired the only real bibliographical treasure owned by my father. That with his relatively limited means he amassed a truly great library is a tribute to his enthusiasm, as well as perhaps to the forbearance of his wife. Towards the end of his days he sold the manuscript collection to the British Museum, which has thus far not done all that is possible to make it properly accessible to students. Some works which he had held back and placed in a safe deposit at the time of the German air-raids on London, were ruined by water from a water-main in the immediate neighbourhood that had been damaged. What remained, however, including many important Samaritan MSS., were acquired by the famous John Rylands Library in Manchester—one of the greatest libraries in the British Isles, which contains much Hebraica, including also some truly magnificent illuminated MSS.

The third of the great Anglo-Jewish trio, David Solomon Sassoon, had advantages neither of the other two possessed. He belonged to a famous Anglo-Iraqi-Indian family, with international connections in the Far East which gave him unique opportunities; and he also enjoyed great affluence which enabled him to acquire any work he found desirable. And he did, lavishly, learnedly, and discriminatingly. On one occasion, while on a boat which put in at Port Said on its way to or from India, he learned that a Jewish peddler who came aboard had a rare book at home. David Sassoon looked after his stock and, to the great amusement of the fellow-passengers, did a thriving business, while the peddler went ashore to fetch his treasure. Moreover, Sassoon was a very considerable scholar; and his catalogue of his manuscripts, in two splendid volumes, is perhaps the most satisfactory description of any Hebrew collection that has ever been published. There is another feature about his collection which is almost unique. His son, Rabbi Solomon Sassoon, who inherited it, devotes to it the same loving care as did his father; and this is perhaps the only truly great library of Hebrew printed books and manuscripts which remains in the world still in private hands.

SELECTED PRIVATE
JEWISH LIBRARY COLLECTIONS

By Salamon Faber

Book collecting reflects man's desire to acquire and preserve knowledge. Numerous factors in mankind's socio-cultural development provided many motivations for the various forms of organization and specialization of this activity. In ancient times, when private collectors were altogether unknown, it was an important means of the realm to maintain its cultural resources. In the Middle Ages only monks were interested in preserving books. Revival of interest in the classics during the Renaissance period inspired many among the wealthy to collect books, some for personal enjoyment, while others performed a valuable social service in organizing or enriching existing libraries. The invention of printing provided incentives to more private collectors. By and large, the activity was a hobby of the wealthy, subject to fluctuations of the economic patterns of supply and demand.

At present, collecting ancient manuscripts, incunabula, early prints, special subject matter—theology, history, linguistics, literature of certain periods—is indicative of tendencies to specialize, especially when these materials are sought by university libraries or research institutes in order to develop those respective departments. Private collectors also concentrate on specific subjects, but often they look for certain forms or external features of the collected materials, such as sizes, bindings, illustrations, typographic variations, and the like. Hobby patterns may vary as whimsically as do fashions.[1]

Book collecting among Jews has been traditionally more than a hobby. The process of learning, requiring book materials as helpful tools, is one of the basic sancta of Judaism. A knowledgeable Jew would take seriously the injunction in Deuteronomy 31,19, "Therefore, write down this poem and teach it to the people of Israel," together with the interpretation by later authorities that one is bound by a religious command to acquire copies of the Pentateuch and rabbinic works.[2] What thoughtful student of Jew-

---

[1] Comp. *Introduction to Book Collecting*, by Colton Storm and Howard Peckham, New York, Bowker, 1947, pp. 35-36.

[2] *Tur Yoreh Deah*, no. 270 and references in the commentaries.

ish lore would disregard Rav Hai Gaon's advice: "Look to three possessions—a field, a friend, a book."[3] Israel M. Goldman points out in his *The Life and Times of Rabbi David Ibn Abi Zimra* (New York, Jewish Theological Seminary, 1970), that large libraries were assembled especially by rabbis who received requests from afar to settle legal disputes, or to interpret difficult statements in the Talmud. The combination of these two factors, the need of materials for study and instruction, and the desire to practice the *mitzvah* to acquire sacred texts, created a reverential aura for the Jewish book, aptly described by Cecil Roth in his essay "The Jewish Love of Books."[4]

The Renaissance, as in Christian circles, brought with it a new form of interest in Jewish literary materials—collecting as a hobby. It began naturally in Italy and spread to other communities.[5]

While contemporary attitudes to Jewish learning are not what they were in past ages, interest in book collecting by individuals, both for pragmatic purposes and as a hobby, is vigorously pursued here and abroad, particularly in Israel. Even in Soviet Russia, according to personal accounts by the well-known book dealer and bibliographer Jacob Twersky of Tel Aviv,[6] collectors of Jewish books are still active. For obvious reasons none could be identified in this essay.

Described below are a number of private Jewish library collections in America, selected from a study of a large number of such libraries possessing unique materials generally classed as collectors' items by bibliographers and commercial dealers. These collections may be divided into four major groupings: Rabbinic and scholarly; Manuscripts, incunabula and early prints; American Jewish history; Art.

All information in this essay is based upon personal communication with the owners of the collections, as well as visits to their libraries in most cases. Whenever statements are quoted verbatim from correspondence between the owners and the writer, they are indicated by quotation marks.

Rabbinic and Scholarly Collections

The collection of the late Rabbi Moses Rokach of Brooklyn, consisting of well over 7,000 volumes in Hebrew, represents a

---

[3] Quoted by Cecil Roth in "Famous Jewish Book Collections and Collectors," *Jewish Book Annual*, vol. 25, 1967, p. 75.
[4] *Jewish Book Annual*, vol. 3, 1944, pp. 1-7.
[5] See essay quoted in note 3.
[6] *Maariv*, Feb. 19th, 1971, pp. 2, 47.

typical library of a rav in an East European community. It includes many editions of the Talmud, midrash, codes, responsa, commentaries on *Tenakh,* liturgy, mysticism and related materials, some of which are highly priced 16th and 17th century prints the owner would use in his regular daily tasks as rabbinic judge, teacher, guide, and arbiter in matters of ritual. Of special interest are many titles, rare collectors' items, because of their associative value —autographs and annotations by famous scholars. Some 300 Pesah Haggadot, many of which are rare editions not found even in special libraries, as well as a number of Cabalah manuscripts from the school of Rabbi Yitzhak Luria, enhance the collection's value. Of considerable interest are also several smaller groups of materials relating to controversies among hasidic sects.

The library of Dr. Arthur Hyman of New York City is similar in scope and variety of materials. Its value gains considerably in that it includes all the publications of *Mekitze Nirdamim,* scores of complete sets of bibliographically important Hebrew periodicals, valuable festschriften, and rare titles in the history and geography of Eretz Yisrael.

The collection of Dr. Solomon B. Freehof in Pittsburgh is famous throughout the world of Jewish scholarship for its comprehensive responsa materials, probably the largest collection of its kind. It includes many hundreds of titles not listed even in the most detailed bibliography on the subject, the well-known *Kuntras ha-Teshuvot* by Boaz Cohen (Budapest, 1930). As an indication of its size and qualitative value, Dr. Freehof stated in a personal note that "he would have to devote months of study to describe the collection." He willed it to the library of the Hebrew Union College.

Based upon research for this essay, it appears that the collection of Rabbi Leonard C. Mishkin in Chicago represents the largest privately owned Jewish library in America. It consists of over 54,500 volumes in a dozen languages covering all fields of Jewish scholarship. Its major strengths are in rabbinics, periodica, jahresberichten, festschriften, Jewish history, Jewish education, and bibliographic materials of all types. It is perhaps the only private library this side of the Iron Curtain with hundreds of Yiddish titles published in the U.S.S.R.

Dr. Walter J. Fischel of Berkeley has a collection which typifies an academician's working library, consisting of approximately 8,000 titles in the areas of Jewish history and literature, in Hebrew, English, Arabic, Persian, and various Asian languages and dialects. Of special interest are many manuscripts and fragmentary documents relating to Jewish diasporas in India, Persia, and communities in the Far East. Foremost in the latter group are the manuscripts in Judeo-Persian.

The collection of the late Dr. Mordekhai M. Kosover of Elmhurst, N.Y. represents another illustration of a professional scholar's wide ranging interests in materials relating to his research. Beyond his direct concerns with Jewish history, folklore, and social studies, Dr. Kosover assembled a sizeable collection of unique items, including hundreds of volumes of pre-modern Yiddish literature, books of unusual appearance in format and size, and many rare prints. This collection also includes an index of about 100,000 cards to the fields of Jewish folklore and philology.

The library of Dr. Fritz Bamberger of New York City specializes in first and early editions in major disciplines of philosophy published before 1850. Of unique interest are some 1,500 titles, either by or about Barukh Spinoza published before 1820, as well as many hundreds of works by and about Moses Mendelssohn published before 1840. Of further special interest are all the writings by Solomon Maimon in their first editions. Other philosophers of Jewish origin are represented in this collection although their respective works are not all related specifically to Judaism and Jewish thought.

Manuscripts, Incunabula and Early Prints

Two outstanding, widely renowned collections belong to this category. Rabbi Manfred Lehrman of Cedarhurst, N.Y., possesses some 400 complete manuscripts in the fields of rabbinics, mysticism, Bible commentaaries, and responsa, approximately dating from the 13th century until the middle of the nineteenth. A number of additional fragmentary manuscripts date back as early as the 10th century. These materials hail from Italy, North Africa, Poland, Russia, Persia, Palestine and Yemen. Of very special significance to the historian are manuscripts of *pinkasim* from the Jewish communities of Hagenau, Hamburg, Halberstadt, and Venice. Rabbi Lehrman has also assembled ten of the rarest Hebrew incunabula, and over fifty titles in rabbinics printed in the first half of the 16th century in Bologna, Fano, Ferrari, Pizzaro, Riva, Venice, Salonica, and Istanbul. All these materials are generally sought as precious collectors' items. Another section of the Lehrman collection includes some 10,000 titles, books and scholarly journals, in many languages, specializing in rabbinics, Jewish history and archeology.

The incunabula collection of Jacob M. Lowy in Montreal, Canada, is perhaps the most significant library of this type in America. It includes thirty-five titles in Hebrew and nine in Latin, covering the fields of Bible, Talmud, Hebrew grammar, Jewish philosophy, Josephus, and Thomas Aquinas. In addition, the Lowy library has some 250 titles which are of extraordinary interest to the private collector, such as early Bible prints in many languages, including Polyglot, unusual Hebrew liturgical materials, entire sets and single copies of the Babylonian and Palestinian Talmuds, various editions of the Zohar, Josephus in all European languages, including Czech. All the materials in this last group are rare prints from the 16th and 17th centuries.

American Jewish History

All types of materials dealing with American Jewish history—manuscripts, books, memoirs, newspapers, magazines, even incidental pages with commercial advertisements—are of interest to private collectors, both scholars and laymen. Typical in this category is Rabbi Abraham J. Karp in Rochester, N.Y. His field of specialization is limited to Jews and Judaism in the United States in the 19th century. Included in this collection are such rare items as Emma Lazarus' *Poems and Translations* (printed for private circulation in New York, 1866), sixteen of the original issues of *The Occident* (Philadelphia, 1843-1868), as well as many "firsts in Hebrew printed in America."

The collection of Irving I. Katz in Detroit, Michigan, contains over 10,000 books and manuscripts relating to American Jewish history, especially Jewish history in Michigan, and other Hebraica. Orginally this collection was much larger, but Mr. Katz has been donating materials in the past ten years to various universities and institutions. Similarly the library of Edwin Wolf 2nd, of Wyncote, Pennsylvania, specializes in American Judaica—books written by and about Jews in the United States—from 1718 to 1875. It consists of some 400 selected volumes and 200 manuscripts.

Art

Various items of Jewish art—paintings, sculptures, illustrated books, especially Pesah Haggadot and Megillot, decorative items for Torahs, ketubot—are among the most eagerly sought collectors' treasures. Since this essay is limited to library collections, the following descriptions may serve as typical examples in that genre.

The collection of Leon L. Gildesgame of Mt. Kisco, N.Y., includes many richly illustrated Arabic and Persian manuscripts from the 15th and 16th centuries, well preserved in their original beautiful bindings. These are appraised by connoisseurs for their artistic value as much as for their literary merits. In addition, this collection has many artistically decorated Bibles from early periods and in several languages. Of equal interest are the many titles representative of contemporary Jewish art. Foremost in this group are Chagall's major masterworks on Biblical themes reproduced in print in limited editions, each copy autographed by the artist with a laudatory note. Works by other famous Jewish artists in Israel, America and France, appropriately decorated to reflect the author's style or school, complete this unusual collection.

Ludwig Jesselson in Riversdale, N.Y., includes in his private library over 400 titles selected with discriminating care for their artistic forms. In addition to twenty-five rare, beautifully decorated manuscripts, this collection has a number of Megillot, Haggadot, *sidurim,* and *mahzorim* which are known for their artistic illustrations. A complete set of the first Venice edition of the Babylonian Talmud, in special binding, lends the Jesselson library an unusual beauty. It is further heightened by the presence of ten incunabula and many first editions of outstanding rabbinic titles from Istanbul, Livorno, and Venice, all in excellent condition and of fine artistic appearance.

The collection of Jakob Michael of New York City—the largest private library of Jewish music assembled in the United States—consisting of approximately 25,000 pieces of notes, manuscripts, records and tapes, was donated several years ago to the National Library of the Hebrew University. It is currently used by scholars, cantors, students of Jewish music, and Kol Israel, for broadcasts of Jewish music.

Rabbi William A. Rosenthal of New York City specializes in Jewish graphic arts. His collection is made up of the following parts: prints, engravings, etchings, woodcuts, lithographs of the last five centuries; books pictorially portraying various areas of Jewish life in the last three centuries; newspaper and magazine illustrations from the 19th century; commemorative medallions and medals from the 19th and early 20th centuries; paintings and postcards from the first two decades of the 20th century. "The collection is extremely large. Many thousands of items . . . Aside from the principal body of the collection are such areas as photographs, contemporary clippings, and commercial reproductions of all subjects, not to mention a creditable specialized collection of philatelic Judaica. . . . The particular value of the collection is that it brings together a largely unknown and unstudied area of Jewish history, religion and culture. The majority of the graphic items have never been reproduced in secondary works."

The Badonna Spertus Art Library of Judaica, sponsored by Maurice Spertus of Highland Park, Ill., contains about a thousand titles in English, Hebrew, Yiddish, German, French, Italian, Russian and Polish, covering all aspects of Jewish art—archeology, ceremonial arts, Bible themes, materials about Jewish artists. Mr.

Spertus' library also harbors some 100 Yemeni manuscripts in Hebrew and Arabic. The University of Chicago Press will soon publish a complete catalog of these manuscripts, edited and annotated by Professor Norman Golb. This material is of much interest on the history of the Jewish community in Yemen and its relations to the Moslems.

This last item suggests that there are no definitive criteria for specializations within library collections. At best, we can indicate collectors' tendencies and general interests in certain categories of materials, whether it be the four alluded to above, or others. In reality, there is overlapping to some degree, even in those cases where a certain group predominates. At times a private collector develops an interest in some unusual subject. For example, the collection of Justin G. Turner of Los Angeles specializes in materials on Jewish cartographers. Another of its distinctive features is a collection of taped statements by all the signers of the Declaration of Independence of the State of Israel.

An example of unusual curiosa is offered by the collection of Dr. S. Z. Yovely of New York City who specializes in Judaica in the Italian language, especially anti-semitic materials of the fascist period. It even includes a complete set of Der Stürmer, called La Difesa della Razza in the Italian language. Another of its unusual features are books and manuscripts on amulets and incantations, know in Jewish folklore as segulot u-refuot.

Some tentative conclusions may be drawn from these descriptions of private Jewish library collections. To begin with, collectors of Judaica seem to be interested in materials with an intrinsic literary value. This explains the demand for incunabula, rare rabbinic materials, Bible commentaries, and the like. The external features of these materials—that is their bindings, sizes, or typographical peculiarities—seem to be of secondary significance to most collectors, while in the general field of book collection such matters assume considerable importance.[7] The only exception in this respect might be an interest frequently noted by collectors in books with an associative value deriving from the fact that they bear annotations or autographs by famous men.

It is noteworthy that materials which might be described as "secular Judaica" have a limited appeal to private collectors, due perhaps to the fact that secularism in Jewish life is a recent phenomenon. Whatever literary products secular Judaism may have inspired, not enough time has elapsed for them to become popular

---

[7] See New Paths in Book Collecting, ed. by John Carter, Freeport, N.Y., Books for Libraries, 1934.

collectors' items. Whatever the reason, few collectors specialize in that genre. Nor are materials pertaining to sects in Jewish history excessively sought by private collectors.

One final observation. Book collecting, unless engaged in exclusively for profit, can become a source of spiritual delight to all involved: the collector who buys the books, the bibliographer who offers guidance, and even the dealer interested solely in a business transaction. However, the most meaningful satisfaction is achieved when a collection is ultimately bequeathed to a library. Through such gifts, Jewish book collectors enrich and add luster to great depositories of Jewish scholarship. If this essay will inspire one more such gift, the writer's humble effort will have served a worthwhile purpose.

THE ISRAEL PL-480 PROGRAM, 1964-1969: A REVIEW

By CHARLES BERLIN

FOR THE PAST FIVE YEARS the United States government has been conducting a program unique in the annals of Judaic librarianship. Within the framework of what is commonly referred to as the Public Law-480 Program, the United States government has been supplying some twenty-five American research libraries with a copy of virtually every book and periodical published currently in the State of Israel.

The government's entry into the world of Hebrew books is the by-product of an earlier humanitarian gesture. In 1954 the Food for Peace Program (Public Law-480) was established, enabling certain needy countries to purchase surplus American agricultural products in their own currency instead of in dollars. Since the local currency was to be spent only in that country, large amounts accumulated to the credit of the United States in these countries. Some of this money was made available as grants and loans to promote economic development; other funds were used for various cultural projects. One such project was to assist American libraries to develop their resources in various areas.

Since the end of the Second World War, American research libraries have been faced with the enormous task of developing collections of materials on new areas of the world now beginning to receive attention from scholars and students. This is especially true of the new nations of Asia and Africa as well as of the countries of Eastern Europe. The task was complicated by the absence in many of these places of a well-organized book trade to fill the needs of these libraries. In an attempt to alleviate this difficulty, the American Library Association, the Asssociation of Research Libraries, the Social Science Research Council and the American Council of Learned Societies recommended—and Congress passed in 1958—an amendment to Public Law-480 authorizing the Library of Congress to use part of the blocked local currency for the purchase of materials published in these countries. The amendment was implemented in 1961 when such acquisition programs were established in India, Pakistan and the United Arab Republic. Since then the program has been extended to other areas including Ceylon, Nepal, Indonesia and Yugoslavia.

25 American Library Participants

The availability of Public Law-480 funds in Israel, the great interest of many American libraries in developing or strengthening collections of Hebraica and Judaica, and the success of the book procurement programs in other areas resulted in the establishment in 1964 of the American Libraries Book Procurement Center of the Library of Congress in the American Embassy in Tel-Aviv. The number of American libraries invited to participate in the Israel program now totals twenty-five. In addition to the accepted criterion governing a library's resources in the field of Jewish studies, invitations were also issued on the basis of interest in developing a collection, especially where wider geographic distribution of this material would be assured. The list of participants reflects these considerations; it includes libraries of Jewish institutions with a strong interest in Judaica: Hebrew Union College, Jewish Theological Seminary of America, Yeshiva University, College of Jewish Studies. Included also are university and public research libraries with distinguished collections in the field of Jewish studies: e.g., Harvard, Yale, Columbia, Library of Congress and New York Public Library. Libraries developing collections in this field and assuring wide geographic distribution include: Brandeis, University of California-Berkeley, University of California-Los Angeles, Cornell, Indiana, Joint University Libraries in Nashville, University of Michigan, Portland (Oregon) State College, Princeton, University of Southern California, Syracuse, Texas, Utah, Virginia, Wayne State (Detroit) and Boston Public Library.

The purpose of the PL-480 Program is to supply each participating library with a copy of every monograph and periodical currently published in Israel that is or may eventually be of research value. The great majority of Israeli publications are, of course, in Hebrew. There is, however, a great deal of publication in other languages, especially in Yiddish, English, German, French and Arabic and to a lesser extent in Rumanian, Russian, Polish, Bulgarian and Spanish—in virtually all the languages used by Jews in their former Diaspora locales. The PL-480 Program acquires materials in these languages as well. A very high percentage of all the material acquired is, understandably, in the field of Jewish studies. Hebrew literature is well represented, from the deluxe editions of collected works of the giants to the pamphlet editions of the budding kibbutz poets. Much of it deals with Jewish history of all periods and places, and especially noteworthy are the many volumes in memory of the European Jewish communities destroyed during the Second World War.

A large proportion consists of rabbinic literature—Biblical and Talmudic commentaries, liturgical texts, responsa, codes, ethical works, homiletics and philosophical, theological and mystical writings. As would be expected, much material is acquired dealing with the State of Israel—its history, politics, economics, geography, sociology, etc. Format ranges from substantial tomes to ephemeral pamphlets, from scholarly volumes to propaganda pamphlets which may some day be the raw material for a scholarly work. Although normally beyond the scope of the Program, reprint editions of various rabbinic works have, at the suggestion of participating libraries, been acquired. These are of special importance since libraries new to the field do not have the original editions (which are, in most cases, impossible to obtain) while established collections which may have the original welcome a chance to acquire a copy usually in much better condition.

Many books dealing with non-Jewish topics are also published in Israel and a selection of the more significant titles is acquired. In the sciences it includes works in the fields of medicine, engineering, agriculture, meteorology, to name a few. The humanities are represented by works in philosophy, the fine arts and literature. The latter range from scholarly Hebrew translations of classical Greek and Latin authors to bilingual editions of the works of modern African poets, often in impressive bibliophilic editions. Works in the social sciences include history, economics, political science and, especially, Middle Eastern studies.

A brief glance through an issue of the monthly accessions list selected at random, February 1967, will serve to illustrate the variety of the material supplied.* Medieval Hebrew poetry is represented by the Jarden edition of the Divan (Ben-Tehilim) of Samuel ha-Nagid; modern Hebrew literature by the works of older writers like Moshe Altman (collected stories) and Joshua Heschel Yeivin (historical fiction), as well as by the works of more recent figures like Itamar Ya'oz-Kest (poetry), Itamar Ben-Hur (fiction), Yitzhak Orpaz (short stories), and Yosi Gamzu (satire). The month's accessions included several juvenile works by established writers, Yehoash Biber and Yitzhak-Yitzhak (Yitzhak Ben-Israel), and a volume of Yiddish poetry by Moshe Gurin. In the area of Jewish history is a collection of source materials dealing with the Jews in Spain from 1391 to 1492, edited by Haim Beinart and published by the Hebrew University; memoirs of a Jewish soldier in World War Two by Tzevi Svet; a Yiddish translation of collected biographies by Nahum Sokolov with an introduction by G. Kressel, and an index in English to the minutes of the first Zionist Congress published by the Institute for Zionist Research of Tel-Aviv University.

---

* Works are in Hebrew unless otherwise noted.

Variety of Rabbinic Literature Available

The various types of rabbinic literature are well represented. Among works dealing with the Bible were *Ktav Sofer* (Abraham Samuel Benjamin Schreiber-Sofer) commentary on the Pentateuch (reprint of the Vienna, 1889 edition), a German work on Biblical exegesis by Issachar Jacobson, a new edition of Nehama Libowitz's weekly studies on the Bible, and a source book dealing with the history of the Biblical text, edited by Professor S. Talmon of the Hebrew University. Talmudic literature was represented by volume one of a new edition of the *Mishnah* with vocalization and notes on Mishnaic realia as well as by a number of traditional commentaries on various parts of the Talmud by medieval scholars such as Isaiah ben Mali di Trani and by later scholars such as Akiba Eger. Jewish law was represented by a new edition of Maimonides' *Mishneh Torah* as well as by Shaul Schaffer's biography of Isaac ben Jacob Alfasi, Baruch Yashar's work on priests and Levites, and Kalman Kahana's bibliography on autopsy. Three collections of responsa were sent: *Lehem Shelomoh* by Solomon Zalman Ehrenreich, *Tzitz Eliezer* by Eliezer Judah Waldenberg, and *Sheelot u-Teshuvot MaHaRAL* by Aryeh Loeb Zuenz. The month's accessions included several works in the field of cabala: a reprint of the Altona, 1755 edition of Jonathan Eybeschuetz's *Luhat Edut* dealing with his controversy with Jacob Emden, a reprint of the Jerusalem, 1868/69-1874/75 edition of Sason ben Mosheh's commentary on Hayyim Vital's cabalistic treatise *Etz Hayyim*. An unusual item was a collection of sermons in Judeo-Persian by Rahamim Melammed.

As usual, the month's accessions included many items dealing with various aspects of the State of Israel. There were a number of publications of government ministries and other bodies: several volumes of the 1961 population and housing census and a report on national income originating in agriculture, both published by the Central Bureau of Statistics; a report by the Ministry of Tourism on the development of tourism in Israel; a survey of electronic technicians in Israel, published by the Ministry of Labour's Manpower Planning Authority. Various monographs on aspects of the Israeli economy included Zvi Livne's history of Hamashbir Hamerkazi (Israel Co-operative Wholesale Society), Itzhak Kanev's study of public expenditure on social security and social services in Israel (in English), Mordecai Reicher's history of Jewish labor in Petah-Tikvah, and a five-year report issued by Hakibbutz Hameuhad (United Kibbutz). Reports of the Bnai Akiba (Religious Zionist Youth) and of the Poale Zion (Socialist Zionist party), memorial volumes issued by Kefar Pines (a moshav) and Daliyya (a kibbutz) in memory of deceased members, a work on Masada (in English) issued by the National Parks

Authority, Samuel Goren's work on the desert of Judea, a technical study published by the Israel Institute of Petroleum—all attest the great variety of material being acquired on Israel. Finally, it should be added that from time to time certain non-book material such as maps, records, sheet-music and film strips are sent.

During the month under review, several items of non-Judaic interest were submitted. They included a book dealing with instruction in drawing, a volume of Liebes' translation of the works of Plato, an anthology of translations from Arabic literature edited by Yehuda Ratzhaby, a teacher's manual on stage art, and a popular work on astronomy by Nahman Jacobi.

More Than 1300 Periodicals Supplied

While the quantity and variety of monograph acquisitions is impressive, one is simply overwhelmed by the more than 1300 periodicals supplied by the PL-480 Program. They reflect virtually every facet of Israeli life. As expected, there are various scholarly journals in the different areas of Jewish studies: *Tarbiz, Zion, Kirjath Sepher,* and *Sinai,* to name but four. There are also many literary journals, those well established like *Moznayim* and *Molad* and more recent ones likes *Keshet* and *Eked.* The proliferation of political parties and ideological groups in Israel is reflected in the veritable flood of journals published by them, primarily but not exclusively in Hebrew: *Ha-Poel ha-Tzair* (Mapai), *Gevilin* (Mizrachi), *Zo ha-Derekh* (Communists), *Matspen* (Israeli Socialist union), *Zot ha-Aretz* (Irredentists), among others. In addition, various immigrant groups publish periodicals dealing with their special interest: *MB* (German language newsletter of immigrants from Central Europe) and *Ba-Ma'arakhah* (organ of the Sephardic and Oriental Jews). Almost every professional, trade and workers' group publishes its own journal: *Niv ha-rofe* (physicians), *Ha-Noked* (sheep breeders), *She'arim* (Tel-Aviv municipal workers), *Ot u-Ma'ot* (Bank of Israel staff organ).

Hundreds of periodical publications issued by governmental bodies on both the national and municipal level are being acquired; these include publications of the various ministries and bureaus, municipalities, kibbutzim and courts. The entire Reshumot series (official gazette) is being sent. Finally, a number of popular periodicals are sent as representatives of mass culture: *La-Ishah* (women's magazine), *Ba-Rekhev* (touring and automobile magazine), *Ha-Adam ve-Khalbo* (dog lovers' journal), *Shemoneh ba-Erev* (radio and television news and programs). While the figure of 1300 titles is impressive to begin with, the quantity of material supplied is staggering when one considers the total number of pieces being sent to an individual library, since many of the periodicals appear on a daily, weekly, monthly, or quarterly basis.

The benefits accruing to libraries participating in this Program are rather obvious. There is, of course, a considerable economic advantage, since participants receive all books free of charge.* A conservative estimate of the annual value of materials supplied to an individual library would be fifteen thousand dollars. Moreover, there is a considerable saving in time and effort that would otherwise be needed to acquire this material through other channels. The field office—in effect, the equivalent of a library's representative in Israel—is close to the source of supply. Since the field office purchases twenty-five copies of a book at a time, many publishers are eager to bring their publications to the Program's attention. On-the-spot representation is especially important with regard to books published outside the regular trade: small private presses and governmental and institutional publications. Thus, the Program is usually able to attain a more comprehensive coverage than an individual library distant from the scene.

Monthly Accessions List

An extremely useful by-product of the Program's activities has been the publication of a monthly accessions list recording all items sent during a given month. Now in its sixth year of publication, it is an invaluable bibliographic reference tool for Israeli publications in the period covered, and comes closer than any other publication to being an Israeli national bibliography. Moreover, items are recorded according to the standard cataloguing rules of the American Library Association and the Library of Congress. Thus, the list supplies a wealth of cataloguing data enabling libraries to catalogue much of this material with greater ease. Indeed, for several years centralized cataloguing of this material by the Library of Congress and supplying participants with full sets of printed Library of Congress catalogue cards were an integral feature of the PL-480 program.

With the advent of the National Program for Acquisitions and Cataloguing under Title IIC of the Higher Education Act of 1965, this phase of the Program has been discontinued. Participants may, however, order Library of Congress catalogue cards on their own initiative from the Library of Congress. Many libraries do this and delay cataloguing of PL-480 material until the Library of Congress catalogues its copy. While some items are catalogued promptly by the Library of Congress, this is not always the case.

---

* A nominal contribution towards the administrative overhead of the program was required for several years but has since been discontinued.

Lack of qualified staff as well as increasing demands on the various facilities of the Library of Congress often cause lengthy delays in the cataloguing of the PL-480 material. This results in large cataloguing arrearages in libraries waiting for Library of Congress cards.

The success of such a program is greatly dependent upon the quality of the selection process. The criteria for "research value" are broad, vague and subject to varying interpretations. To the credit of the Program, a relatively comprehensive and inclusive approach has usually been pursued. Items of no interest may often be sent to participating libraries, but recipients are under no obligation to retain all material sent; therefore, this has not been a problem. Of greater concern is the failure to acquire an item of interest to a participating library. Where differences in interpretation of selection criteria have arisen, they have often been resolved in favor of the library requesting a certain item. Even in certain categories of material usually considered beyond the scope of the program—reprints, albums, text-books, and translations—the Program administration has been most accommodating and, at the request of participants, has included many such items.

The Program's administration has been receptive to suggestions from participating libraries in so far as the budget permitted. This resulted, for example, in the acquisition for all libraries of the costly facsimile edition of the "Bird's Head Haggadah." However, experience has shown that, despite the outstanding efforts of the selection team, some items either escape its attention or are excluded as irrelevant or of no interest. Consequently, a continuous check on various bibliographic sources is necessary to assure the acquisition of all items of value. Assuredly, the effectiveness of the Program would be enhanced with greater cooperation on the part of the participating libraries. However, largely due to a critical shortage of qualified staff, the participants have had to content themselves, with the exception of Harvard and Hebrew Union College, with a rather passive role in the development and refinement of this Program.

A major problem facing any government subsidized program such as this one is a special vulnerability to changes in governmental policy or to international affairs. Thus, the political situation in Poland and Burma has prevented the Library of Congress from even setting up a program in these countries. The Program in the United Arab Republic is at a virtual standstill due to the severing of diplomatic relations between the United Arab Republic and the United States in 1967. Regrettably, at the time of this writing the Israel Program is imperiled by the vicissitudes of governmental budgeting. In March 1969, participants were advised by the Library of Congress that Israeli currency owned by the United

States was diminishing more rapidly than had been anticipated and that additional allocations would not be made available for the rest of 1969 and possibly 1970. Therefore, the Program was discontinuing acquisition of monograph publications for all except the Library of Congress. Participants would continue, however, to receive periodicals. Various solutions to this problem are being explored, and it is to be hoped that a solution will be found to permit the continuation of the Program at its former level, or even increase its activity. The experience of the past five years has shown that the Israel PL-480 Program is making a very significant contribution to the development and strengthening of American library resources in the field of Jewish studies.

Bibliography

Library of Congress. *PL-480 newsletter.* Washington, D.C. no. 1-16 (Oct. 1961-Feb. 1969).
WILLIAMSON, WILLIAM L., ed. *The impact of the Public Law 480 Program on overseas acquisitions by American libraries.* [Madison] University of Wisconsin, Library School, 1967.
Library of Congress. Public Law 480 Project. *Accessions list: Israel.* Tel-Aviv. Vol. 1, no. 1—vol. 6, no. 2 (April 1964-Feb. 1969).

Bibliophilic Sidelights

JEWISH CHARACTERS IN GENTILE FICTION

By Mortimer J. Cohen

Recent fiction, reflecting current influences, often deals with Jewish characters or contains references to Jews. Even the detective story writer does not neglect the Jewish problem. From a brief survey of novels written by gentile authors, it is possible to draw a picture of the Jew as some well-known writers conceive him. It is impossible to encompass the entire field of non-Jewish fiction; it is too vast. The task becomes more manageable when it is realized that, out of the confused welter of our times, well-defined Jewish types have already emerged. It is by these Jewish types that a gentile novelist may be known.

It is no new thing to stereotype the Jew. Modder, in his excellent study *The Jew in the Literature of England,* points out that up to the nineteenth century the dominant Jewish types in English literature were Shylock, the Wandering Jew, the old-clothes peddler, and the unbelieving, worldly Jew or Jewess. Occasionally there appeared the more heroic type, such as George Eliot's Daniel Deronda and Sir Walter Scott's Rebecca in *Ivanhoe.* But on the whole English writers caricatured or attacked Jews mainly because they were not members of the Church, because they were foreigners whose patriotism was questioned, or because they were "usurers."

Out of our stormy and revolutionary world, saturated with the poison of virulent anti-Semitism, gentile writers have added to already existent types other Jewish characters, some adaptations of the old, some newly formed out of the agonies of our times. Whether these Jewish stereotypes portray real Jews is highly questionable. With rare and precious exceptions, Jewish characters in current gentile fiction appear grotesque, distorted, at best but partially realized human beings. "Begin with an individual," wrote F. Scott Fitzgerald, with fine insight, in his novel *All the Sad Young Men,* "and before you know it you have created a type; begin with a type, and you find that you have created—nothing." Gentile novelists who begin with Jewish types today, so far as their Jewish characters are concerned, have created exactly—nothing.

Some of these newly emergent stereotypes of Jews are the following: The Decadent Jew who corrupts the arts and letters as well as the social life of the people among whom he lives; the Materialistic Jew who, like his progenitor Shylock, gives himself wholly to money-getting; the Persecuted or Refugee Jew who in part arouses pity; the Rebel Jew who awakens suspicion because he questions the justice of the prevailing social order; and, finally, a few authors of distinction use the Jew as Symbol through whom they voice their rebellion against the standards and values of our civilization. Sometimes these stereotypes appear in intermingled combinations, sometimes they reflect the opinions of the authors, sometimes they embody not so much the judgments of their authors as what their authors believe are the prevailing notions of public opinion about Jews.

I

Among the novelists who are regarded as realists, Thomas Wolfe creates Jewish characters as decadent and corrupting influences in American society. In his huge novels, *Of Time and the River*, *The Web and the Rock*, and *You Can't Go Home Again*, Wolfe has written a vast story of the America of his times: and in them he recounts his experiences and opinions of Jews.

Wolfe seemed to waver between profound dislike of and exuberant admiration for Jews. He disliked the Jewish girls at the University where he taught for their thrusting sex-awareness; he ridiculed the mercenary attitude of Jewish book-publishers; he hotly excoriated the wealthy Jews and Jewesses who exhibit their vulgar wealth in their Park Avenue homes; he decried Jewish influences in the theater and the arts. Through Esther Jack he had opportunity to meet all kinds of Jews and he was repelled by them, "handsome Jewesses most of them as material-minded in their quest for what was fashionable as were their husbands for what was profitable in the world of business."

He berated the publishers Rawng and Wright, especially Hyman Rawng, who conceived the famous mot, "I don't read books, I publish 'em." He mocked the desire of Jews to change their names. "There's this fellow Burke! Doesn't it want to make you laugh? Nathaniel Burke my eye! . . . His real name is Nathan Berkovich. . . ."

At the same time Wolfe reveals an admiration for certain qualities in Jews. He tells Burke, "Look here, Burke. You'd just better be glad you *are* a Jew." And he writes of Burke's parents, "His mother and father were such nice old people. The old fellow had a store in Grand Street. He wore a beard and a derby hat, and washed his hands in a certain way they have before eating. There's something awfully nice about old Jews like that. . . . Isn't it a shame—to throw away that wonderful thing in order to become imitation Christians?"

He admired the generosity of Jews. Writing of Mr. Rosen, the furrier, he said, "There was in him a vast pride of race, a vast pride in the toil and intelligence which had brought him wealth. For this reason, Mr. Rosen had a very princely quality—the princely quality that almost all rich Jews have, and that few rich Christians ever get."

He extolled the hunger for learning of the Jewish student, and in one of his noblest passages called "The Promise of America," he wrote of the Jewish boy, sitting in a dark room in Brooklyn, poring over books with his near-sighted eyes. Why? "Because, brother, he is burning in the night. He sees the class, the lecture-room, the shining apparatus of gigantic laboratories, the open field of scholarship and pure research, certain knowledge, and the world distinction of an Einstein name."

Similar Jewish types to those found in Thomas Wolfe's novels, or similar remarks about Jews are found in *Europa* by Robert Briffault; *The Last Puritan* by George Santayana. In Eric Knight's popular novel *This Above All*, the American girl responds to the Englishman's assertion that Hitler must be defeated because of what he has done to the little countries of Europe and the Jews with these words, "Oh, the Jews. I'm sick of hearing about them. They're not worth going to war for. Oh, I suppose they're all right. . . . But they're not worth fighting for. They don't fight themselves. . . . No, they just want to sit and make money."

As counterpoint to the Decadent Jew corrupting the arts, F. Scott Fitzgerald has created in his incomplete novel *The Last Tycoon* the figure of Monroe Stahr who created an artistic empire, whose inner force was not primarily the desire for money but the creation of a new artistic medium. It is considered the best piece of creative writing to date about an important phase of American life—Hollywood, and the motion picture industry.

II

The Persecuted and Refugee Jew has become a stereotype in present-day novels. A flood of such stories has appeared, one of the earliest and still among the best being *The Mortal Storm* by Phyllis Bottome. A high point in this tale is reached when the old, disillusioned Professor Johann Roth tells his youngest son to be proud of his Jewishness.

"My boy," he said in his low, deep tones, "to be a Jew is to belong to an old harmless race that has lived in every country of the world; and that has enriched every country it has lived in.

"It is strong with a strength that has outlived persecutions. It is to be wise against ignorance, honest against piracy, harmless against evil, industrious against idleness, kind

against cruelty! It is to belong to a race that has given
Europe its religion, its moral law, and much of its science—
perhaps even more of its genius—in art, literature and music.
"This is to be a Jew; and you know now what is required
of you. You have no country but the world, and you inherit
nothing but wisdom and brotherhood. I do not say there are
no bad Jews—usurers, cowards, corrupt and unjust persons—
but such people are also to be found among Christians. I only
say to you this is to be a good Jew. Every Jew has this aim
brought before him in his youth. He refuses it at his peril;
and at his peril he accepts it."

Anne Parrish's *Pray for a Tomorrow* is a fantasy involving a
Jewish refugee; R. C. Hutchinson's *The Fire and the Wood* is
concerned with a Jewish refugee physician; and Nevile Shute's
delightful *Pied Piper* describes how a Jewish child's soul becomes
bitter with hate at the murder of his parents by the Nazis.

Undoubtedly, the most memorable, perhaps immortal portrait
of a German Jewish family *in extremis* has been created by
Upton Sinclair in his epic novels *World's End, Between Two
Worlds* and *Dragon's Teeth*, with others to come. With remarkable skill Sinclair has chronicled the events of our times from
before 1914 down to 1934. We meet the central Jewish character, Johannes Robin, in *World's End* where he and Robbie
Budd, father of Lanny Budd, the hero of the epic, join in a
business adventure. We follow the Robin family through the
second volume where the coming of Hitler casts its gray shadows
upon the fortunes of the Robins, down to *Dragon's Teeth* where
the storm breaks and the Robin family, persecuted and tortured,
are helped by their American friends to escape to free America.
This third volume is almost entirely taken up with conditions
inside Germany, and the tragedy of the Jewish people there.

Unlike Phyllis Bottome's idealized and romanticized picture
of Jewish life and character, Upton Sinclair strives for realism.
Johannes Robin is a man of the world, an enormous money-
maker, shrewd and capable, but honest and in his own way con-
siderate. His absorption in his business has made him one of the
richest men in Germany. There is much in him to like, considerable to admire, and some little to despise. His sons, Hansi
and Freddi, embody together intellectual and artistic abilities,
and heartily dislike the materialistic pursuits of their father. The
old mother never loses her Ghetto traits, her sweet simplicity and
sincerity, her innate loyalty to Judaism. This is a real Jewish
family, portrayed with fine insight and profound understanding.

Sinclair attempts no heroics so far as these Jews are concerned.
These Jews are not better, and certainly not worse than the rest
of humanity. They are human beings facing agony and death.
Writing of Upton Sinclair's masterpiece, Dr. John Haynes
Holmes in *Opinion*, says:

"With utter objectivity and no slightest mention of anti-Semitism, without a single gesture of the heroic or dramatic, just in the natural and rather easy-going course of a tale which has no moral to teach nor cause to advocate, Upton Sinclair presents in his great trilogy of novels a perfect case for the Jew before the bar of justice. Nay, before the case is half-presented, the tale half-told, it is compassion that is listening at the bar, as well as justice."

III

The Jew as Rebel against the evils of society is, of course, not a new figure. But he takes new form in current fiction. Mary, in Eric Knight's *This Above All,* declares, "Why look at the Jew in this country? They're all Communists." Sinclair Lewis, some time ago, in his *Arrowsmith* created Dr. Gottlieb, the pure scientist in rebellion against political medicine. John Dos Passos writes in his brilliant trilogy, *U.S.A.,* of Benny Compton, the Jewish communist boy who works for the cause of labor and later is sent to Atlanta for opposing the draft during the first World War. The influence of communist thinking upon Jewish life is revealed by Benny, the Marxian Jew, when he declares, "Pop said rabbis were loafers and lived on the blood of the poor, and he and the old woman still ate kosher and kept the Sabbath like their fathers." An interesting mixture of rebellious thinking and traditional observance!

But the Jew as Rebel is not depicted only in communist terms; he is still regarded as a descendant of the social prophets of ancient Israel. D. H. Lawrence has created an interesting Jewish rebel in his neglected novel of genuine power called *Kangaroo.* It is the story of an Englishman who, after the World War, comes to Australia where he meets a strange Jewish character who seeks to redeem the world by setting up a dictatorship of love. In an interesting conversation this Jew, nicknamed the Kangaroo, declares:

". . . The greatest danger to the world to-day is anarchy, not bolshevism. It is anarchy and unrule that are coming upon us—and that is what I, as an order-loving Jew and one of the half-chosen people, do not want. I want one central principle in the world: the principle of love, the maximum of individual liberty, the minimum of human distress."

In Richard Wright's powerful story of Negro life and suffering in the United States, *Native Son,* we meet a Jewish character known as Mr. Max. Mr. Max is a communist and a lawyer who devotes his abilities to the underprivileged in society. He defends a Negro, Bigger Thomas, in court on the charge of murder.

From the first page of the story we are aware of this Negro as an inevitable product of his environment. But he is more than the symbol of social injustice, he is also the victim of "racial" injustice. His essential tragedy was to be born into a minority group, literally, in his own words, to be "whipped before you are born."

Mr. Max feels deeply for this boy. He makes a moving appeal for understanding of his crime. Strange as it may seem, this act of murder for Bigger, hemmed in as he was by all society, was a desperate act of creation, the one moment when he tasted full freedom to act. Of course, no plea could save Bigger from death.

In the trial Mr. Max stands out brilliantly. He pleads for the Negro on the broad basis of an America in grave danger from a conflict of races which only a deeper-going justice can ameliorate. When Mr. Max meets Bigger for the first time in his cell, and seeks to win the confidence of the boy, Bigger warns Mr. Max:

> "Mr. Max, if I was you I wouldn't worry none. If all folks was like you, then maybe I wouldn't be here. But you can't help that now. They're going to hate you for trying to help me. I'm gone. They got me."

To this, Mr. Max answers simply:

> "Oh, they'll hate me, yes . . . But I can take it. That's the difference. I'm a Jew and they hate me, but I know why and I can fight. But sometimes you can't win no matter how you fight. . . . But you need not worry about their hating me for defending you. The fear of hate keeps many whites from trying to help you and your kind. Before I can fight your battle, I've got to fight a battle with them."

In these simple words, we learn how keenly Mr. Max realizes the identity of his position as a Jew with that of Bigger Thomas, the Negro—the identity residing in their being members of minority groups in the complex of American life. But he realizes their difference also; at least Mr. Max, the Jew, knows himself as inheritor of an ancient culture and civilization.

IV

In speaking of the Jew as literary Symbol, it is difficult to differentiate between all art which in essence is working with symbols, and this specific use of symbolism by novelists to convey certain attitudes and values which they cherish.

When Ernest Hemingway in *The Sun Also Rises* depicts Robert Cohn, the prize-fighter, as a symbol of disillusionment after the first Great War, and chooses a prize-fighter because he, Hemingway, at the time believed in violence and force as an arbitral power in human affairs, one can be sure that the author is using the Jew here as a symbol of the age. Yet he realizes Robert Cohn, his hero, as a world-weary character, and as such

Cohn might well represent a Jewish youth amidst the other youths of that generation as a real person.

But, when James Joyce, in his epochal *Ulysses*, writes of the Jew, Leopold Bloom, one can be quite positive that Joyce was not interested in Bloom either as a Jew or as an individual. Joyce was no more interested in Bloom as a Jew than he was interested in Stephen Dedalus, Joyce's *alter ego*, as a Christian. To be sure, as we follow the thoughts of Bloom through his day, we come upon stray débris which might indicate Jewish interests, for example, references to Palestine, Jaffa oranges, the *Haggadah*. Bloom quotes the *Shema* in the Hebrew. He even sings the *Hatikvah* with the "traditional accent of catastrophe." Yet, despite all these evidences of concrete Jewish values floating about in the stream of Bloom's consciousness, the total concern of Joyce in his great work *Ulysses* was not to depict a Jew or create a Jewish character.

Joyce needed a foil, or better still he needed a complementary symbol to Stephen Dedalus. Joyce sought to project into outer symbols the conflicting forces within himself: his aspiration towards the high, the noble, the pure, and his tendency downward toward the low, the base, the ugly. Joyce chose Stephen Dedalus as the symbol of his higher, inner aspirations, and Leopold Bloom as the symbol of his own earth-bound, lesser self.

Just as one can genuinely doubt that Shakespere was an anti-Semite because he created the character of Shylock as a foil for his Antonio and Portia, so one cannot readily accuse Joyce of harboring anti-Semitism in his conceiving the character of Leopold Bloom. Artists speak in terms of the prejudices of their times. Joyce unfortunately utilized prevailing prejudices in one of the great literary masterpieces of all times. In this he has rendered a disservice to the Jewish people.

All the more is this brought home to us when we realize that since Joyce elevated the Jew, Leopold Bloom, into the important role of Ulysses, he has begotten a veritable brood of them in American literature: Fitzgerald's Bloeckman in *The Beautiful and the Damned;* Hemingway's Robert Cohn in *The Sun Also Rises;* William Faulkner's Julius Kauffman in *Mosquitoes.* All of them are symbols, rather than fully realized human beings, symbols of physically arrogant, earth-bound men.

The greatest novelist of our times is Thomas Mann. Philosopher, humanist, prophet, artist, Thomas Mann dominates world literature today. Starting from the realistic *Buddenbrooks* in which he sought to justify art in a commercialistic world, Mann is now engaged in one of the immortal novels of all time—*Joseph*—in which he seeks to justify the ways of God to men.

To convey this immortal theme to mankind, Thomas Mann has chosen a Jewish character out of the pages of the Bible—Joseph, son of Jacob. Through Joseph he symbolizes the strivings of our age; he makes him the prophet-symbol of the age that is to be. In a world flooded by anti-Semitism, coming from a land saturated with hatred of the Jewish people, Thomas Mann courageously holds out to the world Joseph the Jew as the symbol of his richest, most fruitful and noblest thought about God and man. In his choice of Joseph the Jew as his protagonist before the world, Thomas Mann has consciously paid high tribute to the inherent greatness and significance of the Jewish tradition for all Humanity.

In Joseph's life—described in *Joseph and His Brethren, Young Joseph* and *Joseph in Egypt,* soon to be followed by *Joseph the Nourisher*—Mann discerns the origin, growth and fulfillment of the destiny of the human race as planned by God. Just as Joseph moved from his childish egotism through sufferings and tragic descents into the Pit many times, each time to emerge on a higher plane, so, too, mankind is moving through similar experiences to fulfill the pattern of its destiny. And as, in the end, Joseph is cleansed, and begins to discern that the ruling destiny of his life is away from egoistic individualism towards the social-man aware of his social responsibilities, the nourisher of his fellows, so deep within creation God has intended Mankind to develop. This is the high purpose of all creation to which God is calling man. It is the voice of God in the soul of man. Abraham, the Jew, first heard that voice. He taught it to those who came after him. Joseph in the span of his lifetime lived its full meaning, thus transmitting to the future the pattern of God by which man is to fulfill his destiny.

It is significant that Thomas Mann should have begun publishing his work just at the time when Jew-baiting in Germany reached its maniacal height.

Apart from his general message through *Joseph,* Thomas Mann has specific messages for our times, that rise out of the very core of Jewish life and tradition clothed by Mann in words and concepts of our times.

Mann regards the Jews as an interracial people, an amalgam of many races begun with Hagar, the Egyptian woman, wife of Abraham; it was made more complex when Jacob took Bilhah and Zilpah in whom there was Babylonian-Sumerian blood. These mixtures of races form the originals. Thus, Thomas Mann, choosing his theme in the face of Alfred Rosenberg's "Pan-Aryanism," denies the Nazi racial theory that would abolish the Semitic race. There is no such thing as a pure race.

Joseph's escape from Mut, the wife of Potiphar, was more than a personal escape. It was the escape of civilization from death, for Mut was a devotee of the reactionary god, Amun-Re. Mut's narrow nationalism sought to engulf Joseph in her narrow, reactionary, exclusive nationalism; but Joseph escaped her kiss of death. Thus, Mann adjudges the narrow nationalism of our times, especially that of the Nazis, as belonging to the dead Egypt that must perish before the rising sun of an internationalist world and spirit. Of Joseph, when he came to Egypt, Mann writes: "He learns his kind were not alone in the world. That what his fathers stood for was not so much better as different. He meets all races of people, black and yellow. He sees Humanity."

Through Joseph, Mann proclaims the supremacy of the spirit over the sword. Joseph is the dreamer, the man of visions, the man of words. Against him, in the form of his brothers, the jealous masses would rise and unite in hatred. This struggle symbolized the revolt of the masses against reason, against the intellectual. They would tear him limb from limb. So the Nazi masses, relying on brute force, believe they can build a new world order.

But that is not the way, proclaims Thomas Mann. The way is through the spirit of Joseph, the man of intelligence, the man of spirit, the man of words. As Joseph moved from introspection and aloneness to social-mindedness and the sense of collective humanity, so will Humanity move through much sorrow and suffering and grief until, using his divine gift of reason and spirit and words, he will achieve a world of truth and justice and peace. Thus, Thomas Mann protests against Nazi violence and cruel force, and asserts his faith, drawn from Jewish sources, in the triumph of mind and reason and spirit.

In truth, Thomas Mann, in one of the supremely great novels of all times—a novel rich in wisdom, resplendent in beauty, prophetic in hopefulness—through the symbol of the Jew, speaks the voice of all Humanity at its noblest and best.

On completing a survey of the more significant gentile writers of fiction who either treat of Jewish characters or merely allude to Jews, one must confess that on the whole gentile writers do not deal successfully with Jews as human beings. For the most part Jews are treated as stereotypes; their humanity, their individualities, their uniquenesses as persons are overlooked. Jews may or may not be Decadents, Persecuted and Refugees, Rebels and Symbols. They are persons. As Jews they have problems particularly their own; but essentially they are made of the same human stuff as all the rest of God's children. Unfortunately, gentile authors deal with what differentiates Jews from human beings in general. Hence, most portraits of Jews are caricatures or cartoons or grotesques.

Writing in the *Contemporary Review* on "The Jew in Gentile Fiction," D. L. Hobman has well said, "They are, in fact, frequently nothing more than a microphone used for the broadcasting of the author's own view of Semitism, whether friendly or the reverse."

To write of Jews, gentile authors (and one might add, Jewish authors) need a comprehensive understanding of Jews against the backgrounds of history and environment. They ought to be familiar with all factors, external and internal, that make up Jewish experience; above all, they must be able to grasp the essential oneness of Jews with the rest of mankind. At the same time gentile authors must recognize the Jews' spiritual uniqueness which is their glory and despair. Then tellers of tales will create Jewish characters that might well find an honorable place among the creations of world literature.

OF LADIES AND CONVERTS AND TOMES

An Essay in Hebrew Book Lore

By Solomon Feffer

THE word *sefer,* meaning "book," is derived from one of the most important roots in the Hebrew language. The letters *samek, pe, resh* spell out not only the word with which the Jewish people is identified *par excellence,* but also a long list including the verbs *to count, to recount, to relate, to reckon, to take account,* and the nouns *enumerator, muster-officer, secretary, scribe, copyist, member of the class of men learned in the Law, enumeration, census, number, tale,* and *letter.* In later and modern Hebrew these three meaningful and pregnant letters beget, in addition, *to cut, to shear, to speak, to have one's hair cut, to shave, barber, Bible teacher,* as well as *mark, boundary, border district, document, library, shears, scissors, barber shop* and, in mystical literature, *the ten degrees that emanate from the Divinity.* What new words may be created between the writing of this paper and its printing is anybody's guess. The permutations and combinations of these three modest letters are almost endless.

It is natural, therefore, that in the Book of Books words deriving from *sefer* occur with great frequency and that forms of the word "book" are mentioned in it no fewer than 182 times. Indeed, the author of Ecclesiastes remarks, "And furthermore, my son, be admonished: of making many books there is no end . . ." If this was true of the period when the Sacred Scriptures were composed—a time that did not encourage the facile multiplication of the written word—how much truer was this of the Talmudic era when the copyist's art became a recognized occupation, since books which hitherto were not permitted to be written now passed from the oral into the written stage.

It was at this time that precise regulations were formulated for the copying of the Holy Scriptures. These rules, which are collected in the twenty-one chapters of the apocryphal Talmudic treatise *Masseket Soferim,* serve as a guide to every scribe who makes a copy of the Bible, either for his own or for public reading. The scribe must be a learned man, able to comprehend and follow the many detailed instructions, and his work should be performed in a spirit of holiness. He must rule the parchment with a special reed so that the letters will form straight lines and

365

the words parallel columns. He must use a prescribed type of ink and avoid the gaudiness of illumination in gold. He must refrain from making the slightest emendation in the text, retaining the traditional spelling, spacing and size of letter. Where usage decrees an outsize letter, larger or smaller or dangling above the line, he must follow it without alteration. Proper spacing between columns and ample margins at top and bottom assure clarity and beauty.

Thus the Book of Books has been preserved unchanged through centuries of toil and tribulation, of wandering and weariness, bloodshed and massacre. When the art of printing was introduced, the tradition of perfection in the writing of the Torah scrolls was perpetuated in the beautiful editions of the Bible which sparkled like gems in the diadem of Hebrew incunabula.

Début of the Jewish Printed Book

The first Jewish use of the epoch-making art of printing was in Italy. As early as February 1475, Abraham ben Garton ben Isaac printed Rashi's commentary on the Pentateuch at his press in Reggio di Calabria. Less than five months later Meshullam Kozi issued Jacob ben Asher's code of Jewish law in the town of Pieve di Sacco. The following year saw another edition of this book in Mantua by Abraham Conath. At about the same time the art spread to Germany, Belgium, France, Portugal, Switzerland and Turkey. Jewish printing was in the cradle only a short time after the first printed books had made their appearance.

Colophon of Rashi's Commentary on the Pentateuch, printed by Abraham ben Garton ben Isaac in Reggio di Calabria, February, 1475.

It is interesting to note the dates when books employing Hebrew letters had their début in different parts of the world. The first such book to be printed in the British Isles was by Robert Wakefield on Arabic, Aramaic and Hebrew, issued in London in 1524. Palestine waited until 1577, when Abraham and Eliezer Ashkenazi published a commentary on Esther in the town of Safed. The city of cities—Jerusalem—did not appear on a Hebrew title page until 1841, the year Charleston, South Carolina, first issued a book with Hebrew characters. The American colonies honored the Hebrew types as early as 1640. In that year Stephen Daye of Cambridge, Massachusetts, published *The Whole Booke of Psalmes,* known today as the Bay Psalm Book. This was the first book printed in the British American colonies. A few words in Hebrew letters, appearing in the preface, may have been cut for the occasion in wood or in metal, as they apparently do not belong to any regular font of Hebrew type.

Vilna, a name that was to ring like a bell wherever Jewish books were read and revered, did not issue its first Hebrew book until 1799. The press, established by the brothers Aryeh Loeb and Gershon Luria and Moses ben Menahem Mendel, was enlarged by Joseph Reuben Romm in the second quarter of the nineteenth century. It reached its apex under the direction of Deborah Romm, widow of Joseph Reuben's son David, who took over the press after her husband's sudden death in 1860. Under her dynamic guidance the printing house of "The Widow and Brothers Romm" remained in the forefront of Hebrew printing and publishing for over half a century. Thousands of Hebrew and Yiddish books poured from her improved presses, among them the best editions of the Babylonian and Palestinian Talmuds. The imprint of the Widow and Brothers Romm became a household word wherever the Jewish book was read. What the Widow Clicquot was to champagne-loving France, the Widow Romm was to lovers of the Hebrew book the world over.

Printing and the Distaff Side

Deborah Romm is not the only woman's name associated with Hebrew printing. There is a theory (suggested by the historian of Hebrew typography, A. M. Habermann) that as early as 1477 the type for a Hebrew book was set up by a woman typesetter. He based his information on the colophon at the end of *Behinat 'Olam* printed, according to him, in Mantua in 1477: "I, Estalina, the wife of my worthy lord husband, Abraham Conath, wrote this epistle *Behinat 'Olam* with the aid of Jacob . . ." Habermann interprets "I wrote" to mean "I set up," although it could mean "I copied" before the book was set up. At any rate, the learned Estalina indubitably had an important part in the printing of this popular volume on ethics.

התעבש׃　מעשכ　יביצד　צריד　סומא

יהי שם יֹי מבורד　　כתב　אדם הקורצן

פה נשלם טור שלישי　　שבח לֹא מדים ראשי

חזק סליק

Colophon of Jacob Ben Asher's CODE OF JEWISH LAW, *printed in Pieve di Sacco by Meshullam Kozi, July, 1475.*

Title page showing the characteristic imprint of The Widow and Brothers Romm. Vilna, 1909.

370   JEWISH BOOK ANNUAL

מגדת חברה החכם הגדול העשמדד
אנבוגיט אברס הנקראת בחינת
העולם

סעיס לרוס ואדך לעומק חדיחב לב גבון מין
חקח מוהב התחיתק על סדסי עחרסי פחרכב מנושותי מין
חקך לתבונצו רבים חקרי לב אסד אתר רבנ פחשבות
בלב כרי־ק כרחות אהב בקרבני יתרש ידוס יסדיל ובש
ובשפתיו יכבר לק הכבוד מין חכמה מין עבה ואין
תבונה אשר מין להם רועה עי מהשפלי בלעדי השלם
יתכחסו לי היכלכל לב סעים היכלל לב יסים פחיך פ
כללוהו קידות לב היסונבר כנפי רוח על רוח חכמה
מריחפת על פי ענוחות וגחלי עדן היקפנ רחבי ארד
פחשבה פוסבה עלית קד חטנה כנף איש ראה זה
חלק ארס על וחלץ לזה מעולמד האליים בסעוים וזה
לברו על הארך הולך נכומחר דורש רשומות בכתב אמ
גפלאני מעשיו כרת ודין ולדל בעתיות ומנו יבהלההו
נרוח עז נו מבעתו אל יעצרו לי לרכוב סעים לחבק
זרועות עולם עד כיזת כלקים לרעב טוב עלואת
יטרימס כל חסיד יבכל כי אזולת יד כי חרמה מסת
ושור בעיר כלעי חבוה כי אתכונך לתעורות במדרגות
שנאתי נפטי אמרתי־הן הארס הלו בתבלל־היה כאחד
מ ס וג כמרוס כפרוס לכבד עע יס רחבג גרות־י יברוס

עוד בחכמות מטתיות ומושכלות נקיות בעבודס ידוע
להס בראטונה עס חכס וכבון וסאיחדרי,זאת · בכבד ל
מעבה פגע טגנותיהס בין האור העלהי ובינם כמעצ
כדעך עליהכ קטת מכבהידדמ התסגחה להעזב אל
המקדר המאהרי־ והיתה אדיכס לשטה:ולחדסה וחלסה
בהס ידיעת אמיתית התודה וסתרי־ה והסתתריה חכמת
וביניתס דיחוק להס העונש עד כ־ימאסכ רשאוה
פוריחס במדרכות הנרייס אט נעתקו מט אחר כן בטה
שיבא מהומן תשובבה הסגרלות כלס אל עצמותס
הקרומכ יטוב המלכו ותכמ ח החכמה ותחוק ההשגה
וחזרו עיע הלבבות בחדרי הסתרי־ העני־ בטוב א
שיב עמו ועיעגו תחוינה ותכל־ כל הטובצ הזטעו חז
מ צי יסרל בגרחס וגפטותם המאשוגג להחחות בהס
מת מעט־ ה כי גורא הוא סוף דבר תטמי־ל
לבב־ מו תאמין תאגיי בכל מכ שהאמין בו אחירון
הקרומעס בוטן ואטס בחסי־בות הטורס הגדול רב־
מטה עה־ אטר מ־ן עירך הליו בכל חכמי־ יסריל אחר
חתוטמכ התלמור בזאת אע בוטר אטר בכל חרד־
החכמה וה גורה את ה עליך תידא
חוץ
אנכי אטטריל־גה אטת אדע ה־יסי הכנבר כטף־ אברהס
כונת וזיי כבטכי זאת הארכת בחיגת עולם עס עוף
ביכעיר יטע זב לר־ מהרץ פדוונג־טה מטרטיוֹן יחי חמן

"I, Estalina . . . wrote this Epistle BEHINAT OLAM . . ." from the
Mantua edition (1477?)

There is, however, no doubt that another woman, Gitel, daughter of Judah Loeb, set up a volume as early as 1621. This is clear from the colophon of a book which appeared that year in Prague. Here Gitel refers to herself as one who engaged in the "heavenly craft." The term "heavenly craft" or "sacred craft" is applied to typesetting in early Hebrew books—signifying the value set upon this exacting work and the esteem in which it was held. In a volume published seventeen years later, another woman typesetter, Charna, actually refers to herself as a "typesetter in the heavenly craft."

The publication of the Talmud was in feminine hands as early as the sixteenth century. In 1597 the tractate *Ketubbot* was published in Kuru Tsheshme (near Constantinople, Turkey) "in the house of the noble lady, the diadem of her lineage, Dona Reyna . . . widow . . . from the types of the above-mentioned lady." Other works from her press included books of the Bible and biblical commentaries. Dona Reyna was the widow of the famous Don Joseph Nasi, Duke of Naxos, who had been given the city of Tiberias in Palestine, where he attempted to plant a colony of expatriated European Jews.

Widowhood apparently went hand in hand with book publication. Aside from the work of Dona Reyna and Deborah Romm, there are records of extensive book publication by Judith Rosanes, widow of Rabbi Hirsch Rosanes, beginning in 1782 in Zolkiev, Galicia, and continuing after 1788 in Lwow. During her lifetime she published more than fifty volumes. Between

ספר אגרת שמואל

נהוא ביאור מגילת רות הברווהחכםהשלם כמ'הר שמו' אוזרה מ'ע
ועל ימינו לסעתו ולתומכו פירוש הרב הגרול ארון הבפרטים
הלא הוא פירוש רט'י זצ'ל

בדפם בכיף ונאותיום פנברת כמעטירה עטרא היחם וכמעלם עם מייכה פכ'ת ·
אלמכא םדוכום פר עדול ביטרא דן יוסף כנטיא אל'פם   פם נכפב
קורונ'שמי הממיך לקוטמאכבריכא סעיר כבזולה אסר סיא קמא
מעמלת המלך הבדול והזביר טולטן המטר יר'ם

From the first page of SEFER IGGERET SHEMUEL, *a commentary on the Book of Ruth, printed by Dona Reyna in Kuru Tsheshme, 1597.*

the middle of the eighteenth century and the years preceding World War II, no fewer than forty-two women publishers flourished in the Diaspora until the Hitler holocaust consumed them.

The youngest female typesetters on record are two sisters, age nine and twelve. The younger, Ella, set type in her father's printing house in Dessau in 1696 and in Frankfurt a. d. Oder in 1697-1700. In the colophon of a prayer book *Tefillah le-Mosheh,* printed in 1696 and containing a translation into Judeo-German, the following stanza appears by the young typesetter-poet:

> These Yiddish letters I set with my own hand—
> Ella the daughter of Moses of Holland.
> My years number no more than nine;
> The only girl among six children fine.
> So, should you find a misprint wild,
> Remember, this was set by a mere child.

In the pamphlet of *Tehinnot*—prayers in Judeo-German to be recited by women—which was appended to this prayer book, young typesetter Ella again gives her pen poetic reign:

> These beautiful new prayers have not appeared before.
> They are titled *Minhat 'Ani*—prayers of the lonely and the poor.
> Added at no cost to the reader, they are proffered
> As the gift of a pious lady who has offered
> To pay their cost. Almighty, smile on her evermore!

Her sister Gella is known to have set the type for two books in her father's printing press, which had moved to Halle. In

1709, at the age of eleven, she boasts in the colophon to a volume of *Selihot* (prayers for forgiveness): "Behold my handiwork and all my labors." In the following year, when she was what would now be known as *bat mitzvah,* she set up type for another prayer book "from beginning to end," as she notes in the rhymed colophon. The family had now grown to the respectable number of twelve; yet she must engage in her exacting labors. In these trying times every member of the family must do his bit until "the Lord God of Israel brings better days and provides food and garments according to our needs."

The father of these two gifted girls was strangely enough a proselyte to Judaism. As early as 1664 we find his signature on the colophon of a Rashi commentary: "by the worker in the sacred craft, Jacob ben Abraham Israel the proselyte, may the Lord guard and protect him." Twenty-two years later we find his name in many books published in Amsterdam. Born in Nickolsburg, he moved to Prague and then to Amsterdam, where he embraced the Jewish faith and worked in several printing-offices, setting type for books and for the Judeo-German newspaper *Amsterdamsch-Joddsche Courant.* He signed every issue: "by the typesetter Moses, son of Abraham our Father." The enterprising Abraham (later he called himself Moses) established his own press in Amsterdam in 1689 and moved to Berlin, Frankfurt a. d. Oder and Halle. In addition to his accomplishments as a printer, he is known for his translation of the New Testament into Hebrew at the request of the Jewish community, which desired it for purposes of defense in the frequent religious controversies of the period.

Abraham-Moses was not unique among printers. The Hebrew bibliographer Abraham Yaari lists many proselytes who labored in this field and who made important contributions to Hebrew typography. The fact that proselytes were permitted to seek employment in the "sacred craft" reflects the sympathetic Jewish attitude to those possessing a burning desire to embrace Judaism. There was no second-class citizenship for them; they were welcomed into the Jewish community and treated with deference.

Maimonides' responsum to Obadiah the proselyte bears repetition here. The latter had inquired whether he was permitted to recite "*our* God and the God of *our* ancestors, who sanctified *us,* who chose *us,*" etc. Maimonides' reply is a magna carta of tolerance:

> You may recite everything as ordained, without any change whatsoever. You may say your prayers and blessings after the manner of every Jewish citizen ... Do not hold your lineage lightly; if we claim descent from Abraham, Isaac and Jacob, you claim descent from the Creator ... It is therefore clear that you may say, "Which the Lord our God

Title page of a Passover Haggadah set up by the family of Jacob the Proselyte in Amsterdam, 1695.

promised our ancestors to give us," and that Abraham is
father to you, to us, and to all righteous men.

The following incident illustrates an unusual link between
the beauty of typography and the leap into faith. Rabbi Samuel
da Medina, who had been chief rabbi of Salonika for almost
half a century, died in 1594. He was the author of Responsa
which was printed in Salonika during his lifetime. After the
rabbi's death one of his sons, dissatisfied with the appearance of
his father's book, brought printing presses, printing fonts and
printers from Venice to reprint it; and it emerged as a very
handsome piece of typography. In the colophon the following
story is told: When two of the Christian printers observed the
elegance of the book they had turned out, they were drawn to
Judaism and were converted!

Errors of Commission and Omission

Typesetters and proofreaders shoulder weighty responsibility;
their errors of commission and omission, products of carelessness
or wilfulness, can do irreparable harm. One can easily imagine
the effect of an edition of the Bible in which "not" is omitted
from the seventh commandment. Yet we find such Bibles which,
despite all precautions, were allowed to leave the printeries and
to be distributed among readers. A German edition of the Bible,
published in Halle in 1731, is known as the "Ehebrecher
(adulterers) Bibel" because the negative was omitted from the
seventh commandment. There are several peculiar Bibles in
English. One is the edition called "breeches Bible" because the
seventh verse in the third chapter of Genesis reads:

> Then the eyes of them both were opened & they knewe
> that they were naked; and they sewed figtre leaves together,
> and made themselves breeches . . .

Another is the "bug Bible," in which Psalm 91. 5 reads:

> So that thou shalt not nede to be afraid for any bugges by
> nighte, nor for the arrow that flyeth by day . . .

A third, and worst of all, is the "wicked Bible" of 1631 which
omitted the "not" in the seventh commandment. Of this terrible,
wicked book only four copies escaped the public executioner,
and the poor printer was fined the then huge sum of £300.

Jewish books have suffered from errors of commission—wilful
mistakes introduced by censors. In the tractate *Berakot* of the
Babylonian Talmud, the MSS and early texts of folio 3a read:
"Woe to the Father whose children have wandered from their
Father's table." The censor, not relishing the expression "Woe

to the Father," changed it to "What matters it to the Father," etc. This faulty reading is found in several editions.

In *Yebamot* 63a the original "A man without a wife is not a man" was altered by the censors to read "A Jew without a wife," in order not to cast aspersions on Catholic priests.

S. S. Feigensohn relates in his *Insult to the Torah*, Berlin, 1929, how the apostate Dr. Biesenthal induced the stereotyper of an edition of the Talmud published in 1864-1865 to remove the letter *he* from the word *yeshuah,* to make the text in the tractate *Shabbat* 31a, read "You have been expecting Jesus." Four thousand corrected sheets had to be sent to the purchasers of that edition.

That proofreading has always been considered an important and sacred occupation is apparent from several Talmudic quotations. In *Ketubbot* 106a we are told that "the revisers of the scrolls in Jerusalem received their salaries from the Temple funds." "When you teach your son," we read in *Pesahim* 112a, "teach him from a book that has been corrected." And *Ketubbot* 19b admonishes: "A scroll that is not corrected, says Rabbi Ammi, may be kept up to thirty days. From then on it is forbidden to keep it, as it is written (Job 11. 14): 'Let not unrighteousness dwell in thy tents'."

In 1807 a proofreader commented in a note to a volume he was assigned to proofread: "I hesitate as I approach the task of emending errors because there exists an ancient threat of excommunication against those who correct books according to mere opinion..."

A woman proofreader seems to have lived in Yemen in the fifteenth century. Her story is related by Yaakob Sappir in *Eben Sappir,* 102a, who quotes from a manuscript of a Pentateuch this touching account of her apology: "Do not judge me too harshly if you find any errors, because I am a nursing mother. Signed, Miriam daughter of Benayah the Scribe."

The proofreader David Grinhut puns in *Sefer ha-Gilgulim,* published in 1864 in Frankfurt a.M.: "Do not judge your fellow-man until you revise in his stead."

Even today, with all the mechanical means at our disposal, books are rarely completely free from error. In scientific and scholarly volumes, where errors can be particulaly damaging, tables of errata are generally appended. The first such table in a Hebrew book appeared in an edition of the Pentateuch published in Italy in 1840, containing the Aramaic Targum and the Haftarot.

Perhaps proofreaders ought to intone the prayer which our sages, aware of the pitfalls created by error and misunderstanding, uttered before and after expounding the Law. We read in Mishnah 4.2 of *Berakot,*

Rabbi Nehunya ben ha-Kanah used to pray a short prayer
when he entered the House of Study and when he came
forth. They said to him, "What occasion is there for this
prayer?" He replied, "When I enter I pray that no offense
be caused by me, and when I come forth I give thanks for
my lot."

The Magnet of the Title Page

When Kohelet complained that "of making many books there
is no end," he did not realize the whole story. When education
was the privilege of the few, writing materials were both limited
and costly and copying was a slow and tedious process. The
production of books was, therefore, necessarily a luxury. Fust
or Schoeffer or Gutenberg—we still do not know for certain who
deserves the laurel wreath for the introduction of printing into
the western hemisphere—unleashed a tornado of ink-stained paper
which draws almost everyone into its vortex. There is a magnetic
attraction in seeing one's name on the title page of a book. If it
be true, as Milton wrote, that "a good book is the precious lifeblood of a master-spirit, embalmed and treasured up on purpose
to a life beyond life," the thirst for immortality is unslaked.
Nothing seems to stifle this urge. People have paid to have
their books published; they have subsidized ghost writers; have
even founded their own presses in order to have their books
printed. Books have been written in trenches, in prisons, in
hospitals. Authors have had their manuscripts lost, stolen or
burned, and then have proceeded patiently to write everything
all over again. The Holy One Himself said to Moses, after he
had broken the tablets of the Law, "Hew thee two tablets of
stone like unto the first; and I will write upon the tablets the
words that were on the first tablets, which thou didst break."

The same compulsion—*lehabdil elef habdalot*—to rewrite a
lost or destroyed MS drove John Stuart Mill, the English philosopher and economist, to rewrite his chef-d'œuvre from beginning to end after the original manuscript had been accidentally
fed to the flames by his servant girl. Losses of MSS were frequent
among Jewish authors because of the enforced wanderings and
expulsions that befell our ancestors. Particularly numerous were
the losses after the Spanish and Portuguese expulsions at the
end of the fifteenth and the beginning of the sixteenth centuries.
Among the better-known authors of that period who were compelled to rewrite their books was Don Isaac Abarbanel, whose
wanderings included Spain, Portugal and the various city-states
of Italy.

Even imprisonment has had no harmful effect on the writing
of books; the human spirit soars beyond the confines of stone
and brick. The classic example of its power is the prophet
Jeremiah: "The word . . . came to Jeremiah from the Lord . . .

and Jeremiah the prophet was shut up in the court of the guard." Such great classics as *Don Quixote* and *The Travels of Marco Polo* were composed after their authors had been incarcerated. Had imprisonment succeeded in stifling the invincible force of creativity, some of our greatest Jewish works would not have seen the light of day. Yohanan ben Zakkai, Akiba and Hanina are but three of the many scholars whom Roman tyranny and vengeance sought in vain to silence by confinement to prison. The names are legion of Hebrew poets whose muse remained lyrical in the darkest dungeons. Their poems are singularly free from complaint and we know of their oppression only through the writings of their contemporaries. One of the great poets of the Golden Age, Moses ben Ezra, was jailed in Christian Spain after his exile from Granada. We hear of this only through the sympathetic lines of Yehudah ha-Levi, who writes of him:

> Unhappy he whose days are spent
> Nor any ear for his lament!

But we hear no lament from Moses himself.

Another poet of the Spanish period, Todros ben Yehudah ha-Levi Abulafia, was not only unconquered by his lonely imprisonment but continued to pen graceful lyrics and exhorted his brethren to remain steadfast in their faith despite their trials. We get a hint of his whereabouts only from the lines accompanying his poems of encouragement, which he sent to the communal leaders for distribution among their people:

> Fly, O my missive, as free as a bird;
> Carry my poems where'er they be heard.

His faith grows even stronger during his affliction, and when he hears that he may be put to death he is ready to sanctify the Name:

> Let me seek solace in tortures divine!
> God hath decreed them—I find them condign.

In the one couplet where we do hear an echo of despair, he suffers not because of his troubles but because he is surrounded by uncleanliness:

> Alas, there is no balm for me:
> My days are spent unshrived by Thee!

Stone walls could not cage the spirit of the numerous scholars, sages, saints and poets who, for months and years, knew only the dismal habitations forced on them by oppression and cruelty. The reader of their works is scarcely made aware of the hostile environment of their creations. No musty odor clings to their pages; no tears blur their words. The horizons they open are high and wide, luminous with faith in the Creator and hope in the future. One is reminded of the *midrash* about the letter *bet* with which the Torah opens: "Why does the story of creation open with the letter *bet?* To teach you that, just as the *bet* is closed on the sides and open in the front, so do you . . . always look to the future!"

A NOVEL SOURCE OF JEWISH HISTORY

By Judah J. Shapiro

IT IS PROBABLY a combination of the intensity of the reaction to the Nazi experience and the greater sophistication of contemporary Jewish historians that the Holocaust is being so well documented and described. The Yad Vashem Authority in Israel, the YIVO Institute for Jewish Research, and numerous other research organizations throughout the world have been compiling records, eyewitness reports, and memorabilia on the years from the rise of Hitler to the close of the Second World War, documenting how the Jews were dealt with in those years. The work of individuals enhances these sources, whether in the form of autobiography, reporting of events, or fictionalized descriptions of experiences under the Nazis and during the war. We shall assuredly acquire more information and greater resources for understanding the years from 1933 to 1945 than we possess about previous Jewish catastrophies, expulsions and persecutions.

There is a dearth of conjectural assesments of losses other than the measurable loss of life and property. We cannot know how many additional manuscripts might have become available for publication by potential writers who were lost or how many more teachers, rabbis, and communal leaders might have been developed to participate in the myriad tasks of Jewish continuity. Speculation about such possibilities derives from our awareness of a Jewish way of life characteristic of many of the areas and populations which were destroyed from 1933 to 1945.

There can be little disagreement that the purpose of all the preoccupation with the contemporary as history and with the documentation of events that occurred in our times, is to compile authoritative records for future generations. Interpreting the character of the Jewish community and its mores usually falls outside this process of documentation; therefore, there is a strong likelihood that in the future we shall fail to comprehend the cultural destruction despite our excellent records of human and material losses. Hopefully, greater encouragement will be accorded every effort to accumulate such interpretive material.

One such project is presently available in an unusual and yet unpublished work by Berl Kagan, a writer and researcher. Mr.

379

Kagan had published an important work in Yiddish on his own war-time experiences in Polish woods, *A Yid in Vald,* and had served as a member of the library staff of the YIVO. In the course of his work, he stumbled upon an aspect of Jewish cultural life of Eastern Europe and pursued it privately to its present state of completion. He had become aware of the excessive losses of Jewish historical sources in that area. The annihilation of Jewries was accompanied by the wanton destruction of communal records, *pinkassim,* minute-books of various societies, journals, and other pertinent documents. Happily, a few Jewish communities had sent their records to organizations or libraries overseas, thereby salvaging them for Jewish historical research. Professor Israel Halpern stated there was a total of only thirteen communal *pinkassim* in the National Library in Jerusalem. The number of communal records in the hands of individuals or other organizations is lamentably small. In such circumstances, other sources of Jewish history and patterns of life must be sought. While they cannot equal the communal records in importance, they might illuminate various areas of Jewish cultural and spiritual life which prevailed in that great diaspora center, Eastern Europe.

Inventory of Subscribers to Books

A productive source is the listing in Jewish books of names of pre-publication subscribers. For a few hundred years up to our own time, it was customary for authors, mainly rabbinical, to collect monies needed for the publication of their books from potential future purchasers. Since no author could hope to raise sufficient funds in his own town, he would canvass the neighboring communities, and at times his excursions led him considerable distances from home. Upon arrival in a town, the author would present himself to the rabbi and submit his manuscript, together with testimonials to the value of the work. If these were lacking, the rabbi would read the manuscript to determine if it was written in the "spirit of the Torah" and merited publication. If so, the rabbi would assign one or two worthies, *baalei-batim,* to accompany the author in visiting individuals who might obligate themselves to purchase the book. The author would record the donors' names, residences and occupations in the book when published, and generally grouped them by the towns in which they lived. Inasmuch as many lists are extant they constitute a significant and interesting source of Jewish cultural history in Eastern and Central Europe.

Mr. Kagan, now Research Librarian at The Jewish Theological Seminary of America in New York City, has spent the past twelve years studying this source. He has searched through tens of thousands of books and has accumulated close to 50,000 entries from over one thousand volumes. His material covers nine thousand communities, listing hundreds of thousands of individual names. Professor Abraham S. Halkin has rightly indicated that Mr. Kagan's material "is a rich mine of information for scholars and students of the period." The pages that follow will attempt to evaluate some of the precious historic ore that has been extracted from that rich mine.

The first gain is in the demographic area. Among the thousands of listings are the names of settlements so obscure as not to be found on general maps, nor do they appear in Jewish maps purposing to establish areas of Jewish residence. The names alone are a treasure, for there is no work in Yiddish, Hebrew, or any other language recording nine thousand places of Jewish settlement. Mr. Kagan gives not only the most recent names of all these places, but also all the variations drawn from books at different times. This could well be the basis for research about place-names in Europe, because of the Jewish tendency to revise and alter the names of towns.

These lists are also a source of inestimable value for genealogical studies. A number of books list the names of thousands of subscribers, and in some smaller towns from thirty to fifty percent of the Jewish community are inscribed. In older volumes families can be traced in particular towns over periods from 100 to 150 years. Cultural zones also emerge in towns and villages where the authors tended to find potential buyers among like-minded subscribers — a hasid among hasidim, a mitnaged among mitnagdim, a maskil among maskilim. The study of Jewish family names, aided by Mr. Kagan's material, is of crucial significance after the Holocaust. Many who bore these names were destroyed, and the adopted modern Jewish names have supplanted many age-old East European names. Such lists are specially valuable in biographical research about Jewish personalities, especially rabbis. Sometimes such listings are the sole source, as was discovered by Dr. J. Shatsky in his monumental work on the Jews of Warsaw, by I. Trunk in his study on the Jews of Vitebsk and by the editor of the Suvalker Memorial Book in finding the name of the first rabbi of that community.

Subscribers were not only individuals, but also included societies, funds, and synagogues. In many volumes the number of inscribed synagogues is so great that it becomes a source of information about Jewish religious life. For example, one volume lists 48 different synagogues in the city of Minsk; in another work, 52 synagogues are listed for Bialystok. The names of the synagogues in themselves are a fascinating study, albeit less quaint in English; for example: "Bet Midrash on the Sand," "Minyan on the Hill," "Klaus at the Station," "Glaziers' Congregation," among numerous others.

Most of the lists are found in rabbinic works; the number of *haskalah* works are probably not even one percent of the total. The great success in obtaining subscriptions derived from the fact that these books were not in the genre of entertainment or of light reading. Being largely related to the *Shulhan Arukh*, their publication was regarded as promoting the observance of the Jewish law, and thereby strengthening the Jewish way of life in the towns of Eastern and Central Europe. To print the book was like spreading the Torah, and therefore a *mitzvah*. The subscribers were categorized not as "benefactors" or "purchasers," but as "supporters of the Torah" (*tomkhei d'ureita*), assured they would earn a *mitzvah* to memorialize their names in a book of Torah.

There were marked differences in fund-raising potentials between various Jewish settlements. Authors from Lithuania were generally not adept in soliciting subscribers for their works. The number of towns they visited was invariably few, and the extent of their travels was limited. A Lithuanian Gaon, Rabbi J. J. Reines, lamented about himself, "I am not blessed with the talents or the faults that are necessary for this purpose."

Among Galician Jews, however, the record is much better. Their books often list thousands of subscribers from numerous towns and villages. The greatest success was achieved by Hungarian Jews, whose publications contain as many as 5,000 names from over 500 different localities. Much folklore and wit, both favorable and unfavorable, are directed in these collections towards the authors and the donors. In the period under discussion, the average author sold more copies of his books through such subscriptions than modern authors of a Yiddish or Hebrew work sell in the United States today.

Identification of Place Names

One of Mr. Kagan's most difficult and complicated problems was to identify the place names in the lists and volumes. Where most of the books had appeared, the official names of the towns were considerably Judaized. Their spelling was phonetic—as the Jews heard and spoke the names, rather than according to the established spelling in the language of the country. For example, the Polish town of Rzeszow became "Reisha" for the Jews; Bielaya Cerkov in Russian, meaning "white cloister," was changed to "*Sadeh Lavan*," or white field. There were also many instances of duplicated names with no indication of their location. It required four years of effort with the aid of maps, atlases, and gazetteers to distinguish many names and differentiate between them. Despite his zeal, the author confesses that some places cannot be precisely located. At times the name of a town was given as an acronym of a Hebrew phrase which was known to Jews. To decipher some of these was often a matter of intuition and luck.

Decoding and deciphering of place names in subscribers' lists offered no problem in books published by Jews in Germany or Holland. Every place is clearly defined, clearly a province, a lake, and the like. The same is true of the people's names. In Eastern Europe many names were listed simply as Reb Moshe, Reb Osher, Reb Binyamin; the rabbi of one town is called merely "head of the local *Beth Din.*" The same applies to the individuals' occupations. Someone is listed in a German list as *"Inhaber einer Pferdehaarzubereitungsfabrik,"* and another as *"Shumacher-meister."* It would never occur to a Lithuanian or Galician author to identify a supporter as "shoemaker."

The subscription lists of these thousands of books present additional facets for the study of Jewish cultural life in Europe. Such sources have been little used thus far because they have been diffuse and inaccessible. In recording the Holocaust this material has special relevance for memorial volumes being prepared about particular towns. Of some eight hundred such volumes only three have used subscribers' lists, and these were drawn from Mr. Kagan's manuscript. Collating all this material in book form would make it highly valuable for research and memorialization.

Projects of this character and scope are ordinarily embarked upon with appropriate staff, equipment, and financial resources. It is a felicitous indication of the sophistication of Jewish culture that such an ambitious undertaking could have been executed privately by a single individual. In the English vernacular Mr. Kagan's effort can be denominated as a "labor of love"; the more apt Hebrew expression is *meshuga l'davar ehad,* impelled by single-minded madness to bring these vast materials into an orderly compendium. The completed work awaits publication under the auspices of the American Academy for Jewish Research, which is seeking funds for this purpose. It is ardently to be hoped that many individuals will make the publication possible through their generous response, and thus have their names listed in the volume when it appears.

HEBREW MINIATURE BOOKS

By Solomon Feffer

T HE SIZE of miniature books has never been precisely fixed. While folios, quartos, octavos, etc., represent more or less definite book sizes—the folio denoting that the printing sheet has been folded once, the quarto twice, and so on—authorities on typography have been reluctant to establish limits for the tiny, charming works of the printing art that are referred to as minibooks, miniature books, microscopic books, microbiblia, or lilliput books. One scholar refers to them as LXIVmos, that is, books whose printing sheet has been folded to provide sixty-four leaves. But the argument has never been settled to everyone's satisfaction.

To unravel the complexities of definition, this article establishes a simple criterion: miniature books are books whose combined measurement—i.e., length multiplied by width—does not exceed eight inches. This means that a book four inches tall and two inches wide, or one that is 3¼" x 2¼", just about falls within our scope; it cannot be larger and still be regarded as a minibook. Actually, most of the items mentioned here are smaller than the two examples given above and are therefore veritable miniatures.

As in the case of the larger book, the miniature is the successor to the manuscript. The scribe was always proud of his skill and therefore searched for unusual avenues to present his artistic handiwork. Very early in the history of manuscript writing appears the embellishment offered by illumination in colors and gold. Combining tiny page size with colored illustration requires extraordinary control on the part of the scribe joined with painterly ability. J. Henry Middleton, in his "Illuminated Manuscripts," describes such miniatures as being "among the greatest marvels of human skill that have ever been produced." He lists manuscripts only two inches square, set in gold and suspended from the owner's belt by chains and rings.

Jewish manuscripts falling within our size range are extant in the more important libraries and in private collections. Especially popular were Purim *Megillot,* with and without illustrations, generally encased in gold, silver or ivory. Tiny unillustrated Purim scrolls were frequently written in Yemen and Palestine; those embellished with illuminations are the products of Italian, German, and Dutch scribes. The Sephardic scribes tended to eschew representational scenes; their Purim scrolls are frequently decorated with leaves and flowers. Since the obligation to hear the story of Esther is not fulfilled if even a single word is not clearly understood, women as well as men were careful to follow the reading in their private scrolls. It was customary, therefore, for a bride's parents to present her bridegroom with a scroll as beautifully written and decorated as they could afford.

The custom of *Sivlonot,* betrothal gifts from the bridegroom to the bride, is responsible for another charming miniature manuscript book—a collection of prayers, excerpts from the sacred writings, explications in old Yiddish, regulations applicable to the female sex—written on vellum with colorful illuminations of Biblical and ritual scenes. This minibook is frequently bound in silver or in embroidered cloth. The *Sivlonot* booklets are extremely rare because only those amply blessed with material goods could afford to engage an artist-scribe and a bookbinder of superior talent.

The need to provide oneself with the means to execute religious obligations has created two other types of miniature manuscript books. The author has in his collection a tiny *Sefirah* book of German origin, measuring 1¾ by 2½ inches, dated 1785. It contains the blessing for the counting of the *Omer,* the prayer for the restoration of the Temple service, and Psalm LXVII voicing the hope that "Thy way may be known upon the earth, Thy salvation among all the nations." The paper of this manuscript is as crisp today as the day it was written, and its encased parchment has maintained its freshness all these years. The booklet is decorated with red scrollwork framing each page. A much more intriguing *Sefirah* booklet has a page size measuring 2 by 3 inches. It contains the blessing, psalm and prayer on the first three pages, and is embellished with fifty-one miniature paintings (one facing each date page and two more for good measure), each executed in five brilliant colors. The subjects range from the first, which pictures Adam and Eve and the serpent coiled around a tree, to the last, a scene depicting a trumpet blower followed by a figure riding on a capering horse, while a tall, imposing man playing a stringed instrument brings up the rear. Below this miniature is the verse from Malachi 3.23: "Behold, I will send you Elijáh the prophet." Each date page and each miniature painting is bordered in dark sepia. Below each scene is a descriptive portion of a Biblical verse (in one instance a verse from the apocryphal book of *Judith*). The painting style and the silver binding are eighteenth-century Italian. A silver clasp shaped like a fleur-de-lys permits the book to be locked. The first owner's initials LTD and his family's heraldic crest—a stork holding a stalk of wheat in its mouth—are engraved on the covers.

The Zohar mentions the practice of devoting to study the whole first night of *Shavuot,* commemorating the giving of the Torah. For this purpose a *Tikkun shel Shavuot* was compiled, containing excerpts from the beginning and end of every book in the Bible and Mishnah, selected Biblical passages, extracts from *Sefer Yetzirah* and the Zohar, and the 613 commandments. In many communities the *Tikkun* was read also during the nights preceding Hoshana Rabbah and Adar 7, the legendary anniversary of the birth and death of Moses. Before the invention of printing such *Tikkunim* were frequently written as tiny volumes, generally in the rabbinic characters known as "Rashi script."

Larger than the miniatures described above but belonging to their genre, are the numerous miniature Torah scrolls written in various countries and at different periods. While not so tiny as the books mentioned earlier, they frequently measure no more than six inches in height and reveal the skill and artistry expended on them. The beauty of the vellum and the lettering is occasionally enhanced by artistically wrought staves around which they are rolled and the tiny finials which surmount them.

The Challenge of Tiny Books

What prompted the scribes, and later the printers, to devote their skills to the production of these tiny manuscripts and books? Undoubtedly, one reason is the challenge these miniature masterpieces offer their creators. To work within difficult limitations, to extract the utmost from inflexible materials, to outdo other practitioners in the field—these considerations certainly encouraged scribes, printers and bookbinders to their best efforts in this most difficult medium. Another reason is their handiness. The observant Jew requires many books for his religious obligations, and it is more convenient to extract a tiny *Siddur* from one's pocket for the afternoon and evening prayers than to carry a heavy tome.

A painful consideration is the Jewish pattern of mobility, sometimes voluntary but in most cases compulsory. To be able to pack prayer books and scrolls at a moment's notice and in the smallest possible space was of considerable value. Julian I. Edison of St. Louis, a noted collector of miniature books and publisher of the quarterly *Miniature Book News,* quotes from a statement by the London bookseller, Louis Bondy, also a specialist in this field: "When I left Germany as a refugee from Nazi persecution and during later travels as an exile in France and Spain, my then still small miniature library was almost the only property I could easily take along with me." His tiny books survived both Hitler and the Spanish civil war, unfortunately a statement inapplicable to the many irreplaceable treasures destroyed in the Nazi holocaust.

A sorrowful note is perhaps not out of place here. When the Nazis organized street collections for their so-called Winter Help campaign, they issued tiny booklets approximately 2 by 1½ inches as receipts. Twenty of these mementos of evil, extolling the Führer's feats and containing extracts from his speeches, are now extremely rare, much sought after by collectors of Nazi memorabilia.

On a happier note, attention is called to a series of miniature political booklets published during the 1904 presidential campaign when Theodore Roosevelt ran for re-election against Alton B. Parker. These booklets were issued in several languages, including Yiddish. A copy is extant measuring 2¼ by 1⅞ inches, entitled *Facts about the Candidate: a Biography of Theodore Roosevelt.* This little book of 200 pages bound in colored paper contains a portrait of Theodore Roosevelt on the inner front cover and many line drawings of various incidents in the life of Roosevelt from his cowboy days to his experiences as president, including those of the martyred McKinley. Used as a campaign document, it is not only fascinating but also the smallest Roosevelt book recorded. It is, in addition, a reminder of the important role Yiddish once played in Jewish life and in the political life of the United States.

Printing Spurs Minibook Production

The invention of printing in the middle of the fifteenth century spurred a notable proliferation of books and of book ownership. Records of Renaissance booksellers reflect instances of veritable bibliomania, purchasers frequently going into debt in order to acquire the outstanding productions of the great early presses. Together with the elegant folios and stately quartos, there appeared the miniature books which found eager buyers the moment the sheets were pulled from the press. By the last decade of the fifteenth century such books made frequent appearances. Improvements and refinements in the art of punch cutting and type casting led to the production of the tiny types which were the *sine qua non* in the printing of the minibooks.

Among the popular types of printed miniatures were compendia of Jewish law. One of these, once owned by the eminent collector Lee M. Friedman, was printed in Hebrew and Italian in Venice in 1672. Containing 218 pages and measuring 3½ by 2½ inches, it is entitled *Sefer Emet ve-Emunah* (Book of Truth and Faith), compiled by Yitzhak Arubash. It lists the 613 commandments and the 13 fundamentals according to Maimonides.

By far the largest number of editions comprised prayer books, the *vade mecum* of the traditional Jew. Who does not recall the small, thick cube of a prayer book which was the constant companion of our grandfathers? These *siddurim*, as wide and thick as they were high, were not real miniatures because they exceeded the dimensions cited earlier. There were, however, many others which fit into our classification. One was published in Amsterdam by Naphtali Herz Levi. The date of publication appears at the bottom of the title page in the pattern of a chronogram,* which this writer reads as 1739. This tiny *siddur,* containing 318 leaves measuring 2⅜ by 1⅝ inches, is the order of prayers according to the Sephardic rite and has been in the possession of Rabbi D.A. Jessurun Cardozo's family since its publication. There is an interesting introduction in Hebrew by Meir Crescas:

> I have seen in the city of Amsterdam (may the Lord preserve it!) a miniature prayer book with tiny letters but without vowel points. As a result, the young people find it difficult to read the prayers therein. Realizing their grief, I have printed this miniature prayer book in a manner hitherto unparalleled. Although the letters are tiny, they are provided with attractive new vowel points so that the young may be trained to read correctly and thus perform their religious obligations with propriety.

Although this book is diminutive, its print is quite easy on the eyes and, at least as regards this copy, Meir Crescas' pious wishes have been eminently fulfilled.

Many miniature prayer books contained only the afternoon and evening services for weekdays. Since the morning prayers, requiring the donning of prayer shawl and phylacteries, were read either at home or in the synagogue, no problem in carrying was involved. The other obligatory prayers, however, were frequently recited in unexpected locations, and a tiny tome which could be carried inconspicuously was a distinct desideratum. Since the counting of the Omer is part of the evening prayers, these specialized *siddurim* frequently include the order of counting. One such prayer book is *Seder Maariv bi-Zemano im Seder Sefirat ha-Omer* printed in Sulzbach in 1759 and measuring 3⁵⁄₁₆ by 2 inches.

Overtones of the Sabbetaian controversy emerge from a *Sefirat ha-Omer* booklet published in Pisa in 1786. This work, measuring 3½ by 2³⁄₁₆ inches, contains notes from a cabbalistic work, *Hemdat*

---

* Many Hebrew books indicate their date of publication by means of an appropriate Biblical verse, utilizing several letters printed in larger type to denote the year. Since it is not always possible to ascertain—especially in the case of a letter like the *yod*—which are the letters to be considered in adding up the chronogram, there may be differences of opinion regarding the date of publication. In this miniature *siddur* one of the *yods* appears to be printed in large type; if this be so, the date is 1739; it may, on the other hand, be read as 1729.

ha-Yamim, by Nathan, "a prophet of Sabbetai Zevi"! One type page is set up in the shape of a seven-branched menorah.

Not infrequently events in Jewish history are reflected in these tiny volumes. A special prayer book, *Tefillah mikkol ha-Shanah Minhah Ketannah*, was issued for the benefit of German Jews immigrating to the United States, undoubtedly to offset the dangers of assimilation in the distant wilds of America. This was printed in Furth, Germany, in 1860 by J. Sommer and measures 3¼ by 2⅛ inches.

As if to hint that the exodus of the Jews from Czarist oppression would be facilitated by means of an easy-to-carry Passover Haggadah, the famous printers and publishers, the Brothers and Widow Romm of Vilna, issued a miniature Haggadah in 1889. The little book contains 64 pages, measuring 2¾ by 2⅛ inches, and is bound in green boards with blindstamped borders. Even this well-known text required the approval of the Czarist censor and his imprimatur, issued in Kiev on 17 July 1889, appears on the verso of the title page. A copy of this rare item is in the possession of a New York collector of miniatures, Dr. Samuel Hordes.

Distance did not affect the printing of these little prayer books. The ancient Jewish community of the Island of Djerba, Tunisia, although cut off by the sea from contacts with their fellow Jews, was nonetheless a seat of learning and piety. A *Tefillah Ketannah*, containing evening prayers for weekday and Sabbath, was issued there in the middle of the nineteenth century.

The Bible, either in its entirety or in part, has been a frequent subject for small format printing. An edition of the Bible based upon the text edited by M. L. Letteris was reproduced in minuscule facsimile by Menahem M. Shalz of Berlin in 1866. It consists of 605 small pages measuring 1³⁄₁₆ by ¾ inches and is protected by a metal case. A somewhat larger version, measuring 3 by 2½ inches and printed in double columns, was issued in an edition limited to 1000 copies on the occasion of the International Bible Contest held in the amphitheatre of the Hebrew University on August 19, 1958. This edition displays in prominent letters the passage from Joshua 1.8: "Thou shalt meditate therein day and night." Of the Book of Psalms numerous tiny editions have been issued. To make certain that the reader make the proper daily selections, Suwalski (father and son) of Warsaw issued in 1886 a miniature edition of 228 pages, measuring 3 by 2¼ inches. The text is so arranged as to render completion possible in seven days. To help those pressed for time, it is also divided into thirty parts, one for each day of the month.

The greatest challenge to typography is the clear reproduction of illustrations in miniature. Yet such a feat was accomplished in 1884 by Tobiah ben J. M. Salomon of Jerusalem in a 3⅛ by 2⅝ inch book called *Sefer Yerushalayim*. This little volume of 54 pages contains detailed historical descriptions of the Holy City, including some of its famous buildings and ancient sites. It is illustrated with ten charming engravings, some of considerable historical value because they reproduce two edifices, the so-called New Synagogue and the Tiferet Israel Synagogue, which were destroyed after 1948.

Even from behind the Iron Curtain, where very little is being done in the production of Hebrew books, a lone voice may soon be heard. The writer has a recent letter from a Mr. Jenó Vértes, a printer and publisher of miniature books in Budapest, announcing his plans "to make next year an 'Eszter Book' with Hebrew script. It will be about 3 by 4 cm." Let us hope his plans will be carried out successfully "according to the law; none compelling" to the contrary.

Now that current booksellers' catalogues are offering a number of Hebrew miniatures recently published in Israel and in the United States, one may ask: What of the future? A business magazine devoted an article not long ago to the subject of mini-printing:

> ## LASER System Can Record 44 Pages of Text in a Space No Bigger Than a Pinhead
>
> Imagine being able to record 44 pages of text on an area the size of the head of a pin. That's the promise of a Laser recording system announced last week by Precision Instrument Co. of Palo Alto. The system, trademarked Unicorn, can store the total contents of the Library of Congress on four 2,400 ft. reels of tape.

Every Jew will shortly be able to possess on a single small reel the Talmud, the Zohar, all the midrashim, commentaries, Hebrew *belles lettres*, and the great monumental religious, literary and scholarly pyramids constructed by Jewish genius. There is only one obstacle, however; the computer required to scan the tape and print the required pages will cost $250,000.00.

THE LITERATURE OF JEWISH RELIGIOUS DISPUTATIONS

By Judah M. Rosenthal

JULY 1963 marked the 700th anniversary of the public disputation between the famous rabbinic scholar, Biblical exegete and communal leader Rabbi Moses Nahmanides (Moses ben Nahman, RaMBaN, or Bonastruc da Porta as he was called in Spanish sources) and Pablo Christiani, a convert to Christianity. The disputation took place in Barcelona in the presence of the royal family and an assemblage of Church nobles and princes.

The anniversary of this disputation offers an opportune occasion for a brief survey of the literature of the disputations between the Synagogue and the Church, or between Judaism and Christianity in the western world. Since its early advent on the stage of history, Judaism as a religion found itself in conflict with the surrounding world. It appeared to be a negation of values and concepts cherished by other peoples and cultures. The Bible abounds in polemics against the beliefs and ways of worship of other nations. However, since the Bible does not record arguments of the other side, the dispute is a monologue rather than a dialogue. The dialogue form originated in the Hellenistic period with the historical encounter between Judaism and Hellenism and the subsequent emergence of antisemitic literature and Jewish apologetics written in Greek. The Greco-Jewish colloquia are not our concern in the present study. They are dealt with in the classical works on the history of the Jewish people during the Second Commonwealth, for which the writings of Emil Schurer, Joseph Klausner, Victor Tcherikower and Jean Juster, to mention only the most important, should be consulted. The articles on Apologetics, Disputations and Polemics in the standard Jewish encyclopedias also include the Hellenistic period.

The main challenge to Judaism came from its daughter religions, Christianity and Islam. The latter will not concern us here; those interested are referred to the standard work by Moritz Steinschneider, *Polemische und apologetische Literatur in arabischer Sprache* (Leipzig, 1877), and to recent studies by Professor Moshe Perlman of the University of California in Los

Angeles. An authority on Jewish-Muslim polemics, Professor Perlman is now preparing for publication the anti-Jewish polemic *Ifkham al-Yahud* by the convert to Islam, Samuel Ibn Abbas (Morocco, 12th century).

Jewish-Christian polemics commenced with the appearance of Jesus. The New Testament records disputations between Jesus and the Pharisees. The Talmud and the Midrash cite discussions between Talmudic scholars and *Minim,* Jewish Christians. They also contain much material pertaining to the Jewish attitude to Jesus and early Christianity. These sources were dealt with by a number of scholars, the best collection being R. Travers Herford's *Christianity in Talmud and Midrash* (London, 1903).

There are no extant Jewish records of religious disputations between Jews and Christians in the early Middle Ages. The controversies become prominent in the 12th century, after the First Crusade, when the Church policy toward the Jews crystalized and renewed efforts were made by the newly established ecclesiastical orders to gain the Synagogue for the Church. The eminent scholar Professor Harry A. Wolfson succinctly characterized Jewish-Christian polemics in his introduction to the second edition of the book *Jesus as Others Saw Him,* by Joseph Jacobs (New York, 1925). Wolfson writes: "Throughout the history of religious controversies between Christians and Jews in the Middle Ages Christianity was on the defensive. The Christians considered themselves called upon to prove the claims they made on behalf of Jesus by endeavoring to show that the vague prophetic promises were all fulfilled in Christ. The Jews had no counter claims to make; they simply refused to be impressed. As the historical custodians of the Bible text as well as of its interpretations, the Jews looked rather amazed at times even amused at the confidence with which the erstwhile heathen interpreted at their own pleasure the mistaken Scriptures quoted from the Vulgate. The attitude of aloofness and incredulity was sufficient to enrage saints among Christians, for it gave them uneasiness of feeling. . ." The characterization of Professor Wolfson is true also today when the theological assertions of the Church about the fate of the Jewish people as a result of the crucifixion are seriously challenged by the establishment of the State of Israel.

The Jewish-Christian polemical literature can be divided into the following four categories: 1. Public disputations of which reports were preserved by both sides. 2. Private disputations recorded only by one side. 3. Polemical works by Jewish authors without a disputation background. 4. Christian anti-Jewish polemical works of the same nature. To the last two categories, which may be written in the form of a dialogue solely as a literary device, belong also compilations of Biblical passages.

The Christians compiled such lists for Christological purposes. The Jews did so in order to prove that the Messiah had not yet arrived.

The vast literature of Christian Apologiae under the name Contra or Adversus Judaeos was dealt with by a number of scholars. A British scholar, A. Lukyn Williams, in his book *Adversus Judaeos*, gives a bird's-eye view of Christian Apologiae until the Renaissance. This book is highly recommendable (an *Adversus Christianos* of the same nature by a Jewish scholar is long overdue). The French Jewish historian, Bernard Blumenkranz, an authority on the attitude of the Church to the Synagogue in the Middle Ages, is the author of a series of studies entitled *Les auteurs chrétiens latins du moyen âge sur les Juifs et le Judaïsme* which appeared in installments in the *Revue des Études Juives*.

The Major Public Disputations

Public disputations were forced upon the Jews, who knew in advance that the Church would emerge the victor. The moving spirits behind the scenes were always converts, whom the Church had to use because they claimed to know the Talmud and Rabbinic Judaism. Only four major public disputations were staged in five centuries, from the 13th to the 18th: in Paris, 1240; in Barcelona, 1263; in Tortosa, 1413-14; in Kamenetz Podolski and Lwow (Frankists), 1757-59. The main topics were Christology or proofs that Jesus was the true Messiah. Beginning with the disputation at Barcelona, the converts adduced proofs from the Talmud and the Midrash charging Jewish responsibility for the crucifixion of Jesus, and launched violent attacks on Rabbinic Judaism. The last public disputation, that with the Frankists, where the blood libel was the central issue, reflects on the time and place. It was the period of the demoralized and decadent Polish society of the middle of the 18th century, which witnessed the zenith of fanaticism and clerical rule. It was a black period in Jewish history. The revenge seeking converts found ready helpers among the Catholic clergy.

There were more public disputations, but none compared to those mentioned above, whose historical significance derived from several factors. First, there was the fame of the participating Jewish scholars: in 1240, Rabbi Yehiel of Paris; in 1263, Nahmanides; in 1412-13, a galaxy of scholars and notables; in 1757-59, R. Hayim Rapoport, the chief rabbi of Lwow, and many community leaders. Secondly, the disputations had disastrous consequences: in 1240, the burning of the Talmud; in 1263, Nahmanides' forced departure from Spain; in 1413-14, mass conversions of the elite and the deterioration of the Jewish situation in Spain; in 1757-59, the burning of the Talmud and the conversion of hundreds of Frankists to Christianity.

The Hebrew sources for the first three public disputations are available in the very useful and comprehensive thesaurus Judah David Eisenstein published under the title *Ozar Vikuhim* (New York, 1928). The protocols of the disputations with the Frankists are available in the Hebrew *Le-Toldot Ha-Tenuah Ha-Frankit* ("On the History of the Frankist Movement") by the Polish-Jewish historian Mayer Balaban (2 vols., Tel-Aviv, 1934).

The Hebrew reports of the disputations in Paris and in Barcelona are to be found in English translations (Paris and Barcelona in *Conscience on Trial* by Morris Braude, New York, 1952; Barcelona also in *Religious Polemic* by O. S. Rankin, Edinburg, 1956). The Latin protocols of the disputations in Paris and Barcelona were made available by modern scholars. (See the present writer's study "The Talmud on Trial" in *The Jewish Quarterly Review*, vol. XLVII (1956-57), pp. 58-76, 145-169; Cecil Roth, "The Disputation of Barcelona," *Harvard Theological Review*, XLIII (1950), pp. 117-144.) The complete Latin protocol of the disputation in Tortosa, the longest of all, lasting close to two years with long intervals (69 sessions) under the auspices of Pope Benedict XIII, was recently published by a Spanish scholar, Antonio Pacios Lopez, under the title *La Disputa de Tortosa* (2 vols., Madrid-Barcelona, 1957). The protocols of the disputations with the Frankists were published in Poland shortly after they took place (see Balaban, *op. cit.* I, 14-15).

More numerous were the private disputations recorded only by one side. Some are quite fair to their opponents; they present with true objectivity the arguments of the other side. There were also disputations in the form of an exchange of letters. The most famous is the disputation between Johann Caspar Lavater, a clergyman from Zurich, Switzerland, and Moses Mendelssohn, the famous philosopher and father of the Haskalah movement in Germany. Lavater challenged Mendelssohn either to refute the truth of Christianity as proclaimed in a book by a Swiss professor (Bonnet), or, if he found the book convincing, to embrace Christianity. Mendelssohn proudly replied that the Swiss professor's book, like others of the same character, could not cause him to doubt the validity of Judaism. There is also a spate of books by Jewish authors containing answers for eventual disputations, or to bolster the morale of Jews exposed to Christian missionary propaganda by being forced to listen to the sermons of preaching monks in the churches.

These books were not limited to monotonous repetitions of ready refutations of Christological interpretations of Biblical passages. Some address probing, pertinent questions to the

Church, and voice daring criticism of the New Testament. Some of the arguments in these books have retained their cogency up to our day. They represented a real challenge to the Church, which is one of the reasons the majority of these books remained unpublished until recent years. The Jews were apprehensive about publishing them. It is noteworthy that the first to publish Jewish polemical works were Protestant theologians in the second half of the 17th century. Theodor Hackspan published the polemical work *Nizahon* (Victory) by Yomtov Lipman Muhlhausen (15th century, Germany and Poland) with a Latin translation (Altdorf, 1644). Johan Christoph Wagenseil edited the bulky collection *Tela Ignea Satanae* ("The Fiery Darts of Satan," Altdorf, 1681), containing the following six polemical works: 1. *Zikhron Sefer Nizahon* ("A Memoir of the Book of Victory"), a tract in rhyme by Meshullam Uri of Cologna, Italy (16th century); 2. an exchange of letters between a Jew from Amsterdam and a Christian scholar of Jewish descent, Johan Stephan Rittangel (17th century), concerning the word "Shilo" in Genesis 49.10; 3. the anonymous polemical work *Nizahon* (Germany, 13th century); 4. the Hebrew report of the disputation in Paris; 5. the Hebrew report of the disputation in Barcelona; 6. the polemical work *Hizzuk Emunah* ("The Strengthening of the Faith") by the Karaite scholar Isaac of Troki (Poland, 16th century). Wagenseil published these works with a Latin translation. He refuted the small tract of Uri Meshullam with a long reply of several hundred pages. The very title of Wagenseil's collection betrays the motivation for the interest of these Protestant scholars in the polemical literature of the Jews. They were eager to divulge to the Christian world the "Satanic" contents of these works.

Early Printed Polemical Works

The first printed Hebrew polemical work appeared in Muslim Constantinople. It was the satirical tract *Al Tehi Kaabotekha* ("Don't Be Like Your Fathers") by Profiat Duran (or Efodi, Spain, 14-15th century). It was printed in Constantinople in 1577. The first printed Yiddish polemical tract was *Judischer Theriac* by Zalman Zvi of Aufhausen, which appeared in Hanau, Germany, in 1615. This booklet contains a vigorous defense against the slanderous defamations of an ignorant, vicious and vindictive convert. The first publication of a Hebrew polemical work in a Christian country dates from the beginning of the 18th century. In 1709 there appeared in tolerant Holland a Jewish edition of the above-mentioned *Nizahon* by Yomtov Lipman Muhlhausen. There is a proliferation of polemical works in Spanish and Portuguese by Spanish and Portuguese Jews of Marrano descent. These Jews, more than their Ashkenazic or

Sephardic brethren, felt the need of meeting the challenge of the Church to whose influence they were exposed for centuries. Their spiritual leaders were impelled to compose books to bolster them in their Jewishness. Many of these books, listed by Mayer Kayserling in his *Biblioteca Española-Portugueza-Judaica* (Strassbourg, 1890), still await publication.

Scholarly investigation of Jewish polemical literature is of recent date, beginning with the second half of the 19th century. In 1876 a two volume work appeared, *The Fifty-Third Chapter of Isaiah according to Jewish Interpreters* by Adolf Neubauer and S. R. Driver. Volume one contains sources, and volume two English translations. This work comprises excerpts from exegetical writings and from a large number of unpublished polemics. It includes also excerpts from French, Spanish and Latin sources. Neubauer covers the exegetical and polemical literature until the second half of the 19th century.

There is a book of the same scope by Adolf Posnanski, *Schilo* (vol. I, pp. 512, LXXVI, Leipzig, 1904). It deals with the rendering of the word "Shilo" in Gen. 49.10, which the Church interpreted as referring to Jesus. Posnanski limited his sources to those extant up to the end of the Middle Ages. The authors of the two last mentioned works made use of manuscript material and called attention to the vast amount of polemical books and tracts preserved in European libraries. A great number have since been published. (For a detailed bibliography see the present writer's annotated bibliography in the annual *Areshet,* Mosad Harav Kook, Jerusalem, II, 1960, pp. 130-179; Corrigenda and Addenda, *ibid.*, III, 1961, pp. 433-39; New Addenda, *ibid.*, IV.)

Renewed Interest in Polemical Literature

A renewed interest in the polemical literature is noticeable in the last few years. The following editions of medieval polemical works were published recently: 1. *Milhamot Adonai* ("The Wars of the Lord") by Jacob ben Reuben, a 12th century scholar, edited by the present writer and published by Mosad Harav Kook (Jerusalem, 1963). 2. Excerpts from *Milhemet Mizvah* ("A Religious War") by Meir ben Simeon, a Provencial scholar of the 13th century, published by Professor S. Stein in *The Journal of Jewish Studies*, X, 1-2, 1959, 51 f. Professor Stein is preparing an edition of the entire work from a unique manuscript in the Biblioteca Palatina in Parma, Italy. 3. Excerpts from the polemical work *Edut Adonai Neemanah* ("The Testimony of the Lord is Lasting"), by Solomon ben Moses de Rossi, an Italian scholar of the 13th century, published by the present writer in *Sura* III (Jerusalem, 1957-58, pp. 258-274).

An edition of the entire work will appear in Vol. II of the present writer's *Texts and Studies*. 4. The disputation between Elijah Hayim de Genazzano, an Italian scholar of the 15th century, and a Franciscan monk, Francesco de Aquapendente in Orvieto, published by the present writer in *Sura* I (Jerusalem, 1953), pp. 160-177. 5. The polemical work *Herev Piphiot* ("A Two-edged Sword"), by Yair ben Shabbetai da Corregio, an Italian Jew of the second half of the 16th century, edited by the present writer and published by Mosad Harav Kook (Jerusalem, 1958). 6. The polemical work *Magen Va-Herev* ("Shield and Sword"), by the famous Venetian Rabbi, Leon da Modena, first half of the 17th century, edited by Professor S. Simonsohn of the University of Tel-Aviv and published by the Mekize Nirdamim Society (Jerusalem, 1962).

This brief survey has been concerned only with the literary records of the disputations or polemics, not with the evaluation of the problems they dealt with, which would require special treatment.

EXTERNAL AND INTERNAL

CENSORSHIP OF HEBREW BOOKS

By Moshe Carmilly-Weinberger

"The truth is dangerous and knowledge is harmful only to those who oppose them," wrote Aristotle. Throughout the history of mankind various forces and institutions have fought both truth and knowledge, utilizing varying forms of censorship. Because it is prompted by weakness and fear, power based on suppressive censorship cannot endure. In discussing the history of censorship of Jewish books, we must differentiate between what may be designated as external censorship and internal censorship.[1]

External censorship is that imposed by the outside world on works written by Jews; it originated in the West during the thirteenth century. In a letter dated June 20, 1239, Pope Gregory IX ordered the kings and bishops of France, England, Spain, and Portugal to confiscate Hebrew books.

> . . . The outstanding reason that Jews remain obstinate in their perfidy is the influence of their books; they should, therefore, be forced to give up their books and, if they are found to be against Christ, we, through Apostolic Letters order that, under your discretion, the Jews who live in the King-doms of France, England, Aragon, Navarre, Castile, Leon, and Portugal be forced by the secular arm to surrender their books.[2]

Pope Innocent IV, in a letter dated May 9, 1244, wrote to the king of France:

> . . . [by which] they rear and nurture their children, which traditions are called "Talmud" in Hebrew. It is a big book, exceeding in size the text of the Bible. In it are found blasphemies against God and his Christ, obviously entangled fables about the blessed Virgin, abusive errors, and unheard of follies.[3]

The Talmud was attacked, confiscated, and burned in France,

---

[1] See the writer's *Sepher ve-Sayyiph* (Book and Sword: Freedom of Expression and Thought Among the Jewish People, New York, 1966).
[2] Grayzel, Solomon, *The Church and the Jews in the XIIIth Century* (New York, 1966), p. 243.
[3] Ibid., p. 251.

Spain, and Italy in the ensuing 300 years. During the sixteenth century, Pope Pius IV (1559-1565) and Pope Gregory XIII (1572-1585) were prepared to allow the printing and use of the Talmud under certain conditions: the book should be titled *Gemara, Shishah Sedarim,* or *Limmud,* and any expression or passage which the censors deemed insulting toward Christianity should be eliminated. Even with these caveats, the Talmud was not printed in Italy; it was placed on the *Index librorum prohibitorum* in 1559. At the same time the Church authorities ordered that a committee of rabbis be established to supervise the publication of all Hebrew books. The committee was responsible to the secular and ecclesiastic non-Jewish authorities for any printed book, insuring that the Hebrew books would not contain anything derogatory to Christianity. Thus the Church became the initiator of Jewish self-censorship, coerced by the pressure of external censorship.

It became essential for the Jewish communities to establish their own rules in order to avoid the punishing collisions with the Church. On June 21, 1554, representatives of the Italian Jewish communities met in Ferrara and formulated these regulations: Three rabbis and a *parnas* must pass on a book before it could be printed; having obtained this permission, the author could apply to the governmental authorities for authorization to go to press. Permits given by the Jewish communal representatives were recognized by the government as official documents, and were read publicly in the synagogues of the city. The rabbis in charge of the inspection of books were empowered to punish offenders through excommunication. The Ferrara decision was once more approved in Padua, in 1585. It is possible that these actions spurred the Council of the Four Lands (Vaad Arba Aratzot) in Poland to take similar steps in 1594, as well as in 1603, the Jewish community of Frankfort and the Sephardic community of Amsterdam in 1639.

The Index Expurgatorius

The *Index Expurgatorius* of Hebrew Books *(Sepher ha-Zikkuk)* was established by the Church in 1595. Official revisers, sometimes apostate Jews, were appointed to censor Hebrew books according to the regulations in *De correctione librorum* ("Regarding the correction of books"). The *Sepher ha-Zikkuk,* published in 1903 by N. Porges in the *Festschrift zum ziebzigsten Geburtstage A. Berliners,* contains a list of 420 Hebrew books censored by official revisers. The first book listed is *Seror Hamor* by Rabbi Abraham Saba (Constantinople: 1514), and the last is *Sefer Selihot Ke-Minhag Ashkenazim* (Venice, n.d.).[4] The clumsy work of

---

[4] Popper, William, *The Censorship of Hebrew Books: second edition* (New York, 1969), which has my Introduction, "Censorship and Jewish Writers," p. x.

these revisers is displayed in the appearance of the books they oversaw: whole pages deleted, passages omitted, and sentences changed altering the meaning. A Hebrew book could conceivably go through frequent revisions, because the Church did not trust its own officials appointed for the task. Books were brought to revisers by government authorities who confiscated them; sometimes by the owners themselves. A study of the lists of these confiscated books sheds light on Jewish intellectual life, especially in Italy of the sixteenth to the seventeenth centuries.

The *Index librorum prohibitorum* of 1559, published by Pope Paul IV, lists the books which had been banned until that time. The last issue, published in 1948, enumerates banned works by Jews, converted Jews, and non-Jews dealing with Jewish subjects. Among the forbidden Hebrew books are *En Yaakob* by Rabbi Yaakob ibn Habib, published together with *Sefer Bet Lehem Yehuda* by Rabbi Yehuda Arye de Modena; *Shaare Tsiyyon* by Rabbi Nathan Nata ben Moses Hannover (Prague, 1662); Kabbalistic works, at first accepted but later banned because their publication did not convert Jews to Christianity. This had been the hope of the Church in permitting the *Zohar* in Mantua, 1558/1559. When their expectations were frustrated, the books of the Kabbalah were listed in the *Index of forbidden books,* some under the general heading "Kabbalistic Work," and others by title, like *Eshel Abraham* by Rabbi Mordehai ben Rabbi Yehuda Leb Ashkenazi (Fuerth, 1701) which was banned on October 19, 1702.

Books of general philosophy were not spared; the works of Baruch Spinoza were placed on the *Index* in 1679 and 1690. Joseph Salvador's *Histoire des institutions et du peuple hébreu* (Paris, 1828), *Jésus-Christ et sa doctrine* (Paris, 1838), and Joseph Cohen's *Les Déicides examen de la divinité de Jésus-Christ et de l'église chrétienne au point de vue du Judaisme* (Paris, n.d.) were historical works banned because their depiction of the trial of Jesus was unacceptable to the Church. For the same reason the works of Edmond Fleg (enheimer), *L'Enfant prophète* (Paris, 1926) and *Jésus, raconté par le juif errant* (Paris, 1933), found their way onto the *Index.*

It should come as no surprise that the Latin translation of the Rambam's *Hilkhot Avodah Zara (De idolatria liber cum interpretatione latina et notis Dionysii Vosii)* should have been placed on the *Index* when the very words *avodah zara* had to be deleted. The Latin work by Manasseh ben Israel *De resurrectione mortuorum*, libri III (concerning the resurrection of the dead) did not win the approval of the Church. His ideas about the immortality of the soul did not correspond to those of the Church and on January 11, 1656 the book was banned.

At the end of the eighteenth century the powers of the censor were transferred from the Church to the secular authority of the state. This takeover resulted in severe censorship in many European states, in response to the awakening awareness of the intellectual community of writers and poets in political and social affairs. We find many Jewish writers on this new list of the state. Some had converted to Christianity: Moritz Gottlieb Saphir (1795-1858), Ludwig Börne (1786–1837), Heinrich Heine (1797–1856). Heine's *De L'Allemagne, De La France, Reisebilder* and *Neue Gedichte* appeared in the Church *Index*. In Austria, where Joseph II promulgated on June 11, 1871, the *Grundregeln* (Basic Regulations) to guide the state's censor, many Jewish writers were imprisoned and expelled from the country for their liberal ideas. Among them were Moritz Hartmann (1821–1872), whose poems *Böhmische Elegien* contained recognizable socialist themes, and Ludwig August Frankl, secretary of the Jewish community in Vienna (1810-1894), whose drama *Rudolf von der Wart* printed in the *Aurora* insulted the Hapsburgs and whose *Don Juan of Austria* was printed in Leipzig in 1846 without a permit from the Vienna censor.

Heine and Börne, living in exile in Paris, sent their works to their native land. When published in Germany, however, they were banned and confiscated by the state. All of Heine's poems and prose works were denied publication rights in Prussia and Bavaria, on the grounds that the author, having made his home in France, was a cosmopolite and therefore a traitor to his Fatherland.

The censorship of Jewish books attained a horrifying climax during the Nazi era in Germany (1933–1944). Innumerable scientific and literary works in Hebrew, Yiddish, and other languages written by or about Jews were destroyed in a conflagration that consumed the works of the greatest minds of that unhappy country. The tyranny which so feared the truth discovered that it could not be eliminated through bookburning.[5]

Censorship within Jewish Life

Censorship as an institution was never integral to Jewish life. Whatever self-censorship prevailed differed substantially from that imposed by the non-Jewish world. A ban of a book by a rabbi or a rabbinical court was not automatically binding on other Jewish communities. The rabbis of other communities could and often did reject the ban. Placing a book in *herem* (banning its use) was not lightly undertaken since its validity could be questioned and even countered with a *herem aderabba* (a reciprocal ban). This procedure reveals how exceedingly difficult it was to repress freedom of thought in Jewish life. Censorship was not tolerated without a struggle.

[5] Ibid., pp. xxiv f.

The controversies which raged around the writings of Maimonides *(Sepher Hamada* and *Moreh Nevukhim)* are proof of this attitude: first, that the rabbis were not afraid to ban the books of an authority like the Rambam, and second, that not all the rabbis accepted the decision, and fought back with a *herem aderabba.* Books were criticized, attacked, and their authors were sometimes forced to change or omit passages before they could be republished. For example, Azariah ben Moses de Rossi (c. 1513–1578), a scholar and poet, provoked the opposition of some rabbis and had to alter parts of his *Meor Enayim* which was forbidden to readers under twenty-five. Their number was comparatively small (about 250-300 books in 600 years) and we can classify them according to the point of view from which the rabbis dissented: ideological, halakhic, erotic, economic, and political.

I. Ideological Opposition

Some Rabbis reacted frenetically to the study of philosophy. They opposed the publication of philosophic works, lest the masses be led astray. In this category we find the works of Rambam: *Sefer Hamada* and *Moreh Nevukhim;* Rabbi Levi ben Gershon's *Sepher Milhamot Hashem,* and Yitzhak ben Moses Arama's *Akedat Yitzhak.* Rabbi Shlomo ben Adret restricted the study of philosophy to those over the age of twenty-five, the ban to last for a period of only fifty years.

The censorship of books that threatened the orthodox establishment's hold on the intellectual life of the Jewish communities was rationalized as being for the good of the people. Kabbalists, Hasidim, Frankists, and Reformists fitted into this class of ideological bans. Rabbi Moses Hayyim Luzatto, Nehemiah Hayyah Hayyun, and Abraham Cardoso were authors of kabbalistic literature. Yaakov Yoseph of Polonnoye was the author of *Toledot Yaakov Yoseph,* one of the sources for the teachings of the Baal Shem Tov, which led the Vilna Gaon to issue a ban on Hasidism.

II. Halakhic Grounds

Incorrect renderings of halakhic decisions and incorrect explanations were cause for banning a book, as in the case of the *Sepher Or Israel* by Rabbi Israel ben Eliezer Lifshitz (Cleve, 1770). Books written by apostates, such as Shmuel ibn Azariah-Shmuel al Maghribi's *Ifham al-Yahud* (Silencing the Jews, New York, 1964), books published by apostates (the Helitz family), and books which were printed on Shabbat such as *Sefer Yetaw Lev* (M. Sziget, 1835) by J. L. Teitelbaum, were banned or destroyed.[6]

---

[6] About bibliophagy (destruction of books by the authors themselves) by the Jews, see the article by Moshe Carmilly-Weinberger, "Sepher, Sepher ve-Goralo" (Book; Book and Its Fate), *Hadoar,* vol. 48, no. 3 (November 17, 1967), p. 49.

Prayer books with unauthorized changes were forbidden by rabbis. In this group are *Liebliche Tephilla* by Aharon Shmuel Me-Hergershausen, and *Gebetbuch für die öffentliche und hausliche Andacht der Israeliten* published by Meir Bresla and Zekel Frenkel (Hamburg, 1841).

III. Erotica

Erotic literature was not often written by Jewish authors, but the few books that appeared were banned. The Italian poet, teacher, and philosopher, Immanuel ben Solomon Haromi, whose collected verse in his *Mahbarot* included some of an erotic nature, offended the rabbis by its "low" moral tone. The *Shulhan Arukh* (Orah Hayyim, Hilkhot Shabbat 307:16) speaks of the *Book of Immanuel* as a classic example of a book which should remain unread because of its immoral influence on the reader. It exhorts publishers, printers, and copyists not to render a public disservice by promulgating such literature. During the seventeenth century *Flor de Apollo* by Daniel Halevi Barrios was not permitted to be printed in Amsterdam. The author, who belonged to sabbatian circles, took this book and two other banned works, *Coro de las Musas* and *Imperio de Dios en la Harmonia del Mundo*, to Brussels, where it was printed in 1672.

IV. Economic Factors

In order to defend the copyright privileges of author and publisher, and to avoid unfair competition, the rabbis sometimes intervened on behalf of both. When the two competing publishing firms, Props of Amsterdam and Rabbi Meshullam Zalman ben Aharon in Sulzbach, also Reuben Ram in Vilna and the Shapiro brothers in Slavita, started to print the Talmud simultaneously, one of the publishers was forbidden to print, to keep from flooding the market, or the quantity of volumes was equitably distributed among the publishers. The Council of Four Lands tried to allot publication rights in this manner among the competing houses of Poland.

To defend the author's rights a rabbi could issue a *herem hagana* (ban defending copyright). In the publication of the Mahzor by Anton Schmid, who was the official censor of Hebrew books in Austria, the rabbi's ban was not recognized by the secular authorities. Having obtained permission to publish, Schmid chose the Mahzor of Wolf Benjamin Heidenheim, printed in Rödelheim in 1806 and recognized as the finest edition because of its scientific approach. Heidenheim appealed to Rabbi Horovitz in Frankfurt am Main to issue a *herem hagana*. The Rabbi complied with the request but was overruled by the Austrian government.

In the text of the *haskamot*, the approval given a book by the rabbinic authorities, there is a warning that the author's copyright must not be violated.

V. Politics

In the nineteenth century, marking the struggle of the Jews for emancipation and the beginnings of Zionism, a battle of political ideologies ensued. Many rabbis feared that emancipation would lead to assimilation, de-Judaization, even apostasy. They regarded the secular aspects of Zionism as a potential peril to Judaism. *Hamashiah* by Abir Amieli (Rabbi Joseph Natonek), which was printed in Buda in 1861, was banned because it asserted: "The Jewish people does not need emancipation, for its fatherland is not here [in Hungary] but in Eretz Israel." Only a single copy of the book survived, the one that had been preserved in the author's family.

In the city of Radzymin, the work *Solu solu ha-Mesilah* by Rabbi Nathan Friedland (Lesla, 1866) and *Derishot Zion* (Thorn, 1866) by Rabbi Zevi Hirsch Kalischer were destroyed because of their pro-Zionist ideology. Because the Hebrew poems in *Shirat Moshe* (Pressburg, 1858) by Rabbi Moshe Sopher might remind the Jews of their love for Eretz Israel, they were deleted from the volume.

The Range of Control Over Books

Supervision over publications ranged from a simple warning to drastic steps by rabbinical authorities. The milder approach is exemplified by Rabbi Yehuda Hayyat in the sixteenth century. In the introduction to his commentary *Minhat Yehuda* (Mantua, 1558), he suggested that the kabbalistic works of Rabbi Isaac ben Latif should be avoided, but that other books by the same author were commendable. A more stringent step was the issuance of a prohibition against a particular publication, prior to the promulgation of an outright ban.

Divre Shalom ve-Emet (Berlin, 1782) by Rabbi Naphtali Herz Wesel was under a ban that had been issued by many rabbis, led by Rabbi Yehezkel Landau in Prague. Wesel had endorsed certain educational reforms for Jewish children which had been introduced in Austria by Joseph II for general education. The rabbis so feared assimilation that they rejected the proposed reforms and banned the book. In the nineteenth century, when the ban became less effective, the book was actually destroyed and burned. Burning and destruction were used by both sides; for example, Rabbi Israel Löbel's *Sepher Vikuah* (Warsaw, 1798) which fought Hasidism, was burned by the Hasidim with only a few copies surviving.

In reviewing the history of Jewish self-censorship one must consider the unusual conditions that governed the struggle for Jewish survival before passing harsh judgments in the light of modern ideas. National existence is structured on two foundations: a physical homeland and a unique spirit. In exile, the strength of the Jews derived from their cultural and spiritual patrimony, whose defence was an ineluctable *sine qua non* for self-preservation. The rabbis, as the guardians of this *mekor hayyim* ("source of life"), fought to safeguard and insure its future. It is a tribute to them that, under the almost insuperable handicaps of the exile, there was more freedom of expression among the Jews than among the nations who possessed their own homeland.

ILLUSTRATIONS OF ERETZ-ISRAEL
IN HEBREW MANUSCRIPTS AND PRINTS

By Zev Vilnay

ILLUSTRATIONS of sacred shrines and historical sites in the Holy Land first appeared in medieval Hebrew literature. These were primitive and naive drawings made by folk artists who had never seen the places they depicted. They gave full rein to their imagination, and however puerile their attempts, their artlessness all the better expressed the love of the Jew for his far-away homeland and his longing for its hallowed places.

Various pamphlets about the holy shrines in Eretz-Israel were written in the sixteenth century. For the Jewish people sundered from its native soil for more than fifteen hundred years, they were the main source of information about the remote Fatherland so distant geographically but so near to the nostalgic heart. For the few who had the joy of visiting the Holy Land, these pamphlets were guides which companioned them on their journeys along historic roads to the sites so closely interwoven with cherished memories of the past.

One of the most widespread was the Hebrew pamphlet entitled *Lineage of Forefathers and Prophets,* written in 1537 and copied by Uri ben Shim'on of Safed in 1564. It was first printed in 1659 with a wealth of imaginary pictures of the sacred tombs of significant personalities in Jewish history: Rachel; the sons of Jacob and his daughter, Dinah; the kings of the House of David in Jerusalem and of his father Jesse in Hebron; the shrines of renowned prophets—Samuel, Isaiah, Zechariah, Hosea, Hulda, and Ezekiel in Babylonia; and the legendary tomb of Queen Esther in Kefar-Bir'am in Upper Galilee.

The pamphlet contains reproductions of the monuments of outstanding personages in the Mishna and in the Talmud from the second to the fourth century. It includes the Cave of the Sanhedrin and of Simon the Just in Jerusalem; the tombs of Rabbi Shim'on and his son, Elazar; of Hillel the Elder and his pupils in Meiron; of Rabbi Hanina ben Dosa and his wife in Arav, a village in Lower Galilee; of Yosi the Galilean and his son, Ishmael, in the village of Dalton in Upper Galilee, and numerous others. There are also designs of the Temple in Jerusalem, the Palace of King Solomon and the adjoining Gate of Mercy, which is the Golden Gate of Christian tradition (fig. 1).

In 1598, in the little townlet of Cassel Monferrato in northern Italy, an anonymous Jewish artist copied the text of *Lineage of*

Forefathers and Prophets, and contributed new illustrations of his own fancy. Professor Cecil Roth published this interesting manuscript in 1929, together with its pictures, both in Hebrew and in English translation. The original is preserved in his home in Oxford, England. The illustrations in this work represent mainly the holy places in Eretz-Israel: the synagogue of the Rambam in Jerusalem, the city of Jericho surrounded by seven walls, a view of Gaza, the holy tombs in Tiberias, and others (fig. 2).

At the beginning of the seventeenth century, a leaflet entitled *Epistle Telling the Lineage of the Righteous of the Land. of Israel* was published in Venice, Italy. Printed in 1626, it carried a full description of the holy tombs in Palestine. This pamphlet apparently met with great success in Jewish quarters, for it enjoyed many reprintings in subsequent years. Ya'acov Babani, a Sephardi rabbi of Safed, included this text in his book *Zichron Yerushalayim* (Memorial of Jerusalem), which appeared in Amsterdam in 1759. The publisher wished to enhance the work with pictures of the places described, but possessing none, he added various decorations, circles and lines in bizarre and, in some cases, absurd representations of the holy places. A picture of the Wailing Wall appeared for the first time, with the inscriptions above the tiers of stone: "This is the shape of the Western Wall" and God's words to King Solomon, "Mine eyes and My heart shall be there perpetually" (1 Kings 9. 3).

Another book, printed about 1655, was written in Yiddish and given a Hebrew title from Isaiah (35. 10), "And the ransomed of the Lord shall return and come with singing unto Zion." It carries on its front page a picture of the Holy City with the Hebrew rubric, "The Holy Temple and Jerusalem." This drawing which retains the original Latin explanation, was obviously copied from a non-Jewish source. It is noteworthy that a similar drawing, with a like explanation, appeared on the title page of the English edition of Cranmer's Bible in 1540.

A number of Passover Haggadahs in the Middle Ages carried representations of the holy shrines in Eretz-Israel. The famous Haggadah of Sarajevo (Yugoslavia), about the fourteenth century, presents an imaginary drawing of Mt. Sinai and the revelation of the Torah, of the transfer of Jacob's bones from Egypt to Hebron for burial in the Cave of Machpelah, and of Lot's wife being transformed into a block of salt at Sodom (fig. 3). A Haggadah of the fifteenth century, which belonged to Baron E. de Rothschild and is now in the Bezalel Museum in Jerusalem, includes among its beautiful illustrations a picture of Sodom on which the Angel of God is hurling sulphur and fire. It is interesting to note that this picture of Sodom resembles a medieval Italian town.

A Haggadah of the year 1629 depicts Jerusalem with the Messiah approaching on a donkey, preceded by Elijah blowing the horn of redemption (fig. 4). Another interesting Haggadah, which was printed in Amsterdam in 1695 and enjoyed many editions, displays a still wider selection of subjects. These include the Egyptians drowning in the Red Sea, Moses on Mt. Sinai, and the Holy Sanctuary and Jerusalem (fig. 5). A pictorial map of Eretz-Israel is appended. All these illustrations, including the map, are the work of a single artist who styles himself "Abraham, son of Jacob of the family of Abraham the Patriarch." Actually, he was a Christian monk who accepted Judaism and adopted this characteristically Jewish appellation.

Very fanciful picturizations of Jerusalem appeared in marriage contracts (*ketubot*) in earlier days. Their purpose was to embellish the *ketubot* by including as decorations those Hebrew portions of Jeremiah 33. 10-11 which are part of the traditional marriage ritual: "Yet again there shall be heard . . . even in the cities of Judah, and in the streets of Jerusalem . . . the voice of joy and the voice of gladness, the voice of the bridegroom and the voice of the bride." Occasionally, the decoration came from Psalm 137. 5-6: "If I forget thee, O Jerusalem, let my right hand forget its cunning . . . If I set not Jerusalm above my chiefest joy."

A likeness of Jerusalem also decorated *ketubot* issued in various Italian towns; some of them have been reproduced in literature dealing with the subject. A *ketubah* from Mantua, dated 1638, is in the New York Public Library. A beautiful picture of Jerusalem "and mountains around her" appears in an illustrated *ketubah* which was issued in 1727 in the Italian village of Rivarolo. A similar illustration, found in a *ketubah* dated 1738, is preserved in the Jewish Museum in London, while still another comes from Ancona, Italy, and bears the year 1776.

A new edition of *Tsena Vareena,* a Yiddish translation of the Pentateuch, appeared in Amsterdam about 1766. One of the few extant copies of this work is kept in the Schocken Library, Jerusalem. Among other themes, it illustrates the Biblical account of the spies carrying large clusters of grapes from Hebron, Moses contemplating the Land of Canaan from Mt. Nebo, the Holy Ark borne from Kiryat-Yearim to Jerusalem, and Samson carrying off the gates of Gaza. The nineteenth century witnessed the appearance of landscapes of Eretz-Israel in Hebrew books printed mainly in Jerusalem and in Safed. Still very naive and crude, they portrayed holy places whose history was familiar to the Jew from early childhood. If he could not satisfy his yearning to prostrate himself at these hallowed sites, he could at least obtain vicarious enjoyment in viewing their likeness. Pictures of Jerusalem and of other holy shrines were reproduced on napkins used to cover the Sabbath *halah,* on paper sheets with which the booths were decorated during the Feast of Tabernacles, and on banners that were waved on Simhat Torah.

Naturally, Jerusalem is the focal subject of this popular art of prints. Pictures of the Temple site, towards which Jews face while praying, are especially numerous. Ironically, the Temple itself is presented in the likeness of the Mosque of Omar, whose large dome stands out conspicuously on Mt. Moriah (fig. 6). The Wailing Wall, a relic of the ancient western wall of the Temple, is represented in various styles. Overlooking the wall are the Mosque of Omar and the Aksa Mosque, which now occupy the sacred site (fig. 7). In some instances there also appears a reproduction of the monument of the Kings of David lineage, located, according to ancient belief, on the height known as Mt. Zion.

The Mount of Olives rises east of Jerusalem and overlooks the old city. According to legend, the resurrection will take place here "in the fulness of time"; hence many Jews desire to be buried in its precious soil. Some books use it to illustrate Zechariah's description of the Lord's appearance on the Day of Judgment, "Then shall the Lord go forth . . . and His feet shall stand in that day upon the Mount of Olives" (Zech. 14. 1-11) (fig. 8). Zechariah's tomb is traditionally shown at the foot of the Mount, and is reproduced on the front page of *Shevet Musar* (1863), a popular work by Rabbi Shelomo Avraham Hacohen. The book presents pictures also of the Wailing Wall and of the Cave of Machpelah in Hebron.

The monument of Shim'on Hazadik was a venerated shrine among the Jews in Jerusalem. It was he who taught, "Upon three things the world standeth; upon Torah, upon Worship and upon the practice of Charity" (*Abot* 1. 2.). A great popular pilgrimage was made annually to this tomb, until the Arab Legion of Jordan conquered the area during the War of Liberation in 1948. Some prints of Jerusalem include a picture of the tomb.

The ancient town of Ramah, on a height in the vicinity of Jerusalem, is the traditional site of the tomb of Samuel the Prophet, sanctified also in Arab folklore as an-Nabi Samwil. The village built around the tomb, which is variously portrayed in writings published in Jerusalem, bears the same name. Here many pilgrims assemble to pay obeisance to the prophet's memory (fig. 9). The tomb of Rachel, on the highway to Bethlehem, is also a cynosure for numerous bands of pilgrims (fig. 10). The Cave of Machpelah in Hebron, the burial place of the patriarchs and matriarchs in Israel, is pictured in several books. These pictures vary in many respects from the structure now on that spot.

Jericho, the first city captured by the Israelites when they invaded Canaan under Joshua, is known as *Ir Ha-Temorim,* City of the Palms; consequently, it is always depicted in a setting of palm trees (fig. 11). Other pictures portray the historic city of Shechem standing in a narrow vale between Mt. Gerizim and

Mt. Ebal. At the foot of Gerizim is Joseph's tomb, and adjoining it is the sepulchre of his sister Dinah, daughter of Jacob. The tomb of Hamor, recorded in the Torah as the founder of Shechem, is situated on top of the mountain (fig. 12). The word *hamor,* meaning an ass in Hebrew, was apparently regarded as an offensive name; therefore, the grave is often left unmarked.

Pictures of Safed, city of the mystics, and of neighboring Meiron celebrated for the sepulchre of Rabbi Shim'on ben Yohai, appear in several books. Safed is separated from Meiron by a deep rocky vale noted for its wild beauty. This vale is known as *Gei Ha-Tahanot,* Vale of Mills (Wadi at-Tawahin in Arabic), because in ancient times it contained numerous mills operated by water running down the ravine. *Gei Ha-Tahanot* is identified by a wind-mill in the picture, although none actually existed on that site (fig. 13).

The frontispiece of several books printed in Safed display the building in Meiron where the tombs of Rabbi Shim'on ben Yohai and of his son Elazar are shown. Throngs from all over the country and even from abroad are attracted annually to these tombs. Tradition places in the village of Peki'in, amid the mountains of Upper Galilee, west of Meiron, the cave to which Rabbi Shim'on and Elazar escaped from the Romans. Here Rabbi Shim'on is reputed to have written the *Zohar,* the standard text of Cabbalist theosophy. An imaginary etching of this cave is on the front page of *Ben Yohai,* printed in 1815 to eulogize the renowned rabbi. Legend has it that Rabbi Shim'on and his son lived in this cave for thirteen years, eating the fruits of a carob tree that grew at its entrance, and drinking from a spring that flowed miraculously nearby (fig. 14).

Perhaps one final observation should be added. It is a modern aphorism that a single picture is worth a thousand words. The avidity with which prints and illustrations have been made since medieval days to depict sites in Eretz-Israel, demonstrates that this aphorism was first recognized centuries ago.

סערת.שבעים סנהדרין יוטעלייהם ה שילת

1. Cave of the seventy members
of the Sanhedrin.

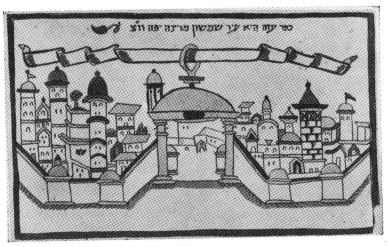

כו עזה היא עיר שמשון מרוה פה ולג

2. View of Gaza. 1598.
"The village of Gaza which is the city of Samson, a fair place."

3. Sodom and Lot's wife.

4. The Messiah approaching Jerusalem. 1629.

5. The Holy Sanctuary and Jerusalem. 1695.

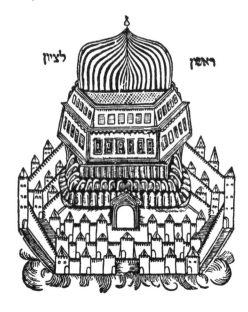

לציון   ראשן

6. The Holy Temple. 1750.
From Rishon Le-Zion,
by Rabbi Hayim Ben-Attar.

7. The Wailing Wall and the Temple Yard.
From Z o h a r , Jerusalem, 1844.

8. Mount of Olives.

רמה

קבר שמואל הנביא

9. Tomb of Samuel the Prophet.

ירחו עיר התמרים

11. Jericho — City of the Palms

10. Tomb of Rachel.

12. Shechem and its holy tombs.

14. Cave
of Shim'on ben Yohai.
1815.

13. Meiron and Safed.